75 Readings

An Anthology

75 Readings

An Anthology

SIXTH EDITION

Boston, Massachusetts   Burr Ridge, Illinois   Dubuque, Iowa
Madison, Wisconsin   New York, New York   San Francisco, California   St. Louis, Missouri

McGraw-Hill

A Division of The McGraw·Hill Companies

This book was set in Palatino by ComCom, Inc.
The editors were Tim Julet and LG; the production supervisor was Leroy A. Young.
The cover was designed by Carla Bauer.
Project supervision was done by Spectrum Publisher Services.
R. R. Donnelley & Sons Company was printer and binder.

Cover photo: Chuck Levey.

75 READINGS
An Anthology

2 3 4 5 6 7 8 9 0 DOC/DOC 9 0 9 8 7

ISBN 0-07-052157-3

Library of Congress Cataloging–in–Publication Data

75 readings: an anthology/[edited by] Santi V. Buscemi, Charlotte
  Smith.—6th ed.
    p.   cm.
  ISBN 0-07-052157-3
    1. College readers.   2. English language—Rhetoric.   I. Buscemi,
Santi V.   II. Smith, Charlotte.
PE1417.A13   1997
808'.0427—dc20   96-26255

http://www.mhhe.com

SANTI BUSCEMI teaches reading and writing and chairs the English Department at Middlesex County College in Edison, New Jersey.

CHARLOTTE SMITH teaches English composition and technical writing at Adirondack Community College in Queensbury, New York.

To Emily Barrosse

Contents

Chapter 7 Illustration   247

Chapter 8 Cause and Effect   296

Chapter 9 Analogy   342

Chapter 10 Argument   382

Thematic Contents

Power and Politics

Problems, Solutions, and Consequences

Health and Medicine

Use and Abuse of Language

Preface

75 Readings: An Anthology is designed to introduce students to a range of traditional and contemporary essays, as well as to topical pieces by international, ethnically diverse, and female writers. The primary aim of this book is to provide the reader with a variety of rhetorical purposes, writing styles, and topics, while retaining maximum pedagogical flexibility for the instructor. We have looked for essays that provide good structural models for rhetorical strategies and that raise complex questions about current or ongoing issues. Thus, the essays do not need to be used merely to illustrate form. Because there is no pedagogical apparatus to direct such use, the anthology can easily be used with a variety of teaching approaches.

The sixth edition features twelve new readings. For this edition we focused on updating the book by removing one or two essays from each of the nine chapters. These essays had been in the book for many editions and thus were replaced with more current essays on a range of topics. Because we added several new additions to Chapter 10 in the last edition, this chapter has no changes. Three of the new readings, those by James Baldwin (Chapter 2), Judith Viorst (Chapter 5), and Philip Meyer (Chapter 8), are well-known essays and can be counted on to promote lively discussion. Another of the new selections is an essay by Barry Lopez (Chapter 1), an author whose essays have appeared in all previous editions; this new selection, although difficult, presents intriguing ideas about the power of narrative.

Other new topics include beekeeping (Sue Hubbell, Chapter 3), painting frescoes (Adam Goodheart, Chapter 3), the northern lights (Claudia Glenn Dowling, Chapter 4), and television talk shows (Nicols Fox, Chapter 9). We also have continued to include essays on culture and language, such as the essays by John Leo (Chapter 4), Lydia Minatoya (Chapter 6), Edward T. Hall (Chapter 7), and Kathy A. Svitil (Chapter 8).

An instructor's manual, prepared by Santi V. Buscemi of Middlesex County College, Skillman, New Jersey, and Charlotte Smith of Adirondack Community College, Queensbury, New York, provides brief author biographies, discussion questions, and journal and paper assignments for each essay in the anthology.

Acknowledgments

Special thanks are due to those instructors who reviewed the anthology and offered their suggestions for the sixth edition: Martha Balusek, San Jacinto College; Betty Bastankhah, San Jacinto College; Geoffrey Bellah, Orange Coast College; Michel de Benedictis, Miami Dade Community College; Sue Bennett, New Mexico Junior College; Timothy J. Dillon, Monroe County Community College; Marilyn Kennedy, Orange Coast College; Kathleen Mayberry, Lehigh Carbon Community College; Jane Mills, Santa Rosa Junior College; C. C. Noordhoorn, Oakland Community College; Hartley Pond, Santa Rosa Junior College; Mary Roberti, Monroe County Community College; and T. Scambray, Fresno City College.

In addition, we want to thank Tim Julet and Christopher Fitzpatrick at McGraw-Hill; and Kelly Ricci and Kristin Steffeck at Spectrum Publisher Services.

Santi V. Buscemi
Charlotte Smith

CHAPTER 1

Narration

A Hanging

George Orwell

It was in Burma, a sodden morning of the rains. A sickly [1]
light, like yellow tinfoil, was slanting over the high walls into
the jail yard. We were waiting outside the condemned cells, a
row of sheds fronted with double bars, like small animal cages.
Each cell measured about ten feet by ten and was quite bare
within except for a plank bed and a pot of drinking water. In
some of them brown silent men were squatting at the inner
bars, with their blankets draped round them. These were the
condemned men, due to be hanged within the next week or
two.

One prisoner had been brought out of his cell. He was a [2]
Hindu, a puny wisp of a man, with a shaven head and vague
liquid eyes. He had a thick, sprouting moustache, absurdly too
big for his body, rather like the moustache of a comic man in
the films. Six tall Indian warders were guarding him and getting him ready for the gallows. Two of them stood by with rifles and fixed bayonets, while the others handcuffed him,
passed a chain through his handcuffs and fixed it to their belts,
and lashed his arms tight to his sides. They crowded very close
about him, with their hands always on him in a careful, caress-
ing grip, as though all the while feeling him to make sure he was
there. It was like men handling a fish which is still alive and may
jump back into the water. But he stood quite unresisting, yield-

ing his arms limply to the ropes, as though he hardly noticed what was happening.

Eight o'clock struck and a bugle call, desolately thin in the wet air, floated from the distant barracks. The superintendent of the jail, who was standing apart from the rest of us, moodily prodding the gravel with his stick, raised his head at the sound. He was an army doctor, with a grey toothbrush moustache and a gruff voice. "For God's sake hurry up, Francis," he said irritably. "The man ought to have been dead by this time. Aren't you ready yet?" 3

Francis, the head jailer, a fat Dravidian in a white drill suit and gold spectacles, waved his black hand. "Yes sir, yes sir," he bubbled. "All iss satisfactorily prepared. The hangman iss waiting. We shall proceed." 4

"Well, quick march, then. The prisoners can't get their breakfast till this job's over." 5

We set out for the gallows. Two warders marched on either side of the prisoner, with their rifles at the slope; two others marched close against him, gripping him by arm and shoulder, as though at once pushing and supporting him. The rest of us, magistrates and the like, followed behind. Suddenly, when we had gone ten yards, the procession stopped short without any order or warning. A dreadful thing had happened—a dog, come goodness knows whence, had appeared in the yard. It came bounding among us with a loud volley ot barks, and leapt round us wagging its whole body, wild with glee at finding so many human beings together. It was a large woolly dog, half Airedale, half pariah. For a moment it pranced round us, and then, before anyone could stop it, it had made a dash for the prisoner, and jumping up tried to lick his face. Everyone stood aghast, too taken aback even to grab at the dog. 6

"Who let that bloody brute in here?" said the superintendent angrily. "Catch it, someone!" 7

A warder, detached from the escort, charged clumsily after the dog, but it danced and gambolled just out of his reach, taking everything as part of the game. A young Eurasian jailer picked up a handful of gravel and tried to stone the dog away, but it dodged the stones and came after us again. Its yaps 8 echoed from the jail walls. The prisoner, in the grasp of the two warders, looked on incuriously, as though this was another formality of the hanging. It was several minutes before someone managed to catch the dog. Then we put my handkerchief through its collar and moved off once more, with the dog still straining and whimpering.

It was about forty yards to the gallows. I watched the bare 9 brown back of the prisoner marching in front of me. He walked clumsily with his bound arms, but quite steadily, with that bobbing gait of the Indian who never straightens his knees. At each step his muscles slid neatly into place, the lock of hair on his scalp danced up and down, his feet printed themselves on the wet gravel. And once, in spite of the men who gripped him by each shoulder, he stepped slightly aside to avoid a puddle on the path.

It is curious, but till that moment I had never realised what 10 it means to destroy a healthy, conscious man. When I saw the prisoner step aside to avoid the puddle, I saw the mystery, the unspeakable wrongness, of cutting a life short when it is in full tide. This man was not dying, he was alive just as we were alive. All the organs of his body were working—bowels digesting food, skin renewing itself, nails growing, tissues forming—all toiling away in solemn foolery. His nails would still be growing when he stood on the drop, when he was falling through the air with a tenth of a second to live. His eyes saw the yellow gravel and the grey walls, and his brain still remembered, foresaw, reasoned—reasoned even about puddles. He and we were a party of men walking together, seeing, hearing, feeling, understanding the same world; and in two minutes, with a sudden snap, one of us would be gone—one mind less, one world less.

The gallows stood in a small yard, separate from the main 11 grounds of the prison, and overgrown with tall prickly weeds. It was a brick erection like three sides of a shed, with planking on top, and above that two beams and a crossbar with the rope dangling. The hangman, a grey-haired convict in the white uniform of the prison, was waiting beside his machine. He greeted us with a servile crouch as we entered. At a word from Francis the two warders, gripping the prisoner more closely than ever, half led, half pushed him to the gallows and helped him clumsily up the ladder. Then the hangman climbed up and fixed the rope round the prisoner's neck.

We stood waiting, five yards away. The warders had 12 formed in a rough circle round the gallows. And then, when the noose was fixed, the prisoner began crying out on his god. It was a high, reiterated cry of "Ram! Ram! Ram! Ram!", not urgent and fearful like a prayer or a cry for help, but steady, rhythmical, almost like the tolling of a bell. The dog answered the sound with a whine. The hangman, still standing on the gallows, produced a small cotton bag like a flour bag and drew it down over the prisoner's face. But the sound, muffled by the cloth, still persisted, over and over again: "Ram! Ram! Ram! Ram! Ram!"

The hangman climbed down and stood ready, holding the 13 lever. Minutes seemed to pass. The steady, muffled crying from the prisoner went on and on, "Ram! Ram! Ram!" never faltering for an instant. The superintendent, his head on his chest, was slowly poking the ground with his stick; perhaps he was counting the cries, allowing the prisoner a fixed number—fifty, perhaps, or a hundred. Everyone had changed colour. The Indians had gone grey like bad coffee, and one or two of the bayonets were wavering. We looked at the lashed, hooded man on the drop, and listened to his cries—each cry another second of life; the same thought was in all our minds: oh, kill him quickly, get it over, stop that abominable noise!

Suddenly the superintendent made up his mind. Throwing 14 up his head he made a swift motion with his stick. "Chalo!" he shouted almost fiercely.

There was a clanking noise, and then dead silence. The pris- 15 oner had vanished, and the rope was twisting on itself. I let go of the dog, and it galloped immediately to the back of the gallows; but when it got there it stopped short, barked, and then retreated into a corner of the yard, where it stood among the weeds, looking timorously out at us. We went round the gallows to inspect the prisoner's body. He was dangling with his toes pointed straight downwards, very slowly revolving, as dead as a stone.

The superintendent reached out with his stick and poked 16 the bare body; it oscillated slightly. *"He's* all right," said the superintendent. He backed out from under the gallows, and blew out a deep breath. The moody look had gone out of his face quite suddenly. He glanced at his wrist-watch. "Eight minutes past eight. Well, that's all for this morning, thank God."

The warders unfixed bayonets and marched away. The dog, 17 sobered and conscious of having misbehaved itself, slipped after them. We walked out of the gallows yard, past the condemned cells with their waiting prisoners, into the big central yard of the prison. The convicts, under the command of warders armed with lathis, were already receiving their breakfast. They squatted in long rows, each man holding a tin pannikin, while two warders with buckets marched round ladling out rice; it seemed quite a homely, jolly scene, after the hanging. An enormous relief had come upon us now that the job was done. One felt an impulse to sing, to break into a run, to snigger. All at once everyone began chattering gaily.

The Eurasian boy walking beside me nodded towards the 18 way we had come, with a knowing smile: "Do you know, sir, our friend (he meant the dead man), when he heard his appeal had been dismissed, he pissed on the floor of his cell. From fright.—Kindly take one of my cigarettes, sir. Do you not admire my new silver case, sir? From the boxwallah, two rupees eight annas. Classy European style."

Several people laughed—at what, nobody seemed certain. 19

Francis was walking by the superintendent, talking garru- 20 lously: "Well, sir, all has passed off with the utmost satisfactoriness. It wass all finished—flick! like that. It iss not always so—oah, no! I have known cases where the doctor wass obliged to go beneath the gallows and pull the prisoner's legs to ensure decease. Most disagreeable!"

"Wriggling about, eh? That's bad," said the superintendent. 21

"Ach, sir, it iss worse when they become refractory! One 22 man, I recall, clung to the bars of hiss cage when we went to take him out. You will scarcely credit, sir, that it took six warders to dislodge him, three pulling at each leg. We reasoned with him. 'My dear fellow,' we said, 'think of all the pain and trouble you are causing to us!' But no, he would not listen! Ach, he wass very troublesome!"

I found that I was laughing quite loudly. Everyone was 23 laughing. Even the superintendent grinned in a tolerant way. "You'd better all come out and have a drink," he said quite genially. "I've got a bottle of whisky in the car. We could do with it."

We went through the big double gates of the prison, into the 24 road. "Pulling at his legs!" exclaimed a Burmese magistrate suddenly, and burst into a loud chuckling. We all began laughing again. At that moment Francis's anecdote seemed extraordinarily funny. We all had a drink together, native and European alike, quite amicably. The dead man was a hundred yards away.

1931

Salvation

Langston Hughes

I was saved from sin when I was going on thirteen. But not 1 really saved. It happened like this. There was a big revival at my Auntie Reed's church. Every night for weeks there had been much preaching, singing, praying, and shouting, and some very hardened sinners had been brought to Christ, and the membership of the church had grown by leaps and bounds. Then just before the revival ended, they held a special meeting for children, "to bring the young lambs to the fold." My aunt spoke of it for days ahead. That night I was escorted to the front row and placed on the mourners' bench with all the other young sinners, who had not yet been brought to Jesus.

My aunt told me that when you were saved you saw a light, 2 and something happened to you inside! And Jesus came into your life! And God was with you from then on! She said you could see and hear and feel Jesus in your soul. I believed her. I had heard a great many old people say the same thing and it seemed to me they ought to know. So I sat there calmly in the hot, crowded church, waiting for Jesus to come to me.

The preacher preached a wonderful rhythmical sermon, all moans and shouts and lonely cries and dire pictures of hell, and then he sang a song about the ninety and nine safe in the fold, but one little lamb was left out in the cold. Then he said: "Won't you come? Won't you come to Jesus? Young lambs, won't you come?" And he held out his arms to all us young sinners there on the mourners' bench. And the little girls cried. And some of them jumped up and went to Jesus right away. But most of us just sat there. 3

A great many old people came and knelt around us and prayed, old women with jet-black faces and braided hair, old men with work-gnarled hands. And the church sang a song about the lower lights are burning, some poor sinners to be saved. And the whole building rocked with prayer and song. 4

Still I kept waiting to *see* Jesus. 5

Finally all the young people had gone to the altar and were saved, but one boy and me. He was a rounder's son named Westley. Westley and I were surrounded by sisters and deacons praying. It was very hot in the church, and getting late now. Finally Westley said to me in a whisper: "God damn! I'm tired o' sitting here. Let's get up and be saved." So he got up and was saved. 6

Then I was left all alone on the mourners' bench. My aunt came and knelt at my knees and cried, while prayers and songs swirled all around me in the little church. The whole congregation prayed for me alone, in a mighty wail of moans and voices. And I kept waiting serenely for Jesus, waiting, waiting—but he didn't come. I wanted to see him, but nothing happened to me. Nothing! I wanted something to happen to me, but nothing happened. 7

I heard the songs and the minister saying: "Why don't you come? My dear child, why don't you come to Jesus? Jesus is waiting for you. He wants you. Why don't you come? Sister Reed, what is this child's name?" 8

"Langston," my aunt sobbed.   9
"Langston, why don't you come? Why don't you come and   10
be saved? Oh, Lamb of God! Why don't you come?"
Now it was really getting late. I began to be ashamed of my-   11
self, holding everything up so long. I began to wonder what
God thought about Westley, who certainly hadn't seen Jesus either, but who was now sitting proudly on the platform, swinging his knickerbockered legs and grinning down at me, surrounded by deacons and old women on their knees praying.
God had not struck Westley dead for taking his name in vain
or for lying in the temple. So I decided that maybe to save further trouble, I'd better lie, too, and say that Jesus had come, and
get up and be saved.
So I got up.   12
Suddenly the whole room broke into a sea of shouting, as   13
they saw me rise. Waves of rejoicing swept the place. Women
leaped in the air. My aunt threw her arms around me. The minister took me by the hand and led me to the platform.
When things quieted down, in a hushed silence, punctuated   14
by a few ecstatic "Amens," all the new young lambs were
blessed in the name of God. Then joyous singing filled the room.
That night, for the last time in my life but one—for I was a   15
big boy twelve years old—I cried. I cried, in bed alone, and
couldn't stop. I buried my head under the quilts, but my aunt
heard me. She woke up and told my uncle I was crying because
the Holy Ghost had come into my life, and because I had seen
Jesus. But I was really crying because I couldn't bear to tell her
that I had lied, that I had deceived everybody in the church, that
I hadn't seen Jesus, and that now I didn't believe there was a
Jesus any more, since he didn't come to help me.

                                                    1940

Grandmother's Victory

Maya Angelou

"Thou shall not be dirty" and "Thou shall not be impu- 1
dent" were the two commandments of Grandmother Henderson upon which hung our total salvation.

Each night in the bitterest winter we were forced to wash 2
faces, arms, necks, legs and feet before going to bed. She used
to add, with a smirk that unprofane people can't control when
venturing into profanity, "and wash as far as possible, then
wash possible."

We would go to the well and wash in the ice-cold, clear 3
water, grease our legs with the equally cold stiff Vaseline, then
tiptoe into the house. We wiped the dust from our toes and settled down for schoolwork, cornbread, clabbered milk, prayers
and bed, always in that order. Momma was famous for pulling
the quilts off after we had fallen asleep to examine our feet. If
they weren't clean enough for her, she took the switch (she kept
one behind the bedroom door for emergencies) and woke up the
offender with a few aptly placed burning reminders.

The area around the well at night was dark and slick, and 4
boys told about how snakes love water, so that anyone who had
to draw water at night and then stand there alone and wash
knew that moccasins and rattlers, puff adders and boa con-
strictors were winding their way to the well and would arrive
just as the person washing got soap in her eyes. But Momma
convinced us that not only was cleanliness next to Godliness,
dirtiness was the inventor of misery.

The impudent child was detested by God and a shame to 5
its parents and could bring destruction to its house and line. All
adults had to be addressed as Mister, Missus, Miss, Auntie,
Cousin, Unk, Uncle, Buhbah, Sister, Brother and a thousand
other appellations indicating familial relationship and the low-
liness of the addressor.

Everyone I knew respected these customary laws, except for 6
the powhitetrash children.

Some families of powhitetrash lived on Momma's farm land 7
behind the school. Sometimes a gaggle of them came to the
Store, filling the whole room, chasing out the air and even
changing the well-known scents. The children crawled over the
shelves and into the potato and onion bins, twanging all the
time in their sharp voices like cigar-box guitars. They took liberties in my Store that I would never dare. Since Momma told
us that the less you say to whitefolks (or even powhitetrash) the
better, Bailey and I would stand, solemn, quiet, in the displaced
air. But if one of the playful apparitions got close to us, I pinched
it. Partly out of angry frustration and partly because I didn't believe in its flesh reality.

They called my uncle by his first name and ordered him 8
around the Store. He, to my crying shame, obeyed them in his
limping dip-straight-dip fashion.

My grandmother, too, followed their orders, except that 9
she didn't seem to be servile because she anticipated their needs.

"Here's sugar, Miz Potter, and here's baking powder. You 10
didn't buy soda last month, you'll probably be needing some."

Momma always directed her statements to the adults, but 11
sometimes, Oh painful sometimes, the grimy, snotty-nosed girls
would answer her.

"Naw, Annie . . ."—to Momma? Who owned the land they 12
lived on? Who forgot more than they would ever learn? If there
was any justice in the world, God should strike them dumb at
once!—"Just give us some extra sody crackers, and some more
mackerel."

At least they never looked in her face, or I never caught 13
them doing so. Nobody with a smidgen of training, not even the
worst roustabout, would look right in a grown person's face. It
meant the person was trying to take the words out before they
were formed. The dirty little children didn't do that, but they
threw their orders around the Store like lashes from a cat-o'-
nine-tails.

When I was around ten years old, those scruffy children 14
caused me the most painful and confusing experience I had
ever had with my grandmother.

One summer morning, after I had swept the dirt yard of 15

leaves, spearmint-gum wrappers and Vienna-sausage labels, I raked the yellow-red dirt, and made half-moons carefully, so that the design stood out clearly and mask-like. I put the rake behind the Store and came through the back of the house to find Grandmother on the front porch in her big, wide white apron. The apron was so stiff by virtue of the starch that it could have stood alone. Momma was admiring the yard, so I joined her. It truly looked like a flat redhead that had been raked with a big-toothed comb. Momma didn't say anything but I knew she liked it. She looked over toward the school principal's house and to the right at Mr. McElroy's. She was hoping one of those community pillars would see the design before the day's business wiped it out. Then she looked upward to the school. My head had swung with hers, so at just about the same time we saw a troop of powhitetrash kids marching over the hill and down by the side of the school.

I looked to Momma for direction. She did an excellent job 16 of sagging from her waist down, but from the waist up she seemed to be pulling for the top of the oak tree across the road. Then she began to moan a hymn. Maybe not to moan, but the tune was so slow and the meter so strange that she could have been moaning. She didn't look at me again. When the children reached halfway down the hill, halfway to the Store, she said without turning, "Sister, go on inside."

I wanted to beg her, "Momma, don't wait for them. Come 17 on inside with me. If they come in the Store, you go to the bedroom and let me wait on them. They only frighten me if you're around. Alone I know how to handle them." But of course I couldn't say anything, so I went in and stood behind the screen door.

Before the girls got to the porch I heard their laughter crack- 18 ling and popping like pine logs in a cooking stove. I suppose my lifelong paranoia was born in those cold, molasses-slow minutes. They came finally to stand on the ground in front of Momma. At first they pretended seriousness. Then one of them wrapped her right arm in the crook of her left, pushed out her mouth and started to hum. I realized that she was aping my grandmother. Another said, "Naw, Helen, you ain't standing

like her. This here's it." Then she lifted her chest, folded her
arms and mocked that strange carriage that was Annie Henderson. Another laughed, "Naw, you can't do it. Your mouth
ain't pooched out enough. It's like this."

I thought about the rifle behind the door, but I knew I'd   19
never be able to hold it straight, and the .410, our sawed-off
shotgun, which stayed loaded and was fired every New Year's
night, was locked in the trunk and Uncle Willie had the key on
his chain. Through the fly-specked screen-door, I could see that
the arms of Momma's apron jiggled from the vibrations of her
humming. But her knees seemed to have locked as if they would
never bend again.

She sang on. No louder than before, but no softer either. No   20
slower or faster.

The dirt of the girls' cotton dresses continued on their legs,   21
feet, arms and faces to make them all of a piece. Their greasy
uncolored hair hung down, uncombed, with a grim finality. I
knelt to see them better, to remember them for all time. The tears
that had slipped down my dress left unsurprising dark spots,
and made the front yard blurry and even more unreal. The
world had taken a deep breath and was having doubts about
continuing to revolve.

The girls had tired of mocking Momma and turned to other   22
means of agitation. One crossed her eyes, stuck her thumbs in
both sides of her mouth and said, "Look here, Annie." Grandmother hummed on and the apron strings trembled. I wanted
to throw a handful of black pepper in their faces, to throw lye
on them, to scream that they were dirty, scummy peckerwoods,
but I knew I was as clearly imprisoned behind the scene as the
actors outside were confined to their roles.

One of the smaller girls did a kind of puppet dance while   23
her fellow clowns laughed at her. But the tall one, who was almost a woman, said something very quietly, which I couldn't
hear. They all moved backward from the porch, still watching
Momma. For an awful second I thought they were going to
throw a rock at Momma, who seemed (except for the apron
strings) to have turned into stone herself. But the big girl turned
her back, bent down and put her hands flat on the ground—she

didn't pick up anything. She simply shifted her weight and did a hand stand.

Her dirty bare feet and long legs went straight for the sky. 24
Her dress fell down around her shoulders, and she had on no drawers. The slick pubic hair made a brown triangle where her legs came together. She hung in the vacuum of that lifeless morning for only a few seconds, then wavered and tumbled. The other girls clapped her on the back and slapped their hands.

Momma changed her song to "Bread of Heaven, bread of 25 Heaven, feed me till I want no more."

I found that I was praying too. How long could Momma 26 hold out? What new indignity would they think of to subject her to? Would I be able to stay out of it? What would Momma really like me to do?

Then they were moving out of the yard, on their way to 27 town. They bobbed their heads and shook their slack behinds and turned, one at a time:

" 'Bye, Annie."   28
" 'Bye, Annie."   29
" 'Bye, Annie."   30

Momma never turned her head or unfolded her arms, but 31 she stopped singing and said, " 'Bye, Miz Helen, 'bye, Miz Ruth, 'bye, Miz Eloise."

I burst. A firecracker July-the-Fourth burst. How could 32 Momma call them Miz? The mean nasty things. Why couldn't she have come inside the sweet, cool store when we saw them breasting the hill? What did she prove? And then if they were dirty, mean and impudent, why did Momma have to call them Miz?

She stood another whole song through and then opened the 33 screen door to look down on me crying in rage. She looked until I looked up. Her face was a brown moon that shone on me. She was beautiful. Something had happened out there, which I couldn't completely understand, but I could see that she was happy. Then she bent down and touched me as mothers of the church "lay hands on the sick and afflicted" and I quieted.

"Go wash your face, Sister." And she went behind the candy 34 counter and hummed, "Glory, glory, hallelujah, when I lay my burden down."

I threw the well water on my face and used the weekday handkerchief to blow my nose. Whatever the contest had been out front, I knew Momma had won. 35

I took the rake back to the front yard. The smudged footprints were easy to erase. I worked for a long time on my new design and laid the rake behind the wash pot. When I came back in the Store, I took Momma's hand and we both walked outside to look at the pattern. 36

It was a large heart with lots of hearts growing smaller inside, and piercing from the outside rim to the smallest heart was an arrow. Momma said, "Sister, that's right pretty." Then she turned back to the Store and resumed, "Glory, glory, hallelujah, when I lay my burden down." 37

1970

No Name Woman

Maxine Hong Kingston

"You must not tell anyone," my mother said, "what I am about to tell you. In China your father had a sister who killed herself. She jumped into the family well. We say that your father has all brothers because it is as if she had never been born. 1

"In 1924 just a few days after our village celebrated seventeen hurry-up weddings—to make sure that every young man who went 'out on the road' would responsibly come home—your father and his brothers and your grandfather and his brothers and your aunt's new husband sailed for America, the Gold Mountain. It was your grandfather's last trip. Those lucky enough to get contracts waved goodbye from the decks. They fed and guarded the stowaways and helped them off in Cuba, 2

New York, Bali, Hawaii. 'We'll meet in California next year
they said. All of them sent money home.

"I remember looking at your aunt one day when she and I 3
were dressing; I had not noticed before that she had such a protruding melon of a stomach. But I did not think, 'She's pregnant,' until she began to look like other pregnant women, her
shirt pulling and the white tops of her black pants showing. She
could not have been pregnant, you see, because her husband
had been gone for years. No one said anything. We did not discuss it. In early summer she was ready to have the child, long
after the time when it could have been possible.

"The village had also been counting. On the night the baby 4
was to be born the villagers raided our house. Some were crying. Like a great saw, teeth strung with lights, files of people
walked zigzag across our land, tearing the rice. Their lanterns
doubled in the disturbed black water, which drained away
through the broken bunds. As the villagers closed in, we could
see that some of them, probably men and women we knew
well, wore white masks. The people with long hair hung it over
their faces. Women with short hair made it stand up on end.
Some had tied white bands around their foreheads, arms, and
legs.

"At first they threw mud and rocks at the house. Then they 5
threw eggs and began slaughtering our stock. We could hear the
animals scream their deaths—the roosters, the pigs, a last great
roar from the ox. Familiar wild heads flared in our night windows; the villagers encircled us. Some of the faces stopped to
peer at us, their eyes rushing like searchlights. The hands flattened against the panes, framed heads, and left red prints.

"The villagers broke in the front and the back doors at the 6
same time, even though we had not locked the doors against
them. Their knives dripped with the blood of our animals. They
smeared blood on the doors and walls. One woman swung a
chicken, whose throat she had slit, splattering blood in red arcs
about her. We stood together in the middle of our house, in the
family hall with the pictures and tables of the ancestors around
us, and looked straight ahead.

"At that time the house had only two wings. When the men 7

came back, we would build two more to enclose our courtyard and a third one to begin a second courtyard. The villagers pushed through both wings, even your grandparents' rooms, to find your aunt's, which was also mine until the men returned. From this room a new wing for one of the younger families would grow. They ripped up her clothes and shoes and broke her combs, grinding them underfoot. They tore her work from the loom. They scattered the cooking fire and rolled the new weaving in it. We could hear them in the kitchen breaking our bowls and banging the pots. They overturned the great waist-high earthenware jugs; duck eggs, pickled fruits, vegetables burst out and mixed in acrid torrents. The old woman from the next field swept a broom through the air and loosed the spirits-of-the-broom over our heads. 'Pig.' 'Ghost.' 'Pig,' they sobbed and scolded while they ruined our house.

"When they left, they took sugar and oranges to bless them-   8
selves. They cut pieces from the dead animals. Some of them took bowls that were not broken and clothes that were not torn. Afterward we swept up the rice and sewed it back up into sacks. But the smells from the spilled preserves lasted. Your aunt gave birth in the pigsty that night. The next morning when I went for the water, I found her and the baby plugging up the family well.

"Don't let your father know that I told you. He denies her.   9
Now that you have started to menstruate, what happened to her could happen to you. Don't humiliate us. You wouldn't like to be forgotten as if you had never been born. The villagers are watchful."

Whenever she had to warn us about life, my mother told   10
stories that ran like this one, a story to grow up on. She tested our strength to establish realities. Those in the emigrant gener-ations who could not reassert brute survival died young and far from home. Those of us in the first American generations have had to figure out how the invisible world the emigrants built around our childhoods fits in solid America.

The emigrants confused the gods by diverting their curses,   11
misleading them with crooked streets and false names. They must try to confuse their offspring as well, who, I suppose, threaten them in similar ways—always trying to get things

straight, always trying to name the unspeakable. The Chinese I know hide their names; sojourners take new names when their lives change and guard their real names with silence.

Chinese-Americans, when you try to understand what 12 things in you are Chinese, how do you separate what is peculiar to childhood, to poverty, insanities, one family, your mother who marked your growing with stories, from what is Chinese? What is Chinese tradition and what is the movies?

If I want to learn what clothes my aunt wore, whether flashy 13 or ordinary, I would have to begin, "Remember Father's drowned-in-the-well sister?" I cannot ask that. My mother has told me once and for all the useful parts. She will add nothing unless powered by Necessity, a riverbank that guides her life. She plants vegetable gardens rather than lawns; she carries the odd-shaped tomatoes home from the fields and eats food left for the gods.

Whenever we did frivolous things, we used up energy; we 14 flew high kites. We children came up off the ground over the melting cones our parents brought home from work and the American movie on New Year's Day—*Oh, You Beautiful Doll* with Betty Grable one year, and *She Wore a Yellow Ribbon* with John Wayne another year. After the one carnival ride each, we paid in guilt; our tired father counted his change on the dark walk home.

Adultery is extravagance. Could people who hatch their 15 own chicks and eat the embryos and the heads for delicacies and boil the feet in vinegar for party food, leaving only the gravel, eating even the gizzard lining—could such people engender a prodigal aunt? To be a woman, to have a daughter in starvation time was a waste enough. My aunt could not have been the lone romantic who gave up everything for sex. Women in the old China did not choose. Some man had commanded her to lie with him and be his secret evil. I wonder whether he masked himself when he joined the raid on her family.

Perhaps she had encountered him in the fields or on the 16 mountain where the daughters-in-law collected fuel. Or perhaps he first noticed her in the marketplace. He was not a stranger because the village housed no strangers. She had to have dealings with him other than sex. Perhaps he worked an adjoining field, or he sold her the cloth for the dress she sewed and wore. His demand must have surprised, then terrified her. She obeyed him; she always did as she was told.

When the family found a young man in the next village to be her husband, she had stood tractably beside the best rooster, his proxy, and promised before they met that she would be his forever. She was lucky that he was her age and she would be the first wife, an advantage secure now. The night she first saw him, he had sex with her. Then he left for America. She had almost forgotten what he looked like. When she tried to envision him, she only saw the black and white face in the group photograph the men had had taken before leaving. 17

The other man was not, after all, much different from her husband. They both gave orders: she followed. "If you tell your family, I'll beat you. I'll kill you. Be here again next week." No one talked sex, ever. And she might have separated the rapes from the rest of living if only she did not have to buy her oil from him or gather wood in the same forest. I want her fear to have lasted just as long as rape lasted so that the fear could have been contained. No drawn-out fear. But women at sex hazarded birth and hence lifetimes. The fear did not stop but permeated everywhere. She told the man, "I think I'm pregnant." He organized the raid against her. 18

On nights when my mother and father talked about their life back home, sometimes they mentioned an "outcast table" whose business they still seemed to be settling, their voices tight. In a commensal tradition, where food is precious, the powerful older people made wrongdoers eat alone. Instead of letting them start separate new lives like the Japanese, who could become samurais and geishas, the Chinese family, faces averted but eyes glowering sideways, hung on to the offenders and fed them leftovers. My aunt must have lived in the same house as my parents and eaten at an outcast table. My mother spoke about the raid as if she had seen it, when she and my aunt, a daughter-in-law to a different household, should not have been living together at all. Daughters-in-law lived with their husbands' parents, not their own; a synonym for marriage in 19

Chinese is "taking a daughter-in-law." Her husband's parents could have sold her, mortgaged her, stoned her. But they had sent her back to her own mother and father, a mysterious act hinting at disgraces not told me. Perhaps they had thrown her out to deflect the avengers.

She was the only daughter; her four brothers went with her 20 father, husband, and uncles "out on the road" and for some years became western men. When the goods were divided among the family, three of the brothers took land, and the youngest, my father, chose an education. After my grandparents gave their daughter away to her husband's family, they had dispensed all the adventure and all the property. They expected her alone to keep the traditional ways, which her brothers, now among the barbarians, could fumble without detection. The heavy, deep-rooted women were to maintain the past against the flood, safe for returning. But the rare urge west had fixed upon our family, and so my aunt crossed boundaries not delineated in space.

The work of preservation demands that the feelings play- 21 ing about in one's guts not be turned into action. Just watch their passing like cherry blossoms. But perhaps my aunt, my forerunner, caught in a slow life, let dreams grow and fade and after some months or years went toward what persisted. Fear at the enormities of the forbidden kept her desires delicate, wire and bone. She looked at a man because she liked the way the hair was tucked behind his ears, or she liked the question-mark line of a long torso curving at the shoulder and straight at the hip. For warm eyes or a soft voice or a slow walk—that's all—a few hairs, a line, a brightness, a sound, a pace, she gave up family. She offered us up for a charm that vanished with tiredness, a pigtail that didn't toss when the wind died. Why, the wrong lighting could erase the dearest thing about him.

It could very well have been, however, that my aunt did not 22 take subtle enjoyment of her friend, but, a wild woman, kept rollicking company. Imagining her free with sex doesn't fit, though. I don't know any women like that, or men either. Unless I see her life branching into mine, she gives me no ancestral help.

To sustain her being in love, she often worked at herself in 23

the mirror, guessing at the colors and shapes that would interest him, changing them frequently in order to hit on the right
combination. She wanted him to look back.

   On a farm near the sea, a woman who tended her appear-   24
ance reaped a reputation for eccentricity. All the married
women blunt-cut their hair in flaps about their ears or pulled it
back in tight buns. No nonsense. Neither style blew easily into
heart-catching tangles. And at their weddings they displayed
themselves in their long hair for the last time. "It brushed the
backs of my knees," my mother tells me. "It was braided, and
even so, it brushed the backs of my knees."

   At the mirror my aunt combed individuality into her bob.   25
A bun could have been contrived to escape into black stream-
ers blowing in the wind or in quiet wisps about her face, but
only the older women in our picture album wear buns. She
brushed her hair back from her forehead, tucking the flaps behind her ears. She looped a piece of thread, knotted into a circle between her index fingers and thumbs, and ran the double
strand across her forehead. When she closed her fingers as if she
were making a pair of shadow geese bite, the string twisted together catching the little hairs. Then she pulled the thread away
from her skin, ripping the hairs out neatly, her eyes watering
from the needles of pain. Opening her fingers, she cleaned the
thread, then rolled it along her hairline and the tops of her eye-
brows. My mother did the same to me and my sisters and herself. I used to believe that the expression "caught by the short
hairs" meant a captive held with a depilatory string. It especially
hurt at the temples, but my mother said we were lucky we
didn't have to have our feet bound when we were seven. Sisters used to sit on their beds and cry together, she said, as their
mothers or their slaves removed the bandages for a few minutes each night and let the blood gush back into their veins. I
hope that the man my aunt loved appreciated a smooth brow,
that he wasn't just a tits-and-ass man.

   Once my aunt found a freckle on her chin, at a spot that the   26
almanac said predestined her for unhappiness. She dug it out
with a hot needle and washed the wound with peroxide.

   More attention to her looks than these pullings of hairs and   27

pickings at spots would have caused gossip among the villagers. They owned work clothes and good clothes, and they
wore good clothes for feasting the new seasons. But since a
woman combing her hair hexes beginnings, my aunt rarely
found an occasion to look her best. Women looked like great sea
snails—the corded wood, babies, and laundry they carried were
the whorls on their backs. The Chinese did not admire a bent
back; goddesses and warriors stood straight. Still there must
have been a marvelous freeing of beauty when a worker laid
down her burden and stretched and arched.

Such commonplace loveliness, however, was not enough   28
for my aunt. She dreamed of a lover for the fifteen days of New
Year's, the time for families to exchange visits, money, and
food. She plied her secret comb. And sure enough she cursed
the year, the family, the village, and herself.

Even as her hair lured her imminent lover, many other men   29
looked at her. Uncles, cousins, nephews, brothers would have
looked, too, had they been home between journeys. Perhaps
they had already been restraining their curiosity, and they left,
fearful that their glances, like a field of nesting birds, might be
startled and caught. Poverty hurt, and that was their first reason for leaving. But another, final reason for leaving the
crowded house was the never-said.

She may have been unusually beloved, the precious only   30
daughter, spoiled and mirror gazing because of the affection the
family lavished on her. When her husband left, they welcomed
the chance to take her back from the in-laws; she could live like
the little daughter for just a while longer. There are stories that
my grandfather was different from other people, "crazy ever
since the little Jap bayoneted him in the head." He used to put
his naked penis on the dinner table, laughing. And one day he
brought home a baby girl, wrapped up inside his brown
western-style greatcoat. He had traded one of his sons, probably my father, the youngest, for her. My grandmother made him
trade back. When he finally got a daughter of his own, he doted
on her. They must have all loved her, except perhaps my father,
the only brother who never went back to China, having once
been traded for a girl.

Brothers and sisters, newly men and women, had to efface ₃₁
their sexual color and present plain miens. Disturbing hair and
eyes, a smile like no other, threatened the ideal of five generations living under one roof. To focus blurs, people shouted face
to face and yelled from room to room. The immigrants I know
have loud voices, unmodulated to American tones even after
years away from the village where they called their friendships
out across the fields. I have not been able to stop my mother's
screams in public libraries or over telephones. Walking erect
(knees straight, toes pointed forward, not pigeon-toed, which
is Chinese-feminine) and speaking in an inaudible voice, I have
tried to turn myself American-feminine. Chinese communication was loud, public. Only sick people had to whisper. But at
the dinner table, where the family members came nearest one
another, no one could talk, not the outcasts nor any eaters.
Every word that falls from the mouth is a coin lost. Silently
they gave and accepted food with both hands. A preoccupied
child who took his bowl with one hand got a sideways glare. A
complete moment of total attention is due everyone alike. Children and lovers have no singularity here, but my aunt used a
secret voice, a separate attentiveness.

She kept the man's name to herself throughout her labor ₃₂
and dying; she did not accuse him that he be punished with her.
To save her inseminator's name she gave silent birth.

He may have been somebody in her own household, but in- ₃₃
tercourse with a man outside the family would have been no
less abhorrent. All the village were kinsmen, and the titles
shouted in loud country voices never let kinship be forgotten.
Any man within visiting distance would have been neutralized
as a lover—"brother," "younger brother," "older brother"—
one hundred and fifteen relationship titles. Parents researched
birth charts probably not so much to assure good fortune as to
circumvent incest in a population that has but one hundred
surnames. Everybody has eight million relatives. How useless
then sexual mannerisms, how dangerous.

As if it came from an atavism deeper than fear, I used to add ₃₄
"brother" silently to boys' names. It hexed the boys, who would
or would not ask me to dance, and made them less scary and
as familiar and deserving of benevolence as girls.

But, of course, I hexed myself also—no dates. I should have 35
stood up, both arms waving, and shouted out across libraries,
"Hey, you! Love me back." I had no idea, though, how to make
attraction selective, how to control its direction and magnitude.
If I made myself American-pretty so that the five or six Chinese
boys in the class fell in love with me, everyone else—the Caucasian, Negro, and Japanese boys—would too. Sisterliness, dignified and honorable, made much more sense.

Attraction eludes control so stubbornly that whole societies 36
designed to organize relationships among people cannot keep
order, not even when they bind people to one another from
childhood and raise them together. Among the very poor and
the wealthy, brothers married their adopted sisters, like doves.
Our family allowed some romance, paying adult brides' prices
and providing dowries so that their sons and daughters could
marry strangers. Marriage promises to turn strangers into
friendly relatives—a nation of siblings.

In the village structure, spirits shimmered among the live 37
creatures, balanced and held in equilibrium by time and land.
But one human being flaring up into violence could open up a
black hole, a maelstrom that pulled in the sky. The frightened
villagers, who depended on one another to maintain the real,
went to my aunt to show her a personal, physical representa-
tion of the break she had made in the "roundness." Misallying
couples snapped off the future, which was to be embodied in
true offspring. The villagers punished her for acting as if she
could have a private life, secret and apart from them.

If my aunt had betrayed the family at a time of large grain 38
yields and peace, when many boys were born, and wings were
being built on many houses, perhaps she might have escaped
such severe punishment. But the men—hungry, greedy, tired
of planting in dry soil—had been forced to leave the village in
order to send food-money home. There were ghost plagues,
bandit plagues, wars with the Japanese, floods. My Chinese
brother and sister had died of an unknown sickness. Adultery,
perhaps only a mistake during good times, became a crime
when the village needed food.

The round moon cakes and round doorways, the round ta- 39
bles of graduated sizes that fit one roundness inside another,

round windows and rice bowls—these talismans had lost their
power to warn this family of the law: a family must be whole,
faithfully keeping the descent line by having sons to feed the
old and the dead, who in turn look after the family. The villagers
came to show my aunt and her lover-in-hiding a broken house.
The villagers were speeding up the circling of events because
she was too shortsighted to see that her infidelity had already
harmed the village, that waves of consequences would return
unpredictably, sometimes in disguise, as now, to hurt her. This
roundness had to be made coin-sized so that she would see its
circumference: punish her at the birth of her baby. Awaken her
to the inexorable. People who refused fatalism because they
could invent small resources insisted on culpability. Deny accidents and wrest fault from the stars.

    After the villagers left, their lanterns now scattering in var-   40
ious directions toward home, the family broke their silence
and cursed her. "Aiaa, we're going to die. Death is coming.
Death is coming. Look what you've done. You've killed us.
Ghost! Dead ghost! Ghost! You've never been born." She ran
out into the fields, far enough from the house so that she could
no longer hear their voices, and pressed herself against the
earth, her own land no more. When she felt the birth coming,
she thought that she had been hurt. Her body seized together.
"They've hurt me too much," she thought. "This is gall, and it
will kill me." With forehead and knees against the earth, her
body convulsed and then relaxed. She turned on her back, lay
on the ground. The black well of sky and stars went out and
out and out forever; her body and her complexity seemed to
disappear. She was one of the stars, a bright dot in blackness,
without home, without a companion, in eternal cold and silence. An agoraphobia rose in her, speeding higher and higher,
bigger and bigger; she would not be able to contain it; there
would be no end to fear.

    Flayed, unprotected against space, she felt pain return, fo-   41
cusing her body. This pain chilled her—a cold, steady kind of
surface pain. Inside, spasmodically, the other pain, the pain of
the child, heated her. For hours she lay on the ground, alter-
nately body and space. Sometimes a vision of normal comfort

obliterated reality: she saw the family in the evening gambling
at the dinner table, the young people massaging their elders'
backs. She saw them congratulating one another, high joy on the
mornings the rice shoots came up. When these pictures burst,
the stars drew yet further apart. Black space opened.

She got to her feet to fight better and remembered that old- 42
fashioned women gave birth in their pigsties to fool the jealous,
pain-dealing gods, who do not snatch piglets. Before the next
spasms could stop her, she ran to the pigsty, each step a rushing out into emptiness. She climbed over the fence and knelt in
the dirt. It was good to have a fence enclosing her, a tribal person alone.

Laboring, this woman who had carried her child as a for- 43
eign growth that sickened her every day, expelled it at last. She
reached down to touch the hot, wet, moving mass, surely
smaller than anything human, and could feel that it was human
after all—fingers, toes, nails, nose. She pulled it up on to her
belly, and it lay curled there, butt in the air, feet precisely tucked
one under the other. She opened her loose shirt and buttoned
the child inside. After resting, it squirmed and thrashed and she
pushed it up to her breast. It turned its head this way and that
until it found her nipple. There, it made little snuffling noises.
She clenched her teeth at its preciousness, lovely as a young calf,
a piglet, a little dog.

She may have gone to the pigsty as a last act of responsi- 44
bility: she would protect this child as she had protected its father. It would look after her soul, leaving supplies on her grave.
But how would this tiny child without family find her grave
when there would be no marker for her anywhere, neither in
the earth nor the family hall? No one would give her a family
hall name. She had taken the child with her into the wastes. At
its birth the two of them had felt the same raw pain of separation, a wound that only the family pressing tight could close. A
child with no descent line would not soften her life but only trail
after her, ghostlike, begging her to give it purpose. At dawn the
villagers on their way to the fields would stand around the
fence and look.

Full of milk, the little ghost slept. When it awoke, she hard- 45 ened her breasts against the milk that crying loosens. Toward morning she picked up the baby and walked to the well.

Carrying the baby to the well shows loving. Otherwise 46 abandon it. Turn its face into the mud. Mothers who love their children take them along. It was probably a girl; there is some hope of forgiveness for boys.

"Don't tell anyone you had an aunt. Your father does not 47 want to hear her name. She has never been born." I have believed that sex was unspeakable and words so strong and fathers so frail that "aunt" would do my father mysterious harm. I have thought that my family, having settled among immigrants who had also been their neighbors in the ancestral land, needed to clean their name, and a wrong word would incite the kinspeople even here. But there is more to this silence: they want me to participate in her punishment. And I have.

In the twenty years since I heard this story I have not asked 48 for details nor said my aunt's name; I do not know it. People who can comfort the dead can also chase after them to hurt them further—a reverse ancestor worship. The real punishment was not the raid swiftly inflicted by the villagers, but the family's deliberately forgetting her. Her betrayal so maddened them, they saw to it that she would suffer forever, even after death. Always hungry, always needing, she would have to beg food from other ghosts, snatch and steal it from those whose living descendants give them gifts. She would have to fight the ghosts massed at crossroads for the buns a few thoughtful citizens leave to decoy her away from village and home so that the ancestral spirits could feast unharassed. At peace, they could act like gods, not ghosts, their descent lines providing them with paper suits and dresses, spirit money, paper houses, paper automobiles, chicken, meat, and rice into eternity—essences delivered up in smoke and flames, steam and incense rising from each rice bowl. In an attempt to make the Chinese care for people outside the family, Chairman Mao encourages us now to give our paper replicas to the spirits of outstanding soldiers and workers, no matter whose ancestors they may be. My aunt remains forever hungry. Goods are not distributed evenly among the dead.

My aunt haunts me—her ghost drawn to me because now,   49 after fifty years of neglect, I alone devote pages of paper to her, though not origamied into houses and clothes. I do not think she always means me well. I am telling on her, and she was a spite suicide, drowning herself in the drinking water. The Chinese are always very frightened of the drowned one, whose weeping ghost, wet hair hanging and skin bloated, waits silently by the water to pull down a substitute.

1975

The Stunt Pilot

Annie Dillard

Dave Rahm lived in Bellingham, Washington, north of Seat-   1 tle. Bellingham, a harbor town, lies between the alpine North Cascade Mountains and the San Juan Islands in Haro Strait above Puget Sound. The latitude is that of Newfoundland. Dave Rahm was a stunt pilot, the air's own genius.

In 1975, with a newcomer's willingness to try anything once,   2 I attended the Bellingham Air Show. The Bellingham airport was a wide clearing in a forest of tall Douglas firs; its runways suited small planes. It was June. People wearing blue or tan zipped jackets stood loosely on the concrete walkways and runways outside the coffee shop. At that latitude in June, you stayed outside because you could, even most of the night, if you could think up something to do. The sky did not darken until ten o'clock or so, and it never got very dark. Your life parted and opened in the sunlight. You tossed your dark winter routines, thought up mad projects, and improvised everything

from hour to hour. Being a stunt pilot seemed the most reasonable thing in the world; you could wave your arms in the
air all day and all night, and sleep next winter.

I saw from the ground a dozen stunt pilots; the air show   3
scheduled them one after the other, for an hour of aerobatics.
Each pilot took up his or her plane and performed a batch of
tricks. They were precise and impressive. They flew upside
down, and straightened out; they did barrel rolls, and straightened out; they drilled through dives and spins, and landed gently on a far runway.

For the end of the day, separated from all other perfor-   4
mances of every sort, the air show director had scheduled a program titled "Dave Rahm." The leaflet said that Rahm was a geologist who taught at Western Washington University. He had
flown for King Hussein in Jordan. A tall man in the crowd told
me Hussein had seen Rahm fly on a visit the king made to the
United States; he had invited him to Jordan to perform at ceremonies. Hussein was a pilot, too. "Hussein thought he was the
greatest thing in the world."

Idly, paying scant attention, I saw a medium-sized, rugged   5
man dressed in brown leather, all begoggled, climb in a black
biplane's open cockpit. The plane was a Bücker Jungman, built
in the thirties. I saw a tall, dark-haired woman seize a propeller
tip at the plane's nose and yank it down till the engine caught.
He was off; he climbed high over the airport in his biplane,
very high until he was barely visible as a mote, and then seemed
to fall down the air, diving headlong, and streaming beauty in
spirals behind him.

The black plane dropped spinning, and flattened out spin-   6
ning the other way; it began to carve the air into forms that built
wildly and musically on each other and never ended. Reluctantly, I started paying attention. Rahm drew high above the
world an inexhaustibly glorious line; it piled over our heads in
loops and arabesques. It was like a Saul Steinberg fantasy; the
plane was the pen. Like Steinberg's contracting and billowing
pen line, the line Rahm spun moved to form new, punning

shapes from the edges of the old. Like a Klee line, it smattered the sky with landscapes and systems.

    The air show announcer hushed. He had been squawking 7 all day, and now he quit. The crowd stilled. Even the children watched dumbstruck as the slow, black biplane buzzed its way around the air. Rahm made beauty with his whole body; it was pure pattern, and you could watch it happen. The plane moved every way a line can move, and it controlled three dimensions, so the line carved massive and subtle slits in the air like sculptures. The plane looped the loop, seeming to arch its back like a gymnast; it stalled, dropped, and spun out of it climbing; it spiraled and knifed west on one side's wings and back east on another; it turned cartwheels, which must be physically impossible; it played with its own line like a cat with yarn. How did the pilot know where in the air he was? If he got lost, the ground would swat him.

    Rahm did everything his plane could do: tailspins, four- 8 point rolls, flat spins, figure eights, snap rolls, and hammerheads. He did pirouettes on the plane's tail. The other pilots could do these stunts too, skillfully, one at a time. But Rahm used the plane inexhaustibly, like a brush marking thin air.

    His was pure energy and naked spirit. I have thought about 9 it for years. Rahm's line unrolled in time. Like music, it split the bulging rim of the future along its seam. It pried out the present. We watchers waited for the split-second curve of beauty in the present to reveal itself. The human pilot, David Rahm, worked in the cockpit right at the plane's nose; his very body tore into the future for us and reeled it down upon us like a curling peel.

    Like any fine artist, he controlled the tension of the audi- 10 ence's longing. You desired, unwittingly, a certain kind of roll or climb, or a return to a certain portion of the air, and he fulfilled your hope slanting, like a poet, or evaded it until you thought you would burst, and then fulfilled it surprisingly, so you gasped and cried out.

    The oddest, most exhilarating and exhausting thing was 11 this: he never quit. The music had no periods, no rests or end-

ings; the poetry's beautiful sentence never ended; the line had
no finish; the sculptured forms piled overhead, one into another
without surcease. Who could breathe, in a world where rhythm
itself had no periods?

It had taken me several minutes to understand what an ex-   12
traordinary thing I was seeing. Rahm kept all that embellished
space in mind at once. For another twenty minutes I watched
the beauty unroll and grow more fantastic and unlikely before
my eyes. Now Rahm brought the plane down slidingly, and just
in time, for I thought I would snap from the effort to compass
and remember the line's long intelligence; I could not add another curve. He brought the plane down on a far runway. After
a pause, I saw him step out, an ordinary man, and make his way
back to the terminal.

The show was over. It was late. Just as I turned from the run-   13
way, something caught my eye and made me laugh. It was a
swallow, a blue-green swallow, having its own air show, apparently inspired by Rahm. The swallow climbed high over the
runway, held its wings oddly, tipped them, and rolled down the
air in loops. The inspired swallow. I always want to paint, too,
after I see the Rembrandts. The blue-green swallow tumbled
precisely, and caught itself and flew up again as if excited, and
looped down again, the way swallows do, but tensely, holding
its body carefully still. It was a stunt swallow.

I went home and thought about Rahm's performance that   14
night, and the next day, and the next.

I had thought I knew my way around beauty a little bit. I   15
knew I had devoted a good part of my life to it, memorizing poetry and focusing my attention on complexity of rhythm in particular, on force, movement, repetition, and surprise, in both poetry and prose. Now I had stood among dandelions between
two asphalt runways in Bellingham, Washington, and begun
learning about beauty. Even the Boston Museum of Fine Arts
was never more inspiriting than this small northwestern airport
on this time-killing Sunday afternoon in June. Nothing on earth
is more gladdening than knowing we must roll up our sleeves

and move back the boundaries of the humanly possible once more.

Later I flew with Dave Rahm; he took me up. A generous 16
geographer, Dick Smith, at Western Washington University,
arranged it, and came along. Rahm and Dick Smith were colleagues at the university. In geology, Rahm had published two
books and many articles. Rahm was handsome in a dull sort of
way, blunt-featured, wide-jawed, wind-burned, keen-eyed, and
taciturn. As anyone would expect. He was forty. He wanted to
show me the Cascade Mountains; these enormous peaks, only
fifty miles from the coast, rise over nine thousand feet; they are
heavily glaciated. Whatcom County has more glaciers than the
lower forty-eight states combined; the Cascades make the Rocky
Mountains look like hills. Mount Baker is volcanic, like most
Cascade peaks. That year, Mount Baker was acting up. Even
from my house at the shore I could see, early in the morning on
clear days, volcanic vapor rise near its peak. Often the vapor
made a cloud that swelled all morning and hid the snows. Every
day the newspapers reported on Baker's activity: Would it
blow? (A few years later, Mount St. Helens did blow.)
    Rahm was not flying his trick biplane that day, but a faster, 17
enclosed plane, a single-engine Cessna. We flew from a bumpy
grass airstrip near my house, out over the coast and inland.
There was coastal plain down there, but we could not see it for
clouds. We were over the clouds at five hundred feet and inside
them too, heading for an abrupt line of peaks we could not see.
I gave up on everything, the way you do in airplanes; it was out
of my hands. Every once in a while Rahm saw a peephole in the
clouds and buzzed over for a look. "That's Larsen's pea farm,"
he said, or "That's Nooksack Road," and he changed our course
with a heave.
    When we got to the mountains, he slid us along Mount 18
Baker's flanks sideways.
    Our plane swiped at the mountain with a roar. I glimpsed 19
a windshield view of dirty snow traveling fast. Our shaking,
swooping belly seemed to graze the snow. The wings shud-
dered; we peeled away and the mountain fell back and the en-

gines whined. We felt flung, because we were in fact flung; parts of our faces and internal organs trailed pressingly behind on the curves. We came back for another pass at the mountain, and another. We dove at the snow headlong like suicides; we jerked up, down, or away at the last second, so late we left our hearts, stomachs, and lungs behind. If I forced myself to hold my heavy head up against the G's, and to raise my eyelids, heavy as barbells, and to notice what I saw, I could see the wrinkled green crevasses cracking the glaciers' snow.

Pitching snow filled all the windows, and shapes of dark 20 rock. I had no notion which way was up. Everything was black or gray or white except the fatal crevasses; everything made noise and shook. I felt my face smashed sideways and saw rushing abstractions of snow in the windshield. Patches of cloud obscured the snow fleetingly. We straightened out, turned, and dashed at the mountainside for another pass, which we made, apparently, on our ear, an inch or two away from the slope. Icefalls and cornices jumbled and fell away. If a commercial plane's black box, such as the FAA painstakingly recovers from crash sites, could store videotapes as well as pilots' last words, some videotapes would look like this: a mountainside coming up at the windows from all directions, ice and snow and rock filling the screen up close and screaming by.

Rahm was just being polite. His geographer colleague 21 wanted to see the fissure on Mount Baker from which steam escaped. Everybody in Bellingham wanted to see that sooty fissure, as did every geologist in the country; no one on earth could fly so close to it as Rahm. He knew the mountain by familiar love and feel, like a face; he knew what the plane could do and what he dared to do.

When Mount Baker inexplicably let us go, he jammed us 22 into cloud again and soon tilted. "The Sisters!" someone shouted, and I saw the windshield fill with red rock. This mountain looked infernal, a drear and sheer plane of lifeless rock. It was red and sharp; its gritty blades cut through the clouds at random. The mountain was quiet. It was in shade. Careening, we made sideways passes at these brittle peaks too steep for snow. Their rock was full of iron, somebody shouted at me then or later; the iron had rusted, so they were red. Later, when I was back on the ground, I recalled that, from a distance, the two jagged peaks called the Twin Sisters looked translucent against the sky; they were sharp, tapered, and fragile as arrowheads.

I talked to Rahm. He was flying us out to the islands now. ₂₃ The islands were fifty or sixty miles away. Like many other people, I had picked Bellingham, Washington, by looking at an atlas. It was clear from the atlas that you could row in the salt water and see snow-covered mountains; you could scale a glaciated mountainside with an ice ax in August, skirting green crevasses two hundred feet deep, and look out on the islands in the sea. Now, in the air, the clouds had risen over us; dark forms lay on the glinting water. There was almost no color to the day, just blackened green and some yellow. I knew the islands were forested in dark Douglas firs the size of skyscrapers. Bald eagles scavenged on the beaches; robins the size of herring gulls sang in the clearings. We made our way out to the islands through the layer of air between the curving planet and its held, thick clouds.

"When I started trying to figure out what I was going to do ₂₄ with my life, I decided to become an expert on mountains. It wasn't much to be, it wasn't everything, but it was something. I was going to know everything about mountains from every point of view. So I started out in geography." Geography proved too pedestrian for Rahm, too concerned with "how many bushels of wheat an acre." So he ended up in geology. Smith had told me that geology departments throughout the country used Rahm's photographic slides—close-ups of geologic features from the air.

"I used to climb mountains. But you know, you can get a bet- ₂₅ ter feel for a mountain's power flying around it, flying all around it, than you can from climbing it tied to its side like a flea."

He talked about his flying performances. He thought of the ₂₆ air as a line, he said. "This end of the line, that end of the line— like a rope." He improvised. "I get a rhythm going and stick with it." While he was performing in a show, he paid attention, he said, to the lighting. He didn't play against the sun. That was all he said about what he did.

In aerobatic maneuvers, pilots pull about seven positive 27
G's on some stunts and six negative G's on others. Some gyra-
tions push; others pull. Pilots alternate the pressures carefully,
so they do not gray out or black out.

Later I learned that some stunt pilots tune up by wearing 28
gravity boots. These are boots made to hook over a doorway;
wearing them, you hang in the doorway upside down. It must
startle a pilot's children to run into their father or mother in the
course of their home wanderings—the parents hanging wide-
eyed, upside down in the doorway like a bat.

We were landing; here was the airstrip on Stuart Island—that 29
island to which Ferrar Burn was dragged by the tide. We put
down, climbed out of the plane, and walked. We wandered a dirt
track through fields to a lee shore where yellow sandstone ledges
slid into the sea. The salt chuck, people there called salt water.
The sun came out. I caught a snake in the salt chuck; the snake,
eighteen inches long, was swimming in the green shallows.

I had a survivor's elation. Rahm had found Mount Baker in 30
the clouds before Mount Baker found the plane. He had wiped
it with the fast plane like a cloth and we had lived. When we
took off from Stuart Island and gained altitude, I asked if we
could turn over—could we do a barrel roll? The plane was making a lot of noise, and Dick Smith did not hear any of this, I
learned later. "Why not?" Rahm said, and added surprisingly,
"It won't hurt the plane." Without ado he leaned on the wheel
and the wing went down and we went somersaulting over it.
We upended with a roar. We stuck to the plane's sides like
flung paint. All the blood in my body bulged on my face; it piled
between my skull and skin. Vaguely I could see the chrome sea
twirling over Rahm's head like a baton, and the dark islands
sliding down the skies like rain.

The G's slammed me into my seat like thugs and pinned me 31
while my heart pounded and the plane turned over slowly and
compacted each organ in turn. My eyeballs were newly spher-
ical and full of heartbeats. I seemed to hear a crescendo; the
wing rolled shuddering down the last 90 degrees and settled on
the flat. There were the islands, admirably below us, and the

clouds, admirably above. When I could breathe, I asked if we could do it again, and we did. He rolled the other way. The brilliant line of the sea slid up the side window bearing its heavy islands. Through the shriek of my blood and the plane's shakes I glimpsed the line of the sea over the windshield, thin as a spear. How in performance did Rahm keep track while his brain blurred and blood roared in his ears without ceasing? Every performance was a tour de force and a show of will, a *Machtspruch*. I had seen the other stunt pilots straighten out after a trick or two; their blood could drop back and the plane simmer down. An Olympic gymnast, at peak form, strings out a line of spins ten stunts long across a mat, and is hard put to keep his footing at the end. Rahm endured much greater pressure on his faster spins using the plane's power, and he could spin in three dimensions and keep twirling till he ran out of sky room or luck.

When we straightened out, and had flown straightfor- ₃₂ wardly for ten minutes toward home, Dick Smith, clearing his throat, brought himself to speak. "What was that we did out there?"

"The barrel rolls?" Rahm said. "They were barrel rolls." He ₃₃ said nothing else. I looked at the back of his head; I could see the serious line of his cheek and jaw. He was in shirtsleeves, tanned, strong-wristed. I could not imagine loving him under any circumstance; he was alien to me, unfazed. He looked like GI Joe. He flew with that matter-of-fact, bored gesture pilots use. They click overhead switches and turn dials as if only their magnificent strength makes such dullness endurable. The half circle of wheel in their big hands looks like a toy they plan to crush in a minute; the wiggly stick the wheel mounts seems barely attached.

A crop-duster pilot in Wyoming told me the life expectancy ₃₄ of a crop-duster pilot is five years. They fly too low. They hit buildings and power lines. They have no space to fly out of trouble, and no space to recover from a stall. We were in Cody, Wyoming, out on the north fork of the Shoshone River. The crop duster had wakened me that morning flying over the ranch house and clearing my bedroom roof by half an inch. I saw the bolts on the wheel assembly a few feet from my face. He was spraying with pesticide the plain old grass. Over breakfast I asked him how long he had been dusting crops. "Four years," he said, and the figure stalled in the air between us for a moment. "You know you're going to die at it someday," he added. "We all know it. We accept that; it's part of it." I think now that, since the crop duster was in his twenties, he accepted only that he had to say such stuff; privately he counted on skewing the curve.

I suppose Rahm knew the fact too. I do not know how he felt about it. "It's worth it," said the early French aviator Mermoz. He was Antoine de Saint-Exupéry's friend. "It's worth the final smashup."

Rahm smashed up in front of King Hussein, in Jordan, during a performance. The plane spun down and never came out of it; it nosedived into the ground and exploded. He bought the farm. I was living then with my husband out on that remote island in the San Juans, cut off from everything. Battery radios picked up the Canadian Broadcasting Company out of Toronto, half a continent away; island people would, in theory, learn if the United States blew up, but not much else. There were no newspapers. One friend got the Sunday *New York Times* by mail boat on the following Friday. He saved it until Sunday and had a party, every week; we all read the Sunday *Times* and no one mentioned that it was last week's.

One day, Paul Glenn's brother flew out from Bellingham to visit; he had a seaplane. He landed in the water in front of the cabin and tied up to our mooring. He came in for coffee, and he gave out news of this and that, and—Say, did we know that stunt pilot Dave Rahm had cracked up? In Jordan, during a performance: he never came out of a dive. He just dove right down into the ground, and his wife was there watching. "I saw it on CBS News last night." And then—with a sudden sharp look at my filling eyes—"What, did you know him?" But no, I did not know him. He took me up once. Several years ago. I admired his flying. I had thought that danger was the safest thing in the world, if you went about it right.

Later I found a newspaper. Rahm was living in Jordan that

year; King Hussein invited him to train the aerobatics team, the
Royal Jordanian Falcons. He was also visiting professor of geology at the University of Jordan. In Amman that day he had
been flying a Pitt Special, a plane he knew well. Katy Rahm, his
wife of six months, was sitting beside Hussein in the viewing
stands, with her daughter. Rahm died performing a Lomcevak
combined with a tail slide and hammerhead. In a Lomcevak, the
pilot brings the plane up on a slant and pirouettes. I had seen
Rahm do this: the falling plane twirled slowly like a leaf. Like
a ballerina, the plane seemed to hold its head back stiff in concentration at the music's slow, painful beauty. It was one of
Rahm's favorite routines. Next the pilot flies straight up, stalls
the plane, and slides down the air on his tail. He brings the nose
down—the hammerhead—kicks the engine, and finishes with
a low loop.

It is a dangerous maneuver at any altitude, and Rahm was 39
doing it low. He hit the ground on the loop; the tail slide had
left him no height. When Rahm went down, King Hussein
dashed to the burning plane to pull him out, but he was already
dead.

A few months after the air show, and a month after I had 40
flown with Rahm, I was working at my desk near Bellingham,
where I lived, when I heard a sound so odd it finally pene-
trated my concentration. It was the buzz of an airplane, but it
rose and fell musically, and it never quit; the plane never flew
out of earshot. I walked out on the porch and looked up: it was
Rahm in the black and gold biplane, looping all over the air. I
had been wondering about his performance flight: could it really have been so beautiful? It was, for here it was again. The
little plane twisted all over the air like a vine. It trailed a line like
a very long mathematical proof you could follow only so far,
and then it lost you in its complexity. I saw Rahm flying high
over the Douglas firs, and out over the water, and back over
farms. The air was a fluid, and Rahm was an eel.

It was as if Mozart could move his body through his notes, 41
and you could walk out on the porch, look up, and see him in
periwig and breeches, flying around in the sky. You could hear

the music as he dove through it; it streamed after him like a con-
trail.

I lost myself; standing on the firm porch, I lost my direction   42
and reeled. My neck and spine rose and turned, so I followed
the plane's line kinesthetically. In his open-cockpit black plane,
Rahm demonstrated curved space. He slid down ramps of air,
he vaulted and wheeled. He piled loops in heaps and praised
height. He unrolled the scroll of the air, extended it, and bent it
into Möbius strips; he furled line in a thousand new ways, as if
he were inventing a script and writing it in one infinitely re-
curving utterance until I thought the bounds of beauty must
break.

From inside, the looping plane had sounded tinny, like a   43
kazoo. Outside, the buzz rose and fell to the Doppler effect as
the plane looped near or away. Rahm cleaved the sky like a
prow and tossed out time left and right in his wake. He performed for forty minutes; then he headed the plane, as small as
a wasp, back to the airport inland. Later I learned Rahm often
practiced acrobatic flights over this shore. His idea was that if
he lost control and was going to go down, he could ditch in the
salt chuck, where no one else would get hurt.

If I had not turned two barrel rolls in an airplane, I might   44
have fancied Rahm felt good up there, and playful. Maybe
Jackson Pollock felt a sort of playfulness, in addition to the
artist's usual deliberate and intelligent care. In my limited experience, painting, unlike writing, pleases the senses while you
do it, and more while you do it than after it is done. Drawing
lines with an airplane, unfortunately, tortures the senses. Jet
bomber pilots black out. I knew Rahm felt as if his brain were
bursting his eardrums, felt that if he let his jaws close as tight
as centrifugal force pressed them, he would bite through his
lungs.

"All virtue is a form of acting," Yeats said. Rahm deliber-   45
ately turned himself into a figure. Sitting invisible at the controls of a distant airplane, he became the agent and the instrument of art and invention. He did not tell me how he felt when
we spoke of his performance flying; he told me instead that he

paid attention to how his plane and its line looked to the audience against the lighted sky. If he had noticed how he felt, he could not have done the work. Robed in his airplane, he was as featureless as a priest. He was lost in his figural aspect like an actor or a king. Of his flying, he had said only, "I get a rhythm and stick with it." In its reticence, this statement reminded me of Veronese's "Given a large canvas, I enhanced it as I saw fit." But Veronese was ironic, and Rahm was not; he was as literal as an astronaut; the machine gave him tongue.

When Rahm flew, he sat down in the middle of art and 46 strapped himself in. He spun it all around him. He could not see it himself. If he never saw it on film, he never saw it at all— as if Beethoven could not hear his final symphonies not because he was deaf but because he was inside the paper on which he wrote. Rahm must have felt it happen, that fusion of vision and metal, motion and idea. I think of this man as a figure, a college professor with a Ph.D. upside down in the loud band of beauty. What are we here for? *Propter chorum,* the monks say: for the sake of the choir.

"Purity does not lie in separation from but in deeper pene- 47 tration into the universe," Teilhard de Chardin wrote. It is hard to imagine a deeper penetration into the universe than Rahm's last dive in his plane, or than his inexpressible wordless selfless line's inscribing the air and dissolving. Any other art may be permanent. I cannot recall one Rahm sequence. He improvised. If Christo wraps a building or dyes a harbor, we join his poignant and fierce awareness that the work will be gone in days. Rahm's plane shed a ribbon in space, a ribbon whose end unraveled in memory while its beginning unfurled as surprise. He may have acknowledged that what he did could be called art, but it would have been, I think, only in the common misusage, which holds art to be the last extreme of skill. Rahm rode the point of the line to the possible; he discovered it and wound it down to show. He made his dazzling probe on the run. "The world is filled, and filled with the Absolute," Teilhard de Chardin wrote. "To see this is to be made free."

1989

The Day the Fire Came

Virginia Bell Dabney

The last rain in these mountains this summer was about July   1
11. It is now the twenty-first day of August and it has not rained
for one month and ten hot days. All of us who live here think
some computer glitch has been made in weather deliveries and
we are getting Arizona weather by mistake. Days that usually
have a high of eighty degrees now reach into the parching
nineties. Thunderheads rise in the west, look us over, and then
go somewhere else to rain. Grass crackles underfoot, the birds
quit singing after the sun is up. Many have packed it up and left;
the indigo buntings are gone and the wood thrush has taken his
flute to damper places.

I sit limply on the porch with a cold drink; the dog lies at   2
my feet eyeing my glass. Finally I give him an ice cube and he
crunches it, licking up the tiny ice puddles. I give him another
and he wants it, but not now, so he takes it over to a dusty bush
and buries it. It is the first drink the bush has had in forty-two
days.

A wind comes up in the afternoon, leaving the dogwoods   3
limp and the poplars yellowing prematurely. There is a smell
in the air that I remember from another time; it is of green leaves
hot and burned in the sun. I keep watching the horizon and
sniffing for any faint whiff of fire starting in the woods, made
wary for all time by what happened when I was eleven.

On a Sunday in April 1930, my mother was pacing from the   4
yard to our upstairs hallway window and then down again. She
was watching a column of smoke rising beyond our woods to
the west. I caught her nervousness and watched also, but without her added awareness that there had been very little rainfall
during the winter and early spring. There were new leaves on
the trees, but on the forest floor the old leaves were as dry and
separate as cornflakes.

I heard Mother report to my sister Allison that the smoke   5
seemed to be moving our way. Allison was in bed, feverish and

coughing. She wanted to get up and help us, but my mother said, "Only if necessary," and started gathering possessions we could take with us if the fire came nearer. Allison was coughing more, the smoke was bothering her. Mother was dumping drawer contents into a box. I lugged down books I wanted to save and Mother told me, "There's no room in the car for those, Vallie."

Our neighbor Carl Stevens drove into the yard and my   6
mother met him on the porch. There was a tense conversation. "Mrs. Bell, you and the girls better get out right quick. That fire is picking up fast. You all better come over to our house. It's got so much plowed land around it I think it will be safe."

"Allison is sick in bed," Mother told him. "You can take the   7
girls and I can come behind you."

But she had hardly finished when I burst into tears. I   8
grabbed her arm and said, "I won't go unless you go too!" I was sure she would be caught in the fire if we left first. Carl looked at my stricken face and said, "I'll just take Allison." He went into the bedroom with my mother, picked Allison up in her blankets, and carried her out to his car.

The wind picked up, smoke was blueing the air around us,   9
and the smell of burning leaves stung our noses. My mother pulled her Model T near the porch and put a box with our silver, her photographs, and her handmade linens into the tiny trunk space. She had already put our suitcases on the running board. Now she hastily gathered up some new WearEver pots and pans packed in salesmen's suitcases and flung them on the bare sand of the tennis court. Burning ash was flying over us. "Get in," Mother yelled at me, and I did so only because she had her foot on the running board itself. She backed the car out, and as we fled through smoke growing thicker every minute, she leaned out of the window and called Mac, the dog. He came running. "Lean out and call him," she told me, and I did. He ran easily not far behind us; he had never followed the car before but understood this was a crisis.

I thought but didn't ask about the cows in the pasture and   10
the chickens in the chicken houses. There were new chicks under the brooder, and I told myself that the brooder house was off by itself and maybe . . .

At Carl's house my mother parked the car near their drive. 11
We all ran toward the open field on the north side of the
Stevenses' big house to watch the fire. I could see our house
standing calmly among its oak trees. Behind it to the north the
fire seemed to be going away, though the smoke was so thick
it was hard to tell. We could see great rolling balls of fire in the
treetops and I thought I could feel the heat on my face.

"If the wind just doesn't change . . . ," my mother said.   12

We stood there until I couldn't stand the tension and began 13
to cry, but Mother said, "Hush, that only makes things worse,"
and I stopped, wanting to watch and at the same time afraid to
see what would happen. The whole woods beyond our house,
our orchard in its grassy clearing, were in flames. There was a
crackling sound as branches broke and fell from trees like burning logs in a fireplace, showering sparks. Over our heads birds
were flying from the fire. Our house stood peacefully silhouet-
ted against the orange-and-black swirl of smoke and flame.

Suddenly I heard my mother say tightly, "The wind's 14
shifted," and we watched as a great ball of fire, tumbling and
rolling on the wind, came toward our house. It caught first in
the highest oak-tree branches, and they flared like torches. My
mother turned away and said, "That's it." I stared long enough
to see burning branches drop on our roof and the entire scene
obliterated by smoke that had tongues of flames roaring
through it.

My mother and I walked back to the Stevenses' back porch 15
and sat on the steps, she silent and her face white. After a while
Carl came over and said, "It's not coming here. Your fields just
burned over and it stopped at the road."

"The house gone?" she said, looking up.   16

"It's gone," he said. "All those trees dropped fire on it."   17

I can remember almost nothing else about the rest of that 18
day. My mother could not go back to our place because some
of the old trees were still burning and the ground was still hot.

We had supper at the Stevenses' big table, and afterward 19
Miss Lou, Carl's wife, took me upstairs to a tiny room under
sloping eaves and showed me a bed with a feather mattress.

When I sank into it its billows rose around me. It was warm and cozy and I snuggled in deeply.

I was still asleep at faint daylight when Mother, unable to [20] rest, went to the kitchen and found Carl, Miss Lou, and Carl's mother fixing breakfast. They gave her coffee and a hot biscuit and then Carl went with her to look at the smoking ruins of our farm.

The barn was gone, the machine shed vanished, the wood- [21] shed and its attached room, where my mother kept her equipment for developing photographs, were ash heaps. One of the chicken houses was a mass of hot melted asphalt roofing over incinerated birds and twisted metal feeders. Another still stood, the new one set off by itself and built for the largest new brood of chickens, which were now gone with the brooder house.

My mother and Carl walked down the pasture hill, seeking [22] the cows they believed might have escaped. At the bottom, up to their knees in the stream, the devastated woods behind them, both of them stood, their udders distended with milk. Carl went back to his house to get milk buckets.

Neither Allison nor I was allowed to go back to view the [23] ruins. We stood with Miss Lou looking across the fields at the black skeletons of trees around the dark pile of rubble that had been our house. We stared numbly, trying to sort out what had happened.

My mother was walking from one pile of rubble to another, [24] feeling, she said later, in a daze, when our neighbors the Woodfords drove up in their wagon. Their own house and buildings were safe but they had lost some good forest. Mrs. Woodford put her arm around Mother and said, "We've been praying for you and the girls. Now we want you all to come stay with us until things are straightened out. We'll be so glad to have you, you know."

Her earnest goodness touched my mother, but it was not [25] her way to turn to others. "I'm not sure yet what I have to do," she said, "but it's wonderfully kind of you to offer." She laid a hand briefly on Mrs. Woodford's arm. "I just have to work things out."

Mother and Mrs. Woodford moved from ruin to ruin, pick- [26]

ing up pieces of things, trying to identify them. One was a darkened dish with a garland of roses; looking at it in her neighbor's
hand, Mother said, "Those were my best dessert bowls." She
carried it around with her as they walked.

Before the day was half over, people from miles around   27
were coming to find out what had happened to the Bells, to ask
if they could help, and to wander about the stricken farmyard.
Tom Walker came on foot and asked my mother what she was
going to do now. "Ye ain't wantin' to stay here, are ye?"

"I don't have any other home, Mr. Walker."   28

He spat with no change of expression. "I tole my wife that's   29
what ye'd say. Ye ain't no quitter, I tole her."

The Painters also urged my mother to move in with them   30
until she could decide what to do, but she thanked them with
the same words she'd said to others. She did not say that she
had already decided what to do; she was probably not ready to
put it into words. When the others had gone, she asked Carl to
come with her to look at the chicken house that had been untouched by fire. It still smelled of recently poured cement and
new wood. As she opened the door she said, "You see this little room we set off for feed? I think I can stay in here while a
place is fixed up for all of us."

"It's right small . . . ," Carl said doubtfully.   31

"But look, I could put a cot over there, and some kind of   32
stove here. And a table and chair. That's all I need right now."

He shook his head. "You know you can stay with us. You'd   33
be comfortable and real close by."

"But Carl, I need to be *here*. I'll have the dog, you know."   34

That, of course, is how it was. I was sent to stay with my   35
other sister, Daphne, so I could finish out the school year. Allison, still running a fever, was put to bed at the home of a friend
who was a nurse. As she had already decided, Mother moved
into the feed room of the chicken house, from which she directed and helped with the cleanup of all that was left of our
house, barn, and sheds. She kept finding remnants of her life
that she turned over and over: a solidified aluminum puddle
on the tennis court where the pots and pans she'd tried to save
had melted; the handles to her bread mixer and meat grinder,

the wooden parts burned off, the machines twisted and useless; fragments of rose glass from the shattered hanging lamp in the living room.

Before they were hauled away, she touched the warped brass bedsteads, the broken shards of pitchers and basins, and the cracked, streaked pieces of my father's plate collection that had once shone from a plate rail in our new dining room.   36

Mother did not allow herself to sigh over these things for long; there was too much to do. One of the first things she did was to walk through deep ash in the ruined woods to see what was left. The young silver-green white pines were gone, and the hollies, once so thick, were unrecognizable. But the trunks of the large blackened oaks and maples still stood, two or three large barren branches left pointing upward. Walking behind my mother with an ax, our hired man, Solomon, cut a notch here and there in the charred bark; underneath there was solid, un-burned wood.   37

"There's a lot of timber here good for building if we can get it out," my mother told Solomon. "Enough for all of us," she said thoughtfully. In her mind, a plan was already taking shape that would distract her from despair and keep her from always watching the skies and listening for rain.   38

1990

Landscape and Narrative

Barry Lopez

One summer evening in a remote village in the Brooks Range of Alaska, I sat among a group of men listening to hunting stories about the trapping and pursuit of animals. I was particularly interested in several incidents involving wolverine, in part because a friend of mine was studying wolverine in Canada, among the Cree, but, too, because I find this animal   1 such an intense creature. To hear about its life is to learn more about fierceness.

Wolverines are not intentionally secretive, hiding their lives 2 from view, but they are seldom observed. The range of their known behavior is less than that of, say, bears or wolves. Still, that evening no gratuitous details were set out. This was somewhat odd, for wolverine easily excite the imagination; they can loom suddenly in the landscape with authority, with an aura larger than their compact physical dimensions, drawing one's immediate and complete attention. Wolverine also have a deserved reputation for resoluteness in the worst winters, for ferocious strength. But neither did these attributes induce the men to embellish.

I listened carefully to these stories, taking pleasure in the 3 sharply observed detail surrounding the dramatic thread of events. The story I remember most vividly was about a man hunting a wolverine from a snow machine in the spring. He followed the animal's tracks for several miles over rolling tundra in a certain valley. Soon he caught sight ahead of a dark spot on the crest of a hill—the wolverine pausing to look back. The hunter was catching up, but each time he came over a rise the wolverine was looking back from the next rise, just out of range. The hunter topped one more rise and met the wolverine bounding toward him. Before he could pull his rifle from its scabbard the wolverine flew across the engine cowl and the windshield, hitting him square in the chest. The hunter scrambled his arms wildly, trying to get the wolverine out of his lap, and fell over as he did so. The wolverine jumped clear as the snow machine rolled over, and fixed the man with a stare. He had not bitten, not even scratched the man. Then the wolverine walked away. The man thought of reaching for the gun, but no, he did not.

The other stories were like this, not so much making a point 4 as evoking something about contact with wild animals that would never be completely understood.

When the stories were over, four or five of us walked out 5 of the home of our host. The surrounding land, in the persistent light of a far northern summer, was still visible for miles— the striated, pitched massifs of the Brooks Range; the shy, willow-lined banks of the John River flowing south from Anak-tuvuk Pass; and the flat tundra plain, opening with great affirmation to the north. The landscape seemed alive because of the stories. It was precisely these ocherous tones, this kind of willow, exactly this austerity that had informed the wolverine narratives. I felt exhilaration, and a deeper confirmation of the stories. The mundane tasks which awaited me I anticipated now with pleasure. The stories had renewed in me a sense of the purpose of my life.

This feeling, an inexplicable renewal of enthusiasm after storytelling, is familiar to many people. It does not seem to matter greatly what the subject is, as long as the context is intimate and the story is told for its own sake, not forced to serve merely as the vehicle for an idea. The tone of the story need not be solemn. The darker aspects of life need not be ignored. But I think intimacy is indispensable—a feeling that derives from the listener's trust and a storyteller's certain knowledge of his subject and regard for his audience. This intimacy deepens if the storyteller tempers his authority with humility, or when terms of idiomatic expression, or at least the physical setting for the story, are shared. 6

I think of two landscapes—one outside the self, the other within. The external landscape is the one we see—not only the line and color of the land and its shading at different times of the day, but also its plants and animals in season, its weather, its geology, the record of its climate and evolution. If you walk up, say, a dry arroyo in the Sonoran Desert you will feel a mounding and rolling of sand and silt beneath your foot that is distinctive. You will anticipate the crumbling of the sedimentary earth in the arroyo bank as your hand reaches out, and in that tangible evidence you will sense a history of water in the region. Perhaps a black-throated sparrow lands in a paloverde bush—the resiliency of the twig under the bird, that precise shade of yellowish-green against the milk-blue sky, the fluttering whir of the arriving sparrow, are what I mean by "the landscape." Draw on the smell of creosote bush, or clack stones together in the dry air. Feel how light is the desiccated dropping 7 of the kangaroo rat. Study an animal track obscured by the wind. These are all elements of the land, and what makes the landscape comprehensible are the relationships between them. One learns a landscape finally not by knowing the name or identity of everything in it, but by perceiving the relationships in it—like that between the sparrow and the twig. The difference between the relationships and the elements is the same as that between written history and a catalog of events.

The second landscape I think of is an interior one, a kind of 8
projection within a person of a part of the exterior landscape. Relationships in the exterior landscape include those that are named and discernible, such as the nitrogen cycle, or a vertical sequence of Ordovician limestone, and others that are uncodified or ineffable, such as winter light falling on a particular kind of granite, or the effect of humidity on the frequency of a black-poll warbler's burst of song. That these relationships have purpose and order, however inscrutable they may seem to us, is a tenet of evolution. Similarly, the speculations, intuitions, and formal ideas we refer to as "mind" are a set of relationships in the interior landscape with purpose and order; some of these are obvious, many impenetrably subtle. The shape and character of these relationships in a person's thinking, I believe, are deeply influenced by where on this earth one goes, what one touches, the patterns one observes in nature—the intricate history of one's life in the land, even a life in the city, where wind, the chirp of birds, the line of a falling leaf, are known. These thoughts are arranged, further, according to the thread of one's moral, intellectual, and spiritual development. The interior landscape responds to the character and subtlety of an exterior landscape; the shape of the individual mind is affected by land as it is by genes.

In stories like those I heard at Anaktuvuk Pass about 9
wolverine, the relationship between separate elements in the land is set forth clearly. It is put in a simple framework of sequential incidents and apposite detail. If the exterior landscape is limned well, the listener often feels that he has heard something pleasing and authentic—trustworthy. We derive this sense of confidence I think not so much from verifiable truth as

from an understanding that lying has played no role in the narrative. The storyteller is obligated to engage the reader with a precise vocabulary, to set forth a coherent and dramatic rendering of incidents—and to be ingenuous.

When one hears a story one takes pleasure in it for differ- 10 ent reasons—for the euphony of its phrases, an aspect of the plot, or because one identifies with one of the characters. With certain stories certain individuals may experience a deeper, more profound sense of well-being. This latter phenomenon, in my understanding, rests at the heart of storytelling as an elevated experience among aboriginal peoples. It results from bringing two landscapes together. The exterior landscape is organized according to principles or laws or tendencies beyond human control. It is understood to contain an integrity that is beyond human analysis and unimpeachable. Insofar as the storyteller depicts various subtle and obvious relationships in the exterior landscape accurately in his story, and insofar as he orders them along traditional lines of meaning to create the narrative, the narrative will "ring true." The listener who "takes the story to heart" will feel a pervasive sense of congruence within himself and also with the world.

Among the Navajo and, as far as I know, many other native 11 peoples, the land is thought to exhibit a sacred order. That order is the basis of ritual. The rituals themselves reveal the power in that order. Art, architecture, vocabulary, and costume, as well as ritual, are derived from the perceived natural order of the universe—from observations and meditations on the exterior landscape. An indigenous philosophy—metaphysics, ethics, epistemology, aesthetics, and logic—may also be derived from a people's continuous attentiveness to both the obvious (scientific) and ineffable (artistic) orders of the local landscape. Each individual, further, undertakes to order his interior landscape according to the exterior landscape. To succeed in this means to achieve a balanced state of mental health.

I think of the Navajo for a specific reason. Among the var- 12 ious sung ceremonies of this people—Enemyway, Coyoteway, Red Antway, Uglyway—is one called Beautyway. In the Navajo view, the elements of one's interior life—one's psychological

makeup and moral bearing—are subject to a persistent principle of disarray. Beautyway is, in part, a spiritual invocation of
the order of the exterior universe, that irreducible, holy complexity that manifests itself as all things changing through time
(a Navajo definition of beauty, hozhǫ́ǫ́). The purpose of this invocation is to recreate in the individual who is the subject of the
Beautyway ceremony that same order, to make the individual
again a reflection of the myriad enduring relationships of the
landscape.

I believe story functions in a similar way. A story draws on [13]
relationships in the exterior landscape and projects them onto
the interior landscape. The purpose of storytelling is to achieve
harmony between the two landscapes, to use all the elements
of story—syntax, mood, figures of speech—in a harmonious
way to reproduce the harmony of the land in the individual's
interior. Inherent in story is the power to reorder a state of psychological confusion through contact with the pervasive truth
of those relationships we call "the land."

These thoughts, of course, are susceptible to interpreta- [14]
tion. I am convinced, however, that these observations can be
applied to the kind of prose we call nonfiction as well as to traditional narrative forms such as the novel and the short story,
and to some poems. Distinctions between fiction and nonfiction are sometimes obscured by arguments over what constitutes "the truth." In the aboriginal literature I am familiar with,
the first distinction made among narratives is to separate the
authentic from the inauthentic. Myth, which we tend to regard
as fictitious or "merely metaphorical," is as authentic, as real,
as the story of a wolverine in a man's lap. (A distinction is
made, of course, about the elevated nature of myth—and frequently the circumstances of myth-telling are more rigorously
prescribed than those for the telling of legends or vernacular
stories—but all of these narratives are rooted in the local landscape. To violate *that* connection is to call the narrative itself
into question.)

The power of narrative to nurture and heal, to repair a spirit [15]
in disarray, rests on two things: the skillful invocation of unim-

peachable sources and a listener's knowledge that no hypocrisy or subterfuge is involved. This last simple fact is to me one of the most imposing aspects of the Holocene history of man.

We are more accustomed now to thinking of "the truth" as [16] something that can be explicitly stated, rather than as something that can be evoked in a metaphorical way outside science and Occidental culture. Neither can truth be reduced to aphorism or formulas. It is something alive and unpronounceable. Story creates an atmosphere in which it becomes discernible as a pattern. For a storyteller to insist on relationships that do not exist is to lie. Lying is the opposite of story. (I do not mean to confuse ignorance with deception, or to imply that a storyteller can perceive all that is inherent in the land. Every storyteller falls short of a perfect limning of the landscape—perception and language both fail. But to make up something that is not there, something which can never be corroborated in the land, to knowingly set forth a false relationship, is to be lying, no longer telling a story.)

Because of the intricate, complex nature of the land, it is not [17] always possible for a storyteller to grasp what is contained in a story. The intent of the storyteller, then, must be to evoke, honestly, some single aspect of all that the land contains. The storyteller knows that because different individuals grasp the story at different levels, the focus of his regard for truth must be at the primary one—with who was there, what happened, when, where, and why things occurred. The story will then possess similar truth at other levels—the integrity inherent at the primary level of meaning will be conveyed everywhere else. As long as the storyteller carefully describes the order before him, and uses his storytelling skill to heighten and emphasize certain relationships, it is even possible for the story to be more successful than the storyteller himself is able to imagine.

I would like to make a final point about the wolverine stories I heard at Anaktuvuk Pass. I wrote down the details afterward, concentrating especially on aspects of the biology and ecology of the animals. I sent the information on to my friend living with the Cree. When, many months later, I saw him, I

asked whether the Cree had enjoyed these insights of the
Nunamiut into the nature of the wolverine. What had they said?

"You know," he told me, "how they are. They said, 'That 19
could happen.' "

In these uncomplicated words the Cree declared their own 20
knowledge of the wolverine. They acknowledged that although
they themselves had never seen the things the Nunamiut spoke
of, they accepted them as accurate observations, because they
did not consider story a context for misrepresentation. They also
preserved their own dignity by not overstating their confidence
in the Nunamiut, a distant and unknown people.

Whenever I think of this courtesy on the part of the Cree I 21
think of the dignity that is ours when we cease to demand the
truth and realize that the best we can have of those substantial
truths that guide our lives is metaphorical—a story. And the
most of it we are likely to discern comes only when we accord
one another the respect the Cree showed the Nunamiut. Beyond
this—that the interior landscape is a metaphorical representa-
tion of the exterior landscape, that the truth reveals itself most
fully not in dogma but in the paradox, irony, and contradictions
that distinguish compelling narratives—beyond this there are
only failures of imagination: reductionism in science; funda-
mentalism in religion; fascism in politics.

Our national literatures should be important to us insofar 22
as they sustain us with illumination and heal us. They can always do that so long as they are written with respect for both
the source and the reader, and with an understanding of why
the human heart and the land have been brought together so
regularly in human history.

1984

CHAPTER 2

Description

Where the World Began

Margaret Laurence

A strange place it was, that place where the world began. 1
A place of incredible happenings, splendors and revelations, de-
spairs like multitudinous pits of isolated hells. A place of
shadow-spookiness, inhabited by the unknowable dead. A
place of jubilation and of mourning, horrible and beautiful.

It was, in fact, a small prairie town. 2

Because that settlement and that land were my first and for 3
many years my only real knowledge of this planet, in some
profound way they remain my world, my way of viewing. My
eyes were formed there. Towns like ours, set in a sea of land,
have been described thousands of times as dull, bleak, flat, uninteresting. I have had it said to me that the railway trip across
Canada is spectacular, except for the prairies, when it would be
desirable to go to sleep for several days, until the ordeal is over.
I am always unable to argue this point effectively. All I can say
is—well, you really have to live there to know that country. The
town of my childhood could be called bizarre, agonizingly repressive or cruel at times, and the land in which it grew could
be called harsh in the violence of its seasonal changes. But never
merely flat or uninteresting. Never dull.

In winter, we used to hitch rides on the back of the milk 4
sleigh, our moccasins squeaking and slithering on the hard
rutted snow of the roads, our hands in ice-bubbled mitts hang-

ing onto the box edge of the sleigh for dear life, while Bert grinned at us through his great frosted mustache and shouted the horse into speed, daring us to stay put. Those mornings, rising, there would be the perpetual fascination of the frost feathers on windows, the ferns and flowers and eerie faces traced there during the night by unseen artists of the wind. Evenings, coming back from skating, the sky would be black but not dark, for you could see a cold glitter of stars from one side of the earth's rim to the other. And then the sometime astonishment when you saw the Northern Lights flaring across the sky, like the scrawled signature of God. After a blizzard, when the snowplow hadn't yet got through, school would be closed for the day, the assumption being that the town's young could not possibly flounder through five feet of snow in the pursuit of education. We would then gaily don snowshoes and flounder for miles out into the white dazzling deserts, in pursuit of a different kind of knowing. If you came back too close to night, through the woods at the foot of the town hill, the thin black branches of poplar and chokecherry now meringued with frost, sometimes you heard coyotes. Or maybe the banshee wolf-voices were really only inside your head.

Summers were scorching, and when no rain came and the 5 wheat became bleached and dried before it headed, the faces of farmers and townsfolk would not smile much, and you took for granted, because it never seemed to have been any different, the frequent knocking at the back door and the young men standing there, mumbling or thrusting defiantly their requests for a drink of water and a sandwich if you could spare it. They were riding the freights, and you never knew where they had come from, or where they might end up, if anywhere. The Drought and Depression were like evil deities which had been there always. You understood and did not understand.

Yet the outside world had its continuing marvels. The 6 poplar bluffs and the small river were filled and surrounded with a zillion different grasses, stones, and weed flowers. The meadowlark sang undaunted from the twanging telephone wires along the gravel highway. Once we found an old flat-bottomed scow, and launched her, poling along the shallow brown waters, mending her with wodges of hastily chewed Spearmint, grounding her among the tangles of yellow marsh marigolds that grew succulently along the banks of the shrunken river, while the sun made our skins smell dusty-warm.

My best friend lived in an apartment above some stores on Main Street (its real name was Mountain Avenue, goodness knows why), an elegant apartment with royal-blue velvet curtains. The back roof, scarcely sloping at all, was corrugated tin, of a furnace-like warmth on a July afternoon, and we would sit there drinking lemonade and looking across the back lane at the Fire Hall. Sometimes our vigil would be rewarded. Oh joy! Somebody's house burning down! We had an almost-perfect callousness in some ways. Then the wooden tower's bronze bell would clonk and toll like a thousand speeded funerals in a time of plague, and in a few minutes the team of giant black horses would cannon forth, pulling the fire wagon like some scarlet chariot of the Goths, while the firemen clung with one hand, adjusting their helmets as they went.

The oddities of the place were endless. An elderly lady used to serve, as her afternoon tea offering to other ladies, soda biscuits spread with peanut butter and topped with a whole marshmallow. Some considered this slightly eccentric, when compared with chopped egg sandwiches, and admittedly talked about her behind her back, but no one ever refused these delicacies or indicated to her that they thought she had slipped a cog. Another lady dyed her hair a bright and cherry orange, by strangers often mistaken at twenty paces for a feather hat. My own beloved stepmother wore a silver fox neckpiece, a whole pelt, *with the embalmed (?) head still on.* My Ontario Irish grandfather said, "sparrow grass," a more interesting term than asparagus. The town dump was known as "the nuisance grounds," a phrase fraught with weird connotations, as though the effluvia of our lives was beneath contempt but at the same time was subtly threatening to the determined and sometimes hysterical propriety of our ways.

Some oddities were, as idiom had it, "funny ha ha"; others

were "funny peculiar." Some were not so very funny at all. An old man lived, deranged, in a shack in the valley. Perhaps he wasn't even all that old, but to us he seemed a wild Methuselah figure, shambling among the underbrush and the tall couchgrass, muttering indecipherable curses or blessings, a prophet who had forgotten his prophecies. Everyone in town knew him, but no one knew him. He lived among us as though only occasionally and momentarily visible. The kids called him Andy Gump, and feared him. Some sought to prove their bravery by tormenting him. They were the medieval bear baiters, and he the lumbering bewildered bear, half blind, only rarely turning to snarl. Everything is to be found in a town like mine. Belsen, writ small but with the same ink.

All of us cast stones in one shape or another. In grade school, 10 among the vulnerable and violet girls we were, the feared and despised were those few older girls from what was charmingly termed "the wrong side of the tracks." Tough in talk and tougher in muscle, they were said to be whores already. And may have been, that being about the only profession readily available to them.

The dead lived in that place, too. Not only the grandparents 11 who had, in local parlance, "passed on" and who gloomed, bearded or bonneted, from the sepia photographs in old albums, but also the uncles, forever eighteen or nineteen, whose names were carved on the granite family stones in the cemetery, but whose bones lay in France. My own young mother lay in that graveyard, beside other dead of our kin, and when I was ten, my father, too, only forty, left the living town for the dead dwelling on the hill.

When I was eighteen, I couldn't wait to get out of that town, 12 away from the prairies. I did not know then that I would carry the land and town all my life within my skull, that they would form the mainspring and source of the writing I was to do, wherever and however far away I might live.

This was my territory in the time of my youth, and in a sense 13 my life since then has been an attempt to look at it, to come to terms with it. Stultifying to the mind it certainly could be, and sometimes was, but not to the imagination. It was many things, but it was never dull.

The same, I now see, could be said for Canada in general. Why on earth did generations of Canadians pretend to believe this country dull? We knew perfectly well it wasn't. Yet for so long we did not proclaim what we knew. If our upsurge of so-called nationalism seems odd or irrelevant to outsiders, and even to some of our own people *(what's all the fuss about?)*, they might try to understand that for many years we valued ourselves insufficiently, living as we did under the huge shadows of those two dominating figures, Uncle Sam and Britannia. We have only just begun to value ourselves, our land, our abilities. We have only just begun to recognize our legends and to give shape to our myths. 14

There are, God knows, enough aspects to deplore about this country. When I see the killing of our lakes and rivers with industrial wastes, I feel rage and despair. When I see our industries and natural resources increasingly taken over by America, I feel an overwhelming discouragement, especially as I cannot simply say "damn Yankees." It should never be forgotten that it is we ourselves who have sold such a large amount of our birthright for a mess of plastic Progress. When I saw the War Measures Act being invoked in 1970, I lost forever the vestigial remains of the naïve wish-belief that repression could not happen here, or would not. And yet, of course, I had known all along in the deepest and often hidden caves of the heart that anything can happen anywhere, for the seeds of both man's freedom and his captivity are found everywhere, even in the microcosm of a prairie town. But in raging against our injustices, our stupidities, I do so *as family*, as I did, and still do in writing, about those aspects of my town which I hated and which are always in some ways aspects of myself. 15

The land still draws me more than other lands. I have lived in Africa and in England, but splendid as both can be, they do not have the power to move me in the same way as, for example, that part of southern Ontario where I spent four months last summer in a cedar cabin beside a river. "Scratch a Canadian, 16 and you find a phony pioneer," I used to say to myself in warning. But all the same it is true, I think, that we are not yet totally alienated from physical earth, and let us only pray we do not become so. I once thought that my lifelong fear and mistrust of cities made me a kind of old-fashioned freak; now I see it differently.

The cabin has a long window across its front western wall, 17 and sitting at the oak table there in the mornings, I used to look out at the river and at the tall trees beyond, green-gold in the early light. The river was bronze; the sun caught it strangely, reflecting upon its surface the near-shore sand ripples underneath. Suddenly, the crescenting of a fish, gone before the eye could clearly give image to it. The old man next door said these leaping fish were carp. Himself, he preferred muskie, for he was a real fisherman and the muskie gave him a fight. The wind most often blew from the south, and the river flowed toward the south, so when the water was windriffled, and the current was strong, the river seemed to be flowing both ways. I liked this, and interpreted it as an omen, a natural symbol.

A few years ago, when I was back in Winnipeg, I gave a talk 18 at my old college. It was open to the public, and afterward a very old man came up to me and asked me if my maiden name had been Wemyss. I said yes, thinking he might have known my father or my grandfather. But no. "When I was a young lad," he said, "I once worked for your great-grandfather, Robert Wemyss, when he had the sheep ranch at Raeburn." I think that was a moment when I realized all over again something of great importance to me. My long-ago families came from Scotland and Ireland, but in a sense that no longer mattered so much. My true roots were here.

I am not very patriotic, in the usual meaning of that word. 19 I cannot say "My country right or wrong" in any political, social or literary context. But one thing is inalterable, for better or worse, for life.

This is where my world began. A world which includes the 20 ancestors—both my own and other people's ancestors who become mine. A world which formed me, and continues to do so, even while I found it in some of its aspects, and continue to do so. A world which gave me my own lifework to do, because it was here that I learned the sight of my own particular eyes.

1976

The Metropolitan Cathedral in San Salvador

Joan Didion

During the week before I flew down to El Salvador a Salvadoran woman who works for my husband and me in Los Angeles gave me repeated instructions about what we must and must not do. We must not go out at night. We must stay off the street whenever possible. We must never ride in buses or taxis, never leave the capital, never imagine that our passports would protect us. We must not even consider the hotel a safe place: people were killed in hotels. She spoke with considerable vehemence, because two of her brothers had been killed in Salvador in August of 1981, in their beds. The throats of both brothers had been slashed. Her father had been cut but stayed alive. Her mother had been beaten. Twelve of her other relatives, aunts and uncles and cousins, had been taken from their houses one night the same August, and their bodies had been found some time later, in a ditch. I assured her that we would remember, we would be careful, we would in fact be so careful that we would probably (trying for a light touch) spend all our time in church.

She became still more agitated, and I realized that I had spoken as a *norteamericana:* churches had not been to this woman the neutral ground they had been to me. I must remember: Archbishop Romero killed saying mass in the chapel of the Divine Providence Hospital in San Salvador. I must remember: more than thirty people killed at Archbishop Romero's funeral in the Metropolitan Cathedral in San Salvador. I must remember: more than twenty people killed before that on the steps of the Metropolitan Cathedral. CBS had filmed it. It had been on television, the bodies jerking, those still alive crawling over the dead as they tried to get out of range. I must understand: the Church was dangerous.

I told her that I understood, that I knew all that, and I did,   3
abstractly, but the specific meaning of the Church she knew eluded me until I was actually there, at the Metropolitan Cathedral in San Salvador, one afternoon when rain sluiced down its corrugated plastic windows and puddled around the supports of the Sony and Philips billboards near the steps. The effect of the Metropolitan Cathedral is immediate, and entirely literary. This is the cathedral that the late Archbishop Oscar Arnulfo Romero refused to finish, on the premise that the work of the Church took precedence over its display, and the high walls of raw concrete bristle with structural rods, rusting now, staining the concrete, sticking out at wrenched and violent angles. The wiring is exposed. Fluorescent tubes hang askew. The great high altar is backed by warped plyboard. The cross on the altar is of bare incandescent bulbs, but the bulbs, that afternoon, were unlit: there was in fact no light at all on the main altar, no light on the cross, no light on the globe of the world that showed the northern American continent in gray and the southern in white; no light on the dove above the globe, *Salvador del Mundo*. In this vast brutalist space that was the cathedral, the unlit altar seemed to offer a single ineluctable message: at this time and in this place the light of the world could be construed as out, off, extinguished.

In many ways the Metropolitan Cathedral is an authentic   4
piece of political art, a statement for El Salvador as *Guernica* was for Spain. It is quite devoid of sentimental relief. There are no decorative or architectural references to familiar parables, in fact no stories at all, not even the Stations of the Cross. On the afternoon I was there the flowers laid on the altar were dead. There were no traces of normal parish activity. The doors were

open to the barricaded main steps, and down the steps there was a spill of red paint, lest anyone forget the blood shed there. Here and there on the cheap linoleum inside the cathedral there was what seemed to be actual blood, dried in spots, the kind of spots dropped by a slow hemorrhage, or by a woman who does not know or does not care that she is menstruating.

There were several women in the cathedral during the hour 5 or so I spent there, a young woman with a baby, an older woman in house slippers, a few others, all in black. One of the women walked the aisles as if by compulsion, up and down, across and back, crooning loudly as she walked. Another knelt without moving at the tomb of Archbishop Romero in the right transept. "LOOR A MONSENOR ROMERO," the crude needlepoint tapestry by the tomb read, "Praise to Monsignor Romero from the Mothers of the Imprisoned, the Disappeared, and the Murdered," the *Comité de Madres y Familiares de Presos, Desaparecidos, y Asesinados Politicos de El Salvador.*

The tomb itself was covered with offerings and petitions, 6 notes decorated with motifs cut from greeting cards and cartoons. I recall one with figures cut from a Bugs Bunny strip, and another with a pencil drawing of a baby in a crib. The baby in this drawing seemed to be receiving medication or fluid or blood intravenously, through the IV line shown on its wrist. I studied the notes for a while and then went back and looked again at the unlit altar, and at the red paint on the main steps, from which it was possible to see the guardsmen on the balcony of the National Palace hunching back to avoid the rain. Many Salvadorans are offended by the Metropolitan Cathedral, which is as it should be, because the place remains perhaps the only unambiguous political statement in El Salvador, a metaphorical bomb in the ultimate power station.

1983

Fifth Avenue, Uptown

James Baldwin

There is a housing project standing now where the house   1
in which we grew up once stood, and one of those stunted city
trees is snarling where our doorway used to be. This is on the
rehabilitated side of the avenue. The other side of the avenue—
for progress takes time—has not been rehabilitated yet and it
looks exactly as it looked in the days when we sat with our noses
pressed against the windowpane, longing to be allowed to go
"across the street." The grocery store which gave us credit is still
there, and there can be no doubt that it is still giving credit. The
people in the project certainly need it—far more, indeed, than
they ever needed the project. The last time I passed by, the Jewish proprietor was still standing among his shelves, looking
sadder and heavier but scarcely any older. Farther down the
block stands the shoe-repair store in which our shoes were re-
paired until reparation became impossible and in which, then,
we bought all our "new" ones. The Negro proprietor is still in
the window, head down, working at the leather.

These two, I imagine, could tell a long tale if they would   2
(perhaps they would be glad to if they could), having watched
so many, for so long, struggling in the fishhooks, the barbed
wire, of this avenue.

The avenue is elsewhere the renowned and elegant Fifth.   3
The area I am describing, which, in today's gang parlance,
would be called "the turf," is bounded by Lenox Avenue on the
west, the Harlem River on the east, 135th Street on the north,
and 130th Street on the south. We never lived beyond these
boundaries; this is where we grew up. Walking along 145th
Street—for example—familiar as it is, and similar, does not
have the same impact because I do not know any of the people
on the block. But when I turn east on 131st Street and Lenox Avenue, there is first a soda-pop joint, then a shoeshine "parlor,"
then a grocery store, then a dry cleaners', then the houses. All
along the street there are people who watched me grow up, peo-

ple who grew up with me, people I watched grow up along with my brothers and sisters; and, sometimes in my arms, some-times underfoot, sometimes at my shoulder—or on it—their children, a riot, a forest of children, who include my nieces and nephews.

When we reach the end of this long block, we find our-selves on wide, filthy, hostile Fifth Avenue, facing that project which hangs over the avenue like a monument to the folly, and the cowardice, of good intentions. All along the block, for any-one who knows it, are immense human gaps, like craters. These gaps are not created merely by those who have moved away, inevitably into some other ghetto; or by those who have risen, almost always into a greater capacity for self-loathing and self-delusion; or yet by those who, by whatever means—World War II, the Korean war, a policeman's gun or billy, a gang war, a brawl, madness, an overdose of heroin, or, simply, unnatural exhaustion—are dead. I am talking about those who are left, and I am talking principally about the young. What are they doing? Well, some, a minority, are fanatical churchgoers, mem-bers of the more extreme of the Holy Roller sects. Many, many more are "moslems," by affiliation or sympathy, that is to say that they are united by nothing more—and nothing less—than a hatred of the white world and all its works. They are present, for example, at every Buy Black street-corner meeting—meet-ings in which the speaker urges his hearers to cease trading with white men and establish a separate economy. Neither the speaker nor his hearers can possibly do this, of course, since Ne-groes do not own General Motors or RCA or the A & P, nor, in-deed, do they own more than a wholly insufficient fraction of anything else in Harlem (those who *do* own anything are more interested in their profits than in their fellows). But these meet-ings nevertheless keep alive in the participators a certain pride of bitterness without which, however futile this bitterness may be, they could scarcely remain alive at all. Many have given up. They stay home and watch the TV screen, living on the earn-ings of their parents, cousins, brothers, or uncles, and only leave the house to go to the movies or to the nearest bar. "How're you making it?" one may ask, running into them along the block, or in the bar. "Oh, I'm TV-ing it"; with the saddest, sweetest, most shamefaced of smiles, and from a great distance. This distance one is compelled to respect; anyone who has traveled so far will not easily be dragged again into the world. There are further retreats, of course, than the TV screen or the bar. There are those who are simply sitting on their stoops, "stoned," animated for a moment only, and hideously, by the approach of someone who may lend them the money for a "fix." Or by the approach of someone from whom they can purchase it, one of the shrewd ones, on the way to prison or just coming out.

And the others, who have avoided all of these deaths, get 5 up in the morning and go downtown to meet "the man." They work in the white man's world all day and come home in the evening to this fetid block. They struggle to instill in their children some private sense of honor or dignity which will help the child to survive. This means, of course, that they must struggle, stolidly, incessantly, to keep this sense alive in themselves, in spite of the insults, the indifference, and the cruelty they are certain to encounter in their working day. They patiently browbeat the landlord into fixing the heat, the plaster, the plumbing; this demands prodigious patience; nor is patience usually enough. In trying to make their hovels habitable, they are perpetually throwing good money after bad. Such frustration, so long endured, is driving many strong, admirable men and women whose only crime is color to the very gates of paranoia.

One remembers them from another time—playing handball 6 in the playground, going to church, wondering if they were going to be promoted at school. One remembers them going off to war—gladly, to escape this block. One remembers their return. Perhaps one remembers their wedding day. And one sees where the girl is now—vainly looking for salvation from some other embittered, trussed, and struggling boy—and sees the all-but-abandoned children in the streets.

1948

The Death of the Moth

Virginia Woolf

Moths that fly by day are not properly to be called moths;   1
they do not excite that pleasant sense of dark autumn nights and
ivy-blossom which the commonest yellow-underwing asleep in
the shadow of the curtain never fails to rouse in us. They are
hybrid creatures, neither gay like butterflies nor sombre like
their own species. Nevertheless the present specimen, with his
narrow hay-coloured wings, fringed with a tassel of the same
colour, seemed to be content with life. It was a pleasant morning, mid-September, mild, benignant, yet with a keener breath
than that of the summer months. The plough was already scoring the field opposite the window, and where the share had
been, the earth was pressed flat and gleamed with moisture.
Such vigour came rolling in from the fields and the down beyond that it was difficult to keep the eyes strictly turned upon
the book. The rooks too were keeping one of their annual fes-
tivities; soaring round the tree tops until it looked as if a vast
net with thousands of black knots in it had been cast up into the
air; which, after a few moments sank slowly down upon the
trees until every twig seemed to have a knot at the end of it.
Then, suddenly, the net would be thrown into the air again in
a wider circle this time, with the utmost clamour and vocifera-
tion, as though to be thrown into the air and settle slowly down
upon the tree tops were a tremendously exciting experience.

The same energy which inspired the rooks, the ploughmen,   2
the horses, and even, it seemed, the lean bare-backed downs,
sent the moth fluttering from side to side of his square of the
window-pane. One could not help watching him. One was, indeed, conscious of a queer feeling of pity for him. The possibilities of pleasure seemed that morning so enormous and so various that to have only a moth's part in life, and a day moth's at
that, appeared a hard fate, and his zest in enjoying his meagre
opportunities to the full, pathetic. He flew vigorously to one corner of his compartment, and, after waiting there a second, flew

across to the other. What remained for him but to fly to a third corner and then to a fourth? That was all he could do, in spite of the size of the downs, the width of the sky, the far-off smoke of houses, and the romantic voice, now and then, of a steamer out at sea. What he could do he did. Watching him, it seemed as if a fibre, very thin but pure, of the enormous energy of the world had been thrust into his frail and diminutive body. As often as he crossed the pane, I could fancy that a thread of vital light became visible. He was little or nothing but life.

Yet, because he was so small, and so simple a form of the   3 energy that was rolling in at the open window and driving its way through so many narrow and intricate corridors in my own brain and in those of other human beings, there was something marvellous as well as pathetic about him. It was as if someone had taken a tiny bead of pure life and decking it as lightly as possible with down and feathers, had set it dancing and zig-zagging to show us the true nature of life. Thus displayed one could not get over the strangeness of it. One is apt to forget all about life, seeing it humped and bossed and garnished and cumbered so that it has to move with the greatest circumspection and dignity. Again, the thought of all that life might have been had he been born in any other shape caused one to view his simple activities with a kind of pity.

After a time, tired by his dancing apparently, he settled on   4 the window ledge in the sun, and, the queer spectacle being at an end, I forgot about him. Then, looking up, my eye was caught by him. He was trying to resume his dancing, but seemed either so stiff or so awkward that he could only flutter to the bottom of the windowpane; and when he tried to fly across it he failed. Being intent on other matters I watched these futile attempts for a time without thinking, unconsciously waiting for him to resume his flight, as one waits for a machine, that has stopped momentarily, to start again without considering the reason of its failure. After perhaps a seventh attempt he slipped from the wooden ledge and fell, fluttering his wings, on to his back on the window sill. The helplessness of his attitude roused me. It flashed upon me that he was in difficulties; he could no longer raise himself; his legs struggled vainly. But, as I stretched out a pencil, meaning to help him to right himself, it came over me that the failure and awkwardness were the approach of death. I laid the pencil down again.

The legs agitated themselves once more. I looked as if for the enemy against which he struggled. I looked out of doors. What had happened there? Presumably it was midday, and work in the fields had stopped. Stillness and quiet had replaced the previous animation. The birds had taken themselves off to feed in the brooks. The horses stood still. Yet the power was there all the same, massed outside, indifferent, impersonal, not attending to anything in particular. Somehow it was opposed to the little hay-coloured moth. It was useless to try to do anything. One could only watch the extraordinary efforts made by those tiny legs against an oncoming doom which could, had it chosen, have submerged an entire city, not merely a city, but masses of human beings; nothing, I knew, had any chance against death. Nevertheless after a pause of exhaustion the legs fluttered again. It was superb this last protest, and so frantic that he succeeded at last in righting himself. One's sympathies, of course, were all on the side of life. Also, when there was nobody to care or to know, this gigantic effort on the part of an insignificant little moth, against a power of such magnitude, to retain what no one else valued or desired to keep, moved one strangely. Again, somehow, one saw life, a pure bead. I lifted the pencil again, useless though I knew it to be. But even as I did so, the unmistakable tokens of death showed themselves. The body relaxed, and instantly grew stiff. The struggle was over. The insignificant little creature now knew death. As I looked at the dead moth, this minute wayside triumph of so great a force over so mean an antagonist filled me with wonder. Just as life had been strange a few minutes before, so death was now as strange. The moth having righted himself now lay most decently and uncomplainingly composed. O yes, he seemed to say, death is stronger than I am.

1942

The Way to Rainy Mountain

N. Scott Momaday

A single knoll rises out of the plain in Oklahoma, north and   1
west of the Wichita Range. For my people, the Kiowas, it is an
old landmark, and they gave it the name Rainy Mountain. The
hardest weather in the world is there. Winter brings blizzards,
hot tornadic winds arise in the spring, and in summer the
prairie is an anvil's edge. The grass turns brittle and brown, and
it cracks beneath your feet. There are green belts along the rivers
and creeks, linear groves of hickory and pecan, willow and
witch hazel. At a distance in July or August the steaming foliage
seems almost to writhe in fire. Great green-and-yellow
grasshoppers are everywhere in the tall grass, popping up like
corn to sting the flesh, and tortoises crawl about on the red
earth, going nowhere in the plenty of time. Loneliness is an aspect of the land. All things in the plain are isolate; there is no
confusion of objects in the eye, but *one* hill or *one* tree or *one*
man. To look upon that landscape in the early morning, with
the sun at your back, is to lose the sense of proportion. Your
imagination comes to life, and this, you think, is where Creation
was begun.

I returned to Rainy Mountain in July. My grandmother had   2
died in the spring, and I wanted to be at her grave. She had lived
to be very old and at last infirm. Her only living daughter was
with her when she died, and I was told that in death her face
was that of a child.

I like to think of her as a child. When she was born, the   3
Kiowas were living that last great moment of their history. For
more than a hundred years they had controlled the open range
from the Smoky Hill River to the Red, from the headwaters of
the Canadian to the fork of the Arkansas and Cimarron. In alliance with the Comanches, they had ruled the whole of the
southern Plains. War was their sacred business, and they were
among the finest horsemen the world has ever known. But war-
fare for the Kiowas was preeminently a matter of disposition

rather than of survival, and they never understood the grim, un-relenting advance of the U.S. Cavalry. When at last, divided and ill-provisioned, they were driven onto the Staked Plains in the cold rains of autumn, they fell into panic. In Palo Duro Canyon they abandoned their crucial stores to pillage and had nothing then but their lives. In order to save themselves, they surrendered to the soldiers at Fort Sill and were imprisoned in the old stone corral that now stands as a military museum. My grandmother was spared the humiliation of those high gray walls by eight or ten years, but she must have known from birth the affliction of defeat, the dark brooding of old warriors.

Her name was Aho, and she belonged to the last culture to 4 evolve in North America. Her forebears came down from the high country in western Montana nearly three centuries ago. They were a mountain people, a mysterious tribe of hunters whose language has never been positively classified in any major group. In the late seventeenth century they began a long migration to the south and east. It was a long journey toward the dawn, and it led to a golden age. Along the way the Kiowas were befriended by the Crows, who gave them the culture and religion of the Plains. They acquired horses, and their ancient nomadic spirit was suddenly free of the ground. They acquired Tai-me, the sacred Sun Dance doll, from that moment the object and symbol of their worship, and so shared in the divinity of the sun. Not least, they acquired the sense of destiny, therefore courage and pride. When they entered upon the southern Plains, they had been transformed. No longer were they slaves to the simple necessity of survival; they were a lordly and dangerous society of fighters and thieves, hunters and priests of the sun. According to their origin myth, they entered the world through a hollow log. From one point of view, their migration was the fruit of an old prophecy, for indeed they emerged from a sunless world.

Although my grandmother lived out her long life in the 5 shadow of Rainy Mountain, the immense landscape of the continental interior lay like memory in her blood. She could tell of the Crows, whom she had never seen, and of the Black Hills, where she had never been. I wanted to see in reality what she had seen more perfectly in the mind's eye, and traveled fifteen hundred miles to begin my pilgrimage.

Yellowstone, it seemed to me, was the top of the world, a   6
region of deep lakes and dark timber, canyons and waterfalls. But, beautiful as it is, one might have the sense of confinement there. The skyline in all directions is close at hand, the high wall of the woods and deep cleavages of shade. There is a perfect freedom in the mountains, but it belongs to the eagle and the elk, the badger and the bear. The Kiowas reckoned their stature by the distance they could see, and they were bent and blind in the wilderness.

Descending eastward, the highland meadows are a stair-   7
way to the plain. In July the inland slope of the Rockies is lux-uriant with flax and buckwheat, stonecrop and larkspur. The earth unfolds and the limit of the land recedes. Clusters of trees and animals grazing far in the distance cause the vision to reach away and wonder to build upon the mind. The sun follows a longer course in the day, and the sky is immense beyond all comparison. The great billowing clouds that sail upon it are shadows that move upon the grain like water, dividing light. Farther down, in the land of the Crows and Blackfeet, the plain is yellow. Sweet clover takes hold of the hills and bends upon itself to cover and seal the soil. There the Kiowas paused on their way; they had come to the place where they must change their lives. The sun is at home on the plains. Precisely there does it have the certain character of a god. When the Kiowas came to the land of the Crows, they could see the dark lees of the hills at dawn across the Bighorn River, the profusion of light on the grain shelves, the oldest deity ranging after the solstices. Not yet would they veer southward to the caldron of the land that lay below; they must wean their blood from the northern win-ter and hold the mountains a while longer in their view. They bore Tai-me in procession to the east.

A dark mist lay over the Black Hills, and the land was like   8
iron. At the top of a ridge I caught sight of Devil's Tower up-thrust against the gray sky as if in the birth of time the core of the earth had broken through its crust and the motion of the world was begun. There are things in nature that engender an

awful quiet in the heart of man; Devil's Tower is one of them. Two centuries ago, because they could not do otherwise, the Kiowas made a legend at the base of the rock. My grandmother said:

> Eight children were there at play, seven sisters and their brother. Suddenly the boy was struck dumb; he trembled and began to run upon his hands and feet. His fingers became claws, and his body was covered with fur. Directly there was a bear where the boy had been. The sisters were terrified; they ran, and the bear after them. They came to the stump of a great tree, and the tree spoke to them. It bade them climb upon it, and as they did so, it began to rise into the air. The bear came to kill them, but they were just beyond its reach. It reared against the tree and scored the bark all around with its claws. The seven sisters were borne into the sky, and they became the stars of the Big Dipper.

From that moment, and so long as the legend lives, the Kiowas have kinsmen in the night sky. Whatever they were in the mountains, they could be no more. However tenuous their well-being, however much they had suffered and would suffer again, they had found a way out of the wilderness.

My grandmother had a reverence for the sun, a holy regard that now is all but gone out of mankind. There was a wariness in her, and an ancient awe. She was a Christian in her later years, but she had come a long way about, and she never forgot her birthright. As a child she had been to the Sun Dances; she had taken part in those annual rites, and by them she had learned the restoration of her people in the presence of Tai-me. She was about seven when the last Kiowa Sun Dance was held in 1887 on the Washita River above Rainy Mountain Creek. The buffalo were gone. In order to consummate the ancient sacrifice—to impale the head of a buffalo bull upon the medicine tree—a delegation of old men journeyed into Texas, there to beg and barter for an animal from the Goodnight herd. She was ten when the Kiowas came together for the last time as a living Sun Dance culture. They could find no buffalo; they had to hang an old hide from the sacred tree. Before the dance could begin, a company of soldiers rode out from Fort Sill under orders to disperse the tribe. Forbidden without cause the essential act of their faith, having seen the wild herds slaughtered and left to rot upon the ground, the Kiowas backed away forever from the medicine tree. That was July 20, 1890, at the great bend of the Washita. My grandmother was there. Without bitterness, and for as long as she lived, she bore a vision of deicide.

Now that I can have her only in memory, I see my grand-   10
mother in the several postures that were peculiar to her: standing at the wood stove on a winter morning and turning meat in a great iron skillet; sitting at the south window, bent above her beadwork, and afterwards, when her vision had failed, looking down for a long time into the fold of her hands; going out upon a cane, very slowly as she did when the weight of age came upon her; praying. I remember her most often at prayer. She made long, rambling prayers out of suffering and hope, having seen many things. I was never sure that I had the right to hear, so exclusive were they of all mere custom and company. The last time I saw her she prayed standing by the side of her bed at night, naked to the waist, the light of a kerosene lamp moving upon her dark skin. Her long, black hair, always drawn and braided in the day, lay upon her shoulders and against her breasts like a shawl. I do not speak Kiowa, and I never understood her prayers, but there was something inherently sad in the sound, some merest hesitation upon the syllables of sorrow. She began in a high and descending pitch, exhausting her breath to silence; then again and again—and always the same intensity of effort, of something that is, and is not, like urgency in the human voice. Transported so in the dancing light among the shadows of her room, she seemed beyond the reach of time. But that was illusion; I think I knew then that I should not see her again.

1969

Alias Benowitz Shoe Repair

David Quammen

I first heard about George Ochenski from a friend of mine   1
who happens to be president of the Montana River-Snorkelers
Association. We were in a fancy restaurant, as I recall, and there
was wine involved. Ochenski had come to my friend's attention
in the course of his (the friend's) presidential duties, which are
in strict point of fact nonexistent. I should explain that the
MRSA presidency is a purely honorary title, self-bestowed actually, because the MRSA is a mythical organization. This is all
quite different, please note, from labeling the organization itself nonexistent. Certainly the Montana River-Snorkelers Association does exist (mainly over wine and beer at various bars
and restaurants, occasionally also around a campfire); it just
isn't *real*. An actual mythical entity, then, the MRSA, of roughly
the same ontological status as the NCAA national champi-
onship in football, or the domino theory of international relations. You should look into this fellow Ochenski, my friend told
me. He can be reached care of Benowitz Shoe Repair, in a tiny
town called Southern Cross, up in the Flint Mountains above
Anaconda. Have some more cabernet, I said. But sure enough
it turned out to be true. Benowitz Shoe Repair is another mythical entity, existent in its own way but not real. George Ochenski is both mythical and real. Are you with me so far?

George Ochenski must certainly be the preeminent river-   2
snorkeler in the Rocky Mountains. He has talent, commitment,
infectious enthusiasm, broad experience, state-of-the-art equipment, and a measure of lunatic daring. He has precious little
competition. Most important, he has self-abnegating dedica-
tion to a larger purpose.

Sometimes you have to snorkel a river, Ochenski believes,   3
in order to save it.

So dedicated is George Ochenski, and so scornful of risk,   4
that—if necessary to make a point—he is willing even to snorkel
the Clark Fork River downstream from the Anaconda smelter.

Now a river-snorkeler (in case this isn't self-evident) is ⁵
someone who swims downstream in a river with his face under
water, enjoying the ride, watching the scenery, breathing
through his little tube. A lazy, hypnotic pastime best practiced
on pellucid trout streams in midsummer. A few of us have been
toying at it for years.

But George Ochenski does not toy. He jimmies himself into ⁶
a full wet suit, adds fins and a hood and neoprene gloves and
a fanny pack holding three cans of beer, pulls a pair of skateboarding knee pads into place, defogs his mask, and jumps into
rivers. Gentle rivers and raging whitewater monsters. Last year,
for instance, he did thirty-eight miles of the Salmon in Idaho
without benefit of a boat. Also last year, he leapt into the Quake
Lake trench—an earthquake-contorted stretch of the Madison
River famous for biting kayaks in half—and nearly died. On that
run his mask was ripped off six times while he tumbled head
over teakettle through a garden of sharp boulders; the trench,
George admits today, was a miscalculation. In Montana this
kind of behavior does not pass unnoticed. By word, and more
discreetly by the looks on their faces, people frequently tell him:
Son, you must be out of your everlovin' skull. But they said that to
Orville Wright, and they were wrong. Then again, they said it
to Evel Knievel, and they were right. George Ochenski figures
somewhere in between.

He has an enduring though ambivalent attraction to what ⁷
he himself classifies "death sports." Huge squinting grin from
George as he acknowledges this ambivalence. Mountaineering.
Iceclimbing. Scuba. Never a major injury, never a bad accident—unless you count the time he fell 600 feet down a steep
rock slope in the Alaska Range and did a self-arrest on his nose.
Back in those years he traveled exotically for serious climbing,
with generous sponsorship from the equipment people, and
took part in the first successful ascent of the west face of
Alaska's Mt. Hayes. Scaled some breathtaking frozen waterfalls.
Around the same time, a consummate autodidact, he turned
himself into an expert cobbler, because he wasn't satisfied with
the professional repair work on his climbing boots; before long
he was doing work for his friends too, and they had rechris-

tened him, whimsically and metonymically, "Benowitz Shoe Repair." Today he mostly stays close to the little wood-heated cabin at Southern Cross, in the front room of which stands a bass fiddle. The fiddle is a logical switch from tuba, which he played for thirteen years. Benowitz is a man of many skills.

Several years ago, in response to pressure both internal and external, he gave up the glorious climbing, thanked the sponsors, and settled down to being useful politically. He had come to feel that he owed something back to the mountains and rivers; meanwhile there happened to be a certain crisis brewing near home. He now makes his living as an editorial assistant to an author of textbooks on environmental science. The cabin is filled ceiling-high with an eclectic library. On one wall is a quote from Congressman Ron Dellums: "Democracy is not about being a damn spectator against the backdrop of tap-dancing politicians swinging in the winds of expediency." By disposition, George is certainly no spectator. Some people, particularly of the opposition, might still take him on first impression for a wild-haired, good-timing, reckless flake. They would be grievously mistaken. George Ochenski has an excellent brain, he has chutzpah, he has focus.

And in a small trailer up the hill behind his own cabin, where the ash from his cook stove can't fuddle its circuits, he has an Apple II computer, its floppy discs full of damning information concerning the Anaconda Minerals Company.

On September 29, 1980, the Anaconda Company announced that it was closing its copper-smelting operations at the town of Anaconda. This came as a severe shock to the 1,000 smelter workers suddenly unemployed, and marked the end of a century of awesome environmental pillage. For one hundred years the Company had cut down forests, poisoned streams, smelted copper, piled up vast mounds of slag, and filled the air of the country with a sulfurous smog, in exchange for the regular paychecks dispensed. Now the economics of copper had shifted. Goodbye, thanks for everything. "The Company thought they could just lock the doors and walk away," says George Ochenski.

He and a few other Anaconda folk, some of them former 11
smelter workers, think otherwise. They are after the Company
like a fierce dog after a bear. They have formed an enraged-
citizens' organization, pressured the governor, pressured the
senators, pressured the EPA. They want more than goodbyes.
They want reclamation. They want accountability. At very least
they want precise information about the nature and magnitude
of the poisonous mess left behind.

With sulfur dioxide no longer pouring from the smelter 12
stack, the chief concern now is over toxic metals: lead, cadmium, mercury, zinc, copper itself, and especially arsenic. One
hundred years of copper-smelting have left various concentrations of some or all of these in the waters, in the plants, in the
soil, in the animals of the county. George Ochenski and his
compatriots want to know: *How much?* How much was dumped
in the ponds, how much was buried, how much is still blowing
free off the smelter site? How much is already in our lungs and
our bones? How much is ingested with each brown trout from
the Clark Fork River, if a person should be so lucky as to catch
one of the surviving fish, and so foolhardy as to eat it?

How much lead? How much cadmium? How much ar- 13
senic? The Anaconda Company, no doubt, devoutly wishes
that these questions would go away.

Sometimes you have to snorkel a river in order to save it. 14
Guided by this dictum, George Ochenski loaded his gear into
the back of my car. It was late in the season, Labor Day weekend, with the air already growing cool. We paused briefly,
where the gravel lane down from Southern Cross joined the
larger road, to check the Benowitz Shoe Repair mailbox. Then
George led me off on a pair of brief but illuminating tours.

We went to the Big Hole River, across the Continental Di- 15
vide from Anaconda and clear of the war zone over heavy metals. The Big Hole is still a pellucid trout stream. We jimmied ourselves into wet suits, added fins and hoods and neoprene
gloves; I pulled George's one extra skateboarding pad into position over my favorite knee. Masks were defogged, snorkels ad-
justed, and we jumped in.

The view was beautiful. Trout and whitefish looked me in 16

the eye, aghast, and skittered away. Sculpins darted discreetly for cover. I observed the differences in underwater behavior among three different species of stonefly. I gazed at the funnel webs of *Arctopsyche* caddisfly larvae, down between rocks in the fast water, that I had read about often but never before seen. I found a mayfly nymph equipped with an elephantine pair of tusks. We passed through a few modest sets of rapids, where the current abruptly accelerated and the boulders came at me like blitzing linebackers who must be straight-armed away. After two hours of cruising we were nearly hypothermic, but the experience had been delightful.

Our second tour was to the Clark Fork River, downstream ₁₇ from the settling ponds into which the Anaconda Company has voided its years of industrial offal. "We're off to snorkel the Clark Fork," George told a friend as we pulled out of town. The friend looked puzzled. Huge squinting grin from George. "Then we'll come back and glow in the dark."

We snorkeled a long section of the Clark Fork. Here the ₁₈ water was turbid, visibility was poor. The rocks of the stream bed were largely cemented together with silt, leaving no habitat for stoneflies or *Arctopsyche*. I didn't see a single fish. I didn't see a single insect. Some people claim that the Clark Fork today is actually much improved over its sorry condition two decades ago, before the Company adopted certain technical measures to mitigate the toxicity of its releases. Maybe those people are right. But I remain skeptical. The river I was swimming through, with my eyes open and my nose very close to the bottom, was definitely no basis for passing out congratulations.

This dramatic lack of vitality proves nothing, of course, ₁₉ about what causal role the smelter wastes, and the erosion from denuded hillsides around Anaconda, may or may not still be playing. It simply correlates. Consider it, if you wish to, purest coincidence. It is not, however, mythical. It is real.

Later Benowitz and I were careful to shower ourselves ₂₀ down with clean water. "River-snorkeling," he told me, and he should know, "is not supposed to be a death sport."

1985

My Father

Doris Lessing

We use our parents like recurring dreams, to be entered into 1
when needed; they are always there for love or for hate; but it
occurs to me that I was not always there for my father. I've written about him before, but novels, stories, don't have to be "true."
Writing this article is difficult because it has to be "true." I knew
him when his best years were over.

There are photographs of him. The largest is of an officer in 2
the 1914–18 war. A new uniform—buttoned, badged, strapped,
tabbed—confines a handsome, dark young man who holds
himself stiffly to confront what he certainly thought of as his
duty. His eyes are steady, serious, and responsible, and show
no signs of what he became later. A photograph at sixteen is of
a dark, introspective youth with the same intent eyes. But it is
his mouth you notice—a heavily-jutting upper lip contradicts
the rest of a regular face. His moustache was to hide it: "Had to
do something—a damned fleshy mouth. Always made me uncomfortable, that mouth of mine."

Earlier a baby (eyes already alert) appears in a lace water- 3
fall that cascades from the pillowy bosom of a fat, plain woman
to her feet. It is the face of a head cook. "Lord, but my mother
was a practical female—almost as bad as you!" as he used to say,
or throw at my mother in moments of exasperation. Beside her
stands, or droops, arms dangling, his father, the source of the
dark, arresting eyes, but otherwise masked by a long beard.

The birth certificate says: Born 3rd August, 1886, Walton 4
Villa, Creffield Road, S. Mary at the Wall, R.S.D. Name, Alfred
Cook. Name and surname of Father: Alfred Cook Tayler. Name
and maiden name of Mother: Caroline May Batley. Rank or
Profession: Bank Clerk. Colchester, Essex.

They were very poor. Clothes and boots were a problem. 5
They "made their own amusements." Books were mostly the
Bible and *The Pilgrim's Progress*. Every Saturday night they
bathed in a hipbath in front of the kitchen fire. No servants.

Church three times on Sundays. "Lord, when I think of those Sundays! I dreaded them all week, like a nightmare coming at you full tilt and no escape." But he rabbited with ferrets along the lanes and fields, bird-nested, stole fruit, picked nuts and mushrooms, paid visits to the blacksmith and the mill and rode a farmer's carthorse.

They ate economically, but when he got diabetes in his for- 6 ties and subsisted on lean meat and lettuce leaves, he remembered suet puddings, treacle puddings, raisin and currant puddings, steak and kidney puddings, bread and butter pudding, "batter cooked in the gravy with the meat," potato cake, plum cake, butter cake, porridge with treacle, fruit tarts and pies, brawn, pig's trotters and pig's cheek and homesmoked ham and sausages. And "lashings of fresh butter and cream and eggs." He wondered if this diet had produced the diabetes, but said it was worth it.

There was an elder brother described by my father as: "Too 7 damned clever by half. One of those quick, clever brains. Now I've always had a slow brain, but I get there in the end, damn it!"

The brothers went to a local school and the elder did well, 8 but my father was beaten for being slow. They both became bank clerks in, I think, the Westminster Bank, and one must have found it congenial, for he became a manager, the "rich brother," who had cars and even a yacht. But my father did not like it, though he was conscientious. For instance, he changed his writing, letter by letter, because a senior criticised it. I never saw his unregenerate hand, but the one he created was elegant, spiky, careful. Did this mean he created a new personality for himself, hiding one he did not like, as he hid his "damned fleshy mouth"? I don't know.

Nor do I know when he left home to live in Luton, or why. 9 He found family life too narrow? A safe guess—he found everything too narrow. His mother was too down-to-earth? He had to get away from his clever elder brother?

Being a young man in Luton was the best part of his life. It 10 ended in 1914, so he had a decade of happiness. His reminiscences of it were all of pleasure, the delight of physical movement, of dancing in particular. All his girls were "a beautiful dancer, light as a feather." He played billiards and ping-pong (both for his country); he swam, boated, played cricket and football, went to picnics and horse races, sang at musical evenings. One family of a mother and two daughters treated him "like a son only better. I didn't know whether I was in love with the mother or the daughters, but oh I did love going there; we had such good times." He was engaged to one daughter, then, for a time, to the other. An engagement was broken off because she was rude to a waiter. "I could not marry a woman who allowed herself to insult someone who was defenseless." He used to say to my wryly smiling mother: "Just as well I didn't marry either of *them;* they would never have stuck it out the way you have, old girl."

Just before he died he told me he had dreamed he was   11
standing in a kitchen on a very high mountain holding X in his arms. "Ah, yes, that's what I've missed in my life. Now don't you let yourself be cheated out of life by the old dears. They take all the colour out of everything if you let them."

But in that decade—"I'd walk 10, 15 miles to a dance two   12
or three times a week and think nothing of it. Then I'd dance every dance and walk home again over the fields. Sometimes it was moonlight, but I liked the snow best all crisp and fresh. I loved walking back and getting into my digs just as the sun was rising. My little dog was so happy to see me, and I'd feed her, and make myself porridge and tea, then I'd wash and shave and go off to work."

The boy who was beaten at school, who went too much to   13
church, who carried the fear of poverty all his life, but who nevertheless was filled with the memories of country pleasures; the young bank clerk who worked such long hours for so little money, but who danced, sang, played, flirted—this naturally vigorous, sensuous being was killed in 1914, 1915, 1916. I think the best of my father died in that war, that his spirit was crippled by it. The people I've met, particularly the women, who knew him young, speak of his high spirits, his energy, his enjoyment of life. Also of his kindness, his compassion and—a word that keeps recurring—his wisdom. "Even when he was just a boy he understood things that you'd think even an old

man would find it easy to condemn." I do not think these people would have easily recognised the ill, irritable, abstracted, hypochondriac man I knew.

He "joined up" as an ordinary soldier out of a characteristically quirky scruple: it wasn't right to enjoy officers' privileges when the Tommies had such a bad time. But he could not stick the communal latrines, the obligatory drinking, the collective visits to brothels, the jokes about girls. So next time he was offered a commission he took it. 14

His childhood and young man's memories, kept fluid, were added to, grew, as living memories do. But his war memories were congealed in stories that he told again and again, with the same words and gestures, in stereotyped phrases. They were anonymous, general, as if they had come out of a communal war memoir. He met a German in no-man's-land, but both slowly lowered their rifles and smiled and walked away. The Tommies were the salt of the earth, the British fighting men the best in the world. He had never known such comradeship. A certain brutal officer was shot in a sortie by his men, but the other officers, recognising rough justice, said nothing. He had known men intimately who saw the Angels at Mons. He wished he could force all the generals on both sides into the trenches for just one day, to see what the common soldiers endured—*that* would have ended the war at once. 15

There was an undercurrent of memories, dreams, and emotions much deeper, more personal. This dark region in him, fate-ruled, where nothing was true but horror, was expressed inarticulately, in brief, bitter exclamations or phrases of rage, incredulity, betrayal. The men who went to fight in that war believed it when they said it was to end war. My father believed it. And he was never able to reconcile his belief in his country with his anger at the cynicism of its leaders. And the anger, the sense of betrayal, strengthened as he grew old and ill. 16

But in 1914 he was naïve, the German atrocities in Belgium inflamed him, and he enlisted out of idealism, although he knew he would have a hard time. He knew because a fortuneteller told him. (He could be described as uncritically superstitious or as psychically gifted.) He would be in great dan- 17 ger twice, yet not die—he was being protected by a famous soldier who was his ancestor. "And sure enough, later I heard from the Little Aunties that the church records showed we were descended the backstairs way from the Duke of Wellington, or was it Marlborough? Damn it, I forget. But one of them would be beside me all through the war, she said." (He was romantic, not only about this solicitous ghost, but also about being a descendant of the Huguenots, on the strength of the "e" in Tayler; and about "the wild blood" in his veins from a great uncle who, sent unjustly to prison for smuggling, came out of a ten-year sentence and earned it, very efficiently, along the coasts of Cornwall until he died.)

The luckiest thing that ever happened to my father, he said,   18
was getting his leg shattered by shrapnel ten days before Passchendaele. His whole company was killed. He knew he was going to be wounded because of the fortuneteller, who had said he would know. "I did not understand what she meant, but both times in the trenches, first when my appendix burst and I nearly died, and then just before Passchendaele, I felt for some days as if a thick, black velvet pall was settled over me. I can't tell you what it was like. Oh, it was awful, awful, and the second time it was so bad I wrote to the old people and told them I was going to be killed."

His leg was cut off at mid-thigh, he was shell-shocked, he   19
was very ill for many months, with a prolonged depression afterwards. "You should always remember that sometimes people are all seething underneath. You don't know what terrible things people have to fight against. You should look at a person's eyes, that's how you tell. . . . When I was like that, after I lost my leg, I went to a nice doctor man and said I was going mad, but he said, don't worry, everyone locks up things like that. You don't know—horrible, horrible, awful things. I was afraid of myself, of what I used to dream. I wasn't myself at all."

In the Royal Free Hospital was my mother, Sister McVeagh.   20
He married his nurse which, as they both said often enough (though in different tones of voice), was just as well. That was 1919. He could not face being a bank clerk in England, he said, not after the trenches. Besides, England was too narrow and

conventional. Besides, the civilians did not know what the soldiers had suffered, they didn't want to know, and now it wasn't done even to remember "The Great Unmentionable." He went off to the Imperial Bank of Persia, in which country I was born.

The house was beautiful, with great stone-floored high- 21 ceilinged rooms whose windows showed ranges of snow-streaked mountains. The gardens were full of roses, jasmine, pomegranates, walnuts. Kermanshah he spoke of with liking, but soon they went to Teheran, populous with "Embassy people," and my gregarious mother created a lively social life about which he was irritable even in recollection.

Irritableness—that note was first struck here, about Persia. 22 He did not like, he said, "the graft and the corruption." But here it is time to try and describe something difficult—how a man's good qualities can also be his bad ones, or if not bad, a danger to him.

My father was honourable—he always knew exactly what 23 that word meant. He had integrity. His "one does not do that sort of thing," his "no, it is *not* right," sounded throughout my childhood and were final for all of us. I am sure it was true he wanted to leave Persia because of "the corruption." But it was also because he was already unconsciously longing for something freer, because as a bank official he could not let go into the dream-logged personality that was waiting for him. And later in Rhodesia, too, what was best in him was also what prevented him from shaking away the shadows: it was always in the name of honesty or decency that he refused to take this step or that out of the slow decay of the family's fortunes.

In 1925 there was leave from Persia. That year in London 24 there was an Empire Exhibition, and on the Southern Rhodesian stand some very fine maize cobs and a poster saying that fortunes could be made on maize at 25/-a bag. So on an impulse, turning his back forever on England, washing his hands of the corruption of the East, my father collected all his capital, £800, I think, while my mother packed curtains from Liberty's, clothes from Harrods, visiting cards, a piano, Persian rugs, a governess and two small children.

Soon, there was my father in a cigar-shaped house of thatch 25 and mud on the top of a kopje that overlooked in all directions a great system of mountains, rivers, valleys, while overhead the sky arched from horizon to empty horizon. This was a couple of hundred miles south from the Zambesi, a hundred or so west from Mozambique, in the district of Banket, so called because certain of its reefs were of the same formation as those called *banket* on the Rand. Lomagundi—gold country, tobacco country, maize country—wild, almost empty. (The Africans had been turned off it into reserves.) Our neighbours were four, five, seven miles off. In front of the house . . . no neighbours, nothing; no farms, just wild bush with two rivers but no fences to the mountains seven miles away. And beyond these mountains and bush again to the Portuguese border, over which "our boys" used to escape when wanted by the police for pass or other offences.

And then? There was bad luck. For instance, the price of maize dropped from 25/- to 9/-a bag. The seasons were bad, prices bad, crops failed. This was the sort of thing that made it impossible for him ever to "get off the farm," which, he agreed with my mother, was what he most wanted to do. 26

It was an absurd country, he said. A man could "own" a farm for years that was totally mortgaged to the Government and run from the Land Bank, meanwhile employing half-a-hundred Africans at 12/-a month and none of them knew how to do a day's work. Why, two farm labourers from Europe could do in a day what twenty of these ignorant black savages would take a week to do. (Yet he was proud that he had a name as a just employer, that he gave "a square deal.") Things got worse. A fortuneteller had told him that her heart ached when she saw the misery ahead for my father: this was the misery. 27

But it was my mother who suffered. After a period of neurotic illness, which was a protest against her situation, she became brave and resourceful. But she never saw that her husband was not living in a real world, that he had made a captive of her common sense. We were always about to "get off the farm." A miracle would do it—a sweepstake, a goldmine, a legacy. And then? What a question! We would go to England where life would be normal with people coming in for musical evenings and nice supper parties at the Trocadero after a show. Poor woman, for 28 the twenty years we were on the farm, she waited for when life would begin for her and for her children, for she never understood that what was a calamity for her was for them a blessing.

Meanwhile my father sank towards his death (at 61). Everything changed in him. He had been a dandy and fastidious, now he hated to change out of shabby khaki. He had been sociable, now he was misanthropic. His body's disorders—soon diabetes and all kinds of stomach ailments—dominated him. He was brave about his wooden leg, and even went down mine shafts and climbed trees with it, but he walked clumsily and it irked him badly. He greyed fast, and slept more in the day, but would be awake half the night pondering about. . . . 29

It could be gold divining. For ten years he experimented on private theories to do with the attractions and repulsions of metals. His whole soul went into it but his theories were wrong or he was *unlucky*—after all, if he had found a mine he would have had to leave the farm. It could be the relation between the minerals of the earth and of the moon; his decision to make infusions of all the plants on the farm and drink them himself in the interests of science; the criminal folly of the British Government in not realising that the Germans and the Russians were conspiring as Anti-Christ to . . . the inevitability of war because no one would listen to Churchill, but it would be all right because God (by then he was a British Israelite) had destined Britain to rule the world; a prophecy said 10 million dead would surround Jerusalem—how would the corpses be cleared away?; people who wished to abolish flogging should be flogged; the natives understood nothing but a good beating; hanging must not be abolished because the Old Testament said "an eye for an eye and a tooth for a tooth. . . ." 30

Yet, as this side of him darkened, so that it seemed all his thoughts were of violence, illness, war, still no one dared to make an unkind comment in his presence or to gossip. Criticism of people, particularly of women, made him more and more uncomfortable till at last he burst out with: "It's all very well, but no one has the right to say that about another person." 31

In Africa, when the sun goes down, the stars spring up, all of them in their expected places, glittering and moving. In the 32 rainy season, the sky flashed and thundered. In the dry season, the great dark hollow of night was lit by veld fires: the mountains burned through September and October in chains of red fire. Every night my father took out his chair to watch the sky and the mountains, smoking, silent, a thin shabby fly-away figure under the stars. "Makes you think—there are so many worlds up there, wouldn't really matter if we did blow ourselves up—plenty more where we came from."

The Second World War, so long foreseen by him, was a bad 33 time. His son was in the Navy and in danger, and his daughter a sorrow to him. He became very ill. More and more often it was necessary to drive him into Salisbury with him in a coma, or in danger of one, on the back seat. My mother moved him into a pretty little suburban house in town near the hospitals, where he took to his bed and a couple of years later died. For the most part he was unconscious under drugs. When awake he talked obsessively (a tongue licking a nagging sore place) about "the old war." Or he remembered his youth. "I've been dreaming—Lord, to see those horses come lickety-split down the course with their necks stretched out and the sun on their coats and everyone shouting. . . . I've been dreaming how I walked along the river in the mist as the sun was rising. . . . Lord, lord, lord, what a time that was, what good times we all had then, before the old war."

1956

*Easter in Sicily**

Mary Taylor Simeti

Beyond the vague intention of ending up at Prizzi to see the 1 devils dance on Easter afternoon, we have no set itinerary for the rest of the day and decide to drive east along the southern

*Editors' title.

coast, turning or stopping at whim. And whim soon declares itself: only a short distance from Castelvetrano there are road signs indicating the turnoff for Selinunte, and it seems sinful not to make a stop when we have all the time in the world.

Selinunte is to me the least accessible of the Greek sites I have seen in Sicily. The bare bones of a city sacked by man and toppled by earthquake lie in careless heaps on low cliffs overlooking the sea, building blocks abandoned by some infant Titan who has centuries since outgrown them. They are illegible in their very size, with the tourists clambering over the enormous fluted drums of fallen columns like tiny, multicolored ants. Today it is very crowded; parking is difficult and the air rings with a many-tongued babble and with the nagging claxons of the tourist buses gathering their various broods. We mingle with the crowds, wander through the eastern temples, and stroll along the road that leads down into the river valley and up to the acropolis on the opposite cliff until the heat and the confusion persuade us to turn back.   2

Selinunte was a revelation the first time I came, exactly twenty years ago yesterday. Apart from Tonino and me there were no more than a dozen people here, and even these disappeared, swallowed up by the vast sweep of sea and plain and the immoderate proportions of the ruins. We sat for hours on some stones and stared out across sea and centuries, the sea of flowers in the foreground no less brilliant than the Mediterranean that sparkled in the distance. The *selinon,* the wild celery that gave the ancient city its name, was submerged by the red of the sulla, the yellow of mayflowers and mustard, the blue of bugloss and borage, bobbing and trembling under the insistent and noisy prodding of thousands of bees. It was my first immersion in the Sicilian spring, in its colors and its perfumes and its heat, a baptism that caught and held me convert. Today the flowers are still as beautiful, the sun perhaps even hotter, but the crowd and the confusion drown out the bees, and the ruins are silent, unable despite their size to cope with this Lilliputian invasion.   3

We continue eastward and then turn north on the road for Caltabellotta, which winds up over the ridge of low mountains   4

that separates the southern coastal plain east of Selinunte from
the rolling hills of the interior. These mountains are quite barren, with patches of vineyard or wheat exploiting the rare flat
spaces, an occasional olive or almond tree clinging to the steep
and rocky slopes, and, as closer inspection reveals, a sparse car-
peting of the crouching, grasping plants of arid soil and high
altitudes: purple squill, delicate white clusters of star-of-
Bethlehem, the single tiny yellow-and-brown orchids of the
lutea family, and the many-flowered stalks of the *orchis italica*,
bristling with minute pink tentacles.

The village of Caltabellotta lies at the summit of the high-   5
est mountain in this southern ridge, topped only by two great
spurs of rock that thrust up behind it like giant tusks. The streets
are narrow and zigzag steeply up the hillside; a policeman directing all five cars' worth of traffic instructs us to park the car
and continue on foot if we want to see the procession. Of course
we do, so we quickly park and follow the main street up to a
point where it splits, one fork leading farther up a very steep
slope, the other curving down to the right into a tiny piazza. The
"procession" is here—townspeople and bandsmen, their instruments tucked forgotten under their elbows, have gathered
in a circle to cheer and applaud a dancing saint, a life-size plaster statue of the Archangel Michael, the town's patron. Michael,
dressed in the armor of a Roman legionary, is leaning against
a column that has been completely wrapped in purple phlox,
with a young laurel tree tied next to it so that the purple flowers glow against the dark leaves. As in Tràpani and Castelvetrano, the flower-decked platform that bears the statue is
mounted on two poles—in this case very long, thick wooden
beams that of themselves must weigh an enormous amount—
and requires some thirty hefty young men to carry it. But
"carry" is not the right word: they rock and jostle and bounce
the statue in the most extraordinary manner, accompanied and
encouraged by a crescendo of cheering and clapping from the
crowd that presses in around them. Sweat pouring off their
faces, the young men push and pull still harder on their poles,
and the Archangel rocks and sways and reels in a frenzied
dance, until his porters can bear it no longer, the movement sub-

sides into a faint bobbing, and the statue itself seems to pant as the men fight to catch their breath, still holding all the weight on their shoulders.

Bottles of water and beer are passed around, the band re- 6 covers its role and starts to play again, and considerable maneuvering is necessary to effect the passage of the statue around the curve and into the main street, where it pauses at the foot of the rise, gathering strength. Meanwhile another statue arrives, a little winged cherub about two feet high, with platform, poles, and porters in proportion: a handful of boys about twelve years old bounce the baby statue about in great excitement, egged on by an amused crowd.

The music dies out, and, at a sign from one of the porters, 7 the drummer sounds a roll. On the final snap of the drumsticks the men charge up the street, running and stumbling with their heavy burden up a slope so steep that the statue seems almost horizontal. The cheers of the onlookers assist them over the top and around the corner, quickly followed by the angel, who bobs gaily and effortlessly up the rise in the wake of his big brother.

We too turn and climb. We have lost the statues, but echoes 8 of their progress parallel to ours reach us at the street corners. A final hike up a street so sheer that the sidewalk is a flight of stairs brings us out onto the Piano della Matrice, the open square of the mother church, unexpectedly spectacular. In front of us a wide checkerboard of cobble and grass slopes gently up to the steps of the Matrice, built by Count Roger after he took Caltabellotta from the Saracens in 1090. The weathered gray stone of the Norman church blends into the sharp-toothed rock that rises abruptly behind it. On the left-hand side of the square stands the chapel of San Michele, its Gothic portal garlanded in laurel branches, and next to it a gate and a stairway carved into the live rock lead off toward the second, bigger pinnacle, ringed by the trees of the town park where the ruins of the Norman castle lie.

Commotion rising from below tells us that Saint Michael is 9 about to make his final assault on the mountain. The last steep rise is rendered more problematical by telephone wires and shop signs, and considerable measuring accompanied by animated discussion is necessary before a strategy can be agreed upon. At last somebody climbs out on a balcony and unties a laundry line, final directions are shouted out, and the group braces itself. Up they come, the initial momentum waning as they scramble up the cobbled street, their boots slipping and straining to find a grip on the polished stones. A final push and they burst into the square, where they bring up sharply, the statue swaying back and forth, evidently in some confusion as to where to go next.

One of the townsmen who has followed the progress of the 10 statue explains to us that the municipal *pro loco* committee has decided that Caltabellotta should cash in on the "Easter in Sicily" tourist boom and has organized a new procession for the afternoon, a version of the Castelvetrano Aurora, but the details have not been thought out all that well, and no one knows whether Michael should spend his lunch hour in the Matrice or in the chapel of San Michele, where the garlands declare a readiness to receive him sooner or later.

After a few false starts and some rather languishing dis- 11 cussion, Michael is carried up the steps and into the dark interior of the Matrice. We start to follow it, but a priest, heretofore absent from the scene, closes the door firmly in our faces. Lunchtime. The Matrice is closed, the chapel is closed, the gate to the castle is closed. The best we can do is climb up some stone steps that lead around behind the Matrice, to discover that the rock is sheltering a miniature Alpine meadow, shaded by pine trees whose sun-warmed resin fills the air and dotted with tiny daisies, the kind whose white petals have had their tips dipped in red. I remember the flowers from a French children's book I had when I was little, and it is surprising yet suitable to find their smiling faces here in the shadow of the Norman walls. The view from the meadow is spectacular: we can look north toward the mountains of Palermo across the whole of Sicily, the hills and valleys flattened from this height into a gentle pool of green, flecked with the white foam of the blossoming fruit trees.

The priest had something, however. Our stomachs call us 12 to more prosaic questions. We discover that Caltabellotta offers a choice of two restaurants, one in the town itself and one just outside, around the back of the peak that rises above the castle ruins. Walking down toward the car we pass the first, which is occupied by a baptismal party and has no free tables. A winding road takes us out of town, past vegetable plots and tiny vineyards, to a huge baroque monastery, this too flanked by a cliff and by a charming restaurant with a trellised terrace. The proprietor is polite and extremely apologetic: a wedding reception is in progress, and there isn't a free chair in the place. Tonino, undaunted or perhaps desperate, asks if they couldn't fix us a little antipasto to go. After a brief wait the obliging host produces three foil-covered plates, a bottle of mineral water, and a round kilo loaf of fragrant, crusty bread. We drive back along the road a little way to a curve that offers space to park and some rocks to sit on. Our plates turn out to hold spicy olives, some slices of *prosciutto crudo* and of a peppery local salame, and two kinds of pecorino cheese, one fresh and mild, the other aged and sharper. With a bag of oranges from the car, the sun warm on our backs, the mountains rolling down at our feet to the southern coast and the sea beyond, where the heat haze clouds the horizon and hides Africa from view, we have as fine an Easter dinner as I have ever eaten.

The drive north to Prizzi, a rapid descent switchbacking 13 down the north side of the mountain to the green valleys we had seen from above, takes us along luxuriant riverbeds, over hills of green wheat, past isolated pear and apple trees in bloom. The hedgerows are overflowing with flowers, unable to contain such a riot of color, such an exuberance of form and texture. It is difficult to believe that in the space of a few months the velvet softness of the wheat fields, shifting from emerald to chartreuse with the wind, will give way to bristling, colorless stubble; these are the hills that the Lampedusa family cross in the Visconti film of *The Leopard,* in blinding light and smothering dust, their carriages creaking to the shrill song of the locusts.

But the extravagant hand of spring is less and less success- 14 ful in concealing the poverty of the agriculture the farther north we go. Our destination, the village of Prizzi, is quite high, slapped down on a hill of rocky soil and stunted vegetation with none of the cozy shifting and filling with which most Sicilian

towns have accommodated themselves to the bones of the island. The outskirts of the town are ringed with the usual half-
finished houses, fruit of the emigrants' remittances, but once
past them the streets are small and close and we are hard put
to find a parking space and then to fight our way through the
crowds that are thronging toward the center of town, the ranks
of the Prizzitani being very much swollen by both foreign and
Sicilian tourists. Tonino greets several of his students from the
university, then most unexpectedly a hand claps down on my
shoulder. It is Nicolò, a man who served on the school board
with me. He is a native of Prizzi, a linesman for the telephone
company, and after a period of technical schooling in Milan now
lives in Palermo, where, fortified by his northern experience, he
has become very active in the local section of the Communist
party, in the neighborhood council, the trade union, and the
school board. He proved a most unusual and valuable addition
to the school board, able and willing to work on two levels in a
way that is rare among Sicilians, ready to debate the ideologi-
cal or educational implications of a policy decision and at the
same time to fix a light plug or repair a busted slide projector
himself rather than trusting to the lengthy meanderings of the
school bureaucracy. But today he is here in Prizzi to be with his
family and to see the devils dance.

We are lucky to run into him. We have arrived too late for 15
the distribution of the *cannateddi*, Prizzi's special Easter cakes,
but Nicolò carries us off to the Circolo della Caccia, the Hunters'
Club, which the Chamber of Commerce has been using as its
headquarters for the occasion, and there he sets various cousins
scurrying around to unearth some last undistributed *cannateddi*
for us, oval cakes of biscuit dough braided about an egg.

Cannateddi in hand, we follow Nicolò out again and push 16
our way along the main street, which dips sharply down, then
rises again in the distance. Nicolò guides us to the lowest point
in the street, where he tells us to stay put, this being a grand-
stand seat for watching the triumph of Good over Evil. The
street is filled with people, strolling, talking, and shouting
across from one crowded balcony to another. Here at the bottom we can look up in either direction at a sea of faces. A small

and hornèd vortex is descending upon us from the eastern end: the devils are coming, accompanied by the clanking of their chains and the squealing and shouting of a swarm of little boys. There are three masked figures, two devils escorting Death. Death is dressed in yellow, a big, loose-fitting yellow jump suit and a yellow mask of soldered tin covering his whole head in the shape of a skull, in which have been cut eyeholes, a black dent for the nose, and a mouth grinning around a few long and crooked teeth. Under his arm is a crossbow with which he menaces the crowd. The devils have rust-colored jump suits, ample enough to accommodate a variety of figures over the years, and their masks are large, flat tin ovals, painted brown, with curved horns, long noses, and tongues sticking out from leering mouths. The backs of their heads and shoulders are covered by heavy, long-haired goat pelts, black for one, white for the other, a touch of the genuine that is somehow much more menacing than the masks themselves. The multicolored stripes of Adidas sneakers show underneath the baggy trouser legs.

Comfortable shoes are a must for the devils, whose loping, lolloping dance betrays considerable weariness. Well it may, says Nicolò: they have been dancing ever since the hour of the Crucifixion on Friday, chasing about the town making mischief and teasing all they encounter. Nicolò was a devil one year and assures us that the costumes are unbearably hot and heavy, especially on a sunny day like today—the only thing that keeps you going is the wine. Anyone whom Death manages to hit with his crossbow is obliged to stand the devils a round at the nearest tavern, and if Death is a good shot, they all have quite a bit under their jump suits by the end of the day. [17]

There is movement up at either end of the street, and for the second time today we are shoved back against the buildings by white-gloved policemen. The street is long and I can barely make out the Madonna to the east, Christ to the west, and just hear the loudest notes of the band. Down the hill come the forces of Good, two angels in armor, with cardboard wings, red capes, ropes of beads and gilt chains across their breasts, swords in hand, and strange flat-topped helmets that Francesco is quick to notice have been cut out from Alemagna panettone boxes. [18]

The devils at first have the best of these bizarre apparitions; a brief skirmish leads to a hasty retreat, and then a counterattack. Back and forth they run and clash and feint as the statues continue their slow but steady descent. The battlefield shrinks as the statues draw nearer, the dance and the swordwork grow more and more frenzied as the devils find themselves hemmed in between the advancing figures, until a last and desperate leap marks the meeting between the risen Christ and the rejoicing Madonna, and Death and the devils fall to earth, vanquished and immobile.

This scene will be repeated four more times this evening, ₁₉ the last time in the dark in the big piazza in front of the Matrice, at the top of the hill. Nicolò urges us to stay, but it is a long way back to Bosco and it is already half past five, so we say goodbye. Drunk with all that we have seen, my cheeks burning from the sun and wind, and my eyes watering, I can hardly take in the landscape we drive through, nor do I notice where we are when Tonino turns his attention from the road to give me a reproachful glance.

"When I was a boy, I spent all my time *avoiding* proces- ₂₀ sions!"

1986

CHAPTER 3

Process

The Spider and the Wasp

Alexander Petrunkevitch

To hold its own in the struggle for existence, every species 1
of animal must have a regular source of food, and if it happens
to live on other animals, its survival may be very delicately balanced. The hunter cannot exist without the hunted; if the latter
should perish from the earth, the former would, too. When the
hunted also prey on some of the hunters, the matter may become complicated.

This is nowhere better illustrated than in the insect world. 2
Think of the complexity of a situation such as the following:
There is a certain wasp, *Pimpla inquisitor*, whose larvae feed on
the larvae of the tussock moth. *Pimpla* larvae in turn serve as
food for the larvae of a second wasp, and the latter in their turn
nourish still a third wasp. What subtle balance between fertility and mortality must exist in the case of each of these four
species to prevent the extinction of all of them! An excess of
mortality over fertility in a single member of the group would
ultimately wipe out all four.

This is not a unique case. The two great orders of insects, 3
Hymenoptera and Diptera, are full of such examples of inter-
relationship. And the spiders (which are not insects but members of a separate order of arthropods) also are killers and victims of insects.

In the feeding and safeguarding of their progeny the insects 4 and spiders exhibit some interesting analogies to reasoning and some crass examples of blind instinct. The case I propose to describe here is that of the tarantula spiders and their arch-enemy, the digger wasps of the genus Pepsis. It is a classic example of what looks like intelligence pitted against instinct—a strange situation in which the victim, though fully able to defend itself, submits unwittingly to its destruction.

A fertilized female tarantula lays from 200 to 400 eggs at a   5 time; thus it is possible for a single tarantula to produce several thousand young. She takes no care of them beyond weaving a cocoon of silk to enclose the eggs. After they hatch, the young walk away, find convenient places in which to dig their burrows and spend the rest of their lives in solitude. Tarantulas feed mostly on insects and millepedes. Once their appetite is appeased, they digest the food for several days before eating again. Their sight is poor, being limited to sensing a change in the intensity of light and to the perception of moving objects. They apparently have little or no sense of hearing, for a hungry tarantula will pay no attention to a loudly chirping cricket placed in its cage unless the insect happens to touch one of its legs.

But all spiders, and especially hairy ones, have an extremely   6 delicate sense of touch. Laboratory experiments prove that tarantulas can distinguish three types of touch: pressure against the body wall, stroking of the body hair and riffling of certain very fine hairs on the legs called trichobothria. Pressure against the body, by a finger or the end of a pencil, causes the tarantula to move off slowly for a short distance. The touch excites no defensive response unless the approach is from above where the spider can see the motion, in which case it rises on its hind legs, lifts its front legs, opens its fangs and holds this threatening posture as long as the object continues to move. When the motion stops, the spider drops back to the ground, remains quiet for a few seconds and then moves slowly away.

The entire body of a tarantula, especially its legs, is thickly   7 clothed with hair. Some of it is short and woolly, some long and stiff. Touching this body hair produces one of two distinct reactions. When the spider is hungry, it responds with an immediate and swift attack. At the touch of a cricket's antennae the tarantula seizes the insect so swiftly that a motion picture taken at the rate of 64 frames per second shows only the result and not the process of capture. But when the spider is not hungry, the stimulation of its hairs merely causes it to shake the touched limb. An insect can walk under its hairy belly unharmed.

The trichobothria, very fine hairs growing from disklike membranes on the legs, were once thought to be the spider's hearing organs, but we now know that they have nothing to do with sound. They are sensitive only to air movement. A light breeze makes them vibrate slowly without disturbing the common hair. When one blows gently on the trichobothria, the tarantula reacts with a quick jerk of its four front legs. If the front and hind legs are stimulated at the same time, the spider makes a sudden jump. This reaction is quite independent of the state of its appetite. 8

These three tactile responses—to pressure on the body wall, to moving of the common hair and to flexing of the trichobothria—are so different from one another that there is no possibility of confusing them. They serve the tarantula adequately for most of its needs and enable it to avoid most annoyances and dangers. But they fail the spider completely when it meets its deadly enemy, the digger wasp Pepsis. 9

These solitary wasps are beautiful and formidable creatures. Most species are either a deep shiny blue all over, or deep blue with rusty wings. The largest have a wing span of about four inches. They live on nectar. When excited, they give off a pungent odor—a warning that they are ready to attack. The sting is much worse than that of a bee or common wasp, and the pain and swelling last longer. In the adult stage the wasp lives only a few months. The female produces but a few eggs, one at a time at intervals of two or three days. For each egg the mother must provide one adult tarantula, alive but paralyzed. The tarantula must be of the correct species to nourish the larva. The mother wasp attaches the egg to the paralyzed spider's abdomen. Upon hatching from the egg, the larva is many hundreds of times smaller than its living but helpless victim. It eats no other food and drinks no water. By the time it has finished its single gargantuan meal and become ready for wasphood, 10 nothing remains of the tarantula but its indigestible chitinous skeleton.

The mother wasp goes tarantula-hunting when the egg in 11 her ovary is almost ready to be laid. Flying low over the ground late on a sunny afternoon, the wasp looks for its victim or for the mouth of a tarantula burrow, a round hole edged by a bit of silk. The sex of the spider makes no difference, but the mother is highly discriminating as to species. Each species of Pepsis requires a certain species of tarantula, and the wasp will not attack the wrong species. In a cage with a tarantula which is not its normal prey the wasp avoids the spider, and is usually killed by it in the night.

Yet when a wasp finds the correct species, it is the other way 12 about. To identify the species the wasp apparently must explore the spider with her antennae. The tarantula shows an amazing tolerance to this exploration. The wasp crawls under it and walks over it without evoking any hostile response. The molestation is so great and so persistent that the tarantula often rises on all eight legs, as if it were on stilts. It may stand this way for several minutes. Meanwhile the wasp, having satisfied itself that the victim is of the right species, moves off a few inches to dig the spider's grave. Working vigorously with legs and jaws, it excavates a hole 8 to 10 inches deep with a diameter slightly larger than the spider's girth. Now and again the wasp pops out of the hole to make sure that the spider is still there.

When the grave is finished, the wasp returns to the taran- 13 tula to complete her ghastly enterprise. First she feels it all over once more with her antennae. Then her behavior becomes more aggressive. She bends her abdomen, protruding her sting, and searches for the soft membrane at the point where the spider's leg joins its body—the only spot where she can penetrate the horny skeleton. From time to time, as the exasperated spider slowly shifts ground, the wasp turns on her back and slides along with the aid of her wings, trying to get under the tarantula for a shot at the vital spot. During all this maneuvering, which can last for several minutes, the tarantula makes no move to save itself. Finally the wasp corners it against some obstruction and grasps one of its legs in her powerful jaws. Now at last the harassed spider tries a desperate but vain defense. The two contestants roll over and over on the ground. It is a terrifying sight and the outcome is always the same. The wasp finally manages to thrust her sting into the soft spot and holds it there for a few seconds while she pumps in the poison. Almost immediately the tarantula falls paralyzed on its back. Its legs stop twitching; its heart stops beating, yet it is not dead, as is shown by the fact that if taken from the wasp it can be restored to some sensitivity by being kept in a moist chamber for several months.

After paralyzing the tarantula, the wasp cleans herself by 14 dragging her body along the ground and rubbing her feet, sucks the drop of blood oozing from the wound in the spider's abdomen, then grabs a leg of the flabby, helpless animal in her jaws and drags it down to the bottom of the grave. She stays there for many minutes, sometimes for several hours, and what she does all that time in the dark we do not know. Eventually she lays her egg and attaches it to the side of the spider's abdomen with a sticky secretion. Then she emerges, fills the grave with soil carried bit by bit in her jaws, and finally tramples the ground all around to hide any trace of the grave from prowlers. Then she flies away, leaving her descendant safely started in life.

In all this the behavior of the wasp evidently is qualita- 15 tively different from that of the spider. The wasp acts like an intelligent animal. This is not to say that instinct plays no part or that she reasons as man does. But her actions are to the point; they are not automatic and can be modified to fit the situation. We do not know for certain how she identifies the tarantula— probably it is by some olfactory or chemo-tactile sense—but she does it purposefully and does not blindly tackle a wrong species.

On the other hand, the tarantula's behavior shows only con- 16 fusion. Evidently the wasp's pawing gives it no pleasure, for it tries to move away. That the wasp is not simulating sexual stimulation is certain, because male and female tarantulas react in the same way to its advances. That the spider is not anesthetized by some odorless secretion is easily shown by blowing lightly at the tarantula and making it jump suddenly. What, then, makes the tarantula behave as stupidly as it does?

No clear, simple answer is available. Possibly the stimula- 17
tion by the wasp's antennae is masked by a heavier pressure on
the spider's body, so that it reacts as when prodded by a pencil. But the explanation may be much more complex. Initiative
in attack is not in the nature of tarantulas; most species fight
only when cornered so that escape is impossible. Their inherited patterns of behavior apparently prompt them to avoid
problems rather than attack them. For example, spiders always
weave their webs in three dimensions, and when a spider finds
that there is insufficient space to attach certain threads in the
third dimension, it leaves the place and seeks another, instead
of finishing the web in a single plane. This urge to escape seems
to arise under all circumstances, in all phases of life and to take
the place of reasoning. For a spider to change the pattern of its
web is as impossible as for an inexperienced man to build a
bridge across a chasm obstructing his way.

In a way the instinctive urge to escape is not only easier but 18
often more efficient than reasoning. The tarantula does exactly
what is most efficient in all cases except in an encounter with a
ruthless and determined attacker dependent for the existence
of her own species on killing as many tarantulas as she can lay
eggs. Perhaps in this case the spider follows its usual pattern of
trying to escape, instead of seizing and killing the wasp, because
it is not aware of its danger. In any case, the survival of the
tarantula species as a whole is protected by the fact that the spider is much more fertile than the wasp.

1952

How to Cook a Carp

Euell Gibbons

When I was a lad of about eighteen, my brother and I were 1
working on a cattle ranch in New Mexico that bordered on the
Rio Grande. Most Americans think of the Rio Grande as a warm

southern stream, but it rises among the high mountains of Colorado, and in the spring it is fed by melting snows. At this time of the year, the water that rushed by the ranch was turbulent, icy-cold and so silt-laden as to be semisolid. "A little too thick to drink, and a little too thin to plow" was a common description of the waters of the Rio Grande.

A few species of fish inhabited this muddy water. Unfortunately, the most common was great eight- to ten-pound carp, a fish that is considered very poor eating in this country, although the Germans and Asiatics have domesticated this fish, and have developed some varieties that are highly esteemed for the table.   2

On the ranch where we worked, there was a drainage ditch   3
that ran through the lower pasture and emptied its clear waters into the muddy Rio Grande. The carp swimming up the river would strike this clear warmer water and decide they preferred it to the cold mud they had been inhabiting. One spring day, a cowhand who had been riding that way reported that Clear Ditch was becoming crowded with huge carp.

On Sunday we decided to go fishing. Four of us armed ourselves with pitchforks, saddled our horses and set out. Near the   4
mouth of the ditch, the water was running about two feet deep and twelve to sixteen feet wide. There is a saying in that part of the country that you can't get a cowboy to do anything unless it can be done from the back of a horse, so we forced our mounts into the ditch and started wading them upstream, four abreast, herding the carp before us.

By the time we had ridden a mile upstream, the water was   5
less than a foot deep and so crystal clear that we could see our herd of several hundred carp still fleeing from the splashing, wading horses. As the water continued to shallow, our fish began to get panicky. A few of the boldest ones attempted to dart back past us and were impaled on pitchforks. We could see that the whole herd was getting restless and was about to stampede back downstream, so we piled off our horses into the shallow water to meet the charge. The water boiled about us as the huge fish swirled past us and we speared madly in every direction with our pitchforks, throwing each fish we managed to hit over the ditch bank. This was real fishing—cowhand style.

The last of the fish herd was by us in a few minutes and it was all over, but we had caught a tremendous quantity of fish.

Back at the ranch house, after we had displayed our trophies, we began wondering what we were going to do with so many fish. This started a series of typical cowboy tall tales on "how to cook a carp." The best of these yarns was told by a grizzled old *vaquero*, who claimed he had made his great discovery when he ran out of food while camping on a tributary of the Rio Grande. He said that he had found the finest way to cook a carp was to plaster the whole fish with a thick coating of fresh cow manure and bury it in the hot ashes of a campfire. In an hour or two, he said, the casing of cow manure had become black and very hard. He then related how he had removed the fish from the fire, broken the hard shell with the butt of his Winchester and peeled it off. He said that as the manure came off the scales and skin adhered to it, leaving the baked fish, white and clean. He then ended by saying, "Of course, the carp still wasn't fit to eat, but manure in which it was cooked tasted pretty good."

There were also some serious suggestions and experiments. The chief objection to the carp is that its flesh is full of many forked bones. One man said that he had enjoyed carp sliced very thin and fried so crisp that one could eat it, bones and all. He demonstrated, and you really could eat it without the bones bothering you, but it was still far from being an epicurean dish. One cowboy described the flavor as "a perfect blend of Rio Grande mud and rancid hog lard."

Another man said that he had eaten carp that had been cooked in a pressure cooker until the bones softened and became indistinguishable from the flesh. A pressure cooker is almost a necessity at that altitude, so we had one at the ranch house. We tried this method, and the result was barely edible. It tasted like the poorest possible grade of canned salmon flavored with a bit of mud. It was, however, highly appreciated by the dogs and cats on the ranch, and solved the problem of what to do with the bulk of the fish we had caught.

It was my brother who finally devised a method of cooking carp that not only made it fit for human consumption, but actually delicious. First, instead of merely scaling the fish, he skinned them. Then, taking a large pinch, where the meat was thickest, he worked his fingers and thumb into the flesh until he struck the median bones, then he worked his thumb and fingers together and tore off a handful of meat. Using this tearing method, he could get two or three good-sized chunks of flesh from each side of the fish. He then heated a pot of bland vegetable shortening, rubbed the pieces of fish with salt and dropped them into the hot fat. He used no flour, meal, crumbs or seasoning other than salt. They cooked to a golden brown in a few minutes, and everyone pronounced them "mighty fine eating." The muddy flavor seemed to have been eliminated by removing the skin and the large bones. The forked bones were still there, but they had not been multiplied by cutting across them, and one only had to remove several bones still intact with the fork from each piece of fish.

For the remainder of that spring, every few days one or another of the cowboys would take a pitchfork and ride over to Clear Ditch and spear a mess of carp. On these evenings, my brother replaced the regular *cocinero* and we enjoyed some delicious fried carp.   10

The flavor of carp varies with the water from which it is caught. Many years after the above incidents I attended a fish fry at my brother's house. The main course was all of his own catching, and consisted of bass, catfish and carp, all from Elephant Butte Lake farther down the Rio Grande. All the fish were prepared exactly alike, except that the carp was pulled apart as described above, while the bass and catfish, being all twelve inches or less in length, were merely cleaned and fried whole. None of his guests knew one fish from another, yet all of them preferred the carp to the other kinds. These experiences have convinced me that the carp is really a fine food fish when properly prepared.   11

Carp can, of course, be caught in many ways besides spearing them with pitchforks from the back of a horse. In my adopted home state, Pennsylvania, they are classed as "trash fish" and one is allowed to take them almost any way. They will sometimes bite on worms, but they are vegetarians by preference and are more easily taken on dough balls. Some states   12 allow the use of gill nets, and other states, because they would like to reduce the population of this unpopular fish, will issue special permits for the use of nets to catch carp.

A good forager will take advantage of the lax regulations 13 on carp fishing while they last. When all fishermen realize that the carp is really a good food fish when prepared in the right way, maybe this outsized denizen of our rivers and lakes will no longer be considered a pest and will take his rightful place among our valued food and game fishes.

1962

Behind the Formaldehyde Curtain

Jessica Mitford

The drama begins to unfold with the arrival of the corpse 1 at the mortuary.

Alas, poor Yorick! How surprised he would be to see how 2 his counterpart of today is whisked off to a funeral parlor and is in short order sprayed, sliced, pierced, pickled, trussed, trimmed, creamed, waxed, painted, rouged and neatly dressed—transformed from a common corpse into a Beautiful Memory Picture. This process is known in the trade as embalming and restorative art, and is so universally employed in the United States and Canada that the funeral director does it routinely, without consulting corpse or kin. He regards as eccentric those few who are hardy enough to suggest that it might be dispensed with. Yet no law requires embalming, no religious doctrine commends it, nor is it dictated by considerations of health, sanitation, or even of personal daintiness. In no part of the world but in Northern America is it widely used. The purpose of embalming is to make the corpse presentable for viewing in a suitably costly container; and here too the funeral director routinely, without first consulting the family, prepares the body for public display.

Is all this legal? The processes to which a dead body may 3 be subjected are after all to some extent circumscribed by law. In most states, for instance, the signature of next of kin must be obtained before an autopsy may be performed, before the deceased may be cremated, before the body may be turned over to a medical school for research purposes; or such provision must be made in the decedent's will. In the case of embalming, no such permission is required nor is it ever sought. A textbook, *The Principles and Practices of Embalming*, comments on this: "There is some question regarding the legality of much that is done within the preparation room." The author points out that it would be most unusual for a responsible member of a bereaved family to instruct the mortician, in so many words, to *"embalm"* the body of a deceased relative. The very term "embalming" is so seldom used that the mortician must rely upon custom in the matter. The author concludes that unless the family specifies otherwise, the act of entrusting the body to the care of a funeral establishment carries with it an implied permission to go ahead and embalm.

Embalming is indeed a most extraordinary procedure, and 4 one must wonder at the docility of Americans who each year pay hundreds of millions of dollars for its perpetuation, blissfully ignorant of what it is all about, what is done, how it is done. Not one in ten thousand has any idea of what actually takes place. Books on the subject are extremely hard to come by. They are not to be found in most libraries or bookshops.

In an era when huge television audiences watch surgical operations in the comfort of their living rooms, when, thanks to the animated cartoon, the geography of the digestive system has become familiar territory even to the nursery school set, in a land where the satisfaction of curiosity about almost all matters is a national pastime, the secrecy surrounding embalming can, surely, hardly be attributed to the inherent gruesomeness of the subject. Custom in this regard has within this century suffered a complete reversal. In the early days of American embalming, when it was performed in the home of the deceased, it was almost mandatory for some relative to stay by the embalmer's side and witness the procedure. Today, family members who might wish to be in attendance would certainly be dissuaded by the funeral director. All others, except apprentices, are excluded by law from the preparation room.

A close look at what does actually take place may explain   6
in large measure the undertaker's intractable reticence concerning a procedure that has become his major *raison d'être*. It is possible he fears that public information about embalming might lead patrons to wonder if they really want this service? If the funeral men are loath to discuss the subject outside the trade, the reader may, understandably, be equally loath to go on reading at this point. For those who have the stomach for it, let us part the formaldehyde curtain. . . .

The body is first laid out in the undertaker's morgue—or   7
rather, Mr. Jones is reposing in the preparation room—to be readied to bid the world farewell.

The preparation room in any of the better funeral estab-   8
lishments has the tiled and sterile look of a surgery, and indeed the embalmer-restorative artist who does his chores there is beginning to adopt the term "dermasurgeon" (appropriately corrupted by some mortician-writers as "demi-surgeon") to describe his calling. His equipment, consisting of scalpels, scissors, augers, forceps, clamps, needles, pumps, tubes, bowls and basins, is crudely imitative of the surgeon's, as is his technique, acquired in a nine- or twelve-month post-high-school course in an embalming school. He is supplied by an advanced chemical industry with a bewildering array of fluids, sprays, pastes, oils, powders, creams, to fix or soften tissue, shrink or distend it as needed, dry it here, restore the moisture there. There are cosmetics, waxes and paints to fill and cover features, even plaster of Paris to replace entire limbs. There are ingenious aids to prop and stabilize the cadaver: a Vari-Pose Head Rest, the Edwards Arm and Hand Positioner, the Repose Block (to support the shoulders during the embalming), and the Throop Foot Positioner, which resembles an old-fashioned stocks.

Mr. John H. Eckels, president of the Eckels College of Mor-   9 tuary Science, thus describes the first part of the embalming procedure: "In the hands of a skilled practitioner, this work may be done in a comparatively short time and without mutilating the body other than by slight incision—so slight that it scarcely would cause serious inconvenience if made upon a living person. It is necessary to remove the blood, and doing this not only helps in the disinfecting, but removes the principal cause of disfigurements due to discoloration."

Another textbook discusses the all-important time element: 10 "The earlier this is done, the better, for every hour that elapses between death and embalming will add to the problems and complications encountered. . . ." Just how soon should one get going on the embalming? The author tells us, "On the basis of such scanty information made available to this profession through its rudimentary and haphazard system of technical research, we must conclude that the best results are to be obtained if the subject is embalmed before life is completely extinct—that is, before cellular death has occurred. In the average case, this would mean within an hour after somatic death." For those who feel that there is something a little rudimentary, not to say haphazard, about this advice, a comforting thought is offered by another writer. Speaking of fears entertained in early days of premature burial, he points out, "One of the effects of embalming by chemical injection, however, has been to dispel fears of live burial." How true; once the blood is removed, chances of live burial are indeed remote.

To return to Mr. Jones, the blood is drained out through the 11 veins and replaced by embalming fluid pumped in through the arteries. As noted in *The Principles and Practices of Embalming*, "every operator has a favorite injection and drainage point—a fact which becomes a handicap only if he fails or refuses to forsake his favorites when conditions demand it." Typical favorites are the carotid artery, femoral artery, jugular vein, subclavian vein. There are various choices of embalming fluid. If Flextone is used, it will produce a "mild, flexible rigidity. The skin retains a velvety softness, the tissues are rubbery and pliable. Ideal for women and children." It may be blended with B. and G. Products Company's Lyf-Lyk tint, which is guaranteed to reproduce "nature's own skin texture . . . the velvety appearance of living tissue." Suntone comes in three separate tints: Suntan; Special Cosmetic Tint, a pink shade "especially indicated for female subjects"; and Regular Cosmetic Tint, moderately pink.

About three to six gallons of a dyed and perfumed solution 12 of formaldehyde, glycerin, borax, phenol, alcohol and water is soon circulating through Mr. Jones, whose mouth has been sewn together with a "needle directed upward between the upper lip and gum and brought out through the left nostril," with the corners raised slightly "for a more pleasant expression." If he should be buck-toothed, his teeth are cleaned with Bon Ami and coated with colorless nail polish. His eyes, meanwhile, are closed with flesh-tinted eye caps and eye cement.

The next step is to have at Mr. Jones with a thing called a 13 trocar. This is a long, hollow needle attached to a tube. It is jabbed into the abdomen, poked around the entrails and chest cavity, the contents of which are pumped out and replaced with "cavity fluid." This done, and the hole in the abdomen sewn up, Mr. Jones's face is heavily creamed (to protect the skin from burns which may be caused by leakage of the chemicals), and he is covered with a sheet and left unmolested for a while. But not for long—there is more, much more, in store for him. He has been embalmed, but not yet restored, and the best time to start the restorative work is eight to ten hours after embalming, when the tissues have become firm and dry.

The object of all this attention to the corpse, it must be re- 14 membered, is to make it presentable for viewing in an attitude of healthy repose. "Our customs require the presentation of our dead in the semblance of normality . . . unmarred by the ravages of illness, disease or mutilation," says Mr. J. Sheridan Mayer in his *Restorative Art*. This is rather a large order since few people die in the full bloom of health, unravaged by illness and unmarked by some disfigurement. The funeral industry is equal to the challenge: "In some cases the gruesome appearance of a mutilated or disease-ridden subject may be quite discouraging. The task of restoration may seem impossible and shake the confidence of the embalmer. This is the time for intestinal fortitude and determination. Once the formative work is begun and affected tissues are cleaned or removed, all doubts of success vanish. It is surprising and gratifying to discover the results which may be obtained."

The embalmer, having allowed an appropriate interval to 15 elapse, returns to the attack, but now he brings into play the skill and equipment of sculptor and cosmetician. Is a hand missing? Casting one in plaster of Paris is a simple matter. "For replacement purposes, only a case of the back of the hand is necessary; this is within the ability of the average operator and is quite adequate." If a lip or two, a nose or an ear should be missing, the embalmer has at hand a variety of restorative waxes with which to model replacements. Pores and skin texture are simulated by stippling with a little brush, and over this cosmetics are laid on. Head off? Decapitation cases are rather routinely handled. Ragged edges are trimmed, and head joined to torso with a series of splints, wires and sutures. It is a good idea to have a little something at the neck—a scarf or a high collar—when time for viewing comes. Swollen mouth? Cut out tissue as needed from inside the lips. If too much is removed, the surface contour can easily be restored by padding with cotton. Swollen necks and cheeks are reduced by removing tissue through vertical incisions made down each side of the neck. "When the deceased is casketed, the pillow will hide the suture incisions . . . as an extra precaution against leakage, the suture may be painted with liquid sealer."

The opposite condition is more likely to present itself—that 16 of emaciation. His hypodermic syringe now loaded with massage cream, the embalmer seeks out and fills the hollowed and sunken areas by injection. In this procedure the backs of the hands and fingers and the under-chin area should not be neglected.

Positioning the lips is a problem that recurrently challenges 17 the ingenuity of the embalmer. Closed too tightly, they tend to give a stern, even disapproving expression. Ideally, embalmers feel, the lips should give the impression of being ever so slightly parted, the upper lip protruding slightly for a more youthful appearance. This takes some engineering, however, as the lips tend to drift apart. Lip drift can sometimes be remedied by pushing one or two straight pins through the inner margin of the lower lip and then inserting them between the two front upper teeth. If Mr. Jones happens to have no teeth, the pins can just as easily be anchored in his Armstrong Face Former and Denture Replacer. Another method to maintain lip closure is to dislocate the lower jaw, which is then held in its new position by a wire run through holes which have been drilled through the upper and lower jaws at the midline. As the French are fond of saying, *il faut souffrir pour être belle.*

If Mr. Jones has died of jaundice, the embalming fluid will [18] very likely turn him green. Does this deter the embalmer? Not if he has intestinal fortitude. Masking pastes and cosmetics are heavily laid on, burial garments and casket interiors are color-correlated with particular care, and Jones is displayed beneath rose-colored lights. Friends will say "How *well* he looks." Death by carbon monoxide, on the other hand, can be rather a good thing from the embalmer's viewpoint: "One advantage is the fact that this type of discoloration is an exaggerated form of a natural pink coloration." This is nice because the healthy glow is already present and needs but little attention.

The patching and filling completed, Mr. Jones is now [19] shaved, washed and dressed. Cream-based cosmetic, available in pink, flesh, suntan, brunette and blond, is applied to his hands and face, his hair is shampooed and combed (and, in the case of Mrs. Jones, set), his hands manicured. For the horny-handed son of toil special care must be taken; cream should be applied to remove ingrained grime, and the nails cleaned. "If he were not in the habit of having them manicured in life, trimming and shaping is advised for better appearance—never questioned by kin."

Jones is now ready for casketing (this is the present partici- [20] ple of the verb "to casket"). In this operation his right shoulder should be depressed slightly "to turn the body a bit to the right and soften the appearance of lying flat on the back." Positioning the hands is a matter of importance, and special rubber positioning blocks may be used. The hands should be cupped slightly for a more lifelike, relaxed appearance. Proper placement of the body requires a delicate sense of balance. It should lie as high as possible in the casket, yet not so high that the lid, when lowered, will hit the nose. On the other hand, we are cautioned, placing the body too low "creates the impression that the body is in a box."

Jones is next wheeled into the appointed slumber room   21 where a few last touches may be added—his favorite pipe placed in his hand or, if he was a great reader, a book propped into position. (In the case of little Master Jones a Teddy bear may be clutched.) Here he will hold open house for a few days, visiting hours 10 A.M. to 9 P.M.

All now being in readiness, the funeral director calls a staff   22 conference to make sure that each assistant knows his precise duties. Mr. Wilber Kriege writes: "This makes your staff feel that they are a part of the team, with a definite assignment that must be properly carried out if the whole plan is to succeed. You never heard of a football coach who failed to talk to his entire team before they go on the field. They have drilled on the plays they are to execute for hours and days, and yet the successful coach knows the importance of making even the bench-warming third-string substitute feel that he is important if the game is to be won." The winning of *this* game is predicated upon glass-smooth handling of the logistics. The funeral director has notified the pallbearers whose names were furnished by the family, has arranged for the presence of clergyman, organist, and soloist, has provided transportation for everybody, has organized and listed the flowers sent by friends. In *Psychology of Funeral Service* Mr. Edward A. Martin points out: "He may not always do as much as the family thinks he is doing, but it is his helpful guidance that they appreciate in knowing they are proceeding as they should. . . . The important thing is how well his services can be used to make the family believe they are giving unlimited expression to their own sentiment."

The religious service may be held in a church or in the   23 chapel of the funeral home; the funeral director vastly prefers the latter arrangement, for not only is it more convenient for him but it affords him the opportunity to show off his beautiful facilities to the gathered mourners. After the clergyman has had his say, the mourners queue up to file past the casket for a last look at the deceased. The family is *never* asked whether they want an open-casket ceremony; in the absence of their instruction to the contrary, this is taken for granted. Consequently well over 90 percent of all American funerals feature the open casket—a custom unknown in other parts of the world. Foreigners are astonished by it. An English woman living in San Francisco described her reaction in a letter to the writer:

> I myself have attended only one funeral here—that of an elderly fellow worker of mine. After the service I could not understand why everyone was walking towards the coffin (sorry, I mean casket), but thought I had better follow the crowd. It shook me rigid to get there and find the casket open and poor old Oscar lying there in his brown tweed suit, wearing a suntan makeup and just the wrong shade of lipstick. If I had not been extremely fond of the old boy, I have a horrible feeling that I might have giggled. Then and there I decided that I could never face another American funeral—even dead.

The casket (which has been resting throughout the service on a Classic Beauty Ultra Metal Casket Bier) is now transferred by a hydraulically operated device called Porto-Lift to a balloon-tired, Glide Easy casket carriage which will wheel it to yet another conveyance, the Cadillac Funeral Coach. This may be lavender, cream, light green—anything but black. Interiors, of course, are color-correlated, "for the man who cannot stop short of perfection." 24

At graveside, the casket is lowered into the earth. This office, once the prerogative of friends of the deceased, is now performed by a patented mechanical lowering device. A "Lifetime Green" artificial grass mat is at the ready to conceal the sere earth, and overhead, to conceal the sky, is a portable Steril Chapel Tent ("resists the intense heat and humidity of summer and the terrific storms of winter . . . available in Silver Grey, Rose or Evergreen"). Now is the time for the ritual scattering of earth over the coffin, as the solemn words "earth to earth, ashes to ashes, dust to dust" are pronounced by the officiating cleric. This can today be accomplished "with a mere flick of the wrist with the Gordon Leak-Proof Earth Dispenser. No grasping of a handful of dirt, no soiled fingers. Simple, dignified, beautiful, 25 reverent! The modern way!" The Gordon Earth Dispenser (at $5) is of nickel-plated brass construction. It is not only "attractive to the eye and long wearing"; it is also "one of the 'tools' for building better public relations" if presented as "an appropriate non-commercial gift" to the clergyman. It is shaped something like a saltshaker.

Untouched by human hand, the coffin and the earth are now united. 26

It is in the function of directing the participants through this maze of gadgetry that the funeral director has assigned to himself his relatively new role of "grief therapist." He has relieved the family of every detail, he has revamped the corpse to look like a living doll, he has arranged for it to nap for a few days in a slumber room, he has put on a well-oiled performance in which the concept of *death* has played no part whatsoever—unless it was inconsiderately mentioned by the clergyman who conducted the religious service. He has done everything in his power to make the funeral a real pleasure for everybody concerned. He and his team have given their all to score an upset victory over death. 27

1963

Writing Drafts

Richard Marius

Finally the moment comes when you sit down to begin your first draft. It is always a good idea at the start to list the points you want to cover. A list is not as elaborate as a formal outline. In writing your first list, don't bother to set items down in the order of importance. List your main points and trust your mind to organize them. You will probably make one list, study it, make another, study it, and perhaps make another. You can organize each list more completely than the last. This preliminary process may save you hours of starting and stopping. 1

Write with your list outline in front of you. Once you begin
to write, commit yourself to the task at hand. Do not get up until
you have written for an hour. Write your thoughts quickly. Let
one sentence give you an idea to develop in the next. Organization, grammar, spelling, and even clarity of sentences are not
nearly as important as getting the first draft together. No matter how desperate you feel, keep going. 2

Always keep your mind open to new ideas that pop into
your head as you write. Let your list outline help you, but don't
become a slave to it. Writers often start an essay with one topic
in mind only to discover that another pushes the first one aside
as they work. Ideas you had not even thought of before you
began to write may pile onto your paper, and five or six pages
into your first draft you may realize that you are going to write
about something you did not imagine when you started. 3

If such a revelation comes, be grateful and accept it. But
don't immediately tear up or erase your draft and start all over
again. Make yourself keep on writing, developing these new
ideas as they come. If you suddenly start all over again, you may
break the train of thought that has given you the new topic. Let
your thoughts follow your new thesis, sailing on that tack until
the wind changes. 4

When you have said everything you can say in this draft,
print it out if you are working on a computer. Get up from your
desk and go sit in a chair somewhere else to read it without correcting anything. Then put it aside, preferably overnight. If possible, read your rough draft just before you go to sleep. Many
psychological tests have shown that our minds organize and
create while we sleep if we pack them full before bedtime. Study
a draft just before sleep, and you may discover new ideas in the
morning. 5

Be willing to make radical changes in your second draft. If
your thesis changed while you were writing your first draft, you
will base your second draft on this new subject. Even if your thesis has not changed, you may need to shift paragraphs around,
eliminate paragraphs, or add new ones. Inexperienced writers
often suppose that revising a paper means changing only a
word or two or adding a sentence or two. This kind of editing 6

is part of the writing process, but it is not the most important part. The most important part of rewriting is a willingness to turn the paper upside down, to shake out of it those ideas that interest you most, to set them in a form where they will interest the reader, too.

I mentioned earlier that some writers cut up their first drafts   7 with a pair of scissors. They toss some paragraphs into the trash; others they paste up with rubber cement in the order that seems most logical and coherent. Afterward they type the whole thing through again, smoothing out the transitions, adding new material, getting new ideas as they work. The translation of the first draft into the second nearly always involves radical cutting and shifting around. Now and then you may firmly fix the order of your thoughts in your first draft, but I find that the order of my essays is seldom established until the second draft.

With the advent of computers the shifting around of parts   8 of the essays has become easy. We can cut and paste electronically with a few strokes of the keyboard. We can also make back-up copies of our earlier drafts so we can go back to them if we wish. But as I said earlier, computers do not remove from us the necessity to think hard about revising.

Always be firm enough with yourself to cut out thoughts   9 or stories that have nothing to do with your thesis, even if they are interesting. Cutting is the supreme test of a writer. You may create a smashing paragraph or sentence only to discover later that it does not help you make your point. You may develop six or seven examples to illustrate a point and discover you need only one.

Now and then you may digress a little. If you digress too   10 often or too far, readers will not follow you unless your facts, your thoughts, and your style are so compelling that they are somehow driven to follow you. Not many writers can pull such digressions off, and most editors will cut out the digressions even when they are interesting. In our hurried and harried time, most readers get impatient with the rambling scenic route. They want to take the most direct way to their destination. To appeal to most of them, you must cut things that do not apply to your main argument.

In your third draft, you can sharpen sentences, add infor- 11
mation here and there, cut some things, and attend to other details to heighten the force of your writing. In the third draft,
writing becomes a lot of fun (for most of us). By then you have
usually decided what you want to say. You can now play a bit,
finding just the right word, choosing just the right sentence
form, compressing here, expanding there.

I find it helpful to put a printed draft down beside my key- 12
board and type the whole thing through again as a final draft,
letting all the words run through my mind and fingers one
more time rather than merely deleting and inserting on the
computer screen. I wrote four drafts of the first edition of this
book; I have preserved the final draft of that edition on computer diskettes. But I am writing this draft by propping the first
edition up here beside me and typing it all over again. By com-
paring the first draft and the second draft, one can see how
many changes I have made, most of them unforeseen until I sat
down here to work.

I have outlined here my own writing process. It works for 13
me. You must find the process that works for you. It may be different from mine. A friend tells me that his writing process consists of writing a sentence, agonizing over it, walking around
the room, thinking, sitting down, and writing the next sentence.
He does not revise very much. I think it unnecessarily painful
to bleed out prose that way, but he bleeds out enough to write
what he needs to write. Several of my friends tell me they cannot compose at a typewriter; they must first write with a pencil on a yellow pad. These are the people most likely to cut up
their drafts with scissors and paste them together in a different
form. They also tend to be older. Most young writers are learning to compose at a keyboard, and they cannot imagine another
way to write. Neither can I—though on occasion yet I go back
to my pencil for pages at a time.

The main thing is to keep at it. B. F. Skinner has pointed out 14
that if you write only fifty words a night, you will produce a
good-sized book every two or three years. That's not a bad
record for any writer. William Faulkner outlined the plot of his
Nobel Prize-winning novel *A Fable* on a wall inside his house

near Oxford, Mississippi. You can see it there to this day. Once he got the outline on the wall, he sat down with his typewriter and wrote, following the outline to the end. If writing an outline on a kitchen wall does the trick for you, do it. You can always repaint the wall if you must.

Think of writing as a process making its way toward a prod- 15 uct—sometimes painfully. Don't imagine you must know everything you are going to say before you begin. Don't demean yourself and insult your readers by letting your first draft be your final draft. Don't imagine that writing is easy or that you can do it without spending time on it. And don't let anything stand in your way of doing it. Let your house get messy. Leave your magazines unread and your mail unanswered. Put off getting up for a drink of water or a cup of tea. (Never mix alcohol with your writing; true, lots of writers have become alcoholics, but it has not helped their writing.) Don't make a telephone call. Don't straighten up your desk. Sit down and write. And write, and write, and write.

1988

The Rules of the Game: Rodeo

Gretel Ehrlich

Instead of honeymooning in Paris, Patagonia, or the Sahara   1
as we had planned, my new husband and I drove through a series of blizzards to Oklahoma City. Each December the National Finals Rodeo is held in a modern, multistoried colosseum next to buildings that house banks and petroleum companies in a state whose flatness resembles a swimming pool filled not with water but with oil.

The National Finals is the "World Series of Professional   2
Rodeo," where not only the best cowboys but also the most athletic horses and bucking stock compete. All year, rodeo cow-

boys have been vying for the honor to ride here. They've been to Houston, Las Vegas, Pendleton, Tucson, Cheyenne, San Francisco, Calgary; to as many as eighty rodeos in one season, sometimes making two or three on a day like the Fourth of July, and when the results are tallied up (in money won, not points) the top fifteen riders in each event are invited to Oklahoma City.

We climbed to our peanut gallery seats just as Miss Rodeo   3
America, a lanky brunette swaddled in a lavender pantsuit, gloves, and cowboy hat, loped across the arena. There was a hush in the audience; all the hats swimming down in front of us, like buoys, steadied and turned toward the chutes. "Out of chute number three, Pat Linger, a young cowboy from Miles City, Montana, making his first appearance here on a little horse named Dillinger." And as fast as these words sailed across the colosseum, the first bareback horse bumped into the lights.

There's a traditional order to the four timed and three rough   4
stock events that make up a rodeo program. Bareback riders are first, then steer wrestlers, team ropers, saddle bronc riders, barrel racers, and finally, the bull riders.

After Pat Linger came Steve Dunham, J. C. Trujillo, Mickey   5
Young, and the defending champ, Bruce Ford on a horse named Denver. Bareback riders do just that: they ride a horse with no saddle, no halter, no rein, clutching only a handhold riveted into a girth that goes around the horse's belly. A bareback rider's loose style suggests a drunken, comic bout of lovemaking: he lies back on the horse and, with each jump and jolt, flops delightfully, like a libidinous Raggedy Andy, toes turned out, knees flexed, legs spread and pumping, back arched, the back of his hat bumping the horse's rump as if nodding, "Yes, let's do 'er again." My husband, who rode saddle broncs in amateur rodeos, explains it differently: "It's like riding a runaway bicycle down a steep hill and lying on your back; you can't see where you're going or what's going to happen next."

Now the steer wrestlers shoot out of the box on their own   6
well-trained horses: there is a hazer on the right to keep the steer running straight, the wrestler on the left, and the steer between them. When the wrestler is neck and neck with the animal, he slides sideways out of his saddle as if he's been stabbed in the

ribs and reaches for the horns. He's airborne for a second; then his heels swing into the dirt, and with his arms around the horns, he skids to a stop twisting the steer's head to one side so the animal loses his balance and falls to the ground. It's a fast-paced game of catch with a thousand-pound ball of horned flesh.

The team ropers are next. Most of them hail from the hilly, 7 oak-strewn valleys of California where dally roping originated.* Ropers are the graceful technicians, performing their pas de deux (plus steer) with a precision that begins to resemble a larger clarity—an erudition. Header and heeler come out of the box at the same time, steer between them, but the header acts first: he ropes the horns of the steer, dallies up, turns off, and tries to position the steer for the heeler who's been tagging behind this duo, loop clasped in his armpit as if it were a hen. Then the heeler sets his generous, unsweeping loop free and double-hocks the steer. It's a complicated act which takes about six seconds. Concomitant with this speed and skill is a feminine grace: they don't clutch their stiff loop or throw it at the steer like a bag of dirty laundry the way I do, but hold it gently, delicately, as if it were a hoop of silk. One or two cranks and both arm and loop vault forward, one becoming an appendage of the other, as if the tendons and pulse that travel through the wrist had lengthened and spun forward like fishing line until the loop sails down on the twin horns, then up under the hocks like a repeated embrace that tightens at the end before it releases.

The classic event at rodeo is saddle bronc riding. The young 8 men look as serious as academicians: they perch spryly on their high-kicking mounts, their legs flicking forward and back, "charging the point," "going back to the cantle" in a rapid, staccato rhythm. When the horse is at the high point of his buck and the cowboy is stretched out, legs spurring above the horse's shoulder, rein-holding arm straight as a board in front, and free hand lifted behind, horse and man look like a propeller. Even their dismounts can look aeronautical: springing off the back of

---

*The word dally is a corruption of the Spanish *da la vuelta,* meaning to take a turn, as with a rope around the saddle horn.

the horse, they land on their feet with a flourish—hat still on—
as if they had been ejected mechanically from a burning plane
long before the crash.

Barrel racing is the one women's event. Where the men are ⁹
tender in their movements, as elegant as if Balanchine had been
their coach, the women are prodigies of Wayne Gretzky, all
speed, bully, and grit. When they charge into the arena, their
hats fly off; they ride brazenly, elbows, knees, feet fluttering,
and by the time they've careened around the second of three
barrels, the whip they've had clenched between their teeth is
passed to a hand, and on the home stretch they urge the horse
to the finish line.

Calf ropers are the whiz kids of rodeo: they're expert on the ¹⁰
horse and on the ground, and their horses are as quick-witted.
The cowboy emerges from the box with a loop in his hand, a
piggin' string in his mouth, coils and reins in the other, and a
network of slack line strewn so thickly over horse and rider,
they look as if they'd run through a tangle of kudzu before arriving in the arena. After roping the calf and jerking the slack
in the rope, he jumps off the horse, sprints down the length of
nylon, which the horse keeps taut, throws the calf down, and
ties three legs together with the piggin' string. It's said of Roy
Cooper, the defending calf-roping champion, that "even with
pins and metal plates in his arm, he's known for the fastest
groundwork in the business; when he springs down his rope to
flank the calf, the resulting action is pure rodeo poetry." The six
or seven separate movements he makes are so fluid they look
like one continual unfolding.

Bull riding is last, and of all the events it's the only one ¹¹
truly dangerous. Bulls are difficult to ride: they're broadbacked,
loose-skinned, and powerful. They don't jump balletically the
way a horse does; they jerk and spin, and if you fall off, they'll
try to gore you with a horn, kick, or trample you. Bull riders are
built like the animals they ride: low to the ground and hefty.
They're the tough men on the rodeo circuit, and the flirts. Two
of the current champs are city men: Charlie Samson is a small,
shy black from Watts, and Bobby Del Vecchio, a brash Italian
from the Bronx who always throws the audience a kiss after a

ride with a Catskill-like showmanship not usually seen here. What a bull rider lacks in technical virtuosity—you won't see the fast spurring action of a saddle bronc rider in this event—he makes up for in personal flamboyance, and because it's a deadlier game they're playing, you can see the belligerence rise up their necks and settle into their faces as the bull starts his first spin. Besides the bull and the cowboy, there are three other men in the ring—the rodeo clowns—who aren't there to make children laugh but to divert the bull from some of his deadlier tricks, and, when the rider bucks off, jump between the two—like secret service men—to save the cowboy's life.

Rodeo, like baseball, is an American sport and has been 12 around almost as long. While Henry Chadwick was writing his first book of rules for the fledgling ball clubs in 1858, ranch hands were paying $25 a dare to a kid who would ride five outlaw horses from the rough string in a makeshift arena of wagons and carts. The first commercial rodeo in Wyoming was held in Lander in 1895, just nineteen years after the National League was formed. Baseball was just as popular as bucking and roping contests in the West, but no one in Cooperstown, New York, was riding broncs. And that's been part of the problem. After 124 years, rodeo is still misunderstood. Unlike baseball, it's a regional sport (although they do have rodeos in New Jersey, Florida, and other eastern states); it's derived from and stands for the western way of life and the western spirit. It doesn't have the universal appeal of a sport contrived solely for the competition and winning; there is no ball bandied about between opposing players.

Rodeo is the wild child of ranch work and embodies some 13 of what ranching is all about. Horsemanship—not gunslinging—was the pride of western men, and the chivalrous ethics they formulated, known as the western code, became the ground rules for every human game. Two great partnerships are celebrated in this Oklahoma arena: the indispensable one between man and animal that any rancher or cowboy takes on, enduring the joys and punishments of the alliance; and the one between man and man, cowboy and cowboy.

Though rodeo is an individualist's sport, it has everything 14 to do with teamwork. The cowboy who "covers" his bronc (stays on the full eight seconds) has become a team with that animal. The cowboys' competitive feelings amongst each other are so mixed with western tact as to appear ambivalent. When Bruce Ford, the bareback rider, won a go-round he said, "The hardest part of winning this year was taking it away from one of my best friends, Mickey Young, after he'd worked so hard all year." Stan Williamson, who'd just won the steer wrestling, said, "I just drew a better steer. I didn't want Butch to get a bad one. I just got lucky, I guess."

Ranchers, when working together, can be just as diplomatic. 15 They'll apologize if they cut in front of someone while cutting out a calf, and their thanks to each other at the end of the day has a formal sound. Like those westerners who still help each other out during branding and roundup, rodeo cowboys help each other in the chutes. A bull rider will steady the saddle bronc rider's horse, help measure out the rein or set the saddle, and a bareback rider might help the bull rider set his rigging and pull his rope. Ropers lend each other horses, as do barrel racers and steer wrestlers. This isn't a show they put on; they offer their help with the utmost goodwill and good-naturedness. Once, when a bucking horse fell over backward in the chute with my husband, his friend H.A., who rode bulls, jumped into the chute and pulled him out safely.

Another part of the "westernness" rodeo represents is the 16 drifting cowboys do. They're on the road much of their lives the way turn-of-the-century cowboys were on the trail, but these cowboys travel in style if they can—driving pink Lincolns and new pickups with a dozen fresh shirts hanging behind the driver, and the radio on.

Some ranchers look down on the sport of rodeo; they don't 17 want these "drugstore cowboys" getting all the attention and glory. Besides, rodeo seems to have less and less to do with real ranch work. Who ever heard of gathering cows on a bareback horse with no bridle, or climbing on a herd bull? Ranchers are generalists—they have to know how to do many things—from juggling the futures market to overhauling a tractor or curing viral scours (diarrhea) in calves—while rodeo athletes are specialists. Deep down, they probably feel envious of each other: the rancher for the praise and big money; the rodeo cowboy for the stay-at-home life among animals to which their sport only alludes.

People with no ranching background have even more dif- 18 ficulty with the sport. Every ride goes so fast, it's hard to see just what happened, and perhaps because of the Hollywood mythologizing of the West which distorted rather than distilled western rituals, rodeo is often considered corny, anachronistic, and cruel to animals. Quite the opposite is true. Rodeo cowboys are as sophisticated athletically as Bjorn Borg or Fernando Valenzuela. That's why they don't need to be from a ranch any-more, or to have grown up riding horses. And to undo another myth, rodeo is not cruel to animals. Compared to the arduous life of any "using horse" on a cattle or dude ranch, a bucking horse leads the life of Riley. His actual work load for an entire year, i.e., the amount of time he spends in the arena, totals ap-proximately 4.6 minutes, and nothing done to him in the arena or out could in any way be called cruel. These animals aren't bludgeoned into bucking; they love to buck. They're bred to be-have this way, they're athletes whose ability has been nurtured and encouraged. Like the cowboys who compete at the Na-tional Finals, the best bulls and horses from all the bucking strings in the country are nominated to appear in Oklahoma, winning money along with their riders to pay their own way.

The National Finals run ten nights. Every contestant rides 19 every night, so it is easy to follow their progress and setbacks. One evening we abandoned our rooftop seats and sat behind the chutes to watch the saddle broncs ride. Behind the chutes two cowboys are rubbing rosin—part of their staying power—be-hind the saddle swells and on their Easter-egg-colored chaps which are pink, blue, and light green with white fringe. Up above, standing on the chute rungs, the stock contractors direct horse traffic: "Velvet Drums" in chute #3, "Angel Sings" in #5, "Rusty" in #1. Rick Smith, Monty Henson, Bobby Berger, Brad Gjermudson, Mel Coleman, and friends climb the chutes. From where I'm sitting, it looks like a field hospital with five separate operating theaters, the cowboys, like surgeons, bent over their patients with sweaty brows and looks of concern. Horses are being haltered; cowboys are measuring out the long, braided reins, saddles are set: one cowboy pulls up on the swells again and again, repositioning his hornless saddle until it sits just right. When the chute boss nods to him and says, "Pull 'em up, boys," the ground crew tightens front and back cinches on the first horse to go, but very slowly so he won't panic in the chute as the cowboy eases himself down over the saddle, not sitting on it, just hovering there. "Okay, you're on." The chute boss nods to him again. Now he sits on the saddle, taking the rein in one hand, holding the top of the chute with the other. He flips the loose bottoms of his chaps over his shins, puts a foot in each stirrup, takes a breath, and nods. The chute gate swings open releasing a flood—not of water, but of flesh, groans, legs kicking. The horse lunges up and out in the first big jump like a wave breaking whose crest the cowboy rides, "marking out the horse," spurs well above the bronc's shoulders. In that first second under the lights, he finds what will be the rhythm of the ride. Once again he "charges the point," his legs pumping forward, then so far back his heels touch behind the cantle. For a moment he looks as though he were kneeling on air, then he's stretched out again, his whole body taut but released, free hand waving in back of his head like a palm frond, rein-holding hand thrust forward: *"En garde!"* he seems to be saying, but he's airborne; he looks like a wing that has sprouted suddenly from the horse's broad back. Eight seconds. The whistle blows. He's covered the horse. Now two gentlemen dressed in white chaps and satin shirts gallop beside the bucking horse. The cowboy hands the rein to one and grabs the waist of the other—the flank strap on the bronc has been undone, so all three horses move at a run—and the pickup man from whom the cowboy is now dangling slows almost to a stop, letting him slide to his feet on the ground.

Rick Smith from Wyoming rides, looking pale and nervous 20 in his white shirt. He's bucked off and so are the brash Monty "Hawkeye" Henson, and Butch Knowles, and Bud Pauley, but with such grace and aplomb, there is no shame. Bobby Berger, an Oklahoma cowboy, wins the go-round with a score of 83.

By the end of the evening we're tired, but in no way as ex- 21
hausted as these young men who have ridden night after night.
"I've never been so sore and had so much fun in my life," one
first-time bull rider exclaims breathlessly. When the performance is over we walk across the street to the chic lobby of a
hotel chock full of cowboys. Wives hurry through the crowd
with freshly ironed shirts for tomorrow's ride, ropers carry their
rope bags with them into the coffee shop, which is now filled
with contestants, eating mild midnight suppers of scrambled
eggs, their numbers hanging crookedly on their backs, their
faces powdered with dust, and looking at this late hour prematurely old.

We drive back to the motel, where, the first night, they'd 22
"never heard of us" even though we'd had reservations for a
month. "Hey, it's our honeymoon," I told the night clerk and
showed him the white ribbons my mother had tied around our
duffel bag. He looked embarrassed, then surrendered another
latecomer's room.

The rodeo finals in Oklahoma may be a better place to hon- 23
eymoon than Paris. All week, we've observed some important
rules of the game. A good rodeo, like a good marriage, or a musical instrument when played to the pitch of perfection, becomes more than what it started out to be. It is effort transformed into effortlessness; a balance becomes grace, the way
love goes deep into friendship.

In the rough stock events such as the one we watched 24
tonight, there is no victory over the horse or bull. The point of
the match is not conquest but communion: the rhythm of two
beings becoming one. Rodeo is not a sport of opposition; there
is no scrimmage line here. No one bears malice—neither the animals, the stock contractors, nor the contestants; no one wants
to get hurt. In this match of equal talents, it is only acceptance,
surrender, respect, and spiritedness that make for the midair
union of cowboy and horse. Not a bad thought when starting
out fresh in a marriage.

1985

*Honey Harvest**

Sue Hubbell

I keep twenty hives of bees here in my home beeyard, but   1
most of my hives are scattered in outyards across the Ozarks,
where I can find the thickest stands of wild blackberries and
other good things for bees. I always have a waiting list of
farmers who would like the bees on their land, for the clover
in their pastures is more abundant when the bees are there to
pollinate it.

One of the farmers, a third-generation Ozarker and a dairy-   2
man with a lively interest in bees, came over today for a look at
what my neighbors call my honey factory. My honey house contains a shiny array of stainless-steel tanks with clear plastic tub-
ing connecting them, a power uncapper for slicing open honey-
comb, an extractor for spinning honey out of the comb, and a lot
of machinery and equipment that whirs, thumps, hums and
looks very special. The dairyman, shrewd in mountain ways,
looked it all over carefully and then observed, "Well . . . ll . . . ll,
wouldn't say for sure now, but it looks like a still to me."

There have been droughty years and cold wet ones when   3
flowers refused to bloom and I would have been better off with
a still back up here on my mountain top, but the weather this
past year was perfect from a bee's standpoint, and this August
I ran 33,000 pounds of honey through my factory. This was
nearly twice the normal crop, and everything was overloaded,
starting with me. Neither I nor my equipment is set up to handle this sort of harvest, even with extra help.

I always need to hire someone, a strong young man who is   4
not afraid of being stung, to help me harvest the honey from the
hives.

The honey I take is the surplus that the bees will not need   5
for the winter; they store it above their hives in wooden boxes
called supers. To take it from them, I stand behind each hive

*Editor's title.

with a gasoline-powered machine called a beeblower and blow the bees out of the supers with a jet of air. Meanwhile, the strong young man carries the supers, which weigh about sixty pounds each, and stacks them on pallets in the truck. There may be thirty to fifty supers in every outyard, and we have only about half an hour to get them off the hives, stacked and covered before the bees get really cross about what we are doing. The season to take the honey in this part of the country is summer's end, when the temperature is often above ninety-five degrees. The nature of the work and the temper of the bees require that we wear protective clothing while doing the job: a full set of coveralls, a zippered bee veil and leather gloves. Even a very strong young man works up a considerable sweat wrapped in a bee suit in hot weather hustling sixty-pound supers—being harassed by angry bees at the same time.

This year my helper has been Ky, my nephew, who wanted   6 to learn something about bees and beekeeping. He is a sweet, gentle, cooperative giant of a young man who, because of a series of physical problems, lacks confidence in his own ability to get on in the world.

As soon as he arrived, I set about to desensitize him to bee   7 stings. The first day, I put a piece of ice on his arm to numb it; then, holding the bee carefully by her head, I placed her abdomen on the numbed spot and let her sting him there. A bee's stinger is barbed and stays in the flesh, pulling loose from her body as she struggles to free herself. Lacking her stinger, the bee will live only a short time. The bulbous poison sac at the top of the stinger continues to pulsate after the bee has left, its muscles pumping the venom and forcing the barbed stinger deeper into the flesh.

I wanted Ky to have only a partial dose of venom that first   8 day, so after a minute I scraped the stinger out with my fingernail and watched his reaction closely. A few people—about one percent of the population—are seriously sensitive to bee venom. Each sting they receive can cause a more severe reaction than the one before, reactions ranging from hives, difficulty in breathing and accelerated heartbeat, to choking, anaphylactic shock and death. Ky had been stung a few times in his life and didn't think he was seriously allergic, but I wanted to make sure.

The spot where the stinger went in grew red and began to 9
swell. This was a normal reaction, and so was the itchiness that Ky felt the next day. That time I let a bee sting him again, repeating the procedure, but leaving the stinger in his arm a full ten minutes, until the venom sac was emptied. Again the spot was red, swollen and itchy, but had disappeared the next day. Thereafter Ky decided that he didn't need the ice cube any more, and began holding the bee himself to administer his own stings. I kept him at one sting a day until he had no redness or swelling from the full sting, and then had him increase to two stings daily. Again the greater amount of venom caused redness and swelling, but soon his body could tolerate them without an allergic reaction. I gradually had him build up to ten full stings a day with no reaction.

To encourage Ky, I had told him that what he was doing 10
might help protect him from the arthritis that runs in our family. Beekeepers generally believe that getting stung by bees is a healthy thing, and that bee venom alleviates the symptoms of arthritis. When I first began keeping bees, I supposed this to be just another one of the old wives' tales that make beekeeping such an entertaining occupation, but after my hands were stung the pain in my fingers disappeared and I too became a believer. Ky was polite, amused and skeptical of what I told him, but he welcomed my taking a few companionable stings on my knuckles along with him.

In desensitizing Ky to bee venom, I had simply been inter- 11
ested in building up his tolerance to stings so that he could be an effective helper when we took the honey from the hives, for I knew that he would be stung frequently. But I discovered that there had been a secondary effect on Ky that was more important: he was enormously pleased with himself for having passed through what he evidently regarded as a rite of initiation. He was proud and delighted in telling other people about the whole process. He was now one tough guy.

I hoped he was prepared well enough for our first day of 12
work. I have had enough strong young men work for me to

know what would happen the first day: he would be stung roy-
ally.

Some beekeepers insist that bees know their keeper—that   13
they won't sting that person, but *will* sting a stranger. This is
nonsense, for summertime bees live only six weeks and I often
open a particular hive less frequently than that, so I am usually
a stranger to my bees; yet I am seldom stung. Others say that
bees can sense fear or nervousness. I don't know if this is true
or not, but I do know that bees' eyes are constructed in such a
way that they can detect discontinuities and movement very
well and stationary objects less well. This means that a person
near their hives who moves with rapid, jerky motions attracts
their attention and will more often be blamed by the bees when
their hives are being meddled with than will the person whose
motions are calm and easy. It has been my experience that the
strong young man I hire for the honey harvest is always stung
unmercifully for the first few days while he is new to the process
and a bit tense. Then he learns to become easier with the bees
and settles down to his job. As he gains confidence and assur-
ance, the bees calm down too, and by the end of the harvest he
usually is only stung a few times a day.

I knew that Ky very much wanted to do a good job with me   14
that initial day working in the outyards. I had explained the procedures we would follow in taking the honey from the hives,
but of course they were new to him and he was anxious. The
bees from the first hive I opened flung themselves on him. Most
of the stingers could not penetrate his bee suit, but in the act of
stinging a bee leaves a chemical trace that marks the person
stung as an enemy, a chemical sign other bees can read easily.
This sign was read by the bees in each new hive I opened, and
soon Ky's bee suit began to look like a pincushion, bristling with
stingers. In addition, the temperature was starting to climb and
Ky was sweating. Honey oozing from combs broken between
the supers was running down the front of his bee suit when he
carried them to the truck. Honey and sweat made the suit cling
to him, so that the stingers of angry bees could penetrate the suit
and he could feel the prick of each one as it entered his skin.
Hundreds of bees were assaulting him and finally drove him

out of the beeyard, chasing him several hundred yards before they gave up the attack. There was little I could do to help him but try to complete the job quickly, so I took the supers off the next few hives myself, carried them to the truck and loaded them. Bravely, Ky returned to finish the last few hives. We tied down the load and drove away. His face was red with exertion when he unzipped his bee veil. He didn't have much to say as we drove to the next yard, but sat beside me gulping down ice water from the thermos bottle.

At the second yard the bees didn't bother Ky as we set up the equipment. I hoped that much of the chemical marker the bees had left on him had evaporated, but as soon as I began to open the hives they were after him again. Soon a cloud of angry bees enveloped him, accompanying him to the truck and back. Because of the terrain, the truck had to be parked at an odd angle and Ky had to bend from the hips as he loaded it, stretching the fabric of the bee suit taut across the entire length of his back and rear, allowing the bees to sting through it easily. We couldn't talk over the noise of the beeblower's engine, but I was worried about how he was taking hundreds more stings. I was removing the bees from the supers as quickly as I could, but the yard was a good one and there were a lot of supers there.

In about an hour's time Ky carried and stacked what we later weighed in as a load of 2500 pounds. The temperature must have been nearly a hundred degrees. After he had stacked the last super, I drove the truck away from the hives and we tied down the load. Ky's long hair was plastered to his face and I couldn't see the expression on it, but I knew he had been pushed to his limits and I was concerned about him. He tried to brush some of the stingers out of the seat of his bee suit before he sat down next to me in the truck in an uncommonly gingerly way. Unzipping his bee veil, he tossed it aside, pushed the hair back from his sweaty face, reached for the thermos bottle, gave me a sunny and triumphant grin and said, "If I ever get arthritis of the ass, I'll know all that stuff you've been telling me is a lot of baloney."

1983

How to Paint a Fresco

Adam Goodheart

Although it must be painted in a very short time, a fresco   1
will last a very long time—that is its great advantage. Many of
the masterpieces of the golden age of fresco (from the 14th
through the 18th centuries) are as brilliant now as when they
were first painted. If you want to fresco a cathedral or palazzo
today, you may have a few problems—papal and ducal com-
missions are scarcer than they once were, and the great Renaissance masters are no longer accepting applications for ap-
prenticeships. Fortunately, a few of their trade secrets have
come down to us through the ages.

EQUIPMENT   2

Lime

Sand

Water

A trowel

Paper

A needle

A small bag of charcoal dust

The bristles of a white hog

The hair of bears, sables and martens

The quills of vultures, geese, hens and doves

Ocher, burnt grapevines, lapis lazuli

Egg yolks

Goat's milk

1. Preparing the wall. Cennino Cennini, a Tuscan master,   3
advised pupils in 1437 to "begin by decking yourselves with this

attire: Enthusiasm, Reverence, Obedience, and Constancy."
You'd do better to deck yourself with some old clothes, though,
since the first stage of the process is quite messy. Soak the wall
thoroughly and coat it with coarse plaster, two parts sand to one
part lime, leaving the surface uneven. (Andrea Pozzo, a 17th-
century expert, recommended hiring a professional mason to do
this, since "the lime makes a foul odor, which is injurious to the
head.")

    2. Tracing your design. You should already have extensive   4
drawings for your fresco—these will be much sought by scholars and collectors in centuries to come. Make a full-size sketch,
on sturdy paper, of a section of the fresco that you can paint in
a day. Then go over the drawing with a needle, pricking holes
along every line. Lay a coat of fine plaster on a section of the
wall corresponding to the location, size and shape of the sketch,
and press the sketch against the plaster. Fill a loosely woven bag
with charcoal dust and strike it lightly all over the surface of the
paper. Now peel the sketch off. Your design will be outlined in
black dots on the wet plaster, giving you a guide for the day's
work.

    3. Painting. Time is of the essence: You must paint the plas-   5
ter while it is wet, so that the pigments bind chemically with the
lime. That gives you about six hours, although some painters
had tricks to prolong drying. (Piero della Francesca packed the
plaster with wet rags; problem was, this left indentations that
are still visible after 500 years.) Use top-quality brushes. One
17th-century Flemish master recommended those made of "fish
hair" (he probably meant seal fur), but most painters made
brushes from bear, marten or sable hairs inserted in hollow
quills. Cennini suggested the bristles of a white hog for the
coarser work. As for paints, every artist had his own favorite
recipes, but all agreed that mineral pigments such as ocher or
ground stone mixed with water were best. Avoid white lead.
One 14th-century Umbrian used it to paint a nursing infant; the
lime turned the white black and the milky babe into a "devil-
ish changeling." A few pigments, such as dark blue azurite
(often used for the Virgin Mary's mantle), must be mixed with

egg yolk or goat's milk and added after the fresco is dry. Such colors will prove less durable.

Money is a consideration in choosing materials. When 6 Michelangelo frescoed the Sistine ceiling, expenses came out of his fee, so he used cheap blue smalt for the sky. Twenty years later, when he did the *Last Judgment,* Michelangelo used semiprecious lapis lazuli for blue, since the pope was paying for the paint. (He made up for it by using burnt grapevines for black.)

4. Casualties of style. Realism, while a worthy goal, has its 7 perils. Spinello Aretino, a 14th-century Tuscan, is said to have painted a fresco that depicted Lucifer with such hideous accuracy that the Evil One himself came to the artist in a dream and demanded an explanation. Spinello went half-mad with fear and died shortly thereafter. On the other hand, a Florentine woodcut from 1500 depicts a painter who has portrayed the Virgin so skillfully that when he falls off the scaffold, she reaches out of the fresco and saves him.

WARNING

Frescoing ceilings can be rough on your back. While work- 8 ing on the Sistine Chapel, Michelangelo wrote a poem complaining: "I've already grown a goiter at this drudgery. . . . With my beard toward heaven . . . I am bent like a bow." Don't be discouraged, though. Bad posture is a small price to pay for immortality.

1995

CHAPTER 4

Definition

Beauty

Susan Sontag

For the Greeks, beauty was a virtue: a kind of excellence. 1
Persons then were assumed to be what we now have to call—
lamely, enviously—whole persons. If it did occur to the Greeks
to distinguish between a person's "inside" and "outside," they
still expected that inner beauty would be matched by beauty of
the other kind. The well-born young Athenians who gathered
around Socrates found it quite paradoxical that their hero was
so intelligent, so brave, so honorable, so seductive—and so ugly.
One of Socrates' main pedagogical acts was to be ugly—and
teach those innocent, no doubt splendid-looking disciples of his
how full of paradoxes life really was.

They may have resisted Socrates' lesson. We do not. Several 2
thousand years later, we are more wary of the enchantments of
beauty. We not only split off—with the greatest facility—the
"inside" (character, intellect) from the "outside" (looks); but
we are actually surprised when someone who is beautiful is also
intelligent, talented, good.

It was principally the influence of Christianity that deprived 3
beauty of the central place it had in classical ideals of human
excellence. By limiting excellence (*virtus* in Latin) to *moral* virtue
only, Christianity set beauty adrift—as an alienated, arbitrary,
superficial enchantment. And beauty has continued to lose prestige. For close to two centuries it has become a convention to at-

tribute beauty to only one of the two sexes: the sex which, however Fair, is always Second. Associating beauty with women has put beauty even further on the defensive, morally.

A beautiful woman, we say in English. But a handsome 4 man. "Handsome" is the masculine equivalent of—and refusal of—a compliment which has accumulated certain demeaning overtones, by being reserved for women only. That one can call a man "beautiful" in French and in Italian suggests that Catholic countries—unlike those countries shaped by the Protestant version of Christianity—still retain some vestiges of the pagan admiration for beauty. But the difference, if one exists, is of degree only. In every modern country that is Christian or post-Christian, women *are* the beautiful sex—to the detriment of the notion of beauty as well as of women.

To be called beautiful is thought to name something essen- 5 tial to women's character and concerns. (In contrast to men—whose essence is to be strong, or effective, or competent.) It does not take someone in the throes of advanced feminist awareness to perceive that the way women are taught to be involved with beauty encourages narcissism, reinforces dependence and immaturity. Everybody (women and men) knows that. For it is "everybody," a whole society, that has identified being feminine with caring about how one *looks*. (In contrast to being masculine—which is identified with caring about what one *is* and *does* and only secondarily, if at all, about how one looks.) Given these stereotypes, it is no wonder that beauty enjoys, at best, a rather mixed reputation.

It is not, of course, the desire to be beautiful that is wrong 6 but the obligation to be—or to try. What is accepted by most women as a flattering idealization of their sex is a way of making women feel inferior to what they actually are—or normally grow to be. For the ideal of beauty is administered as a form of self-oppression. Women are taught to see their bodies in *parts*, and to evaluate each part separately. Breasts, feet, hips, waistline, neck, eyes, nose, complexion, hair, and so on—each in turn is submitted to an anxious, fretful, often despairing scrutiny. Even if some pass muster, some will always be found wanting. Nothing less than perfection will do.

In men, good looks is a whole, something taken in at a   7
glance. It does not need to be confirmed by giving measure-
ments of different regions of the body, nobody encourages a
man to dissect his appearance, feature by feature. As for perfection, that is considered trivial—almost unmanly. Indeed, in
the ideally good-looking man a small imperfection or blemish
is considered positively desirable. According to one movie critic
(a woman) who is a declared Robert Redford fan, it is having
that cluster of skin-colored moles on one cheek that saves Redford from being merely a "pretty face." Think of the deprecia-
tion of women—as well as of beauty—that is implied in that
judgment.

"The privileges of beauty are immense," said Cocteau. To   8
be sure, beauty is a form of power. And deservedly so. What is
lamentable is that it is the only form of power that most women
are encouraged to seek. This power is always conceived in relation to men; it is not the power to do but the power to attract.
It is a power that negates itself. For this power is not one that
can be chosen freely—at least, not by women—or renounced
without social censure.

To preen, for a woman, can never be just a pleasure. It is also   9
a duty. It is her work. If a woman does real work—and even if
she has clambered up to a leading position in politics, law, medicine, business, or whatever—she is always under pressure to
confess that she still works at being attractive. But in so far as
she is keeping up as one of the Fair Sex, she brings under suspicion her very capacity to be objective, professional, authori-
tative, thoughtful. Damned if they do—women are. And
damned if they don't.

One could hardly ask for more important evidence of the   10
dangers of considering persons as split between what is "inside"
and what is "outside" than that interminable half-comic half-
tragic tale, the oppression of women. How easy it is to start off
by defining women as caretakers of their surfaces, and then to
disparage them (or find them adorable) for being "superficial."
It is a crude trap, and it has worked for too long. But to get out
of the trap requires that women get some critical distance from
that excellence and privilege which is beauty, enough distance
to see how much beauty itself has been abridged in order to prop

up the mythology of the "feminine." There should be a way of
saving beauty *from* women—and *for* them.

1975

What Is Poverty?*

Jo Goodwin Parker

You ask me what is poverty? Listen to me. Here I am, dirty,   1
smelly, and with no "proper" underwear on and with the stench
of my rotting teeth near you. I will tell you. Listen to me. Listen without pity. I cannot use your pity. Listen with understanding. Put yourself in my dirty, worn out, ill-fitting shoes,
and hear me.

Poverty is getting up every morning from a dirt- and illness-   2
stained mattress. The sheets have long since been used for diapers. Poverty is living in a smell that never leaves. This is a smell
of urine, sour milk, and spoiling food sometimes joined with the
strong smell of long-cooked onions. Onions are cheap. If you
have smelled this smell, you did not know how it came. It is the
smell of the outdoor privy. It is the smell of young children who
cannot walk the long dark way in the night. It is the smell of the
mattresses where years of "accidents" have happened. It is the
smell of the milk which has gone sour because the refrigerator
long has not worked, and it costs money to get it fixed. It is the
smell of rotting garbage. I could bury it, but where is the shovel?
Shovels cost money.

Poverty is being tired. I have always been tired. They told   3
me at the hospital when the last baby came that I had chronic
anemia caused from poor diet, a bad case of worms, and that I
needed a corrective operation. I listened politely—the poor are
always polite. The poor always listen. They don't say that there

*From an unpublished speech (Deland, Florida, December 27, 1965). Printed by
permission as it appears in George Henderson (Ed.), *America's Other Children:
Public Schools Outside Suburbia*. Norman: University of Oklahoma Press, pp.30–34.

is no money for iron pills, or better food, or worm medicine. The idea of an operation is frightening and costs so much that, if I had dared, I would have laughed. Who takes care of my children? Recovery from an operation takes a long time. I have three children. When I left them with "Granny" the last time I had a job, I came home to find the baby covered with fly specks, and a diaper that had not been changed since I left. When the dried diaper came off, bits of my baby's flesh came with it. My other child was playing with a sharp bit of broken glass, and my oldest was playing alone at the edge of a lake. I made twenty-two dollars a week, and a good nursery school costs twenty dollars a week for three children. I quit my job.

Poverty is dirt. You can say in your clean clothes coming 4 from your clean house, "Anybody can be clean." Let me explain about housekeeping with no money. For breakfast I give my children grits with no oleo or cornbread without eggs and oleo. This does not use up many dishes. What dishes there are, I wash in cold water and with no soap. Even the cheapest soap has to be saved for the baby's diapers. Look at my hands, so cracked and red. Once I saved for two months to buy a jar of Vaseline for my hands and the baby's diaper rash. When I had saved enough, I went to buy it and the price had gone up two cents. The baby and I suffered on. I have to decide every day if I can bear to put my cracked sore hands into the cold water and strong soap. But you ask, why not hot water? Fuel costs money. If you have a wood fire it costs money. If you burn electricity, it costs money. Hot water is a luxury. I do not have luxuries. I know you will be surprised when I tell you how young I am. I look so much older. My back has been bent over the wash tubs every day for so long, I cannot remember when I ever did anything else. Every night I wash every stitch my school age child has on and just hope her clothes will be dry by morning.

Poverty is staying up all night on cold nights to watch the 5 fire knowing one spark on the newspaper covering the walls means your sleeping child dies in flames. In summer poverty is watching gnats and flies devour your baby's tears when he cries. The screens are torn and you pay so little rent you know they will never be fixed. Poverty means insects in your food, in your nose, in your eyes, and crawling over you when you sleep. Poverty is hoping it never rains because diapers won't dry when it rains and soon you are using newspapers. Poverty is seeing your children forever with runny noses. Paper handkerchiefs cost money and all your rags you need for other things. Even more costly are antihistamines. Poverty is cooking without food and cleaning without soap.

Poverty is asking for help. Have you ever had to ask for   6 help, knowing your children will suffer unless you get it? Think about asking for a loan from a relative, if this is the only way you can imagine asking for help. I will tell you how it feels. You find out where the office is that you are supposed to visit. You circle that block four or five times. Thinking of your children, you go in. Everyone is very busy. Finally, someone comes out and you tell her that you need help. That never is the person you need to see. You go see another person, and after spilling the whole shame of your poverty all over the desk between you, you find that this isn't the right office after all—you must repeat the whole process, and it never is any easier at the next place.

You have asked for help, and after all it has a cost. You are   7 again told to wait. You are told why, but you don't really hear because of the red cloud of shame and the rising cloud of despair.

Poverty is remembering. It is remembering quitting school   8 in junior high because "nice" children had been so cruel about my clothes and my smell. The attendance officer came. My mother told him I was pregnant. I wasn't, but she thought that I could get a job and help out. I had jobs off and on, but never long enough to learn anything. Mostly I remember being married. I was so young then. I am still young. For a time, we had all the things you have. There was a little house in another town, with hot water and everything. Then my husband lost his job. There was unemployment insurance for a while and what few jobs I could get. Soon, all our nice things were repossessed and we moved back here. I was pregnant then. This house didn't look so bad when we first moved in. Every week it gets worse. Nothing is ever fixed. We now had no money. There were a few odd jobs for my husband, but everything went for food then, as it does now. I don't know how we lived through three years and three babies, but we did. I'll tell you something, after the last baby I destroyed my marriage. It had been a good one, but could you keep on bringing children in this dirt? Did you ever think how much it costs for any kind of birth control? I knew my husband was leaving the day he left, but there were no goodbys between us. I hope he has been able to climb out of this mess somewhere. He never could hope with us to drag him down.

That's when I asked for help. When I got it, you know how 9 much it was? It was, and is, seventy-eight dollars a month for the four of us; that is all I ever can get. Now you know why there is no soap, no needles and thread, no hot water, no aspirin, no worm medicine, no hand cream, no shampoo. None of these things forever and ever and ever. So that you can see clearly, I pay twenty dollars a month rent, and most of the rest goes for food. For grits and cornmeal, and rice and milk and beans. I try my best to use only the minimum electricity. If I use more, there is that much less for food.

Poverty is looking into a black future. Your children won't 10 play with my boys. They will turn to other boys who steal to get what they want. I can already see them behind the bars of their prison instead of behind the bars of my poverty. Or they will turn to the freedom of alcohol or drugs, and find themselves enslaved. And my daughter? At best, there is for her a life like mine.

But you say to me, there are schools. Yes, there are schools. 11 My children have no extra books, no magazines, no extra pencils, or crayons, or paper and most important of all, they do not have health. They have worms, they have infections, they have pink-eye all summer. They do not sleep well on the floor, or with me in my one bed. They do not suffer from hunger, my seventy-eight dollars keeps us alive, but they do suffer from malnutrition. Oh yes, I do remember what I was taught about health in school. It doesn't do much good. In some places there is a surplus commodities program. Not here. The country said it cost too much. There is a school lunch program. But I have two children who will already be damaged by the time they get to school.

But, you say to me, there are health clinics. Yes, there are 12
health clinics and they are in the towns. I live out here eight miles from town. I can walk that far (even if it is sixteen miles both ways), but can my little children? My neighbor will take me when he goes; but he expects to get paid, *one way or another*. I bet you know my neighbor. He is that large man who spends his time at the gas station, the barbershop, and the corner store complaining about the government spending money on the immoral mothers of illegitimate children.

Poverty is an acid that drips on pride until all pride is worn 13
away. Poverty is a chisel that chips on honor until honor is worn away. Some of you say that you would do *something* in my situation, and maybe you would, for the first week or the first month, but for year after year after year?

Even the poor can dream. A dream of a time when there is 14
money. Money for the right kinds of food, for worm medicine, for iron pills, for toothbrushes, for hand cream, for a hammer and nails and a bit of screening, for a shovel, for a bit of paint, for some sheeting, for needles and thread. Money to pay *in money* for a trip to town. And, oh, money for hot water and money for soap. A dream of when asking for help does not eat away the last bit of pride. When the office you visit is as nice as the offices of other governmental agencies, when there are enough workers to help you quickly, when workers do not quit in defeat and despair. When you have to tell your story to only one person, and that person can send you for other help and you don't have to prove your poverty over and over and over again.

I have come out of my despair to tell you this. Remember I 15
did not come from another place or another time. Others like me are all around you. Look at us with an angry heart, anger that will help you help me. Anger that will let you tell of me. The poor are always silent. Can you be silent too?

1971

Faith of the Father

Sam Pickering

On weekdays Campbell's store was the center of life in the 1
little Virginia town in which I spent summers and Christmas va-
cations. The post office was in a corner of the store, and the train
station was across the road. In the morning men gathered on
Campbell's porch and drank coffee while they waited for the
train to Richmond. Late in the afternoon, families appeared.
While waiting for their husbands, women bought groceries,
mailed letters, and visited with one another. Children ate cups
of ice cream and played in the woods behind the store. Sometimes a work train was on the siding, and the engineer filled his
cab with children and took them for short trips down the track.
On weekends life shifted from the store to St. Paul's Church.
Built in a grove of pine trees in the nineteenth century, St. Paul's
was a small, white clapboard building. A Sunday School wing
added to the church in the 1920s jutted out into the graveyard.
Beyond the graveyard was a field in which picnics were held
and on the Fourth of July, the yearly Donkey Softball Game was
played.

St. Paul's was familial and comfortable. Only a hundred 2
people attended regularly, and everyone knew everyone else
and his business. What was private became public after the service as people gathered outside and talked for half an hour before going home to lunch. Behind the altar inside the church was
a stained glass window showing Christ's ascension to heaven.
A red carpet ran down the middle aisle, and worn, gold cush-
ions covered the pews. On the walls were plaques in memory
of parishioners killed in foreign wars or who had made large
donations to the building fund. In summer the minister put
fans out on the pews. Donated by a local undertaker, the fans
were shaped like spades. On them, besides the undertaker's
name and telephone number, were pictures of Christ performing miracles: walking on water, healing the lame, and raising
Lazarus from the dead.

Holidays and funerals were special at St. Paul's. Funerals ₃
were occasions for reminiscing and telling stories. When an
irascible old lady died and her daughter had "Gone to Jesus"
inscribed on her tombstone, her son-in-law was heard to say
"poor Jesus"—or so the tale went at the funeral. Christmas Eve
was always cold and snow usually fell. Inside the church at midnight, though, all was cheery and warm as the congregation
sang the great Christmas hymns: "O Come, All Ye Faithful,"
"The First Noel," "O Little Town of Bethlehem," and "Hark! The
Herald Angels Sing." The last hymn was "Silent Night." The
service did not follow the prayer book; inspired by Christmas
and eggnog, the congregation came to sing, not to pray. Bourbon was in the air, and when the altar boy lit the candles, it
seemed a miracle that the first spark didn't send us all to heaven
in a blue flame.

Easter was almost more joyous than Christmas. Men stuck ₄
greenery into their lapels and women blossomed in bright bonnets, some ordering hats not simply from Richmond but from
Baltimore and Philadelphia. On a farm outside town lived Miss
Emma and Miss Ida Catlin. Miss Emma was the practical sister, running the farm and bringing order wherever she went.
Unlike Miss Emma, Miss Ida was shy. She read poetry and
raised guinea fowl and at parties sat silently in a corner. Only
on Easter was she outgoing; then like a day lily she bloomed tri-
umphantly. No one else's Easter bonnet ever matched hers, and
the congregation eagerly awaited her entrance which she always made just before the first hymn.

One year Miss Ida found a catalogue from a New York store ₅
which advertised hats and their accessories. For ten to twenty-
five cents ladies could buy artificial flowers to stick into their
bonnets. Miss Ida bought a counter full, and that Easter her head
resembled a summer garden in bloom. Daffodils, zinnias, and
black-eyed Susans hung yellow and red around the brim of her
hat while in the middle stood a magnificent pink peony.

In all his glory Solomon could not have matched Miss Ida's ₆
bonnet. The congregation could not take its eyes off it; even the
minister had trouble concentrating on his sermon. After the last
hymn, everyone hurried out of the church, eager to get a better

look at Miss Ida's hat. As she came out, the altar boy began ring-
ing the bell. Alas, the noise frightened pigeons who had recently begun to nest and they shot out of the steeple. The congregation scattered, but the flowers on Miss Ida's hat hung over
her eyes, and she did not see the pigeons until it was too late
and the peony had been ruined.

Miss Ida acted like nothing had happened. She greeted   7
everyone and asked their healths and the healths of absent
members of families. People tried not to look at her hat but
were not very successful. For two Sundays Miss Ida's "accident"
was the main subject of after-church conversation; then it was
forgotten for almost a year. But, as Easter approached again,
people remembered the hat. They wondered what Miss Ida
would wear to church. Some people speculated that since she
was a shy, poetic person, she wouldn't come. Even the minister had doubts. To reassure Miss Ida, he and his sons borrowed
ladders two weeks before Easter, and climbing to the top of the
steeple, chased the pigeons away and sealed off their nesting
place with chicken wire.

Easter Sunday seemed to confirm the fears of those who   8
doubted Miss Ida would appear. The choir assembled in the
rear of the church without her. Half-heartedly the congregation
sang the processional hymn, "Hail Thee, Festival Day." Miss
Ida's absence had taken something bright from our lives, and
as we sat down after singing, Easter seemed sadly ordinary.

We were people of little faith. Just as the minister reached   9
the altar and turned to face us, there was a stir at the back of the
church. Silently the minister raised his right hand and pointed
toward the door. Miss Ida had arrived. She was wearing the
same hat she wore the year before; only the peony was missing. In its place was a wonderful sunflower; from one side hung
a black and yellow garden spider building a web while fluttering above was a mourning cloak, black wings, dotted with blue
and a yellow border running around the edges. Our hearts
leaped up, and at the end of the service people in Richmond
must have heard us singing "Christ The Lord Is Risen Today."

St. Paul's was the church of my childhood, that storied time   10
when I thought little about religion but knew that Jesus loved

me, yes, because the Bible told me so. In the Morning Prayer of
life I mixed faith and fairy tale, thinking God a kindly giant,
holding in his hands, as the song put it, the corners of the earth
and the strength of the hills. Thirty years have passed since I last
saw St. Paul's, and I have come down from the cool upland pastures and the safe fold of childhood to the hot lowlands. Instead
of being neatly tucked away in a huge hand, the world now
seems to bound erratically, smooth and slippery, forever beyond the grasp of even the most magical deity. Would that it
were not so, and my imagination could find a way through his
gates, as the prayer says, with thanksgiving. Often I wonder
what happened to the "faith of our fathers." Why if it endured
dungeon, fire, and sword in others, did it weaken so within me?

For me religion is a matter of story and community, a con-   11
gregation rising together to look at an Easter Bonnet, unconsciously seeing it an emblem of hope and vitality, indeed of the
Resurrection itself. For me religion ought to be more concerned
with people than ideas, creating soft feeling rather than sharp
thought. Often I associate religion with small, backwater towns
in which tale binds folk one to another. Here in a university in
which people are separated by idea rather than linked by story,
religion doesn't have a natural place. In the absence of community ceremony becomes important. Changeable and always
controversial, subject to dispassionate analysis, ceremony
doesn't tie people together like accounts of pigeons and pe-
onies and thus doesn't promote good feeling and finally love
for this world and hope for the next. Often when I am discouraged, I turn for sustenance, not to formal faith with articled ceremony but to memory, a chalice winey with story.

Not long ago I thought about Beagon Hackett, a Baptist   12
minister in Carthage, Tennessee. Born in Bagdad in Jackson
County, Beagon answered the call early in life. Before he was
sixteen, he had preached in all the little towns in Jackson
County: Antioch, Nameless, McCoinsville, Liberty, and Gum
Springs. Although popular in country churches, Beagon's specialty was the all-day revival, picnic, and baptizing, usually
held back in the woods near places like Seven Knobs, Booger
Hill, Backbone Ridge, Chigger Hollow, and Twelve Corners.

Beacon made such a name that the big Baptist church in
Carthage selected him as minister. Once in Carthage, Beacon
tempered his faith to suit the mood of the county seat. Only once
a year did he hold a meeting out of doors. For his first four or
five years in Carthage, he led a revival near Dripping Rock
Bluff across Hell Bend on the Caney Fork River, the spot being
selected for name not location.

  The narrows of the river were swift and deep, and crossing   13
Hell Bend was dangerous, a danger Beacon celebrated, first reminding the faithful that Jesus was a fisher of men and then
buoying their spirits up on a raft of watery Christian song:
"Shall We Gather at the River," "The Rock That Is Higher Than
I," and "Sweet By and By." Beacon's meetings across the Caney
Fork were a success with people traveling from as far as Macon
and Trousdale counties to be baptized. But then one spring
Gummert Capron or Doodlebug Healy, depending on whose
memory is accurate, became frightened in mid-river and tipping
over a rowboat changed "Throw Out the Life-Line" from word
to deed. If Hosmer Nye had not grabbed Clara Jakeways by the
hair, the dark waters, as the hymn puts it, would have swept
her to eternity's shore. As it turned out Clara's salvation turned
into romance, and three months later she and Nye were married, much to the disappointment of Silas Jakeways who owned
a sawmill and the Eagle Iron Works and who disapproved of
Nye, until that time an itinerant bricklayer. Clara, Silas was reported to have said, would "have been better off if love hadn't
lifted her from the deep to become the wife of a no-account."
Whatever the case, however, Beacon never led another revival
across Hell Bend; instead he stayed dry on the Carthage side of
the Caney Fork, once a year holding a temperate affair, more
Sunday outing than revival, on Myers Bottom.

  After Beacon had been in Carthage for twenty years, he   14
grew heavy and dignified. No longer would he preside at river
baptizings. In his church he erected, as Silas Jakeways said "a
marble birdbath," a baptismal font, copied from one he saw in
an Episcopal Church at Monteagle. In Carthage, though, pre-
tension was always liable to be tipped over, if not by simple-
minded folk like Gummert Capron or Doodlebug Healy, then

by daily life. Addicted to drink, Horace Armitage, the disreputable brother of Benbow Armitage, occasionally cut hair at King's Barber Shop. One morning after a long night of carousing at Enos Mayfield's in South Carthage, Horace was a bit shaky, and while shaving Beagon cut him slightly on the chin. "That's what comes of taking too much to drink," said Beagon, holding a towel to his chin. "Yes, sir, Reverend," Horace replied, "Alcohol does make the skin tender."

1985

Erotica and Pornography
Gloria Steinem

Human beings are the only animals that experience the 1 same sex drive at times when we can—and cannot—conceive.

Just as we developed uniquely human capacities for lan- 2 guage, planning, memory, and invention along our evolutionary path, we also developed sexuality as a form of expression, a way of communicating that is separable from our need for sex as a way of perpetuating ourselves. For humans alone, sexuality can be and often is primarily a way of bonding, of giving and receiving pleasure, bridging differentness, discovering sameness, and communicating emotion.

We developed this and other human gifts through our abil- 3 ity to change our environment, adapt physically, and in the long run, to affect our own evolution. But as an emotional result of this spiraling path away from other animals, we seem to alternate between periods of exploring our unique abilities to change new boundaries, and feelings of loneliness in the unknown that we ourselves have created; a fear that sometimes sends us back to the comfort of the animal world by encouraging us to exaggerate our sameness.

The separation of "play" from "work," for instance, is a 4

problem only in the human world. So is the difference between
art and nature, or an intellectual accomplishment and a physical one. As a result, we celebrate play, art, and invention as leaps
into the unknown; but any imbalance can send us back to nos-
talgia for our primate past and the conviction that the basics of
work, nature, and physical labor are somehow more worth-
while or even moral.

In the same way, we have explored our sexuality as sepa-   5
rable from conception: a pleasurable, empathetic bridge to
strangers of the same species. We have even invented contraception—a skill that has probably existed in some form since
our ancestors figured out the process of birth—in order to extend this uniquely human difference. Yet we also have times of
atavistic suspicion that sex is not complete—or even legal or
intended-by-god—if it cannot end in conception.

No wonder the concepts of "erotica" and "pornography"   6
can be so crucially different, and yet so confused. Both assume
that sexuality can be separated from conception, and therefore
can be used to carry a personal message. That's a major reason
why, even in our current culture, both may be called equally
"shocking" or legally "obscene," a word whose Latin derivative
means "dirty, containing filth." This gross condemnation of all
sexuality that isn't harnessed to childbirth and marriage has
been increased by the current backlash against women's
progress. Out of fear that the whole patriarchal structure might
be upset if women really had the autonomous power to decide
our reproductive futures (that is, if we controlled the most basic
means of production), right-wing groups are not only de-
nouncing prochoice abortion literature as "pornographic," but
are trying to stop the sending of all contraceptive information
through the mails by invoking obscenity laws. In fact, Phyllis
Schlafly recently denounced the entire Women's Movement as
"obscene."

Not surprisingly, this religious, visceral backlash has a sec-   7
ular, intellectual counterpart that relies heavily on applying the
"natural" behavior of the animal world to humans. That is questionable in itself, but these Lionel Tigerish studies make their
political purpose even more clear in the particular animals they

select and the habits they choose to emphasize. The message is that females should accept their "destiny" of being sexually dependent and devote themselves to bearing and rearing their young.

Defending against such reaction in turn leads to another 8 temptation: to merely reverse the terms, and declare that *all* nonprocreative sex is good. In fact, however, this human activity can be as constructive or destructive, moral or immoral, as any other. Sex as communication can send messages as different as life and death; even the origins of "erotica" and "pornography" reflect that fact. After all, "erotica" is rooted in *eros* or passionate love, and thus in the idea of positive choice, free will, the yearning for a particular person. (Interestingly, the definition of erotica leaves open the question of gender.) "Pornography" begins with a root meaning "prostitution" or "female captives," thus letting us know that the subject is not mutual love, or love at all, but domination and violence against women. (Though, of course, homosexual pornography may imitate this violence by putting a man in the "feminine" role of victim.) It ends with a root meaning "writing about" or "description of" which puts still more distance between subject and object, and replaces a spontaneous yearning for closeness with objectification and a voyeur.

The difference is clear in the words. It becomes even more 9 so by example.

Look at any photo or film of people making love; really 10 making love. The images may be diverse, but there is usually a sensuality and touch and warmth, an acceptance of bodies and nerve endings. There is always a spontaneous sense of people who are there because they *want* to be, out of shared pleasure.

Now look at any depiction of sex in which there is clear 11 force, or an unequal power that spells coercion. It may be very blatant, with weapons or torture or bondage, wounds and bruises, some clear humiliation, or an adult's sexual power being used over a child. It may be much more subtle: a physical attitude of conqueror and victim, the use of race or class difference to imply the same thing, perhaps a very unequal nudity, with one person exposed and vulnerable while the other is clothed. In either case, there is no sense of equal choice or equal power.

The first is erotic: a mutually pleasurable, sexual expression between people who have enough power to be there by positive choice. It may or may not strike the sense-memory in the viewer, or be creative enough to make the unknown seem real; but it doesn't require us to identify with a conqueror or a victim. It is truly sensuous, and may give us a contagion of pleasure.   12

The second is pornographic: its message is violence, dominance, and conquest. It is sex being used to reinforce some inequality, or to create one, or to tell us the lie that pain and humiliation (ours or someone else's) are really the same as pleasure. If we are to feel anything, we must identify with conqueror or victim. That means we can only experience pleasure through the adoption of some degree of sadism or masochism. It also means that we may feel diminished by the role of conqueror, or enraged, humiliated, and vengeful by sharing identity with the victim.   13

Perhaps one could simply say that erotica is about sexuality, but pornography is about power and sex-as-weapon—in the same way we have come to understand that rape is about violence, and not really about sexuality at all.   14

Yes, it's true that there are women who have been forced by violent families and dominating men to confuse love with pain; so much so that they have become masochists. (A fact that in no way excuses those who administer such pain.) But the truth is that, for most women—and for men with enough humanity to imagine themselves into the predicament of women—true pornography could serve as aversion therapy for sex.   15

Of course, there will always be personal differences about what is and is not erotic, and there may be cultural differences for a long time to come. Many women feel that sex makes them vulnerable and therefore may continue to need more sense of personal connection and safety before allowing any erotic feelings. We now find competence and expertise erotic in men, but that may pass as we develop those qualities in ourselves. Men, on the other hand, may continue to feel less vulnerable, and   16 therefore more open to such potential danger as sex with strangers. As some men replace the need for submission from childlike women with the pleasure of cooperation from equals, they may find a partner's competence to be erotic, too.

Such group changes plus individual differences will continue to be reflected in sexual love between people of the same gender, as well as between women and men. The point is not to dictate sameness, but to discover ourselves and each other through sexuality that is an exploring, pleasurable, empathetic part of our lives; a human sexuality that is unchained both from unwanted pregnancies and from violence. 17

But that is a hope, not a reality. At the moment, fear of change is increasing both the indiscriminate repression of all nonprocreative sex in the religious and "conservative" male world, and the pornographic vengeance against women's sexuality in the secular world of "liberal" and "radical" men. It's almost futuristic to debate what is and is not truly erotic, when many women are again being forced into compulsory motherhood, and the number of pornographic murders, tortures, and woman-hating images are on the increase in both popular culture and real life. 18

It's a familiar division: wife or whore, "good" woman who is constantly vulnerable to pregnancy or "bad" woman who is unprotected from violence. *Both* roles would be upset if we were to control our own sexuality. And that's exactly what we must do. 19

In spite of all our atavistic suspicions and training for the "natural" role of motherhood, we took up the complicated battle for reproductive freedom. Our bodies had borne the health burden of endless births and poor abortions, and we had a greater motive for separating sexuality and conception. 20

Now we have to take up the equally complex burden of explaining that all nonprocreative sex is *not* alike. We have a motive: our right to a uniquely human sexuality, and sometimes even to survival. As it is, our bodies have too rarely been enough our own to develop erotica in our own lives, much less in art and literature. And our bodies have too often been the objects of pornography and the womanhating, violent practice that it 21

preaches. Consider also our spirits that break a little each time
we see ourselves in chains or full labial display for the con-
quering male viewer, bruised or on our knees, screaming a real
or pretended pain to delight the sadist, pretending to enjoy
what we don't enjoy, to be blind to the images of our sisters that
really haunt us—humiliated often enough ourselves by the
truly obscene idea that sex and the domination of women must
be combined.

Sexuality *is* human, free, separate—and so are we.   22

But until we untangle the lethal confusion of sex with vio- 23
lence, there will be more pornography and less erotica. There
will be little murders in our beds—and very little love.

1978

Good Souls

Dorothy Parker

All about us, living in our very families, it may be, there ex- 1
ists a race of curious creatures. Outwardly, they possess no
marked peculiarities; in fact, at a hasty glance, they may be
readily mistaken for regular human beings. They are built after
the popular design; they have the usual number of features,
arranged in the conventional manner; they offer no variations
on the general run of things in their habits of dressing, eating,
and carrying on their business.

Yet, between them and the rest of the civilized world, there 2
stretches an impassable barrier. Though they live in the very
thick of the human race, they are forever isolated from it. They
are fated to go through life, congenital pariahs. They live out
their little lives, mingling with the world, yet never a part of it.

They are, in short, Good Souls.   3

And the piteous thing about them is that they are wholly 4
unconscious of their condition. A Good Soul thinks he is just like
anyone else. Nothing could convince him otherwise. It is

heartrending to see him, going cheerfully about, even whistling or humming as he goes, all unconscious of his terrible plight. The utmost he can receive from the world is an attitude of good-humored patience, a perfunctory word of approbation, a praising with faint damns, so to speak—yet he firmly believes that everything is all right with him.

There is no accounting for Good Souls.   5

They spring up anywhere. They will suddenly appear in   6
families which, for generations, have had no slightest stigma attached to them. Possibly they are throw-backs. There is scarcely a family without at least one Good Soul somewhere in it at the present moment—maybe in the form of an elderly aunt, an unmarried sister, an unsuccessful brother, an indigent cousin. No household is complete without one.

The Good Soul begins early; he will show signs of his con-   7
dition in extreme youth. Go now to the nearest window, and look out on the little children playing so happily below. Any group of youngsters that you may happen to see will do perfectly. Do you observe the child whom all the other little dears make "it" in their merry games? Do you follow the child from whom the other little ones snatch the cherished candy, to consume it before his streaming eyes? Can you get a good look at the child whose precious toys are borrowed for indefinite periods by the other playful youngsters, and are returned to him in fragments? Do you see the child upon whom all the other kiddies play their complete repertory of childhood's winsome pranks—throwing bags of water on him, running away and hiding from him, shouting his name in quaint rhymes, chalking coarse legends on his unsuspecting back?

Mark that child well. He is going to be a Good Soul when   8
he grows up.

Thus does the doomed child go through early youth and   9
adolescence. So does he progress towards the fulfillment of his destiny. And then, some day, when he is under discussion, someone will say of him, "Well, he means well, anyway." That settles it. For him, that is the end. Those words have branded him with the indelible mark of his pariahdom. He has come into his majority; he is a full-fledged Good Soul.

The activities of the adult of the species are familiar to us   10 all. When you are ill, who is it that hastens to your bedside bearing molds of blancmange, which, from infancy, you have hated with unspeakable loathing? As usual, you are way ahead of me, gentle reader—it is indeed the Good Soul. It is the Good Souls who efficiently smooth out your pillow when you have just worked it into the comfortable shape, who creak about the room on noisy tiptoe, who tenderly lay on your fevered brow damp cloths which drip ceaselessly down your neck. It is they who ask, every other minute, if there isn't something that they can do for you. It is they who, at great personal sacrifice, spend long hours sitting beside your bed, reading aloud the continued stories in the *Woman's Home Companion,* or chatting cozily on the increase in the city's death rate.

In health, as in illness, they are always right there, ready to 11
befriend you. No sooner do you sit down, than they exclaim that they can see you aren't comfortable in that chair, and insist on your changing places with them. It is the Good Souls who just *know* that you don't like your tea that way, and who bear it masterfully away from you to alter it with cream and sugar until it is a complete stranger to you. At the table, it is they who always feel that their grapefruit is better than yours and who have to be restrained almost forcibly from exchanging with you. In a restaurant the waiter invariably makes a mistake and brings them something which they did not order—and which they refuse to have changed, choking it down with a wistful smile. It is they who cause traffic blocks, by standing in subway entrances arguing altruistically as to who is to pay the fare.

At the theater, should they be members of a box-party, it is 12
the Good Souls who insist on occupying the rear chairs; if the seats are in the orchestra, they worry audibly, all through the performance, about their being able to see better than you, until finally in desperation you grant their plea and change seats with them. If, by so doing, they can bring a little discomfort on themselves—sit in a draught, say, or behind a pillar—then their happiness is complete. To feel the genial glow of martyrdom— that is all they ask of life. . . .

The lives of Good Souls are crowded with Occasions, each 13
with its own ritual which must be solemnly followed. On

Mother's Day, Good Souls conscientiously wear carnations; on St. Patrick's Day, they faithfully don boutonnieres of shamrocks; on Columbus Day, they carefully pin on miniature Italian flags. Every feast must be celebrated by the sending out of cards—Valentine's Day, Arbor Day, Groundhog Day, and all the other important festivals, each is duly observed. They have a perfect genius for discovering appropriate cards of greeting for the event. It must take hours of research.

If it's too long a time between holidays, then the Good Soul 14 will send little cards or little mementoes, just by way of surprises. He is strong on surprises, anyway. It delights him to drop in unexpectedly on his friends. Who has not known the joy of those evenings when some Good Soul just runs in, as a surprise? It is particularly effective when a chosen company of other guests happens to be present—enough for two tables of bridge, say. This means that the Good Soul must sit wistfully by, patiently watching the progress of the rubber, or else must cut in at intervals, volubly voicing his desolation at causing so much inconvenience, and apologizing constantly during the evening.

His conversation, admirable though it is, never receives its 15 just due of attention and appreciation. He is one of those who believe and frequently quote the exemplary precept that there is good in everybody; hanging in his bedchamber is the whimsically phrased, yet vital, statement, done in burned leather— "There is so much good in the worst of us and so much bad in the best of us that it hardly behooves any of us to talk about the rest of us." This, too, he archly quotes on appropriate occasions. Two or three may be gathered together, intimately discussing some mutual acquaintance. It is just getting really absorbing, when comes the Good Soul, to utter his dutiful, "We mustn't judge harshly—after all, we must always remember that many times our own actions may be misconstrued." Somehow, after several of these little reminders, there seems to be a general waning of interest; the little gathering breaks up, inventing quaint excuses to get away and discuss the thing more fully, adding a few really good details, some place where the Good Soul will not follow. While the Good Soul pitifully ignorant of their evil purpose glows with the warmth of conscious virtue, and settles himself to read the Contributors' Club, in the *Atlantic Monthly*, with a sense of duty well done. . . .

Good Souls are no mean humorists. They have a time- 16 honored formula of fun-making, which must be faithfully followed. Certain words or phrases must be whimsically distorted every time they are used. "Over the river," they dutifully say, whenever they take their leave. "Don't you cast any asparagus on me," they warn, archly; and they never fail to speak of "three times in concussion." According to their ritual, these screaming phrases must be repeated several times, for the most telling effect, and are invariably followed by hearty laughter from the speaker, to whom they seem eternally new.

Perhaps the most congenial role of the Good Soul is that of 17 advice-giver. He loves to take people aside and have serious little personal talks, all for their own good. He thinks it only right to point out faults or bad habits which are, perhaps unconsciously, growing on them. He goes home and laboriously writes long, intricate letters, invariably beginning, "Although you may feel that this is no affair of mine, I think that you really ought to know," and so on, indefinitely. In his desire to help, he reminds one irresistibly of Marcelline, who used to try so pathetically and so fruitlessly to be of some assistance in arranging the circus arena, and who brought such misfortunes on his own innocent person thereby.

The Good Souls will, doubtless, gain their reward in 18 Heaven; on this earth, certainly, theirs is what is technically known as a rough deal. The most hideous outrages are perpetrated on them. "Oh, he won't mind," people say. "He's a Good Soul." And then they proceed to heap the rankest impositions upon him. When Good Souls give a party, people who have accepted weeks in advance call up at the last second and refuse, without the shadow of an excuse save that of a subsequent engagement. Other people are invited to all sorts of entertaining affairs; the Good Soul, unasked, waves them a cheery good-bye and hopes wistfully that they will have a good time. His is the uncomfortable seat in the motor; he is the one to ride backwards in the train; he is the one who is always chosen to solicit subscriptions and make up deficits. People borrow his money, steal his servants, lose his golf balls, use him as a sort of errand boy, leave him flat whenever something more attractive offers—and carry it all off with their cheerful slogan, "Oh, he won't mind—he's a Good Soul."

And that's just it—Good Souls never do mind. After each 19 fresh atrocity they are more cheerful, forgiving and virtuous, if possible, than they were before. There is simply no keeping them down—back they come, with their little gifts, and their little words of advice, and their little endeavors to be of service, always anxious for more.

Yes, there can be no doubt about it—their reward will come 20 to them in the next world.

Would that they were even now enjoying it!   21

1919

Fire in the Sky

Claudia Glenn Dowling

Nights are long and bitter in the polar winters, but the com- 1 pensations can be spectacular: The skies blaze in a display of energy called the aurora borealis in the Arctic, aurora australis in the Antarctic. Ancient tribes who saw the lights believed they were caused by the bonfires of spirits; today we know that awe-inspiring physical forces create the heavenly arrays. And we're about to know more: A hardy breed of scientists—who don't mind odd hours or sub-zero temperatures—are investigating the powerful magnetic storms hidden within the aurora's glory. A few years ago some of these researchers put up a sign outside their University of Alaska lab near the tiny village of Poker Flats. It said it all: "Center for the Study of Something which, on the face of it, might seem trivial, but on closer examination takes on Global Significance."

Auroras are born on the sun, where thermonuclear storms ₂
tear apart hydrogen atoms, blasting protons and electrons toward earth at up to 1,000 miles per second. As this solar wind
approaches earth's magnetic field, particles are drawn to the
poles like iron filings to the ends of a bar magnet. When the particles collide with gases in the earth's atmosphere, they create
electrical discharges that glow purple, green, red and white. The
effect is similar to the collision of electrons and gases inside a
color television tube.

The beauty of an auroral storm hides its violence—the re- ₃
lease of millions of amperes of electricity, 20 times that found
in a bolt of lightning. Surges within auroras, called substorms,
tap energy trapped by the earth's magnetic field on the side of
the planet away from the sun. One physicist poetically calls
this energy pool earth's "electromagnetic soul."

A series of such storms knocked out power in all of Quebec ₄
as well as several U.S. states in 1989. Earlier this year surges
damaged two communications satellites. NASA researchers
theorize that the substorms, which produce nitrogen oxides,
may also damage the ozone layer above the poles. No one
knows what effect the electrical charge may have on human beings, although Japanese travel agencies book tours to the Arctic specifically for couples who believe that their chances of
conceiving a child are better under the aurora.

Lately, interest in mapping and predicting substorms has ₅
led to increased government spending. (That may be why, not
long ago, the sign at Poker Flats was changed to read: "This facility is uniquely dedicated to studies of the aurora borealis and
other atmospheric research studies for the paying customer
such as the National Aeronautics and Space Administration, the
United States Air Force. . . .") Last month NASA launched a
satellite—dubbed Wind—to monitor the solar wind as it howls
toward earth. Another, called Polar, the size of a school bus, is
planned to orbit closer to the planet, photographing auroras
with sensitive cameras. Next year Russia will launch two similar probes. And in November a consortium of European nations will open a radar installation in Spitsbergen, Norway,
with high-powered dishes that will collect information about

the velocity, density and temperature of solar particles. A European satellite that is designed to circle the Arctic will collect similar data from above.

Still, a nonscientific observer need only be in the right place at the right time to study this natural wonder. A jargon-filled recorded message from the National Oceanic and Atmospheric Administration in Boulder, Colo. (303-497-3235), tells aficionados when conditions are favorable for a good show. Although the aurora can be seen year-round—the atmosphere is always being bombarded by the solar wind—and is sometimes visible as far away as the equator, it occurs most often in the extreme north and south and is easiest to see on a clear, dark winter night. Photographer Norbert Rosing's favorite site is Churchill, Manitoba, where winter skies are cloudless 80 percent of the time. There, every February and March, he waits in the cold, warming his film with his car heater so it won't crack. "When you see the northern lights," he says, "you're in love." 6

1994

Stop Murdering the Language

John Leo

If you doubt that word games are becoming crucial to our social and political struggles, listen to Derek Humphry. A leading figure in the euthanasia movement, Humphry says his side lost at the polls in Washington State last fall largely because it lost the battle over language. The pro-euthanasia campaigners talked broadly about "aid in dying." But the media and public, Humphry says, "used the real words with relish"—suicide and euthanasia—and Initiative 119 went down. 1

In passing, Humphry pointed out the vagueness of "aid in dying." It can mean, he says, "anything from a physician's lethal injection all the way to holding hands with a dying patient and 2 saying, 'I love you.' " Anyone who stretches a phrase to cover both killing and moral support is a serious player in the language games.

This is, in fact, a big trend in the fast-growing field of language manipulation. Specific terms give way to ever broader and gassier ones. "Blind" or "legally blind" was replaced by "visually impaired," which includes everyone who wears glasses. "Child abuse" now seems to cover almost anything a parent or a parental figure can do wrong. "Substance abusers" (formerly addicts and winos) now include any person who overuses or misuses anything at all. William Lutz, editor of the *Quarterly Review of Doublespeak,* says, "The whole world is composed of substance. . . . This doesn't promote clarity of discussion."

More often word stretching occurs for frankly polemic reasons. "Family" has been stretched to make nonfamilies eligible for various family benefits. Now the word is seriously used to refer to group renters, childless couples and even single people living alone. To circumvent zoning restrictions, two groups of recovering alcoholics in Cherry Hill, N.J., insisted they were families. A spokesman said, "Residents consider themselves a family, and no other family in the country has to announce itself or explain itself." As in "Alice in Wonderland," the word means what the speaker wants it to mean.

FIGHTING WORDS

Another popular form of stretching is to associate some low-level complaint with a higher-level one involving violence, thus presumably startling everyone into paying attention. A *Washington Post* columnist complained recently about "intellectual genocide" in D.C. public schools, meaning that students aren't taught well and aren't learning basic skills. Betty Friedan regularly complains about the media's "symbolic annihilation of women" (she means there still aren't enough news stories by and about women). A Manhattan man, dying of AIDS, said his death should be seen as "a form of political assassination" (he means Bush should have spent more on AIDS).

These stretching exercises are often more than publicity- 6
grabbing hyperbole. Sometimes they are conscious attempts to
ratchet up a minor offense into a major one. Ogling a woman,
once considered harmless, or merely rude, is considered sexual harassment now and is often mentioned in the same breath
as rape. Notice how the University of Minnesota's definition
of sexual harassment blurs all lines between a glance, lack of
sensitivity, serious harassment and rape: "Sexual harassment
can be as blatant as rape or as subtle as a look. Harassment . . .
often consists of callous insensitivity to the experience of
women."

The verbal work of folding the entire category of harass- 7
ment into the category of rape goes on all the time. "Sexual harassment is a subtle rape," a psychologist named John Gottman
told the *New York Times.* "Sexual harassment is a subset of rape
with overtones of blackmail and extortion," columnist Carole
Agus told her readers in *New York Newsday.*

Looser definitions keep blurring categories. The term "do- 8
mestic violence," for instance, once referred to physical assault
in the home. Now it includes psychological abuse. Lenore
Walker, a specialist in the field, defines wife battering to include
bullying and manipulation ("making women do things they
otherwise wouldn't . . . by eroding their self-esteem"). This
mimics what happened when some definitions of date rape
were expanded to include "psychological coercion," presumably including wheedling and pleading for sex.

A similar blurring occurs in the hate crime field. Often it's 9
not very clear whether we are talking about violence or nonvi-
olence, crimes or noncriminal bias incidents, serious social of-
fenses or minor and ambiguous run-ins. The National Institute
Against Prejudice and Violence in Baltimore keeps feeding the
media statistics on campus "ethnoviolence," but it defines violence to include slurs, graffiti and perceptions of slights (e.g., "I
went to talk to someone who was black, and his friend stared
at me the whole time as though she didn't want me there"). The
effect of this tactic is to increase alarm about what's happening
on campus and to raise doubts about the aims and methods of
the statistics keepers.

The constant use of violent language for nonviolent inci- 10
dents reflects the current tensions among races and between
sexes. But it probably also helps magnify those tensions by linking minor incidents to major assaults and putting everyone on
full-time alert for offense. It's one price we're paying for these
polemic word games.

1993

CHAPTER 5

Division and Classification

Thinking as a Hobby
William Golding

While I was still a boy, I came to the conclusion that there   1
were three grades of thinking; and since I was later to claim
thinking as my hobby, I came to an even stranger conclusion—
namely, that I myself could not think at all.

I must have been an unsatisfactory child for grownups to   2
deal with. I remember how incomprehensible they appeared to
me at first, but not, of course, how I appeared to them. It was
the headmaster of my grammar school who first brought the
subject of thinking before me—though neither in the way, nor
with the result he intended. He had some statuettes in his study.
They stood on a high cupboard behind his desk. One was a lady
wearing nothing but a bath towel. She seemed frozen in an eternal panic lest the bath towel slip down any farther; and since
she had no arms, she was in an unfortunate position to pull the
towel up again. Next to her, crouched the statuette of a leopard,
ready to spring down at the top drawer of a filing cabinet labeled A-AH. My innocence interpreted this as the victim's last,
despairing cry. Beyond the leopard was a naked, muscular gentleman, who sat, looking down, with his chin on his fist and his
elbow on his knee. He seemed utterly miserable.

Some time later, I learned about these statuettes. The head- 3
master had placed them where they would face delinquent children, because they symbolized to him the whole of life. The
naked lady was the Venus of Milo. She was Love. She was not
worried about the towel. She was just busy being beautiful. The
leopard was Nature, and he was being natural. The naked, muscular gentleman was not miserable. He was Rodin's Thinker, an
image of pure thought. It is easy to buy small plaster models of
what you think life is like.

I had better explain that I was a frequent visitor to the head- 4
master's study, because of the latest thing I had done or left undone. As we now say, I was not integrated. I was, if anything,
disintegrated; and I was puzzled. Grownups never made sense.
Whenever I found myself in a penal position before the headmaster's desk, with the statuettes glimmering whitely above
him, I would sink my head, clasp my hands behind my back and
writhe one shoe over the other.

The headmaster would look opaquely at me through flash- 5
ing spectacles.

"What are we going to do with you?"   6

Well, what *were* they going to do with me? I would writhe 7
my shoe some more and stare down at the worn rug.

"Look up, boy! Can't you look up?"   8

Then I would look up at the cupboard, where the naked 9
lady was frozen in her panic and the muscular gentleman contemplated the hindquarters of the leopard in endless gloom. I
had nothing to say to the headmaster. His spectacles caught the
light so that you could see nothing human behind them. There
was no possibility of communication.

"Don't you ever think at all?"   10

No, I didn't think, wasn't thinking, couldn't think—I was 11
simply waiting in anguish for the interview to stop.

"Then you'd better learn—hadn't you?"   12

On one occasion the headmaster leaped to his feet, reached 13
up and plonked Rodin's masterpiece on the desk before me.

"That's what a man looks like when he's really thinking."   14

I surveyed the gentleman without interest or comprehen- 15
sion.

"Go back to your class."   16

Clearly there was something missing in me. Nature had en-   17
dowed the rest of the human race with a sixth sense and left me
out. This must be so, I mused, on my way back to the class, since
whether I had broken a window, or failed to remember Boyle's
Law, or been late for school, my teachers produced me one,
adult answer: "Why can't you think?"

As I saw the case, I had broken the window because I had   18
tried to hit Jack Arney with a cricket ball and missed him; I
could not remember Boyle's Law because I had never bothered
to learn it; and I was late for school because I preferred looking
over the bridge into the river. In fact, I was wicked. Were my
teachers, perhaps, so good that they could not understand the
depths of my depravity? Were they clear, untormented people
who could direct their every action by this mysterious business
of thinking? The whole thing was incomprehensible. In my earlier years, I found even the statuette of the Thinker confusing.
I did not believe any of my teachers were naked, ever. Like
someone born deaf, but bitterly determined to find out about
sound, I watched my teachers to find out about thought.

There was Mr. Houghton. He was always telling me to   19
think. With a modest satisfaction, he would tell me that he had
thought a bit himself. Then why did he spend so much time
drinking? Or was there more sense in drinking than there appeared to be? But if not, and if drinking were in fact ruinous to
health—and Mr. Houghton was ruined, there was no doubt
about that—why was he always talking about the clean life and
the virtues of fresh air? He would spread his arms wide with
the action of a man who habitually spent his time striding along
mountain ridges.

"Open air does me good, boys—I know it!"   20

Sometimes, exalted by his own oratory, he would leap from   21
his desk and hustle us outside into a hideous wind.

"Now, boys! Deep breaths! Feel it right down inside you—   22
huge draughts of God's good air!"

He would stand before us, rejoicing in his perfect health, an   23
open-air man. He would put his hands on his waist and take a
tremendous breath. You could hear the wind, trapped in the

cavern of his chest and struggling with all the unnatural im-
pediments. His body would reel with shock and his ruined face
go white at the unaccustomed visitation. He would stagger
back to his desk and collapse there, useless for the rest of the
morning.

Mr. Houghton was given to high-minded monologues   24
about the good life, sexless and full of duty. Yet in the middle
of one of these monologues, if a girl passed the window, tap-
ping along on her neat little feet, he would interrupt his discourse, his neck would turn of itself and he would watch her
out of sight. In this instance, he seemed to me ruled not by
thought but by an invisible and irresistible spring in his nape.

His neck was an object of great interest to me. Normally it   25
bulged a bit over his collar. But Mr. Houghton had fought in the
First World War alongside both Americans and French, and had
come—by who knows what illogic?—to a settled detestation of
both countries. If either happened to be prominent in current
affairs, no argument could make Mr. Houghton think well of
it. He would bang the desk, his neck would bulge still further
and go red. "You can say what you like," he would cry, "but
I've thought about this—and I know what I think!"

Mr. Houghton thought with his neck.   26

There was Miss Parsons. She assured us that her dearest   27
wish was our welfare, but I knew even then, with the mysterious clairvoyance of childhood, that what she wanted most was
the husband she never got. There was Mr. Hands—and so on.

I have dealt at length with my teachers because this was my   28
introduction to the nature of what is commonly called thought.
Through them I discovered that thought is often full of unconscious prejudice, ignorance and hypocrisy. It will lecture on
disinterested purity while its neck is being remorselessly
twisted toward a skirt. Technically, it is about as proficient as
most businessmen's golf, as honest as most politicians' intentions, or—to come near my own preoccupation—as coherent as
most books that get written. It is what I came to call grade-three
thinking, though more properly, it is feeling, rather than
thought.

True, often there is a kind of innocence in prejudices, but in   29 those days I viewed grade-three thinking with an intolerant contempt and an incautious mockery. I delighted to confront a pious lady who hated the Germans with the proposition that we should love our enemies. She taught me a great truth in dealing with grade-three thinkers; because of her, I no longer dismiss lightly a mental process which for nine-tenths of the population is the nearest they will ever get to thought. They have immense solidarity. We had better respect them, for we are outnumbered and surrounded. A crowd of grade-three thinkers, all shouting the same thing, all warming their hands at the fire of their own prejudices, will not thank you for pointing out the contradictions in their beliefs. Man is a gregarious animal, and enjoys agreement as cows will graze all the same way on the side of a hill.

Grade-two thinking is the detection of contradictions. I 30 reached grade two when I trapped the poor, pious lady. Grade-two thinkers do not stampede easily, though often they fall into the other fault and lag behind. Grade-two thinking is a withdrawal, with eyes and ears open. It became my hobby and brought satisfaction and loneliness in either hand. For grade-two thinking destroys without having the power to create. It set me watching the crowds cheering His Majesty and King and asking myself what all the fuss was about, without giving me anything positive to put in the place of that heady patriotism. But there were compensations. To hear people justify their habit of hunting foxes and tearing them to pieces by claiming that the foxes liked it. To hear our Prime Minister talk about the great benefit we conferred on India by jailing people like Pandit Nehru and Gandhi. To hear American politicians talk about peace in one sentence and refuse to join the League of Nations in the next. Yes, there were moments of delight.

But I was growing toward adolescence and had to admit 31 that Mr. Houghton was not the only one with an irresistible spring in his neck. I, too, felt the compulsive hand of nature and began to find that pointing out contradiction could be costly as well as fun. There was Ruth, for example, a serious and attractive girl. I was an atheist at the time. Grade-two thinking is a menace to religion and knocks down sects like skittles. I put my-

self in a position to be converted by her with an hypocrisy worthy of grade three. She was a Methodist—or at least, her parents were, and Ruth had to follow suit. But, alas, instead of relying on the Holy Spirit to convert me, Ruth was foolish enough
to open her pretty mouth in argument. She claimed that the
Bible (King James Version) was literally inspired. I countered
by saying that the Catholics believed in the literal inspiration
of Saint Jerome's *Vulgate,* and the two books were different. Argument flagged.

At last she remarked that there were an awful lot of ³²
Methodists, and they couldn't be wrong, could they—not all
those millions? That was too easy, said I restively (for the nearer
you were to Ruth, the nicer she was to be near to) since there
were more Roman Catholics than Methodists anyway; and they
couldn't be wrong, could they—not all those hundreds of millions? An awful flicker of doubt appeared in her eyes. I slid my
arm around her waist and murmured breathlessly that if we
were counting heads, the Buddhists were the boys for my
money. But Ruth had really wanted to do me good, because I
was so nice. She fled. The combination of my arm and those
countless Buddhists was too much for her.

That night her father visited my father and left, red-cheeked ³³
and indignant. I was given the third degree to find out what had
happened. It was lucky we were both of us only fourteen. I lost
Ruth and gained an undeserved reputation as a potential lib-
ertine.

So grade-two thinking could be dangerous. It was in this ³⁴
knowledge, at the age of fifteen, that I remember making a
comment from the heights of grade two, on the limitations of
grade three. One evening I found myself alone in the school hall,
preparing it for a party. The door of the headmaster's study was
open. I went in. The headmaster had ceased to thump Rodin's
Thinker down on the desk as an example to the young. Perhaps
he had not found any more candidates, but the statuettes were
still there, glimmering and gathering dust on top of the cupboard. I stood on a chair and rearranged them. I stood Venus
in her bath towel on the filing cabinet, so that now the top
drawer caught its breath in a gasp of sexy excitement. "A-ah!"

The portentous Thinker I placed on the edge of the cupboard so that he looked down at the bath towel and waited for it to slip.

Grade-two thinking, though it filled life with fun and excitement, did not make for content. To find out the deficiencies of our elders bolsters the young ego but does not make for personal security. I found that grade two was not only the power to point out contradictions. It took the swimmer some distance from the shore and left him there, out of his depth. I decided that Pontius Pilate was a typical grade-two thinker. "What is truth?" he said, a very common grade-two thought, but one that is used always as the end of an argument instead of the beginning. There is still a higher grade of thought which says, "What is truth?" and sets out to find it.

But these grade-one thinkers were few and far between. They did not visit my grammar school in the flesh though they were there in books. I aspired to them, partly because I was ambitious and partly because I now saw my hobby as an unsatisfactory thing if it went no further. If you set out to climb a mountain, however high you climb, you have failed if you cannot reach the top.

I *did* meet an undeniably grade-one thinker in my first year at Oxford. I was looking over a small bridge in Magdalen Deer Park, and a tiny mustached and hatted figure came and stood by my side. He was a German who had just fled from the Nazis to Oxford as a temporary refuge. His name was Einstein.

But Professor Einstein knew no English at that time and I knew only two words of German. I beamed at him, trying wordlessly to convey by my bearing all the affection and respect that the English felt for him. It is possible—and I have to make the admission—that I felt here were two grade-one thinkers standing side by side; yet I doubt if my face conveyed more than a formless awe. I would have given my Greek and Latin and French and a good slice of my English for enough German to communicate. But we were divided; he was as inscrutable as my headmaster. For perhaps five minutes we stood together on the bridge, undeniable grade-one thinker and breathless aspirant. With true greatness, Professor Einstein realized that my contact was better than none. He pointed to a trout wavering in mid-stream.

He spoke: *"Fisch."*   39

My brain reeled. Here I was, mingling with the great, and   40
yet helpless as the veriest grade-three thinker. Desperately I
sought for some sign by which I might convey that I, too,
revered pure reason. I nodded vehemently. In a brilliant flash
I used up half of my German vocabulary.

"Fisch. Ja Ja."   41

For perhaps another five minutes we stood side by side.   42
Then Professor Einstein, his whole figure still conveying good
will and amiability, drifted away out of sight.

I, too, would be a grade-one thinker. I was irreverent at the   43
best of times. Political and religious systems, social customs,
loyalties and traditions, they all came tumbling down like so
many rotten apples off a tree. This was a fine hobby and a sen-
sible substitute for cricket, since you could play it all the year
round. I came up in the end with what must always remain the
justification for grade-one thinking, its sign, seal and charter. I
devised a coherent system for living. It was a moral system,
which was wholly logical. Of course, as I readily admitted, conversion of the world to my way of thinking might be difficult,
since my system did away with a number of trifles, such as big
business, centralized government, armies, marriage. . . .

It was Ruth all over again. I had some very good friends   44
who stood by me, and still do. But my acquaintances vanished,
taking the girls with them. Young women seemed oddly contented with the world as it was. They valued the meaningless
ceremony with a ring. Young men, while willing to concede the
chaining sordidness of marriage, were hesitant about aban-
doning the organizations which they hoped would give them
a career. A young man on the first rung of the Royal Navy, while
perfectly agreeable to doing away with big business and marriage, got as rednecked as Mr. Houghton when I proposed a
world without any battleships in it.

Had the game gone too far? Was it a game any longer? In   45
those prewar days, I stood to lose a great deal, for the sake of a
hobby.

Now you are expecting me to describe how I saw the folly 46
of my ways and came back to the warm nest, where prejudices
are so often called loyalties, where pointless actions are hallowed into custom by repetition, where we are content to say
we think when all we do is feel.

But you would be wrong. I dropped my hobby and turned 47
professional.

If I were to go back to the headmaster's study and find the 48
dusty statuettes still there, I would arrange them differently. I
would dust Venus and put her aside, for I have come to love
her and know her for the fair thing she is. But I would put the
Thinker, sunk in his desperate thought, where there were shadows before him—and at his back, I would put the leopard,
crouched and ready to spring.

1961

The Climythology of America
David M. Ludlum

History is full of myths, and so is climatology. Every gen- 1
eration of historians gives rise to a revisionist school that rein-
terprets the past in light of new material and facts. Sometimes
the revisions join the body of history; other times they are revised by the next generation. Overall, the process leads to a
richer and more truthful history.

The settlement of America produced a series of myths about 2
the climate of different regions of our country. Even before
the first British settlements in North America, Europeans held
certain concepts concerning the supposed climate of the New
World, and those concepts greatly influenced their efforts to establish colonies from Newfoundland to the Carolinas.

Once the seaboard was occupied, new myths arose about
the lands west of the Allegheny Mountains. Other unfounded 3

beliefs appeared to influence the occupation of the Mississippi Valley and Great Plains until, in the last decade of the nineteenth century, the land office in Washington officially declared the frontier closed, though much territory remained unsettled. Most of this, however, was thought to be wasteland unsuitable for cultivation. This belief would be dispelled in the next century by the introduction of scientific methods of agriculture and the construction of huge irrigation projects.

THE EQUAL-LATITUDE MYTH

The intellectual content of climatology had made little   4
progress from the time of Ptolemy, the Greek astronomer and geographer of the second century A.D., to the year 1601, which marked the beginning of the century of colonization of North America by the English and the French. The concept of *clima*, or parallel bands around the world which shared comparable temperatures and hence weather conditions, was the generally accepted view of global arrangements. So much so, in fact, that the word clima was used by English writers interchangeably with "latitude." This gave rise to what I shall call the equal-latitude myth.

The planners and backers of the new colonies held to the   5
classical view of the distribution of global temperatures and thus were greatly surprised and chagrined when their environmental expectations were not met by the realities of the New World. The French were perplexed by the harsh winter conditions they met in Nova Scotia and the St. Lawrence Valley because both lay at the same latitudes as northern and central France. The British ultimately gave up constant efforts to settle Newfoundland in the early years of the seventeenth century because of the severe winters, despite the fact that it lay at the same latitude as southernmost England, where winters were usually moderate in temperature.

The history of all the British colonies from Maine to the   6
Carolinas ran much the same. The commercial backers of each colony expressed surprise and dismay that these settlements,

though at the latitudes of France and Spain, could not produce the exotic agricultural products of those countries.

Believing Virginia to have a Mediterranean climate, the proprietors tried silk culture until the realities of the winter killed all hopes of producing such a tropical product. 7

Almost a century passed before the backers of the colonies realized that the American climate differed from the European at the same latitudes. By the beginning of the eighteenth century, a more realistic viewpoint prevailed about the climate of the New World. Facts replaced the equal-latitude myth. 8

THE CLIMATE CHANGE MYTH

During the first two centuries of settlement of the American seaboard, a popular misconception arose about the observed climate. Where were the record snows of yesteryear? Why did we not have the harsh winters so often mentioned by grandfather and great-grandfather? Many homespun philosophers pondered these questions and suggested answers. Though no actual facts were brought forth, most colonists believed that conditions had grown milder and that the seasons had changed, with spring coming later and autumn lasting longer. 9

These ideas were expressed in an article by Dr. Hugh Williamson of North Carolina in the first issue of the *Transactions of the American Philosophical Society* in 1771: "An attempt to account for the change observed in the Middle Colonies in North America." 10

Williamson's thesis was that the cutting down of the forests for farms and settlements had produced a warming of the soil for two reasons. First, the felling of the trees allowed easterly winds to penetrate more deeply into the country, bringing temperate marine influences inland. Second, the bare soil received and stored more solar heat than did forested lands, and snow melted more quickly when exposed to direct sunlight. 11

In addition, some colonials suggested that the rise of urban 12

communities with heated buildings and smokepots was leading to a milder climate, as they claimed had occurred in Europe.
These ideas were the first of many about climate change that
were to arise and claim a body of believers among Americans.

THE OHIO COUNTRY MYTH

After almost 200 years of English settlement along the At- 13
lantic seaboard, the vast interior of the North American continent remained a *terra incognita* as far as an exact knowledge of
its geography and climate was concerned. The French had sent
voyageurs, couriers de bois and missionaries deep into the interior, but their first-hand knowledge of the conditions encountered did not reach the seaboard-bound British. Though
the barrier of the Appalachian Mountains was breached during
the war years that marked the closing decades of the eighteenth
century, few scientific men went westward to observe and report on the physical and atmospheric geography of the interior.

A vigorous controversy as to the nature of the climate of the 14
Ohio Country beyond the Allegheny Mountains arose as the
century drew to a close and continued to spark lively arguments well into the next century. The controversy became
known as the Ohio Country myth.

Between October 1795 and June 1796, Constantin Francois 15
de Chaseboeuf, Comte de Volney, traveled from Washington,
D.C., to Vincennes on the Wabash River in Indiana. He was familiar with Jefferson's view, expressed in his *Notes on the State
of Virginia,* that the annual temperature west of the mountains
was several degrees warmer than at the same latitude east of
the mountains along the Atlantic seaboard. Jefferson based his
opinion on the different types of plants thriving on opposite
sides of the mountains. Volney's seeming confirmation of Jefferson's opinion received wide dissemination in the *View of the
Climate and Soil of the United States,* published in London and
Paris in 1804.

The first refutation of the ideas promulgated by Volney 16
came from Dr. Daniel Drake in *Notices concerning Cincinnati,*
published in 1810, which produced actual comparative tem-

perature readings. Others soon took up their scientific cudgels. In an address before the Albany Institute in 1823, Dr. Lewis Beck took each of Volney's statements and demolished them with facts from more recent material.

William Darby, in his *View of the United States: Historical, Geographical and Statistical* (1828), referred to Volney's "by no means innoxious vulgar error." As late as 1842, Dr. Samuel Forry, in the first climatological survey to employ meteorological observations, felt constrained to criticize Volney's opinions as being "barren of precise data." [17]

In 1857, Lorin Blodget put the Ohio Country myth to final rest in his comprehensive *Climatology of the United States:* "The early distinction between the Atlantic States and the Mississippi has been quite dropped, as the progress of observation has shown them to be essentially the same, or to differ only in unimportant particulars." [18]

THE GREAT AMERICAN DESERT MYTH

"When I was a schoolboy my map of the United States showed between the Missouri River and the Rocky Mountains a long, broad white blotch, upon which was printed in small capitals 'THE GREAT AMERICAN DESERT—UNEXPLORED.' " So wrote Colonel Richard Irving Dodge in 1877 when commencing his revealing survey, *The Great Plains of the Great West.* He concluded: "What was then 'unexplored' is now almost thoroughly known. What was regarded as a desert supports, in some portions, thriving populations. The blotch of thirty years ago is now known as 'The Plains'." [19]

Sergeant John Ordway, who had accompanied Lewis and Clark in 1804, had stated ". . . this country may with propriety be called the Deserts of North America." Captain Zebulon Pike in exploring the headwaters of the Arkansas River had declared that ". . . these vast plains of the western hemisphere may become in time as celebrated as the sandy deserts of Africa." And Major Stephen H. Long had written, ". . . the Great Desert at the Base of the Rocky Mountains . . . is almost wholly unfit for cultivation, and of course uninhabitable. . . ." [20]

When Lorin Blodget published his comprehensive *Clima-*   21
tology of the United States in 1857, he marked a zone running east
of the 100° W meridian on his precipitation chart "the eastern
limit of the dry plains," and labeled the area of western Kansas
and Nebraska "the Desert Plains."

Following the Civil War, a counterattack was launched on   22
the pessimistic opinion about the future of the plains. The pressure for new lands to settle caused a change of view regarding
the farming possibilities of the plains west of the Missouri River.
Optimistic projections were penned by enthusiastic travelers,
booster-type editors and eager business promoters. Their hopes
were bolstered by several years of above-normal rainfall in the
late 1860s and early 1870s. The concept that "Rain Follows the
Plough" was broadcast in chamber-of-commerce style by agricultural improvement societies and business enterprises. This
was the "Garden Myth"—that planting trees and crops on the
dry plains would result in increased rainfall in a self-
perpetuating manner. The climate pendulum, however, underwent several swings from adequate to inadequate rainfall
until a nadir was reached in the late 1880s and early 1890s, resulting in disaster for the many cattle ranchers and the abandonment of farming in much of western Kansas and western
Nebraska.

The occupation of the central plains by farmers, the west-   23
ern plains by cattlemen, the mountains by miners, and the Pacific Northwest by lumbermen brought more adequate knowledge of the actual climates of these regions. The filling in of the
nation's climatological charts was completed about 1890, when
the availability of free land ended and the frontier was considered closed.

THE SOUTHERN CALIFORNIA
HEALTH MYTH

During the first 30 years of American settlement Southern   24
California remained a frontier country with ranching and agriculture dominating the economy. The last two decades of the

century, however, brought a change. Promoters and developers exploited the region's prime natural attraction, a beneficent climate, to make it the health frontier of the United States. Its favorable features were widely promoted in a tidal wave of publicity, and hordes of Easterners responded by migrating to the promised land in search of restored health. Thanks to man's ingenuity, the barren outlands had suddenly become habitable and even attractive.

During the decades from 1850 to 1880, native Angelenos 25 might have been forgiven for doubting their climate would turn out to be the most promising feature of the region. Damaging floods occurred in 1862 and 1868, devastating droughts came in 1862–64 and 1876–77 and a long spell of recurrent cold weather in the late 1870s and early 1880s set many still-standing date records for coldness. In addition, a destructive earthquake struck in 1857 and every year there were "tremblos."

Despite the lack of knowledge of the effect of California's 26 climate on disease, publicity for the region's salubrity soon poured forth. A pamphlet entitled *Southern California: The Italy of America* claimed for the area the "only perfect climate in the world and the grandest scenery under the sun." *The Los Angeles Star* in 1872 carried an article, "Land of Glorious Sunsets," which was considered by historian Oscar O. Winther (in 1946) as "the opening trumpet blast of a climate promotion campaign that has not ended."

Concerted efforts to attract visitors and settlers became an 27 increasingly active industry in the 1880s. The local Chamber of Commerce was careful to point out that not all parts of California enjoyed the salubrious climate claimed for the southern region. The results soon became apparent. A great boom in real estate and business developed in the mid-1880s, similar to those previously experienced in other sections of the western frontier country.

In the 1890s, climate continued to be the principal pitch of 28 promotion agencies. In 1892, the Southern California Information Bureau asserted: ". . . we sell the climate at so much an acre and throw in the land." To a complaint that the region had nothing to sell except climate, one enthusiast declared: "That's right, and we sell it, too—$10 for an acre of land, $490 an acre for the climate."

The health angle and longevity prospects were emphasized 29 in the promotional publications of the 1890s. Dr. Peter C. Remondino stated the extreme claim for the region in his book, *The Mediterranean Shores of America: Southern California:* "from my personal observations, I can say that at least an extra ten years' lease on life is gained by a removal to this coast from the Eastern States; not ten years to be added with its extra weight of age and infirmity, but ten years more with additional benefit of feeling ten years younger during the time."

They came at first by the thousands, and finally by the mil- 30 lions; today more than 15 million people live in Southern California where a century ago there were only 32,000.

Ironically, the concentration of population with attendant 31 urban sprawl and congested freeways affected the climate in a way none of its promoters of the late 1800s foresaw. The effusions of millions of combustion engines, trapped in the area's natural basins by the almost daily inversions in the lower atmosphere, have created smog conditions detrimental to health.

ALASKAN CLIMYTHOLOGY

The bill for $7,200,000 to pay for Alaska "loosed a storm in 32 the House of Representatives. I shall not attempt to say whether it was a hurricane or tornado, but it was accompanied by a lot of wind, by a great flood—a flood of oratory and some verbal thunder," declared Senator Ernest Gruening at a meeting of the American Meteorological Society at the University of Alaska on June 27, 1962. The former Russian colony was portrayed as "a frozen waste with a savage climate, where little or nothing could grow, and where few could or would live."

Typical of the statements of these pioneer climythologists 33 was that of Benjamin F. Loan of St. Louis, who declared:

". . . the acquisition of this inhospitable and barren waste 34 will never add a dollar to the wealth of our country or furnish any homes to our people. It is utterly worthless. . . . To suppose that anyone would leave the United States . . . to seek a home

... in the regions of perpetual snow is simply to suppose such a person insane."

Another climatic pessimist, Representative Orange Ferris of Glens Falls, New York, asserted that Alaska "is a barren and unproductive region covered with ice and snow" and "will never be populated by an enterprising people."

A representative from New York, Dennis McCarthy of Syracuse, cited "reports that every foot of the soil of Alaska is frozen from five to six feet in depth" and ventured that his colleagues would soon hear that Greenland was on the market.

And the minority report of the House Committee on Foreign Relations, in a scathing denunciation, declared Alaska "had no capacity as an agricultural country . . . no value as a mineral country. . . . its timber generally of poor quality and growing upon inaccessible mountains. . . . its fur trade . . . of insignificant value, and, will speedily come to an end. . . . the fisheries of doubtful value. . . . in a climate unfit for the habitation of civilized men."

Today, Alaska supports a population of more than one half million people and an annual economy worth more than $9 billion.

1987

Predictable Crises of Adulthood

Gail Sheehy

We are not unlike a particularly hardy crustacean. The lobster grows by developing and shedding a series of hard, protective shells. Each time it expands from within, the confining shell must be sloughed off. It is left exposed and vulnerable until, in time, a new covering grows to replace the old.

With each passage from one stage of human growth to the next we, too, must shed a protective structure. We are left exposed and vulnerable—but also yeasty and embryonic again, capable of stretching in ways we hadn't known before. These sheddings may take several years or more. Coming out of each passage, though, we enter a longer and more stable period in which we can expect relative tranquility and a sense of equilibrium regained. . . .

As we shall see, each person engages the steps of develop- 3 ment in his or her own characteristic *step-style*. Some people never complete the whole sequence. And none of us "solves" with one step—by jumping out of the parental home into a job or marriage, for example—the problems in separating from the caregivers of childhood. Nor do we "achieve" autonomy once and for all by converting our dreams into concrete goals, even when we attain those goals. The central issues or tasks of one period are never fully completed, tied up, and cast aside. But when they lose their primacy and the current life structure has served its purpose, we are ready to move on to the next period.

Can one catch up? What might look to others like listless- 4 ness, contrariness, a maddening refusal to face up to an obvious task may be a person's own unique detour that will bring him out later on the other side. Developmental gains won can later be lost—and rewon. It's plausible, though it can't be proven, that the mastery of one set of tasks fortifies us for the next period and the next set of challenges. But it's important not to think too mechanistically. Machines work by units. The bureaucracy (supposedly) works step by step. Human beings, thank God, have an individual inner dynamic that can never be precisely coded.

Although I have indicated the ages when Americans are 5 likely to go through each stage, and the differences between men and women where they are striking, do not take the ages too seriously. The stages are the thing, and most particularly the sequence.

Here is the briefest outline of the developmental ladder. 6

PULLING UP ROOTS

Before 18, the motto is loud and clear: "I have to get away 7 from my parents." But the words are seldom connected to action. Generally still safely part of our families, even if away at school, we feel our autonomy to be subject to erosion from moment to moment.

After 18, we begin Pulling Up Roots in earnest. College, military service, and short-term travels are all customary vehicles our society provides for the first round trips between family and a base of one's own. In the attempt to separate our view of the world from our family's view, despite vigorous protestations to the contrary—"I know exactly what I want!"—we cast about for any beliefs we can call our own. And in the process of testing those beliefs we are often drawn to fads, preferably those most mysterious and inaccessible to our parents.

Whatever tentative memberships we try out in the world, the fear haunts us that we are really kids who cannot take care of ourselves. We cover that fear with acts of defiance and mimicked confidence. For allies to replace our parents, we turn to our contemporaries. They become conspirators. So long as their perspective meshes with our own, they are able to substitute for the sanctuary of the family. But that doesn't last very long. And the instant they diverge from the shaky ideals of "our group," they are seen as betrayers. Rebounds to the family are common between the ages of 18 and 22.

The tasks of this passage are to locate ourselves in a peer group role, a sex role, an anticipated occupation, an ideology or world view. As a result, we gather the impetus to leave home physically and the identity to *begin* leaving home emotionally.

Even as one part of us seeks to be an individual, another part longs to restore the safety and comfort of merging with another. Thus one of the most popular myths of this passage is: We can piggyback our development by attaching to a Stronger One. But people who marry during this time often prolong financial and emotional ties to the family and relatives that impede them from becoming self-sufficient.

A stormy passage through the Pulling Up Roots years will probably facilitate the normal progression of the adult life cycle. If one doesn't have an identity crisis at this point, it will erupt during a later transition, when the penalties may be harder to bear.

THE TRYING TWENTIES

The Trying Twenties confront us with the question of how   13
to take hold in the adult world. Our focus shifts from the interior turmoils of late adolescence—"Who am I?" "What is
truth?"—and we become almost totally preoccupied with working out the externals. "How do I put my aspirations into effect?"
"What is the best way to start?" "Where do I go?" "Who can
help me?" "How did *you* do it?"

In this period, which is longer and more stable compared   14
with the passage that leads to it, the tasks are as enormous as
they are exhilarating: To shape a Dream, that vision of ourselves which will generate energy, aliveness, and hope. To prepare for a lifework. To find a mentor if possible. And to form
the capacity for intimacy without losing in the process whatever
consistency of self we have thus far mustered. The first test
structure must be erected around the life we choose to try.

Doing what we "should" is the most pervasive theme of the   15
twenties. The "shoulds" are largely defined by family models,
the press of the culture, or the prejudices of our peers. If the pre-
vailing cultural instructions are that one should get married and
settle down behind one's own door, a nuclear family is born. If
instead the peers insist that one should do one's own thing, the
25-year-old is likely to harness himself onto a Harley-Davidson
and burn up Route 66 in the commitment to have no commitments.

One of the terrifying aspects of the twenties is the inner   16
conviction that the choices we make are irrevocable. It is largely
a false fear. Change is quite possible, and some alteration of our
original choices is probably inevitable.

Two impulses, as always, are at work. One is to build a   17
firm, safe structure for the future by making strong commitments, to "be set." Yet people who slip into a ready-made form
without much self-examination are likely to find themselves
locked in.

The other urge is to explore and experiment, keeping any   18
structure tentative and therefore easily reversible. Taken to the
extreme, these are people who skip from one trial job and one

limited personal encounter to another, spending their twenties in the *transient* state.

Although the choices of our twenties are not irrevocable, 19 they do set in motion a Life Pattern. Some of us follow the lock-in pattern, others the transient pattern, the wunderkind pattern, the caregiver pattern, and there are a number of others. Such patterns strongly influence the particular questions raised for each person during each passage. . . .

Buoyed by powerful illusions and belief in the power of the 20 will, we commonly insist in our twenties that what we have chosen to do is the one true course in life. Our backs go up at the merest hint that we are like our parents, that two decades of parental training might be reflected in our current actions and attitudes.

"Not me," is the motto, "I'm different." 21

CATCH-30

Impatient with devoting ourselves to the "shoulds," a new 22 vitality springs from within as we approach 30. Men and women alike speak of feeling too narrow and restricted. They blame all sorts of things, but what the restrictions boil down to are the outgrowth of career and personal choices of the twenties. They may have been choices perfectly suited to that stage. But now the fit feels different. Some inner aspect that was left out is striving to be taken into account. Important new choices must be made, and commitments altered or deepened. The work involves great change, turmoil, and often crisis—a simultaneous feeling of rock bottom and the urge to bust out.

One common response is the tearing up of the life we spent 23 most of our twenties putting together. It may mean striking out on a secondary road toward a new vision or converting a dream of "running for president" into a more realistic goal. The single person feels a push to find a partner. The woman who was previously content at home with children chafes to venture into the world. The childless couple reconsiders children. And almost everyone who is married, especially those married for seven years, feels a discontent.

If the discontent doesn't lead to a divorce, it will, or should, 24
call for a serious review of the marriage and of each partner's
aspirations in their Catch-30 condition. The gist of that condition was expressed by a 29-year-old associate with a Wall Street
law firm:

"I'm considering leaving the firm. I've been there four years 25
now; I'm getting good feedback, but I have no clients of my
own. I feel weak. If I wait much longer, it will be too late, too
close to that fateful time of decision on whether or not to become
a partner. I'm success-oriented. But the concept of being 55
years old and stuck in a monotonous job drives me wild. It
drives me crazy now, just a little bit. I'd say that 85 percent of
the time I thoroughly enjoy my work. But when I get a screw-
ball case, I come away from court saying, 'What am I doing
here?' It's a *visceral* reaction that I'm wasting my time. I'm trying to find some way to make a social contribution or a slot in
city government. I keep saying, 'There's something more.' "

Besides the push to broaden himself professionally, there is 26
a wish to expand his personal life. He wants two or three more
children. "The concept of a home has become very meaningful
to me, a place to get away from troubles and relax. I love my
son in a way I could not have anticipated. I never could live
alone."

Consumed with the work of making his own critical life- 27
steering decisions, he demonstrates the essential shift at this age:
an absolute requirement to be more self-concerned. The self
has new value now that his competency has been proved.

His wife is struggling with her own age-30 priorities. She 28
wants to go to law school, but he wants more children. If she is
going to stay home, she wants him to make more time for the
family instead of taking on even wider professional commitments. His view of the bind, of what he would most like from
his wife, is this:

"I'd like not to be bothered. It sounds cruel, but I'd like not 29
to have to worry about what she's going to do next week. Which
is why I've told her several times that I think she should do
something. Go back to school and get a degree in social work
or geography or whatever. Hopefully that would fulfill her,

and then I wouldn't have to worry about her line of problems. I want her to be decisive about herself."

The trouble with his advice to his wife is that it comes out 30 of concern with *his* convenience, rather than with *her* development. She quickly picks up on this lack of goodwill: He is trying to dispose of her. At the same time, he refuses her the same latitude to be "selfish" in making an independent decision to broaden her horizons. Both perceive a lack of mutuality. And that is what Catch-30 is all about for the couple.

ROOTING AND EXTENDING

Life becomes less provisional, more rational and orderly in 31 the early thirties. We begin to settle down in the full sense. Most of us begin putting down roots and sending out new shoots. People buy houses and become very earnest about climbing career ladders. Men in particular concern themselves with "making it." Satisfaction with marriage generally goes downhill in the thirties (for those who have remained together) compared with the highly valued, vision-supporting marriage of the twenties. This coincides with the couple's reduced social life outside the family and the inturned focus on raising their children.

THE DEADLINE DECADE

In the middle of the thirties we come upon a crossroads. We 32 have reached the halfway mark. Yet even as we are reaching our prime, we begin to see there is a place where it finishes. Time starts to squeeze.

The loss of youth, the faltering of physical powers we have 33 always taken for granted, the fading purpose of stereotyped roles by which we have thus far identified ourselves, the spiritual dilemma of having no absolute answers—any or all of these shocks can give this passage the character of crisis. Such thoughts usher in a decade between 35 and 45 that can be called the Deadline Decade. It is a time of both danger and opportunity. All of us have the chance to rework the narrow identity by which we defined ourselves in the first half of life. And those of us who make the most of the opportunity will have a full-out authenticity crisis.

To come through this authenticity crisis, we must reexam- 34 ine our purposes and reevaluate how to spend our resources from now on. "Why am I doing all this? What do I really believe in?" No matter what we have been doing, there will be parts of ourselves that have been suppressed and now need to find ex-pression. "Bad" feelings will demand acknowledgment along with the good.

It is frightening to step off onto the treacherous footbridge 35 leading to the second half of life. We can't take everything with us on this journey through uncertainty. Along the way, we dis-cover that we are alone. We no longer have to ask permission because we are the providers of our own safety. We must learn to give ourselves permission. We stumble upon feminine or masculine aspects of our natures that up to this time have usu-ally been masked. There is grieving to be done because an old self is dying. By taking in our suppressed and even our un-wanted parts, we prepare at the gut level for the reintegration of an identity that is ours and ours alone—not some artificial form put together to please the culture or our mates. It is a dark passage at the beginning. But by disassembling ourselves, we can glimpse the light and gather our parts into a renewal.

Women sense this inner crossroads earlier than men do. 36 The time pinch often prompts a woman to stop and take an all-points survey at age 35. Whatever options she has already played out, she feels a "my last chance" urgency to review those options she has set aside and those that aging and biology will close off in the *now foreseeable* future. For all her qualms and con-fusion about where to start looking for a new future, she usu-ally enjoys an exhilaration of release. Assertiveness begins ris-ing. There are so many firsts ahead.

Men, too, feel the time push in the mid-thirties. Most men 37 respond by pressing down harder on the career accelerator. It's "my last chance" to pull away from the pack. It is no longer enough to be the loyal junior executive, the promising young novelist, the lawyer who does a little *pro bono* work on the side. He wants now to become part of top management, to be recognized as an established writer, or an active politician with his own legislative program. With some chagrin, he discovers that he has been too anxious to please and too vulnerable to criticism. He wants to put together his own ship.

During this period of intense concentration on external advancement, it is common for men to be unaware of the more difficult, gut issues that are propelling them forward. The survey that was neglected at 35 becomes a crucible at 40. Whatever rung of achievement he has reached, the man of 40 usually feels stale, restless, burdened, and unappreciated. He worries about his health. He wonders, "Is this all there is?" He may make a series of departures from well-established lifelong base lines, including marriage. More and more men are seeking second careers in midlife. Some become self-destructive. And many men in their forties experience a major shift of emphasis away from pouring all their energies into their own advancement. A more tender, feeling side comes into play. They become interested in developing an ethical self. 38

RENEWAL OR RESIGNATION

Somewhere in the mid-forties, equilibrium is regained. A new stability is achieved, which may be more or less satisfying. 39

If one has refused to budge through the midlife transition, the sense of staleness will calcify into resignation. One by one, the safety and supports will be withdrawn from the person who is standing still. Parents will become children; children will become strangers; a mate will grow away or go away; the career will become just a job—and each of these events will be felt as an abandonment. The crisis will probably emerge again around 50. And although its wallop will be greater, the jolt may be just what is needed to prod the resigned middle-ager toward seeking revitalization. 40

On the other hand . . . 41

If we have confronted ourselves in the middle passage and 42 found a renewal of purpose around which we are eager to build a more authentic life structure, these may well be the best years. Personal happiness takes a sharp turn upward for partners who can now accept the fact: "I cannot expect *anyone* to fully understand me." Parents can be forgiven for the burdens of our childhood. Children can be let go without leaving us in collapsed silence. At 50, there is a new warmth and mellowing. Friends become more important than ever, but so does privacy. Since it is so often proclaimed by people past midlife, the motto of this stage might be "No more bullshit."

1976

Why Nothing Is "Wrong" Anymore

Meg Greenfield

There has been an awful lot of talk about sin, crime, and plain old antisocial behavior this summer—drugs and pornography at home, terror and brutality abroad. Maybe it's just the heat; or maybe these categories of conduct (sin, crime, etc.) are really on the rise. What strikes me is our curiously deficient, not to say defective, way of talking about them. We don't seem to have a word anymore for "wrong" in the moral sense, as in, for example, "theft is wrong."

Let me quickly qualify. There is surely no shortage of people condemning other people on such grounds, especially their political opponents or characters they just don't care for. Name-calling is still very much in vogue. But where the concept of wrong is really important—as a guide to one's own behavior or that of one's own side in some dispute—it is missing; and this is as true of those on the religious right who are going around pronouncing great masses of us sinners as it is of their principal antagonists, those on the secular left who can forgive or "understand" just about anything so long as it has not been perpetrated by a right-winger.

There is a fairly awesome literature that attempts to explain 3 how we have changed as a people with the advent of psychiatry, the weakening of religious institutions and so forth, but you don't need to address these matters to take note of a simple fact. As a guide and a standard to live by, you don't hear so much about "right and wrong" these days. The very notion is considered politically, not to say personally, embarrassing, since it has such a repressive, Neanderthal ring to it. So we have developed a broad range of alternatives to "right and wrong." I'll name a few.

> *Right and stupid:* This is the one you use when your can- 4
> didate gets caught stealing, or, for that matter, when anyone on your side does something reprehensible. "It was really so dumb of him"—head must shake here—"I just can't understand it." Bad is dumb, breathtakingly dumb and therefore unfathomable; so, conveniently enough, the effort to fathom it might just as well be called off. This one had a big play during Watergate and has had mini-revivals ever since whenever congressmen and senators investigating administration crimes turn out to be guilty of something similar themselves.

> *Right and not necessarily unconstitutional:* I don't know 5
> at quite what point along the way we came to this one, the avoidance of admitting that something is wrong by pointing out that it is not specifically or even inferentially prohibited by the Constitution or, for that matter, mentioned by name in the criminal code or the Ten Commandments. The various parties that prevail in civil-liberty and civil-rights disputes before the Supreme Court have gotten quite good at making this spurious connection: it is legally permissible, therefore it is morally acceptable, possibly even good. But both as individuals and as a society we do things

every day that we know to be wrong even though they may not fall within the class of legally punishable acts or tickets to eternal damnation.

Right and sick: Crime or lesser wrongdoing defined as 6 physical and/or psychological disorder—this one has been around for ages now and as long ago as 1957 was made the butt of a great joke in the "Gee Officer Krupke!" song in "West Side Story." Still, I think no one could have foreseen the degree to which an originally reasonable and humane assumption (that some of what once was regarded as wrongdoing is committed by people acting out of ailment rather than moral choice) would be seized upon and exploited to exonerate every kind of misfeasance. This route is a particular favorite of caught-out officeholders who, when there is at last no other recourse, hold a press conference, announce that they are "sick" in some wise and throw themselves and their generally stunned families on our mercy. At which point it becomes gross to pick on them; instead we are exhorted to admire them for their "courage."

Right and only to be expected: You could call this the tit- 7 for-tat school; it is related to the argument that holds moral wrongdoing to be evidence of sickness, but it is much more pervasive and insidious these days. In fact it is probably the most popular dodge, being used to justify, or at least avoid owning up to, every kind of lapse: the other guy, or sometimes just plain circumstance, "asked for it." For instance, I think most of us could agree that setting fire to live people, no matter what their political offense, is—dare I say it?— wrong. Yet if it is done by those for whom we have sympathy in a conflict, there is a tendency to extenuate or disbelieve it, receiving it less as evidence of wrongdoing on our side than as evidence of the severity of the provocation or as enemy-supplied disinformation. Thus the hesitation of many in the antiapartheid movement to confront the brutality of so-called "necklacing," and thus the immediate leap of Sen. Jesse Helms to the defense of the Chilean government after the horrifying incineration of protesters there.

Right and complex: This one hardly takes a moment to de- 8
scribe; you know it well. "Complex" is the new "controversial," a word used as "controversial" was for so long to
flag trouble of some unspecified, dismaying sort that the
speaker doesn't want to have to step up to. "Well, you
know, it's very complex. . . ." I still can't get this one out of
my own vocabulary.

In addition to these various sophistries, we also have cre- 9
ated a rash of "ethics committees" in our government, of course,
whose function seems to be to dither around writing rules that
allow people who have clearly done wrong—and should have
known it and probably did—to get away because the rules don't
cover their offense (see Right and not necessarily unconstitu-
tional). But we don't need any more committees or artful
dodges for that matter. As I listen to the moral arguments
swirling about us this summer I become ever more persuaded
that our real problem is this: the "still, small voice" of conscience has become far too small—and utterly still.

1986

Cinematypes

Susan Allen Toth

Aaron takes me only to art films. That's what I call them, 1
anyway: strange movies with vague poetic images I don't always understand, long dreamy movies about a distant Technicolor past, even longer black-and-white movies about the general meaninglessness of life. We do not go unless at least one
reputable critic has found the cinematography superb. We went
to *The Devil's Eye*, and Aaron turned to me in the middle and
said, "My God, this is *funny*." I do not think he was pleased.

When Aaron and I go to the movies, we drive our cars sep- 2

arately and meet by the box office. Inside the theater he sits ten-
tatively in his seat, ready to move if he can't see well, poised to
leave if the film is disappointing. He leans away from me, careful not to touch the bare flesh of his arm against the bare flesh
of mine. Sometimes he leans so far I am afraid he may be touching the woman on his other side. If the movie is very good, he
leans forward, too, peering between the heads of the couple in
front of us. The light from the screen bounces off his glasses; he
gleams with intensity, sitting there on the edge of his seat,
watching the screen. Once I tapped him on the arm so I could
whisper a comment in his ear. He jumped.

After *Belle de Jour* Aaron said he wanted to ask me if he   3
could stay overnight. "But I can't," he shook his head mournfully before I had a chance to answer, "because I know I never
sleep well in strange beds." Then he apologized for asking. "It's
just that after a film like that," he said, "I feel the need to assert
myself."

Pete takes me only to movies that he thinks have redeem-   4
ing social value. He doesn't call them "films." They tend to be
about poverty, war, injustice, political corruption, struggling
unions in the 1930s, and the military-industrial complex. Pete
doesn't like propaganda movies, though, and he doesn't like to
be too depressed, either. We stayed away from *The Sorrow and
the Pity;* it would be, he said, just too much. Besides, he assured
me, things are never that hopeless. So most of the movies we
see are made in Hollywood. Because they are always topical,
these movies offer what Pete calls "food for thought." When we
saw *Coming Home,* Pete's jaw set so firmly with the first half-
hour that I knew we would end up at Poppin' Fresh Pies afterward.

When Pete and I go to the movies, we take turns driving so   5
no one owes anyone else anything. We leave the car far from
the theater so we don't have to pay for a parking space. If it's
raining or snowing, Pete offers to let me off at the door, but I
can tell he'll feel better if I go with him while he finds a spot, so
we share the walk too. Inside the theater Pete will hold my
hand when I get scared if I ask him. He puts my hand firmly on
his knee and covers it completely with his own hand. His knee

never twitches. After a while, when the scary part is past, he loosens his hand slightly and I know that is a signal to take mine away. He sits companionably close, letting his jacket just touch my sweater, but he does not infringe. He thinks I ought to know he is there if I need him.

One night, after *The China Syndrome*, I asked Pete if he wouldn't like to stay for a second drink, even though it was past midnight. He thought a while about that, considering my offer from all possible angles, but finally he said no. Relationships today, he said, have a tendency to move too quickly. 6

Sam likes movies that are entertaining. By that he means movies that Will Jones in the *Minneapolis Tribune* loved and either *Time* or *Newsweek* rather liked; also movies that do not have sappy love stories, are not musicals, do not have subtitles, and will not force him to think. He does not go to movies to think. He liked *California Suite* and *The Seduction of Joe Tynan*, though the plots, he said, could have been zippier. He saw it all coming too far in advance, and that took the fun out. He doesn't like to know what is going to happen. "I just want my brain to be tickled," he says. It is very hard for me to pick out movies for Sam. 7

When Sam takes me to the movies, he pays for everything. He thinks that's what a man ought to do. But I buy my own popcorn, because he doesn't approve of it; the grease might smear his flannel slacks. Inside the theater, Sam makes himself comfortable. He takes off his jacket, puts one arm around me, and all during the movie he plays with my hand, stroking my palm, beating a small tattoo on my wrist. Although he watches the movie intently, his body operates on instinct. Once I inclined my head and kissed him lightly just behind his ear. He beat a faster tattoo on my wrist, quick and musical, but he didn't look away from the screen. 8

When Sam takes me home from the movies, he stands outside my door and kisses me long and hard. He would like to come in, he says regretfully, but his steady girlfriend in Duluth wouldn't like it. When the *Tribune* gives a movie four stars, he has to save it to see with her. Otherwise her feelings might be hurt. 9

I go to some movies by myself. On rainy Sunday afternoons 10

I often sneak into a revival house or a college auditorium for old Technicolor musicals, *Kiss Me Kate, Seven Brides for Seven Brothers, Calamity Jane,* even, once, *The Sound of Music.* Wearing saggy jeans so I can prop my feet on the seat in front, I sit toward the rear where no one can see me. I eat large handfuls of popcorn with double butter. Once the movie starts, I feel completely at home. Howard Keel and I are old friends; I grin back at him on the screen. I know the sound tracks by heart. Sometimes when I get really carried away I hum along with Kathryn Grayson, remembering how I once thought I would fill out a formal like that. I am rather glad now I never did. Skirts whirl, feet tap, acrobatic young men perform impossible feats, and then the camera dissolves into a dream sequence I know I can comfortably follow. It is not, thank God, Bergman.

If I can't find an old musical, I settle for Hepburn and Tracy,   11 vintage Grant or Gable, on adventurous days Claudette Colbert or James Stewart. Before I buy my ticket I make sure it will all end happily. If necessary, I ask the girl at the box office. I have never seen *Stella Dallas* or *Intermezzo.* Over the years I have developed other peccadilloes: I will, for example, see anything that is redeemed by Thelma Ritter. At the end of *Daddy Long Legs* I wait happily for the scene when Fred Clark, no longer angry, at last pours Thelma a convivial drink. They smile at each other, I smile at them, I feel they are smiling at me. In the movies I go to by myself, the men and women always like each other.

1980

Growing Up Asian in America

Kesaya E. Noda

Sometimes when I was growing up, my identity seemed to   1 hurtle toward me and paste itself right to my face. I felt that way, encountering the stereotypes of my race perpetuated by non-

Japanese people (primarily white) who may or may not have had contact with other Japanese in America. "You don't like cheese, do you?" someone would ask. "I know your people don't like cheese." Sometimes questions came making allusions to history. That was another aspect of the identity. Events that had happened quite apart from the me who stood silent in that moment connected my face with an incomprehensible past. "Your parents were in California? Were they in those camps during the war?" And sometimes there were phrases or nicknames: "Lotus Blossom." I was sometimes addressed or referred to as racially Japanese, sometimes as Japanese American, and sometimes as an Asian woman. Confusions and distortions abounded.

How is one to know and define oneself? From the inside— 2 within a context that is self-defined, from a grounding in community and a connection with culture and history that are comfortably accepted? Or from the outside—within terms of messages received from the media and people who are often ignorant? Even as an adult I can still see two sides of my face and past. I can see from the inside out, in freedom. And I can see from the outside in, driven by the old voices of childhood and lost in anger and fear.

I AM RACIALLY JAPANESE

A voice from my childhood says: "You are other. You are 3 less than. You are unalterably alien." This voice has its own history. We have indeed been seen as other and alien since the early years of our arrival in the United States. The very first immigrants were welcomed and sought as laborers to replace the dwindling numbers of Chinese, whose influx had been cut off by the Chinese Exclusion Act of 1882. The Japanese fell natural heir to the same anti-Asian prejudice that had arisen against the Chinese. As soon as they began striking for better wages, they were no longer welcomed.

I can see myself today as a person historically defined by 4 law and custom as being forever alien. Being neither "free white," nor "African," our people in California were deemed "aliens, ineligible for citizenship," no matter how long they intended to stay here. Aliens ineligible for citizenship were prohibited from owning, buying, or leasing land. They did not and could not belong here. The voice in me remembers that I am always a *Japanese*-American in the eyes of many. A third-generation German-American is an American. A third-generation Japanese-American is a Japanese-American. Being Japanese means being a danger to the country during the war and knowing how to use chopsticks. I wear this history on my face.

I move to the other side. I see a different light and claim a   5 different context. My race is a line that stretches across ocean and time to link me to the shrine where my grandmother was raised. Two high, white banners lift in the wind at the top of the stone steps leading to the shrine. It is time for the summer festival. Black characters are written against the sky as boldly as the clouds, as lightly as kites, as sharply as the big black crows I used to see above the fields in New Hampshire. At festival time there is liquor and food, ritual, discipline, and abandonment. There is music and drunkenness and invocation. There is hope. Another season has come. Another season has gone.

I am racially Japanese. I have a certain claim to this crazy   6 place where the prayers intoned by a neighboring Shinto priest (standing in for my grandmother's nephew who is sick) are drowned out by the rehearsals for the pop singing contest in which most of the villagers will compete later that night. The village elders, the priest, and I stand respectfully upon the immaculate, shining wooden floor of the outer shrine, bowing our heads before the hidden powers. During the patchy intervals when I can hear him, I notice the priest has a stutter. His voice flutters up to my ears only occasionally because two men and a woman are singing gustily into a microphone in the compound, testing the sound system. A pre-recorded tape of guitars, samisens, and drums accompanies them. Rock music and Shinto prayers. That night, to loud applause and cheers, a young man is given the award for the most *netsuretsu*—passionate, burning—rendition of a song. We roar our approval of the reward. Never mind that his voice had wandered and slid, now slightly above, now slightly below the given line of the melody. Netsuretsu. Netsuretsu.

In the morning, my grandmother's sister kneels at the foot 7 of the stone stairs to offer her morning prayers. She is too crippled to climb the stairs, so each morning she kneels here upon the path. She shuts her eyes for a few seconds, her motions as matter of fact as when she washes rice. I linger longer than she does, so reluctant to leave, savoring the connection I feel with my grandmother in America, the past, and the power that lives and shines in the morning sun.

Our family has served this shrine for generations. The fam- 8 ily's need to protect this claim to identity and place outweighs any individual claim to any individual hope. I am Japanese.

I AM A JAPANESE-AMERICAN

"Weak." I hear the voice from my childhood years. "Pas- 9 sive," I hear. Our parents and grandparents were the ones who were put into those camps. They went without resistance; they offered cooperation as proof of loyalty to America. "Victim," I hear. And, "Silent."

Our parents are painted as hard workers who were socially 10 uncomfortable and had difficulty expressing even the smallest opinion. Clean, quiet, motivated, and determined to match the American way; that is us, and that is the story of our time here.

"Why did you go into those camps?" I raged at my parents, 11 frightened by my own inner silence and timidity. "Why didn't you do anything to resist? Why didn't you name it the injustice it was?" Couldn't our parents even think? Couldn't they? Why were we so passive?

I shift my vision and my stance. I am in California. My 12 uncle is in the midst of the sweet potato harvest. He is pressed, trying to get the harvesting crews onto the field as quickly as possible, worried about the flow of equipment and people. His big pickup is pulled off to the side, motor running, door ajar. I see two tractors in the yard in front of an old shed; the flatbed harvesting platform on which the workers will stand has already been brought over from the other field. It's early morning. The workers stand loosely grouped and at ease, but my uncle looks as harried and tense as a police officer trying to unsnarl a New York City traffic jam. Driving toward the shed, I pull my car off the road to make way for an approaching tractor. The front wheels of the car sink luxuriously into the soft, white sand by the roadside and the car slides to a dreamy halt, tail still on the road. I try to move forward. I try to move back. The front bites contentedly into the sand, the back lifts itself at a jaunty angle. My uncle sees me and storms down the road, running. He is shouting before he is even near me.

"What's the matter with you?" he screams. "What the hell   13
are you doing?" In his frenzy, he grabs his hat off his head and slashes it through the air across his knee. He is beside himself. "Don't you know how to drive in sand? What's the matter with you? You've blocked the whole roadway. How am I supposed to get my tractors out of here? Can't you use your head? You've cut off the whole roadway, and we've got to get out of here."

I stand on the road before him helplessly thinking. "No, I   14
don't know how to drive in sand. I've never driven in sand."

"I'm sorry, uncle," I say, burying a smile beneath a look of   15
sincere apology. I notice my deep amusement and my affection for him with great curiosity. I am usually devastated by anger. Not this time.

During the several years that follow I learn about the peo-   16
ple and the place, and much more about what has happened in this California village where my parents grew up. The issei, our grandparents, made this settlement in the desert. Their first crops were eaten by rabbits and ravaged by insects. The land was so barren that men walking from house to house sometimes got lost. Women came here too. They bore children in 114-degree heat, then carried the babies with them into the fields to nurse when they reached the end of each row of grapes or other truck-farm crops.

I had had no idea what it meant to buy this kind of land and   17
make it grow green. Or how, when the war came, there was no space at all for the subtlety of being who we were—Japanese-Americans. Either/or was the way. I hadn't understood that

people were literally afraid for their lives then, that their money had been frozen in banks; that there was a five-mile travel limit; that when the early evening curfew came and they were inside their houses, some of them watched helplessly as people they knew went into their barns to steal their belongings. The police were patrolling the road, interested only in violators of curfew. There was no help for them in the face of thievery. I had not been able to imagine before what it must have felt like to be an American—to know absolutely that one is an American—and yet to have almost everyone else deny it. Not only deny it, but challenge that identity with machine guns and troops of white American soldiers. In those circumstances it was difficult to say, "I'm a Japanese-American." "American" had to do.

But now I can say that I am a Japanese-American. It means 18 I have a place here in this country, too. I have a place here on the East Coast, where our neighbor is so much a part of our family that my mother never passes her house at night without glancing at the lights to see if she is home and safe; where my parents have hauled hundreds of pounds of rocks from fields and arduously planted Christmas trees and blueberries, lilacs, asparagus, and crab apples; where my father still dreams of angling a stream to a new bed so that he can dig a pond in the field and fill it with water and fish. "The neighbors already came for their Christmas tree?" he asks in December. "Did they like it? Did they like it?"

I have a place on the West Coast where my relatives still 19 farm, where I heard the stories of feuds and backbiting, and where I saw that people survived and flourished because fundamentally they trusted and relied upon one another. A death in the family is not just a death in a family; it is a death in the community. I saw people help each other with money, materials, labor, attention, and time. I saw men gather once a year, without fail, to clean the grounds of a ninety-year-old woman who had helped the community before, during, and after the war. I saw her remembering them with birthday cards sent to each of their children.

I come from a people with a long memory and a distinctive 20 grace. We live our thanks. And we are Americans. Japanese-Americans.

I AM A JAPANESE-AMERICAN WOMAN

Woman. The last piece of my identity. It has been easier by   21
far for me to know myself in Japan and to see my place in America than it has been to accept my line of connection with my own
mother. She was my dark self, a figure in whom I thought I saw
all that I feared most in myself. Growing into womanhood and
looking for some model of strength, I turned away from her. Of
course, I could not find what I sought. I was looking for a black
feminist or a white feminist. My mother is neither white nor
black.

My mother is a woman who speaks with her life as much   22
as with her tongue. I think of her with her own mother. Grandmother had Parkinson's disease and it had frozen her gait and
set her fingers, tongue, and feet jerking and trembling in a terrible dance. My aunts and uncles wanted her to be able to live
in her own home. They fed her, bathed her, dressed her, awoke
at midnight to take her for one last trip to the bathroom. My
aunts (her daughters-in-law) did most of the care, but my
mother went from New Hampshire to California each summer
to spend a month living with Grandmother, because she wanted
to and because she wanted to give my aunts at least a small rest.
During those hot summer days, mother lay on the couch watching the television or reading, cooking foods that Grandmother
liked, and speaking little. Grandmother thrived under her care.

The time finally came when it was too dangerous for Grand-   23
mother to live alone. My relatives kept finding her on the floor
beside her bed when they went to wake her in the mornings.
My mother flew to California to help clean the house and make
arrangements for Grandmother to enter a local nursing home.
On her last day at home, while Grandmother was sitting in her
big, overstuffed armchair, hair combed and wearing a green
summer dress, my mother went to her and knelt at her feet.
"Here, Mamma," she said. "I've polished your shoes." She lifted
Grandmother's legs and helped her into the shiny black shoes.
My Grandmother looked down and smiled slightly. She left
her house walking, supported by her children, carrying her
pocket book, and wearing her polished black shoes. "Look,

Mamma," my mom had said, kneeling. "I've polished your shoes."

Just the other day, my mother came to Boston to visit. She   24
had recently lost a lot of weight and was pleased with her new shape and her feeling of good health. "Look at me, Kes," she exclaimed, turning toward me, front and back, as naked as the day she was born. I saw her small breasts and the wide, brown scar, belly button to pubic hair, that marked her because my brother and I were both born by Caesarean section. Her hips were small. I was not a large baby, but there was so little room for me in her that when she was carrying me she could not even begin to bend over toward the floor. She hated it, she said.

"Don't I look good? Don't you think I look good?"   25

I looked at my mother, smiling and as happy as she, think-   26
ing of all the times I have seen her naked. I have seen both my parents naked throughout my life, as they have seen me. From childhood through adulthood we've had our naked moments, sharing baths, idle conversations picked up as we moved between showers and closets, hurried moments at the beginning of days, quiet moments at the end of days.

I know this to be Japanese, this ease with the physical, and   27
it makes me think of an old Japanese folk song. A young nursemaid, a fifteen-year-old girl, is singing a lullaby to a baby who is strapped to her back. The nursemaid has been sent as a servant to a place far from her own home. "We're the beggars," she says, "and they are the nice people. Nice people wear fine sashes. Nice clothes."

> If I should drop dead,
>> bury me by the roadside!
>> I'll give a flower
>> to everyone who passes.
>
> What kind of flower?
>> The cam-cam-camellia [tsun-tsun-tsubaki]
>> watered by Heaven:
>> alms water.

The nursemaid is the intersection of heaven and earth, the   28
intersection of the human, the natural world, the body, and the

soul. In this song, with clear eyes, she looks steadily at life, which is sometimes so very terrible and sad. I think of her while looking at my mother, who is standing on the red and purple carpet before me, laughing, without any clothes.

I am my mother's daughter. And I am myself.   29

I am a Japanese-American woman.   30

EPILOGUE

I recently heard a man from West Africa share some mem-   31
ories of his childhood. He was raised Muslim, but when he was a young man, he found himself deeply drawn to Christianity. He struggled against his inner impulse for years, trying to avoid the church yet feeling pushed to return to it again and again. "I would have done anything to avoid the change," he said. At last, he became Christian. Afterwards he was afraid to go home, fearing that he would not be accepted. The fear was groundless, he discovered, when at last he returned—he had separated himself, but his family and friends (all Muslim) had not separated themselves from him.

The man, who is now a professor of religion, said that in the   32
Africa he knew as a child and a young man, pluralism was embraced rather than feared. There was "a kind of tolerance that did not deny your particularity," he said. He alluded to zestful, spontaneous debates that would sometimes loudly erupt between Muslims and Christians in the village's public spaces. His memories of an atheist who harangued the villagers when he came to visit them once a week moved me deeply. Perhaps the man was an agricultural advisor or inspector. He harassed the women. He would say: "Don't go to the fields! Don't even bother to go to the fields. Let God take care of you. He'll send you the food. If you believe in God, why do you need to work? You don't need to work! Let God put the seeds in the ground. Stay home."

The professor said, "The women laughed, you know? They   33
just laughed. Their attitude was, 'Here is a child of God. When will he come home?' "

The storyteller, the professor of religion, smiled a most fan- 34
tastic tender smile as he told this story. "In my country, there
is a deep affirmation of the oneness of God," he said. "The atheist and the women were having quite different experiences in
their encounter, though the atheist did not know this. He saw
himself as quite separate from the women. But the women did
not see themselves as being separate from him. 'Here is a child
of God,' they said. 'When will he come home?' "

1989

The Truth About Lying

Judith Viorst

I've been wanting to write on a subject that intrigues and
challenges me: the subject of lying. I've found it very difficult 1
to do. Everyone I've talked to has a quite intense and personal
but often rather intolerant point of view about what we can—
and can never *never*—tell lies about. I've finally reached the
conclusion that I can't present any ultimate conclusions, for too
many people would promptly disagree. Instead, I'd like to present a series of moral puzzles, all concerned with lying. I'll tell
you what I think about them. Do you agree?

SOCIAL LIES

Most of the people I've talked with say that they find social 2
lying acceptable and necessary. They think it's the civilized way
for folks to behave. Without these little white lies, they say, our
relationships would be short and brutish and nasty. It's arrogant, they say, to insist on being so incorruptible and so brave
that you cause other people unnecessary embarrassment or
pain by compulsively assailing them with your honesty. I basically agree. What about you?

Will you say to people, when it simply isn't true, "I like your   3
new hairdo," "You're looking much better," "It's so nice to see
you," "I had a wonderful time"?

Will you praise hideous presents and homely kids?   4

Will you decline invitations with "We're busy that night—   5
so sorry we can't come," when the truth is you'd rather stay
home than dine with the So-and-sos?

And even though, as I do, you may prefer the polite eva-   6
sion of "You really cooked up a storm" instead of "The soup"—
which tastes like warmed-over coffee—"is wonderful," will
you, if you must, proclaim it wonderful?

There's one man I know who absolutely refuses to tell so-   7
cial lies. "I can't play that game," he says; "I'm simply not
made that way." And his answer to the argument that saying
nice things to someone doesn't cost anything is, "Yes, it does—
it destroys your credibility." Now, he won't, unsolicited, offer
his views on the painting you just bought, but you don't ask
his frank opinion unless you want *frank,* and his silence at those
moments when the rest of us liars are muttering, "Isn't it
lovely?" is, for the most part, eloquent enough. My friend does
not indulge in what he calls "flattery, false praise and mel-
lifluous comments." When others tell fibs he will not go along.
He says that social lying is lying, that little white lies are still
lies. And he feels that telling lies is morally wrong. What about
you?

PEACE-KEEPING LIES

Many people tell peace-keeping lies; lies designed to avoid   8
irritation or argument; lies designed to shelter the liar from possible blame or pain; lies (or so it is rationalized) designed to keep
trouble at bay without hurting anyone.

I tell these lies at times, and yet I always feel they're wrong.   9
I understand why we tell them, but still they feel wrong. And
whenever I lie so that someone won't disapprove of me or think
less of me or holler at me, I feel I'm a bit of a coward, I feel I'm
dodging responsibility, I feel . . . guilty. What about you?

Do you, when you're late for a date because you overslept, 10 say that you're late because you got caught in a traffic jam?

Do you, when you forget to call a friend, say that you called 11 several times but the line was busy?

Do you, when you didn't remember that it was your father's 12 birthday, say that his present must be delayed in the mail?

And when you're planning a weekend in New York City 13 and you're not in the mood to visit your mother, who lives there, do you conceal—with a lie, if you must—the fact that you'll be in New York? Or do you have the courage—or is it the cruelty?—to say, "I'll be in New York, but sorry—I don't plan on seeing you"?

(Dave and his wife Elaine have two quite different points 14 of view on this very subject. He calls her a coward. She says she's being wise. He says she must assert her right to visit New York sometimes and not see her mother. To which she always patiently replies: "Why should we have useless fights? My mother's too old to change. We get along much better when I lie to her.")

Finally, do you keep the peace by telling your husband lies 15 on the subject of money? Do you reduce what you really paid for your shoes? And in general do you find yourself ready, willing and able to lie to him when you make absurd mistakes or lose or break things?

"I used to have a romantic idea that part of intimacy was 16 confessing every dumb thing that you did to your husband. But after a couple of years of that," says Laura, "have I changed my mind!"

And having changed her mind, she finds herself telling 17 peace-keeping lies. And yes, I tell them too. What about you?

PROTECTIVE LIES

Protective lies are lies folks tell—often quite serious lies— 18 because they're convinced that the truth would be too damaging. They lie because they feel there are certain human values that supersede the wrong of having lied. They lie, not for personal gain, but because they believe it's for the good of the person they're lying to. They lie to those they love, to those who trust them most of all, on the grounds that breaking this trust is justified.

They may lie to their children on money or marital matters.   19

They may lie to the dying about the state of their health.   20

They may lie about adultery, and not—or so they insist—   21
to save their own hide, but to save the heart and the pride of the men they are married to.

They may lie to their closest friend because the truth about   22
her talents or son or psyche would be—or so they insist—utterly devastating.

I sometimes tell such lies, but I'm aware that it's quite pre-   23
sumptuous to claim I know what's best for others to know. That's called playing God. That's called manipulation and control. And we never can be sure, once we start to juggle lies, just where they'll land, exactly where they'll roll.

And furthermore, we may find ourselves lying in order to   24
back up the lies that are backing up the lie we initially told.

And furthermore—let's be honest—if conditions were re-   25
versed, we certainly wouldn't want anyone lying to us.

Yet, having said all that, I still believe that there are times   26
when protective lies must nonetheless be told. What about you?

If your Dad had a very bad heart and you had to tell him   27
some bad family news, which would you choose: to tell him the truth or to lie?

If your former husband failed to send his monthly child-   28
support check and in other ways behaved like a total rat, would you allow your children—who believed he was simply wonderful—to continue to believe that he was wonderful?

If your dearly beloved brother selected a wife whom you   29
deeply disliked, would you reveal your feelings or would you fake it?

And if you were asked, after making love, "And how was   30
that for you?" would you reply, if it wasn't too good, "Not too good"?

Now, some would call a sex lie unimportant, little more   31 than social lying, a simple act of courtesy that makes all human intercourse run smoothly. And some would say all sex lies are bad news and unacceptably protective. Because, says Ruth, "a man with an ego that fragile doesn't need your lies—he needs a psychiatrist." Still others feel that sex lies are indeed protective lies, more serious than simple social lying, and yet at times they tell them on the grounds that when it comes to matters sexual, everybody's ego is somewhat fragile.

"If most of the time things go well in sex," says Sue, "I think 32 you're allowed to dissemble when they don't. I can't believe it's good to say, 'Last night was four stars, darling, but tonight's performance rates only a half.' "

I'm inclined to agree with Sue. What about you?   33

TRUST-KEEPING LIES

Another group of lies are trust-keeping lies, lies that in- 34 volve triangulation, with *A* (that's you) telling lies to *B* on behalf of *C* (whose trust you'd promised to keep). Most people concede that once you've agreed not to betray a friend's confidence, you can't betray it, even if you must lie. But I've talked with people who don't want you telling them anything that they might be called on to lie about.

"I don't tell lies for myself," says Fran, "and I don't want to 35 have to tell them for other people." Which means, she agrees, that if her best friend is having an affair, she absolutely doesn't want to know about it.

"Are you saying," her best friend asks, "that if I went off 36 with a lover and I asked you to tell my husband I'd been with you, that you wouldn't lie for me, that you'd betray me?"

Fran is very pained but very adamant. "I wouldn't want to 37 betray you, so . . . don't ask me."

Fran's best friend is shocked. What about you?   38

Do you believe you can have close friends if you're not pre- 39 pared to receive their deepest secrets?

Do you believe you must always lie for your friends?   40

Do you believe, if your friend tells a secret that turns out to ₄₁ be quite immoral or illegal, that once you've promised to keep it, you must keep it?

And what if your friend were your boss—if you were per- ₄₂ haps one of the President's men—would you betray or lie for him over, say, Watergate?

As you can see, these issues get terribly sticky. ₄₃

It's my belief that once we've promised to keep a trust, we ₄₄ must tell lies to keep it. I also believe that we can't tell Watergate lies. And if these two statements strike you as quite contradictory, you're right—they're quite contradictory. But for now they're the best I can do. What about you?

Some say that truth will out and thus you might as well tell ₄₅ the truth. Some say you can't regain the trust that lies lose. Some say that even though the truth may never be revealed, our lies pervert and damage our relationships. Some say . . . well, here's what some of them have to say.

"I'm a coward," says Grace, "about telling close people im- ₄₆ portant, difficult truths. I find that I'm unable to carry it off. And so if something is bothering me, it keeps building up inside till I end up just not seeing them any more."

"I lie to my husband on sexual things, but I'm furious," ₄₇ says Joyce, "that he's too insensitive to know I'm lying."

"I suffer most from the misconception that children can't ₄₈ take the truth," says Emily. "But I'm starting to see that what's harder and more damaging for them is being told lies, is *not* being told the truth."

"I'm afraid," says Joan, "that we often wind up feeling a bit ₄₉ of contempt for the people we lie to."

And then there are those who have no talent for lying. ₅₀

"Over the years, I tried to lie," a friend of mine explained, ₅₁ "but I always got found out and I always got punished. I guess I gave myself away because I feel guilty about any kind of lying. It looks as if I'm stuck with telling the truth."

For those of us, however, who are good at telling lies, for ₅₂ those of us who lie and don't get caught, the question of whether or not to lie can be a hard and serious moral problem. I liked the remark of a friend of mine who said, "I'm willing to lie. But just as a last resort—the truth's always better."

"Because," he explained, "though others may completely 53 accept the lie I'm telling, I don't."

I tend to feel that way too.   54

What about you?   55

1981

CHAPTER 6

Comparison and Contrast

Grant and Lee: A Study in Contrasts

Bruce Catton

When Ulysses S. Grant and Robert E. Lee met in the parlor 1
of a modest house at Appomattox Court House, Virginia, on
April 9, 1865, to work out the terms for the surrender of Lee's
Army of Northern Virginia, a great chapter in American life
came to a close, and a great new chapter began.

These men were bringing the Civil War to its virtual finish. 2
To be sure, other armies had yet to surrender, and for a few days
the fugitive Confederate government would struggle desperately and vainly, trying to find some way to go on living now
that its chief support was gone. But in effect it was all over
when Grant and Lee signed the papers. And the little room
where they wrote out the terms was the scene of one of the
poignant, dramatic contrasts in American history.

They were two strong men, these oddly different generals, 3
and they represented the strengths of two conflicting currents
that, through them, had come into final collision.

Back of Robert E. Lee was the notion that the old aristocratic 4
concept might somehow survive and be dominant in American
life.

Lee was tidewater Virginia, and in his background were 5
family, culture, and tradition . . . the age of chivalry trans-

210

planted to a New World which was making its own legends and its own myths. He embodied a way of life that had come down through the age of knighthood and the English country squire. America was a land that was beginning all over again, dedicated to nothing much more complicated than the rather hazy belief that all men had equal rights, and should have an equal chance in the world. In such a land Lee stood for the feeling that it was somehow of advantage to human society to have a pronounced inequality in the social structure. There should be a leisure class, backed by ownership of land; in turn, society itself should be keyed to the land as the chief source of wealth and influence. It would bring forth (according to this ideal) a class of men with a strong sense of obligation to the community; men who lived not to gain advantage for themselves, but to meet the solemn obligations which had been laid on them by the very fact that they were privileged. From them the country would get its leadership; to them it could look for the higher values—of thought, of conduct, of personal deportment—to give it strength and virtue.

Lee embodied the noblest elements of this aristocratic ideal.   6
Through him, the landed nobility justified itself. For four years, the Southern states had fought a desperate war to uphold the ideals for which Lee stood. In the end, it almost seemed as if the Confederacy fought for Lee; as if he himself was the Confederacy . . . the best thing that the way of life for which the Confederacy stood could ever have to offer. He had passed into legend before Appomattox. Thousands of tired, underfed, poorly clothed Confederate soldiers, long-since past the simple enthusiasm of the early days of the struggle, somehow considered Lee the symbol of everything for which they had been willing to die. But they could not quite put this feeling into words. If the Lost Cause, sanctified by so much heroism and so many deaths, had a living justification, its justification was General Lee.

Grant, the son of a tanner on the Western frontier, was   7
everything Lee was not. He had come up the hard way, and embodied nothing in particular except the eternal toughness and sinewy fiber of the men who grew up beyond the mountains. He was one of a body of men who owed reverence and obei-

sance to no one, who were self-reliant to a fault, who cared hardly anything for the past but who had a sharp eye for the future.

These frontier men were the precise opposites of the tide- 8
water aristocrats. Back of them, in the great surge that had taken people over the Alleghenies and into the opening Western country, there was a deep, implicit dissatisfaction with a past that had settled into grooves. They stood for democracy, not from any reasoned conclusion about the proper ordering of human society, but simply because they had grown up in the middle of democracy and knew how it worked. Their society might have privileges, but they would be privileges each man had won for himself. Forms and patterns meant nothing. No man was born to anything, except perhaps to a chance to show how far he could rise. Life was competition.

Yet along with this feeling had come a deep sense of be- 9
longing to a national community. The Westerner who developed a farm, opened a shop or set up in business as a trader, could hope to prosper only as his own community prospered— and his community ran from the Atlantic to the Pacific and from Canada down to Mexico. If the land was settled, with towns and highways and accessible markets, he could better himself. He saw his fate in terms of the nation's own destiny. As its horizons expanded, so did his. He had, in other words, an acute dollars-and-cents stake in the continued growth and development of his country.

And that, perhaps, is where the contrast between Grant and 10
Lee becomes most striking. The Virginia aristocrat, inevitably, saw himself in relation to his own region. He lived in a static society which could endure almost anything except change. Instinctively, his first loyalty would go to the locality in which that society existed. He would fight to the limit of endurance to defend it, because in defending it he was defending everything that gave his own life its deepest meaning.

The Westerner, on the other hand, would fight with an 11
equal tenacity for the broader concept of society. He fought so because everything he lived by was tied to growth, expansion, and a constantly widening horizon. What he lived by would

survive or fall with the nation itself. He could not possibly stand by unmoved in the face of an attempt to destroy the Union. He would combat it with everything he had, because he could only see it as an effort to cut the ground out from under his feet.

So Grant and Lee were in complete contrast, representing 12
two diametrically opposed elements in American life. Grant was the modern man emerging; beyond him, ready to come on the stage, was the great age of steel and machinery, of crowded cities and a restless, burgeoning vitality. Lee might have ridden down from the old age of chivalry, lance in hand, silken banner fluttering over his head. Each man was the perfect champion of his cause, drawing both his strengths and his weaknesses from the people he led.

Yet it was not all contrast, after all. Different as they were— 13
in background, in personality, in underlying aspiration—these two great soldiers had much in common. Under everything else, they were marvelous fighters. Furthermore, their fighting qualities were really very much alike.

Each man had, to begin with, the great virtue of utter tenac- 14
ity and fidelity. Grant fought his way down the Mississippi Valley in spite of acute personal discouragement and profound military handicaps. Lee hung on in the trenches at Petersburg after hope itself had died. In each man there was an indomitable quality . . . the born fighter's refusal to give up as long as he can still remain on his feet and lift his two fists.

Daring and resourcefulness they had, too; the ability to 15
think faster and move faster than the enemy. These were the qualities which gave Lee the dazzling campaigns of Second Manassas and Chancellorsville and won Vicksburg for Grant.

Lastly, and perhaps greatest of all, there was the ability, at 16
the end, to turn quickly from war to peace once the fighting was over. Out of the way these two men behaved at Appomattox came the possibility of a peace of reconciliation. It was a possibility not wholly realized, in the years to come, but which did, in the end, help the two sections to become one nation again . . . after a war whose bitterness might have seemed to make such a reunion wholly impossible. No part of either man's life became him more than the part he played in their brief meeting

in the McLean house at Appomattox. Their behavior there put all succeeding generations of Americans in their debt. Two great Americans, Grant and Lee—very different, yet under everything very much alike. Their encounter at Appomattox was one of the great moments of American history.

1958

My Brother Shaman

Richard Selzer

In the cult of the Bhagavati, as it has been practiced in south- 1 ern India, there is a ritual in which two entranced shamans dressed in feathered costumes and massive headgear enter a circle of witnesses. All night long in the courtyard of a temple they lunge and thrust at each other, give shouts of defiance, make challenging gestures. It is all done to the sound of drums, conches and horns. Come daybreak, the goddess Kali "slays" the demon Darika, then plunges her hands into the very bowels of Darika, drinking of and smearing herself with blood. At last Kali withdraws from the field of battle having adorned herself with the intestines of the vanquished.

It is a far cry from the bloody trances of shamans to the 2 bloody acts of surgery. Or is it? Take away from Kali and Darika the disciplinary beat of tautened hide and the moaning of flutes, and you have . . . an emergency intestinal resection. The technique is there, the bravado, the zeal. Only lacking in surgery is the ecstasy.

In both surgery and shamanism the business is done largely 3 by the hands of the operator. The surgeon holds his scalpel, hemostat, forceps; the shaman, his amulet of bone, wood, metal. For each there is the hieratic honoring of ritual objects. The handling of these objects induces a feeling of tranquility and power. One's mind is nudged from the path of self-awareness into the pathless glade of the imagination. The nun, too, knows this. She tells her beads, and her heart is enkindled. Surely it is true that the handling of instruments is conducive to the kind of possession or devotion that is the mark of all three—nun, surgeon, shaman. The surgeon and the shaman understand that one must honor, revere and entreat one's tools. Both do their handiwork with a controlled vehemence most dramatically seen in those offshoots of Buddhism wherein the shaman ties his fingers in "knots," giving them a strange distorted appearance. These priests have an uncanny flexibility of their finger joints, each of which has a special name. During these maneuvers the shaman is possessed by finger spirits. He invokes the good spirits and repels the evil ones. Such hand poses, or mudras, seen in Buddhist iconography, are used in trancelike rituals to call down the gods to possess the shaman. In like manner the surgeon restrains his knife even as he gives it rein. He, too, is the medium between man and God.

The shaman has his drum which is the river of sound 4 through which he can descend to the Kingdom of Shadows to retrieve the soul of his tribesfellow. The surgeon listens to the electronic beep of the cardiac monitor, the regulated respiration of anesthesia, and he is comforted or warned. Even the operating table has somewhat the shape and size of the pagan altars I saw in a tiny sixth-century baptistry in the Provençal village of Vénasque. Upon these slabs beasts and, in certain instances, humans were laid open to appease the gods. Should one of these ancient pagans undergo resurrection and be brought to a modern operating room with its blazing lamps and opulence of linen and gleaming gadgetry, where masked and gowned figures dip their hands in and out of the body of someone who has been plunged into magical sleep, what else would he think but that he had happened upon a ritual sacrifice?

Nor is the toilet of decoration less elaborate for surgeon 5 than for shaman. Take the Washing of the Hands: Behold the surgeon at his ablutions. His lavabo is a deep sink, often of white porcelain, with a central faucet controlled by the knee. The soap he uses is thick and red as iodine. It is held in a nozzled bottle on the wall. The surgeon depresses a pedal on the floor. Once, twice, three times and collects in his cupped palm a puddle of the soap. There it would sit, lifeless, if he did not add a little water from the faucet and begin to brush. Self-containment is part of the nature of soap. Now, all at once, suds break as air and water are incorporated. Here and there in the play of the bristles, bubbles, first one, then another and another, lift from the froth and achieve levitation. For a moment each globule sways in front of the surgeon's dazzled eyes, but only long enough to give him its blessing before winking out. Meanwhile, the stern brush travels back and forth through the slush of forearms, raising wakes of gauze, scratching the skin . . . Oh, not to hurt or abrade, but tenderly, as one scratches the ears of a dog. At last the surgeon thrusts his hands into the stream of water. A dusky foam darkens the porcelain and fades like smoke. A moment later the sink is calm and white. The surgeon too is calm. And purified.

The washing of the hands, then, is at once a rational step in the achievement of sterile technique and a ritual act carried out under the glance of God by which one is made ready to behold, to perform. It is not wholly unlike the whirling of dervishes, or the to and fro rocking of the orthodox Jew at his prayers. The mask, cap, gown and gloves that the surgeon puts on prior to surgery echo, do they not, the phylacteries of this same Jew? Prophetic wisdom, if it will come at all, is most likely to come to one so sacredly trussed. By these simple acts of bathing and adorning, both surgeon and shaman are made receptacular.

Time was when, in order to become a shaman, one had to undergo an initiatory death and resurrection. The aspirant had to be taken to the sky or the netherworld; often he would be dismembered by spirits, cooked in a pot and eaten by them. Only then could he be born again as a shaman. No such rite of passage goes into the making of a surgeon, it is true, but there is something about the process of surgical training that is reminiscent of the sacred ur-drama after all. The modern surgical intern must undergo a long and arduous novitiate during which the subjugation of the will and spirit to the craft is virtually complete. After a number of years of abasement and humiliation he or she is led to a room where no one else is permitted. There is the donning of special raiment, the washing of the hands and, at last, the performance of secret rites before the open ark of the body. In this, surgery remains a hieratic pantomime marked by exorcism, propitiation and invocation. God dwells in operating rooms as He does everywhere. More than once I have surmised a presence . . . something between hearing and feeling. . . .

In the selection of students to enter medical school, I won- 8 der whether the present weight given to academic excellence in organic chemistry is justified. At least as valid a selection would be based upon the presence of a bat-shaped mole on the inner aspect of the thigh of the aspirant, or a specific conjunction of the planets on his birthday. Neither seems more prophetic than the other in the matter of intuition, compassion and ingenuity which form the trinity of doctorhood.

The shaman's journey through disorder and illness to health 9 has parallels to the surgeon's journey into the body. Both are like Jason setting out in the Argos, weathering many storms to return at last with the Golden Fleece. Or Galahad with the Holy Grail. The extirpated gallbladder, then, becomes the talisman of the surgeon's journey, the symbol of his hard-won manhood. What is different is that the surgeon practices inherited rites, while the shaman is susceptible to visions. Still, they both perform acts bent upon making chaos into cosmos.

Saint John of the Cross alludes to the mystic as a solitary 10 bird who must seek the heights, admit of no companionship even with its own kind, stretch out its beak into the air, and sing sweetly. I think of such a shaman soaring, plummeting, riding ecstatic thermals to the stars, tumbling head over heels, and at last descending among the fog of dreams. If, as it seems, the mark of the shaman was his ability to take flight, soaring to the sky or plummeting to the earth in search of his quarry, only the astronaut or the poet would now qualify.

Ever since Nietzsche delivered his stunning pronounce- 11 ment—"Dead are all the gods"—man has been forced to assume the burden of heroism without divine assistance. All the connections to the ancestral past have been severed. It is our rashest act. For no good can come to a race that refuses to acknowledge the living spirit of ancient kingdoms. Ritual has receded from the act of surgery. Only the flavor of it is left, giving, if not to the performers, then to the patients and to those forbidden to witness these events, a shiver of mysticism. Few and far between are the surgeons who consider what they do an encounter with the unknown. When all is said and done, I am left with the suspicion that we have gone too far in our arrogant drift from the priestly forebears of surgery. It is pleasing to imagine surgeons bending over their incisions with love, infusing them with the impalpable. Only then would the surgeon, like the shaman, turn himself into a small god and re-create the world.

1986

Talk in the Intimate Relationship: His and Hers

Deborah Tannen

Male-female conversation is cross-cultural communication.   1
Culture is simply a network of habits and patterns gleaned from past experience, and women and men have different past experiences. From the time they're born, they're treated differently, talked to differently, and talk differently as a result. Boys and girls grow up in different worlds, even if they grow up in the same house. And as adults they travel in different worlds, reinforcing patterns established in childhood. These cultural differences include different expectations about the role of talk in relationships and how it fulfills that role.

Everyone knows that as a relationship becomes long-term,   2
its terms change. But women and men often differ in how they expect them to change. Many women feel, "After all this time, you should know what I want without my telling you." Many men feel, "After all this time, we should be able to tell each other what we want."

These incongruent expectations capture one of the key differences between men and women. Communication is always a matter of balancing conflicting needs for involvement and independence. Though everyone has both these needs, women often have a relatively greater need for involvement, and men a relatively greater need for independence. Being understood without saying what you mean gives a payoff in involvement, and that is why women value it so highly.

If you want to be understood without saying what you mean explicitly in words, you must convey meaning somewhere else—in how words are spoken, or by metamessages. Thus it stands to reason that women are often more attuned than men to the metamessages of talk. When women surmise meaning in this way, it seems mysterious to men, who call it "women's intuition" (if they think it's right) or "reading things in" (if they think it's wrong). Indeed, it could be wrong, since metamessages are not on record. And even if it is right, there is still the question of scale: How significant are the metamessages that are there?

Metamessages are a form of indirectness. Women are more likely to be indirect, and to try to reach agreement by negotiation. Another way to understand this preference is that negotiation allows a display of solidarity, which women prefer to the display of power (even though the aim may be the same—getting what you want). Unfortunately, power and solidarity are bought with the same currency: Ways of talking intended to create solidarity have the simultaneous effect of framing power differences. When they think they're being nice, women often end up appearing deferential and unsure of themselves or of what they want.

When styles differ, misunderstandings are always rife. As their differing styles create misunderstandings, women and men try to clear them up by talking things out. These pitfalls are compounded in talks between men and women because they have different ways of going about talking things out, and different assumptions about the significance of going about it.

Sylvia and Harry celebrated their fiftieth wedding anniversary at a mountain resort. Some of the guests were at the resort for the whole weekend, others just for the evening of the celebration: a cocktail party followed by a sit-down dinner. The manager of the dining room approached Sylvia during dinner. "Since there's so much food tonight," he said, "and the hotel prepared a fancy dessert and everyone already ate at the cocktail party anyway, how about cutting and serving the anniversary cake at lunch tomorrow?" Sylvia asked the advice of the others at her table. All the men agreed: "Sure, that makes sense. Save the cake for tomorrow." All the women disagreed: "No, the party is tonight. Serve the cake tonight." The men were focusing on the message: the cake as food. The women were thinking of the metamessage: Serving a special cake frames an occasion as a celebration.

Why are women more attuned to metamessages? Because   8 they are more focused on involvement, that is, on relationships among people, and it is through metamessages that relationships among people are established and maintained. If you want to take the temperature and check the vital signs of a relationship, the barometers to check are its metamessages: what is said and how.

Everyone can see these signals, but whether or not we pay   9 attention to them is another matter—a matter of being sensitized. Once you are sensitized, you can't roll your antennae back in; they're stuck in the extended position.

When interpreting meaning, it is possible to pick up signals   10 that weren't intentionally sent out, like an innocent flock of birds on a radar screen. The birds are there—and the signals women pick up are there—but they may not mean what the interpreter thinks they mean. For example, Maryellen looks at Larry and asks, "What's wrong?" because his brow is furrowed. Since he was only thinking about lunch, her expression of concern makes him feel under scrutiny.

The difference in focus on messages and metamessages can   11 give men and women different points of view on almost any comment. Harriet complains to Morton, "Why don't you ask me how my day was?" He replies, "If you have something to tell me, tell me. Why do you have to be invited?" The reason is that she wants the metamessage of interest: evidence that he cares how her day was, regardless of whether or not she has something to tell.

A lot of trouble is caused between women and men by, of 12
all things, pronouns. Women often feel hurt when their partners
use "I" or "me" in a situation in which they would use "we" or
"us." When Morton announces, "I think I'll go for a walk," Harriet feels specifically uninvited, though Morton later claims she
would have been welcome to join him. She felt locked out by
his use of "I" and his omission of an invitation: "Would you like
to come?" Metamessages can be seen in what is not said as well
as what is said.

It's difficult to straighten out such misunderstandings be- 13
cause each one feels convinced of the logic of his or her position and the illogic—or irresponsibility—of the other's. Harriet
knows that she always asks Morton how his day was, and that
she'd never announce, "I'm going for a walk," without inviting
him to join her. If he talks differently to her, it must be that he
feels differently. But Morton wouldn't feel unloved if Harriet
didn't ask about his day, and he would feel free to ask, "Can I
come along?" if she announced she was taking a walk. So he
can't believe she is justified in feeling responses he knows he
wouldn't have.

These processes are dramatized with chilling yet absurdly 14
amusing authenticity in Jules Feiffer's play *Grown Ups*. To get
a closer look at what happens when men and women focus on
different levels of talk in talking things out, let's look at what
happens in this play.

Jake criticizes Louise for not responding when their daugh- 15
ter, Edie, called her. His comment leads to a fight even though
they're both aware that this one incident is not in itself important.

JAKE: Look, I don't care if it's important or not, when a kid calls
    its mother the mother should answer.
LOUISE: Now I'm a bad mother.
JAKE: I didn't say that.
LOUISE: It's in your stare.
JAKE: Is that another thing you know? My stare?

Louise ignores Jake's message—the question of whether or not
she responded when Edie called—and goes for the metamessage: his implication that she's a bad mother, which Jake insis-

tently disclaims. When Louise explains the signals she's reacting to, Jake not only discounts them but is angered at being held accountable not for what he said but for how he looked—his stare.

As the play goes on, Jake and Louise replay and intensify these patterns: 16

LOUISE: If I'm such a terrible mother, do you want a divorce?

JAKE: I do not think you're a terrible mother and no, thank you, I do not want a divorce. Why is it that whenever I bring up any difference between us you ask me if I want a divorce?

The more he denies any meaning beyond the message, the more she blows it up, the more adamantly he denies it, and so on:

JAKE: I have brought up one thing that you do with Edie that I don't think you notice that I have noticed for some time but which I have deliberately not brought up before because I had hoped you would notice it for yourself and stop doing it and also—frankly, baby, I have to say this—I knew if I brought it up we'd get into exactly the kind of circular argument we're in right now. And I wanted to avoid it. But I haven't and we're in it, so now, with your permission, I'd like to talk about it.

LOUISE: You don't see how that puts me down?

JAKE: What?

LOUISE: If you think I'm so stupid why do you go on living with me?

JAKE: *Dammit! Why can't anything ever be simple around here?!*

It can't be simple because Louise and Jake are responding to different levels of communication. As in Bateson's example of the dual-control electric blanket with crossed wires, each one intensifies the energy going to a different aspect of the problem. Jake tries to clarify his point by over-elaborating it, which gives Louise further evidence that he's condescending to her, making it even less likely that she will address his point rather than his condescension.

What pushes Jake and Louise beyond anger to rage is their different perspectives on metamessages. His refusal to admit that his statements have implications and overtones denies her 17 authority over her own feelings. Her attempts to interpret what he didn't say and put the metamessage into the message makes him feel she's putting words into his mouth—denying his authority over his own meaning.

The same thing happens when Louise tells Jake that he is being manipulated by Edie: 18

LOUISE: Why don't you ever make her come to see you? Why do you always go to her?

JAKE: You want me to play power games with a nine year old? I want her to know I'm interested in her. Someone around here has to show interest in her.

LOUISE: You love her more than I do.

JAKE: I didn't say that.

LOUISE: Yes, you did.

JAKE: You don't know how to listen. You have never learned how to listen. It's as if listening to you is a foreign language.

Again, Louise responds to his implication—this time, that he loves Edie more because he runs when she calls. And yet again, Jake cries literal meaning, denying he meant any more than he said.

Throughout their argument, the point to Louise is her feelings—that Jake makes her feel put down—but to him the point is her actions—that she doesn't always respond when Edie calls: 19

LOUISE: You talk about what I do to Edie, what do you think you do to me?

JAKE: This is not the time to go into what we do to each other.

Since she will talk only about the metamessage, and he will talk only about the message, neither can get satisfaction from their talk, and they end up where they started—only angrier: 20

JAKE: That's not the point!

LOUISE: It's my point.

JAKE: It's hopeless!

LOUISE: Then get a divorce.

American conventional wisdom (and many of our parents and English teachers) tell us that meaning is conveyed by words, so men who tend to be literal about words are supported by conventional wisdom. They may not simply deny but actually miss the cues that are sent by how words are spoken. If they sense something about it, they may nonetheless discount what they sense. After all, it wasn't said. Sometimes that's a dodge—a plausible defense rather than a gut feeling. But sometimes it is a sincere conviction. Women are also likely to doubt the reality of what they sense. If they don't doubt it in their guts, they nonetheless may lack the arguments to support their position and thus are reduced to repeating, "You said it. You did so." Knowing that metamessages are a real and fundamental part of communication makes it easier to understand and justify what they feel.

An article in a popular newspaper reports that one of the ₂₁ five most common complaints of wives about their husbands is "He doesn't listen to me anymore." Another is "He doesn't talk to me anymore." Political scientist Andrew Hacker noted that lack of communication, while high on women's lists of reasons for divorce, is much less often mentioned by men. Since couples are parties to the same conversations, why are women more dissatisfied with them than men? Because what they expect is different, as well as what they see as the significance of talk itself.

First, let's consider the complaint "He doesn't talk to me." ₂₂

One of the most common stereotypes of American men is ₂₃ the strong silent type. Jack Kroll, writing about Henry Fonda on the occasion of his death, used the phrases "quiet power," "abashed silences," "combustible catatonia," and "sense of power held in check." He explained that Fonda's goal was not to let anyone see "the wheels go around," not to let the "machinery" show. According to Kroll, the resulting silence was effective on stage but devastating to Fonda's family.

The image of a silent father is common and is often the ₂₄ model for the lover or husband. But what attracts us can become flypaper to which we are unhappily stuck. Many women find the strong silent type to be a lure as a lover but a lug as a husband. Nancy Schoenberger begins a poem with the lines "It was your silence that hooked me,/so like my father's." Adrienne Rich refers in a poem to the "husband who is frustratingly mute." Despite the initial attraction of such quintessentially male silence, it may begin to feel, to a woman in a long-term relationship, like a brick wall against which she is banging her head.

In addition to these images of male and female behavior—   25 both the result and the cause of them—are differences in how women and men view the role of talk in relationships as well as how talk accomplishes its purpose. These differences have their roots in the settings in which men and women learn to have conversations among their peers, growing up.

Children whose parents have foreign accents don't speak   26 with accents. They learn to talk like their peers. Little girls and little boys learn how to have conversations as they learn how to pronounce words from their playmates. Between the ages of five and fifteen, when children are learning to have conversations, they play mostly with friends of their own sex. So it's not surprising that they learn different ways of having and using conversations.

Anthropologists Daniel Maltz and Ruth Borker point out   27 that boys and girls socialize differently. Little girls tend to play in small groups or, even more common, in pairs. Their social life usually centers around a best friend, and friendships are made, maintained, and broken by talk—especially "secrets." If a little girl tells her friend's secret to another little girl, she may find herself with a new best friend. The secrets themselves may or may not be important, but the fact of telling them is all-important. It's hard for newcomers to get into these tight groups, but anyone who is admitted is treated as an equal. Girls like to play cooperatively; if they can't cooperate, the group breaks up.

Little boys tend to play in larger groups, often outdoors, and   28 they spend more time doing things than talking. It's easy for boys to get into the group, but not everyone is accepted as an equal. Once in the group, boys must jockey for their status in it. One of the most important ways they do this is through talk: verbal display such as telling stories and jokes, challenging and sidetracking the verbal displays of other boys, and withstanding other boys' challenges in order to maintain their own story—and status. Their talk is often competitive talk about who is best at what.

Feiffer's play is ironically named *Grown Ups* because adult 29 men and women struggling to communicate often sound like children: "You said so!" "I did not!" The reason is that when they grow up, women and men keep the divergent attitudes and habits they learned as children—which they don't recognize as attitudes and habits but simply take for granted as ways of talking.

Women want their partners to be a new and improved ver- 30 sion of a best friend. This gives them a soft spot for men who tell them secrets. As Jack Nicholson once advised a guy in a movie: "Tell her about your troubled childhood—that always gets 'em." Men expect to *do* things together and don't feel anything is missing if they don't have heart-to-heart talks all the time.

If they do have heart-to-heart talks, the meaning of those 31 talks may be opposite for men and women. To many women, the relationship is working as long as they can talk things out. To many men, the relationship isn't working out if they have to keep working it over. If she keeps trying to get talks going to save the relationship, and he keeps trying to avoid them because he sees them as weakening it, then each one's efforts to preserve the relationship appear to the other as reckless endangerment.

If talks (of any kind) do get going, men's and women's ideas 32 about how to conduct them may be very different. For example, Dora is feeling comfortable and close to Tom. She settles into a chair after dinner and begins to tell him about a problem at work. She expects him to ask questions to show he's interested; reassure her that he understands and that what she feels is normal; and return the intimacy by telling her a problem of his. Instead, Tom sidetracks her story, cracks jokes about it, questions her interpretation of the problem, and gives her advice about how to solve it and avoid such problems in the future.

All of these responses, natural to men, are unexpected to 33 women, who interpret them in terms of their own habits—negatively. When Tom comments on side issues or cracks jokes, Dora thinks he doesn't care about what she's saying and isn't really listening. If he challenges her reading of what went on, she feels he is criticizing her and telling her she's crazy, when what she wants is to be reassured that she's not. If he tells her how to solve the problem, it makes her feel as if she's the patient to his doctor—a metamessage of condescension, echoing male one-upmanship compared to the female etiquette of equality. Because he doesn't volunteer information about his problems, she feels he's implying he doesn't have any.

His way of responding to her bid for intimacy makes her 34 feel distant from him. She tries harder to regain intimacy the only way she knows how—by revealing more and more about herself. He tries harder by giving more insistent advice. The more problems she exposes, the more incompetent she feels, until they both see her as emotionally draining and problem-ridden. When his efforts to help aren't appreciated, he wonders why she asks for his advice if she doesn't want to take it. . . .

When women talk about what seems obviously interesting 35 to them, their conversations often include reports of conversations. Tone of voice, timing, intonation, and wording are all re-created in the telling in order to explain—dramatize, really—the experience that is being reported. If men tell about an incident and give a brief summary instead of recreating what was said and how, the women often feel that the essence of the experience is being omitted. If the woman asks, "What exactly did he say?," and "How did he say it?," the man probably can't remember. If she continues to press him, he may feel as if he's being grilled.

All these different habits have repercussions when the man 36 and the woman are talking about their relationship. He feels out of his element, even one down. She claims to recall exactly what he said, and what she said, and in what sequence, and she wants him to account for what he said. He can hardly account for it since he has forgotten exactly what was said—if not the whole conversation. She secretly suspects he's only pretending not to remember, and he secretly suspects that she's making up the details.

One woman reported such a problem as being a matter of 37 her boyfriend's poor memory. It is unlikely, however, that his problem was poor memory in general. The question is what types of material each person remembers or forgets.

Frances was sitting at her kitchen table talking to Edward, 38 when the toaster did something funny. Edward began to explain why it did it. Frances tried to pay attention, but very early in his explanation, she realized she was completely lost. She felt very stupid. And indications were that he thought so too.

Later that day they were taking a walk. He was telling her 39 about a difficult situation in his office that involved a complex network of interrelationships among a large number of people. Suddenly he stopped and said, "I'm sure you can't keep track of all these people." "Of course I can," she said, and she retraced his story with all the characters in place, all the details right. He was genuinely impressed. She felt very smart.

How could Frances be both smart and stupid? Did she have 40 a good memory or a bad one? Frances's and Edward's abilities to follow, remember, and recount depended on the subject— and paralleled her parents' abilities to follow and remember. Whenever Frances told her parents about people in her life, her mother could follow with no problem, but her father got lost as soon as she introduced a second character. "Now who was that?" he'd ask. "Your boss?" "No, my boss is Susan. This was my friend." Often he'd still be in the previous story. But whenever she told them about her work, it was her mother who would get lost as soon as she mentioned a second step: "That was your tech report?" "No, I handed my tech report in last month. This was a special project."

Frances's mother and father, like many men and women, 41 had honed their listening and remembering skills in different arenas. Their experience talking to other men and other women gave them practice in following different kinds of talk.

Knowing whether and how we are likely to report events 42 later influences whether and how we pay attention when they happen. As women listen to and take part in conversations, knowing they may talk about them later makes them more likely to pay attention to exactly what is said and how. Since most men aren't in the habit of making such reports, they are less likely to pay much attention at the time. On the other hand, many women aren't in the habit of paying attention to scientific explanations and facts because they don't expect to have to perform in public by reciting them—just as those who aren't in the habit of entertaining others by telling jokes "can't" remember jokes they've heard, even though they listened carefully enough to enjoy them.

So women's conversations with their women friends keep 43 them in training for talking about their relationships with men, but many men come to such conversations with no training at all—and an uncomfortable sense that this really isn't their event.

Most of us place enormous emphasis on the importance of 44 a primary relationship. We regard the ability to maintain such relationships as a sign of mental health—our contemporary metaphor for being a good person.

Yet our expectations of such relationships are nearly— 45 maybe in fact—impossible. When primary relationships are between women and men, male-female differences contribute to the impossibility. We expect partners to be both romantic interests and best friends. Though women and men may have fairly similar expectations for romantic interests, obscuring their differences when relationships begin, they have very different ideas about how to be friends, and these are the differences that mount over time.

In conversations between friends who are not lovers, small 46 misunderstandings can be passed over or diffused by breaks in contact. But in the context of a primary relationship, differences can't be ignored, and the pressure cooker of continued contact keeps both people stewing in the juice of accumulated minor misunderstandings. And stylistic differences are sure to cause misunderstandings—not, ironically, in matters such as sharing values and interests or understanding each other's philosophies of life. These large and significant yet palpable issues can be talked about and agreed on. It is far harder to achieve congruence—and much more surprising and troubling that it is hard—in the simple day-to-day matters of the automatic rhythms and nuances of talk. Nothing in our backgrounds or in the media (the present-day counterpart to religion or grandparents' teachings) prepares us for this failure. If two people share so much in terms of point of view and basic values, how can they continually get into fights about insignificant matters?

If you find yourself in such a situation and you don't know 47 about differences in conversational style, you assume something's wrong with your partner, or you for having chosen your partner. At best, if you are forward thinking and generous minded, you may absolve individuals and blame the relationship. But if you know about differences in conversational style, you can accept that there are differences in habits and assumptions about how to have conversation, show interest, be considerate, and so on. You may not always correctly interpret your partner's intentions, but you will know that if you get a negative impression, it may not be what was intended—and neither are your responses unfounded. If he says he really is interested even though he doesn't seem to be, maybe you should believe what he says and not what you sense.

Sometimes explaining assumptions can help. If a man starts   48
to tell a woman what to do to solve her problem, she may say, "Thanks for the advice but I really don't want to be told what to do. I just want you to listen and say you understand." A man might want to explain, "If I challenge you, it's not to prove you wrong; it's just my way of paying attention to what you're telling me." Both may try either or both to modify their ways of talking and to try to accept what the other does. The important thing is to know that what seem like bad intentions may really be good intentions expressed in a different conversational style. We have to give up our conviction that, as Robin Lakoff put it, "Love means never having to say 'What do you mean?' "

1986

Two Views of the Mississippi

Mark Twain

Now when I had mastered the language of this water, and   1
had come to know every trifling feature that bordered the great river as familiarly as I knew the letters of the alphabet, I had made a valuable acquisition. But I had lost something, too. I had

lost something which could never be restored to me while I lived. All the grace, the beauty, the poetry, had gone out of the majestic river! I still keep in mind a certain wonderful sunset which I witnessed when steamboating was new to me. A broad expanse of the river was turned to blood; in the middle distance the red hue brightened into gold, through which a solitary log came floating black and conspicuous; in one place a long, slanting mark lay sparkling upon the water; in another the surface was broken by boiling, tumbling rings, that were as many-tinted as an opal; where the ruddy flush was faintest, was a smooth spot that was covered with graceful circles and radiating lines, ever so delicately traced; the shore on our left was densely wooded, and the somber shadow that fell from this forest was broken in one place by a long, ruffled trail that shone like silver; and high above the forest wall a clean-stemmed dead tree waved a single leafy bough that glowed like a flame in the unobstructed splendor that was flowing from the sun. There were graceful curves, reflected images, woody heights, soft distances; and over the whole scene, far and near, the dissolving lights drifted steadily, enriching it every passing moment with new marvels of coloring.

I stood like one bewitched. I drank it in, in a speechless rapture. The world was new to me, and I had never seen anything like this at home. But as I have said, a day came when I began to cease from noting the glories and the charms which the moon and the sun and the twilight wrought upon the river's face; another day came when I ceased altogether to note them. Then, if that sunset scene had been repeated, I should have looked upon it without rapture, and should have commented upon it, inwardly, after this fashion: "This sun means that we are going to have wind to-morrow; that floating log means that the river is rising, small thanks to it; that slanting mark on the water refers to a bluff reef which is going to kill somebody's steamboat one of these nights, if it keeps on stretching out like that; those tumbling 'boils' show a dissolving bar and a changing channel there; the lines and circles in the slick water over yonder are a warning that that troublesome place is shoaling up dangerously; that silver streak in the shadow of the forest is the 'break' from a new snag, and he has located himself in the very best place he could have found to fish for steamboats; that tall dead tree, with a single living branch, is not going to last long, and then how is a body ever going to get through this blind place at night without the friendly old landmark?"

No, the romance and beauty were all gone from the river.   3 All the value any feature of it had for me now was the amount of usefulness it could furnish toward compassing the safe piloting of a steamboat. Since those days, I have pitied doctors from my heart. What does the lovely flush in a beauty's cheek mean to a doctor but a "break" that ripples above some deadly disease? Are not all her visible charms sown thick with what are to him the signs and symbols of hidden decay? Does he ever see her beauty at all, or doesn't he simply view her professionally, and comment upon her unwholesome condition all to himself? And doesn't he sometimes wonder whether he has gained most or lost most by learning his trade?

1883

The Rewards of Living
a Solitary Life

May Sarton

The other day an acquaintance of mine, a gregarious and   1 charming man, told me he had found himself unexpectedly alone in New York for an hour or two between appointments. He went to the Whitney and spent the "empty" time looking at things in solitary bliss. For him it proved to be a shock nearly as great as falling in love to discover that he could enjoy himself so much alone.

What had he been afraid of, I asked myself? That, sud-   2 denly alone, he would discover that he bored himself, or that there was, quite simply, no self there to meet? But having taken the plunge, he is now on the brink of adventure; he is about to be launched into his own inner space, space as immense, unexplored and sometimes frightening as outer space to the astronaut. His every perception will come to him with a new freshness and, for a time, seem startlingly original. For anyone who can see things for himself with a naked eye becomes, for a moment or two, something of a genius. With another human being present vision becomes double vision, inevitably. We are busy wondering, what does my companion see or think of this, and what do I think of it? The original impact gets lost, or diffused.

"Music I heard with you was more than music." Exactly.   3
And therefore music *itself* can only be heard alone. Solitude is the salt of personhood. It brings out the authentic flavor of every experience.

"Alone one is never lonely: the spirit adventures, walk-   4
ing / In a quiet garden, in a cool house, abiding single there."

Loneliness is most acutely felt with other people, for with   5
others, even with a lover sometimes, we suffer from our differences of taste, temperament, mood. Human intercourse often demands that we soften the edge of perception, or withdraw at the very instant of personal truth for fear of hurting, or of being inappropriately present, which is to say naked, in a social situation. Alone we can afford to be wholly whatever we are, and to feel whatever we feel absolutely. That is a great luxury!

For me the most interesting thing about a solitary life, and   6
mine has been that for the last twenty years, is that it becomes increasingly rewarding. When I can wake up and watch the sun rise over the ocean, as I do most days, and know that I have an entire day ahead, uninterrupted, in which to write a few pages, take a walk with my dog, lie down in the afternoon for a long think (why does one think better in a horizontal position?), read and listen to music, I am flooded with happiness.

I am lonely only when I am overtired, when I have worked   7
too long without a break, when for the time being I feel empty and need filling up. And I am lonely sometimes when I come back home after a lecture trip, when I have seen a lot of people

and talked a lot, and am full to the brim with experience that
needs to be sorted out.

Then for a little while the house feels huge and empty, and   8
I wonder where my self is hiding. It has to be recaptured slowly
by watering the plants, perhaps, and looking again at each one
as though it were a person, by feeding the two cats, by cooking
a meal.

It takes a while, as I watch the surf blowing up in fountains   9
at the end of the field, but the moment comes when the world
falls away, and the self emerges again from the deep unconscious, bringing back all I have recently experienced to be explored and slowly understood, when I can converse again with
my hidden powers, and so grow, and so be renewed, till death
do us part.

1946

Neat People vs. Sloppy People

Suzanne Britt

I've finally figured out the difference between neat people   1
and sloppy people. The distinction is, as always, moral. Neat
people are lazier and meaner than sloppy people.

Sloppy people, you see, are not really sloppy. Their sloppi-   2
ness is merely the unfortunate consequence of their extreme
moral rectitude. Sloppy people carry in their mind's eye a heavenly vision, a precise plan, that is so stupendous, so perfect, it
can't be achieved in this world or the next.

Sloppy people live in Never-Never Land. Someday is their   3
métier. Someday they are planning to alphabetize all their books
and set up home catalogs. Someday they will go through their
wardrobes and mark certain items for tentative mending and
certain items for passing on to relatives of similar shape and
size. Someday sloppy people will make family scrapbooks into

which they will put newspaper clippings, postcards, locks of hair, and the dried corsage from their senior prom. Someday they will file everything on the surface of their desks, including the cash receipts from coffee purchases at the snack shop. Someday they will sit down and read all the back issues of *The New Yorker*.

For all these noble reasons and more, sloppy people never   4
get neat. They aim too high and wide. They save everything, planning someday to file, order, and straighten out the world. But while these ambitious plans take clearer and clearer shape in their heads, the books spill from the shelves onto the floor, the clothes pile up in the hamper and closet, the family mementos accumulate in every drawer, the surface of the desk is buried under mounds of paper and the unread magazines threaten to reach the ceiling.

Sloppy people can't bear to part with anything. They give   5
loving attention to every detail. When sloppy people say they're going to tackle the surface of the desk, they really mean it. Not a paper will go unturned; not a rubber band will go unboxed. Four hours or two weeks into the excavation, the desk looks exactly the same, primarily because the sloppy person is meticulously creating new piles of papers with new headings and scrupulously stopping to read all the old book catalogs before he throws them away. A neat person would just bulldoze the desk.

Neat people are bums and clods at heart. They have cava-   6
lier attitudes toward possessions, including family heirlooms. Everything is just another dust-catcher to them. If anything collects dust, it's got to go and that's that. Neat people will toy with the idea of throwing the children out of the house just to cut down on the clutter.

Neat people don't care about process. They like results.   7
What they want to do is get the whole thing over with so they can sit down and watch the rasslin' on TV. Neat people operate on two unvarying principles: Never handle any item twice, and throw everything away.

The only thing messy in a neat person's house is the trash   8
can. The minute something comes to a neat person's hand, he

will look at it, try to decide if it has immediate use and, finding none, throw it in the trash.

Neat people are especially vicious with mail. They never go 9 through their mail unless they are standing directly over a trash can. If the trash can is beside the mailbox, even better. All ads, catalogs, pleas for charitable contributions, church bulletins and money-saving coupons go straight into the trash can without being opened. All letters from home, postcards from Europe, bills and paychecks are opened, immediately responded to, then dropped in the trash can. Neat people keep their receipts only for tax purposes. That's it. No sentimental salvaging of birthday cards or the last letter a dying relative ever wrote. Into the trash it goes.

Neat people place neatness above everything, even eco- 10 nomics. They are incredibly wasteful. Neat people throw away several toys every time they walk through the den. I knew a neat person once who threw away a perfectly good dish drainer be- cause it had mold on it. The drainer was too much trouble to wash. And neat people sell their furniture when they move. They will sell a La-Z-Boy recliner while you are reclining in it.

Neat people are no good to borrow from. Neat people buy 11 everything in expensive little single portions. They get their flour and sugar in two-pound bags. They wouldn't consider clipping a coupon, saving a leftover, reusing plastic nondairy whipped cream containers or rinsing off tin foil and draping it over the unmoldy dish drainer. You can never borrow a neat person's newspaper to see what's playing at the movies. Neat people have the paper all wadded up and in the trash by 7:05 A.M.

Neat people cut a clean swath through the organic as well 12 as the inorganic world. People, animals, and things are all one to them. They are so insensitive. After they've finished with the pantry, the medicine cabinet, and the attic, they will throw out the red geranium (too many leaves), sell the dog (too many fleas), and send the children off to boarding school (too many scuffmarks on the hardwood floors).

1983

At the Mercy of the Cure

Mark Mathabane

Upon returning to Dowling in the new year, 1982, I found   1
a letter from home waiting for me with the miraculous news:
my mother had finally been cured of her insanity. I was over-
whelmed with joy. The contents of the letter related how Aunt
Queen, the *isangoma*, had spent over a year treating my mother.
She was said to have used *muti* (tribal medicine), consisting of
special herbs, bark, and roots—and divination, a seeing into the
past and future using bones.

Apparently my mother's kindness had done her in. While   2
in South Africa she had, against my protestations and those of
the family, taken in as boarders from the Giyani homeland in
the Northern Transvaal a tall, raw-boned *nyanga* (medicine
man) with bloodshot eyes, named Mathebula, and his family of
five. They had nowhere else to go. The shack became home for
about fifteen people; some slept under the tables, others curled
up in corners and near the stove; there was no privacy. My
mother had made it clear that their moving in with us was only
a temporary measure, to provide them a roof over their heads
while they hunted for their own shack. When months passed
without the Mathebulas making any attempts at finding alternative housing, my mother had politely requested them to
leave. This angered the wizard, a proud and chauvinistic man.
Nonetheless he speedily constructed a shack in one of the rat-
infested alleyways. But he never forgave my mother.

From strands of my mother's hair and pieces of her cloth-   3
ing, which he had gathered while he lived in our house, he al-
legedly concocted his voodoo and drove my mother mad. It
took Aunt Queen almost a year to piece together what she
deemed a "dastardly plot." Daily, out in the yard, under the hot
African sun, with my mother seated cross-legged across from
her, my aunt shook bones and tossed them onto the ground.
From interpreting their final positions she believed that she
was able to name the sorcerer and the method he used to be-

witch my mother. To a Western mind this of course sounds incredible and primitive. But witchcraft is a time-honored tradition among many African tribes, where convenient scapegoats
are always blamed for events which, through limited knowledge and technology, seem inexplicable. Belief in witchcraft
can be compared to a Westerner's belief in astrology holding answers to man's future and fate.

"Now you know the truth," Aunt Queen said to my mother   4
at the end of her confinement, when she was finally cured. The
two spoke in Tsonga. "What do you want me to do?"

"Protect my family from further mischief."   5

"Is that all?"   6

"That's all."   7

"Don't you want revenge? Are you simply going to let him   8
go scot-free?"

"I'm not a witch. I'm a child of God. I harbor no malice to- 9
ward him or his family. I seek no revenge." My mother, despite
her belief in witchcraft, still considered the Christian God to be
all-powerful. This position of course had its contradictions, and
since this episode occurred I have pointed them out to her from
time to time. She has modified her beliefs and is now more
under the sway of Christianity.

"But your ancestors must be satisfied," Aunt Queen said.   10
"And what about the pain he caused you? Do you know that
he intended to kill you?"

"But Christ prevented that. He led me to you and gave you   11
the power to cure me."

"You know, Mudjaji [my mother's maiden name], you're so   12
loving that it's impossible for me to understand why anyone
would want to harm you. The only thing left for me to do to
complete your cure and prevent a relapse is to send the mischief
back to its perpetrator." It was believed that no cure of witchcraft was complete until the black magic had reverted to the sorcerer.

"Please don't do anything that would harm him or his fam-   13
ily," my mother pleaded.

"The gods will decide," Aunt Queen said.   14

Two weeks after my mother returned to Alexandra, the sor-   15 cerer's favorite son was stabbed to death during an argument in a *shebeen*. Hardly had he been buried when another of his sons was stabbed to death by *tsotsis* (gangsters) during a robbery and dumped in a ditch. My mother felt remorse over the deaths and grieved for the sorcerer's family. Aunt Queen told her that there was nothing she could have done to prevent their fate.

Here I was in America, in the heart of Western civilization itself, having to grapple with the reality or unreality of witchcraft. I remember how my mother's incredible story tested my "civilized mentality," my Western education, my dependency on reason, my faith in science and philosophy. But in the end I realized that her insanity, of course, had rational causes, just as did Uncle Piet's gambling, matrimonial problems, my father's alcoholism, and the family's poverty—all of which they tended to blame on witchcraft. Either my mother's undiagnosed and untreated diabetes or the oppressive conditions under which she lived, or a combination of the two, had deranged her. Aunt Queen was the tribal equivalent of a shrink. Her "magical" treatments of diseases owed much to the power of suggestion and her keen knowledge of the medicinal effects of certain herbs, bark, leaves, and roots, from which, it has been discovered, a good deal of Western medicine has gained real remedies. As for the deaths of the Wizard's sons, this was, of course, pure coincidence, since Alexandra, especially the neighborhood in which my family lived, was an extremely violent place: on one weekend over a dozen murders were committed.

I realized all this from the knowledge I had gained since coming to America and discovering that there was a branch of medicine of which I had been completely ignorant while I lived in South Africa: psychoanalysis and psychiatry. The inhuman suffering experienced by blacks under apartheid had devastating effects on their mental and physical well-being. Given the primitive state of health care in the ghettos, endemic illiteracy, and the sway of tribal beliefs, my mother and most blacks were ignorant of causal relationships. They therefore blamed witchcraft for mental illnesses like schizophrenia and paranoia; diseases like malnutrition and tuberculosis; problems like unem-

ployment, alcoholism, and gambling; and unlucky coinci-
dences, such as being arrested during a pass raid while neighbors escaped, or being fired from a job. Their lack of access to
qualified medical doctors, psychotherapists, and social workers forced them to rely on the dubious and often dangerous
"cures" of *isangomas*, especially since such "cures" at least offered the victim much-needed psychological relief.

Superstition is present in Western societies as well, as-   18
trology being one example. Some people also blame their misfortunes on the Devil. And many govern their lives through
card-reading and palmistry, and rely on charlatans to cure
them of cancer, AIDS, blindness, varicose veins, and other diseases. Until education dispelled my ignorance and fortified my
reason I was to a degree superstitious and believed in witchcraft.

The psychological problems experienced by blacks in South   19
African ghettos are somewhat similar to those experienced by
inmates of concentration camps during the Second World War.
From Death-Camp to Existentialism, by Viktor E. Frankl, explains
how psychotic behavior can become a "normal" way of life, a
means of survival, for helpless people whose sense of identity
and self-worth are under constant attack by an all-powerful op-
pressor. Jews in concentration camps were at the mercy of their
Nazi guards, just as blacks in the ghettos of South Africa are at
the mercy of apartheid's Gestapo-like police. Some victims of
oppression even come to identify with their oppressors and
persecute with relish their own kind. There are cases of Jews,
known as Capos, who, in return for special privileges like food
and cigarettes doled out by SS guards, treated other Jews sadis-
tically and even herded them into crematoriums and gas chambers. In South Africa black policemen, in return for special privileges such as better housing, residential permits, and passbooks
for relatives, shoot and kill unarmed black protesters, torture
them in jail, uproot black communities under the homeland
policy, and launch brutal raids into the ghettos to enforce
Kafkaesque apartheid laws. Such are the evil consequences of
unbearable pressures.

1989

Discordant Fruit

Lydia Minatoya

Once, in a cross-cultural training manual, I came across a   1
riddle. In Japan, a young man and woman meet and fall in love.
They decide they would like to marry. The young man goes to
his mother and describes the situation. "I will visit the girl's family," says the mother. "I will seek their approval." After some
time, a meeting between mothers is arranged. The boy's mother
goes to the girl's ancestral house. The girl's mother has prepared
tea. The women talk about the fine spring weather: will this be
a good year for cherry blossoms? The girl's mother serves a
plate of fruit. Bananas are sliced and displayed in an exquisite
design. Marriage never is mentioned. After the tea, the boy's
mother goes home. "I am so sorry," she tells her son. "The other
family has declined the match."

In the training manual, the following question was posed.   2
How did the boy's mother know the marriage was unacceptable? That is easy, I thought when I read it. To a Japanese, the
answer is obvious. Bananas do not go well with tea.

All of my life, I have been fluent in communicating through   3
discordant fruit.

"You're not serious about applying to be a foreign exchange   4
student!" exclaims a high school teacher. "The point is to spon-
sor an *American* kid." On my application, I deliberately misspell
the teacher's name. I cross it out with an unsightly splotch.
"Take that you mean narrow man," I gloat in triumph.

"Your mother is so deferential, so *quiet*," says a boyfriend.   5
"Women like that drive me crazy." *His* mother is an attorney.
That morning, I scorch his scrambled eggs. I hide the sports section of the Sunday news. "No insight, loud-mouth fool," I mutter. Vengeance, I think, is mine.

The Japanese raise their daughters differently than their   6
sons. "*Gambatte!*" they exhort their sons. "Have courage, be like
the carp, swim upstream!" "*Kiotsukete*," they caution their
daughters. "Be careful, be modest, keep safe."

In the old stories, men are warriors: fierce and bold. But a lady   7
never lunges to slash the throat of an assailant. Instead, she writes
a poem about harsh winter; how it can snap a slender stalk. Then
she kills *herself* in protest. How the old stories galled me!

My mother was raised in a world such as this, in a house of   8
tradition and myth. And although she has traveled across continents, oceans, and time, although she considers herself a modern woman—a believer in the sunlight of science—it is a world
that surrounds her still. Feudal Japan floats around my mother.
Like an unwanted pool of ectoplasm, it quivers with supernatural might. It followed her into our American home and gov-
erned my girlhood life.

And so, I was shaped. In that feudal code, all females were   9
silent and yielding. Even their possessions were accorded more
rights. For, if mistreated, belongings were granted an annual
holiday when they could spring into life and complain.

And so, I was haunted. If I left my clothes on the floor, or   10
my bicycle in the rain; if I yanked on my comb with roughness;
if it splintered and lost its teeth (and I did these things often and
deliberately, trying to challenge their spell); then my misdeeds
pursued me in dreams.

Emitting a hair-raising keening, my mittens would mourn   11
for their mates. The floors I had scuffed, the doors I had
slammed, herded me into the street. Broken dishes and dulled
scissors joined them to form a large, shrill, and reproachful parade of dutiful ill-treated items. How I envied white children
and the simple absolution of a spanking.

While other children were learning that in America you get   12
what you ask for, I was being henpecked by inanimate objects.
While other children were learning to speak their minds, I was
locked in a losing struggle for dominance with my clothing, my
toys, and my tools.

The objects meant me no harm; they meant to humble and   13
educate me. "Ownership," they told me "means obligation,
caretaking, reciprocity." And although I was a resistant student, in time I was trained. Well-maintained, my possessions
live long, useful, and mercifully quiet lives of service.

The consequence, however, is that I cannot view my be-   14

longings as mere conveniences. They cannot serve as simple timesavers. For me, acquisitiveness holds little allure. The indebtedness is much too great.

I am a woman who apologizes to her furniture. "Excuse 15 me," I say when I bump into a chair. My voice resonates with solicitude. In America, such behavior is viewed as slightly loony.

I am a woman caught between standards of East and West. 16 "I disagree," I say to elders, to the men in my life. My voice rises and cracks with shame. "Razor-tongue," relatives say with the pleasure of knowing. "No wonder she still is unmarried."

All these incongruities came flooding back while visiting 17 my Japanese family. The pull to be deferent. The push to be bold. The tension and richness between.

In the evening, after we left the patriarch's house, Sachiko- 18 san prepared a feast. She kneeled before us, cooking a huge skillet of sukiyaki. She plucked plump morsels of tender beef from the pot and popped them onto my plate. Her teenaged daughters slipped shyly in and out of the room, bearing flasks of sake and platters of sushi.

Tadao-san, Yoshi, Mark, and I were seated at the table. 19 Sachiko-san and the girls ate in the kitchen. "Where are the other women?" Mark asked Yoshi. "Yuri-chan is the guest," he replied. "She is being paid the house's high honor."

Loosened by the sake, chaffing from days of communicat- 20 ing only with me or through me, Mark bombarded Yoshi with questions. Did Yoshi like American rock and roll? Who were his favorite performers?

Uncomfortable with being the focus of attention, Yoshi at- 21 tempted to generalize every query. "How familiar are Japanese youth with popular American music?" he translated for Tadao-san.

But Tadao-san was not fooled. Excluded in his own house, 22 shunned in favor of his translator, Tadao-san grew increasingly irritable.

"How long has this one been riding autobikes?" he sud- 23

denly interjected. "Has he ever had an accident? Would he know how to make repairs should the autobike become disabled?"

At first, the American in me grinned. Clearly Tadao-san 24 had grown weary of his subordinate role. He was asserting his authority. "How are you providing for Yuri-chan's safety?" his questions implied. "Do not forget you are welcome only in so far as you provide service to members of my house."

But quickly, the Japanese in me surfaced. The evening was 25 not going smoothly and I was responsible.

"You're putting Yoshi on the spot!" I hissed into Mark's ear. 26 "After all, he is not your host. Address your comments to the household head and try to act with more deference!"

"No kidding!" exclaimed Mark. He thought everything had 27 been going along just fine.

I smiled apologetically at Yoshi and Tadao-san. My annoy- 28 ance and bossy instructiveness had not gone unnoticed. I flushed mightily. I knew my behavior was most unseemly for a lady.

"So Tadao-san," said Mark heartily, "what do you think 29 about all these protests of American military presence in Japan?"

Yoshi reeled in horror. How could he translate, with deli- 30 cacy, such an openly confrontational question?

"Don't you think it's a little, uhmmm, *ungrateful?*" contin- 31 ued Mark. "After all, by picking up the bill for your country's defense, America has allowed Japan to become an economic competitor."

"How can you be so rude!" I croaked in anger. I staggered 32 under the responsibility of having brought a boor into the ancestral house.

"Relax. You're overreacting," snapped Mark. "Besides, this 33 is *my* conversation." Mark was growing tired of my conduct coaching. I could hardly blame him. Only a few days earlier, as we sat in a coffee shop and I instructed him on the proper method of ordering, I had overheard a comment. *"Rimokon,"* a woman had murmured to her companion. She had nodded in

Mark's direction. *Rimokon* is a shortened form of *rimoto-kontororu*. It is the Japanese pronunciation of remote control: slang for a henpecked man.

Tadao-san looked questioningly at Yoshi. What was the   34
meaning of all this clamor? Yoshi rushed to translate.

"This is a most difficult question," said Tadao-san after   35
hearing an edited translation.

I cringed. When a Japanese says a question is difficult he is   36
requesting release from an uncomfortable situation.

"I work on a military base," said Mark, "and the sentiment   37
is that Japan is complaining about a free ride."

I wished we never had left the subject of rock and roll. I   38
wished I were not the honored guest. I wished I was with
Sachiko-san, in the refuge of the kitchen.

Tadao-san and Yoshi caucused for a while. "Some Japanese   39
believe that America's motives are not fully benevolent," said
Yoshi. His voice hesitated with the task of defusing the situation. "They say Americans do not fully view Asians as people.
Japan and her people are expendable. Perhaps the point is not
to defend Japan but rather to move the site of possible conflict.
Asia may be a buffer zone. If war is based from Japan, South
Korea, or the Philippines, the soil and civilians of these countries, not America, would be the first at risk."

"I don't know about that," muttered Mark.   40

"In each country, there are prejudices," said Tadao-san.   41
"We Japanese are prejudiced against the Koreans. I have read
your history. Has there not been discrimination against Japanese in America? Is there not discrimination today?"

"No," said Mark flatly.   42

"Of course there is!" I cried. We argued hotly for a minute.   43
Then, remembering that I was trying to act like a credit to my
mother's upbringing, I demurred.

"Mark and I share slight disagreement about this point," I   44
murmured with sudden modesty.

Perhaps Mark was right. Perhaps I was overreacting. Per-   45
haps among men, even in Japan, verbal confrontations and po-

sitioning for power are acceptable social forms. Perhaps when two samurai meet, they must engage in hostile sword play and find themselves well matched, before they can be friends.

The exchange of political opinions left me shaken, but Mark, 46 Tadao-san, and Yoshi seemed unscathed. They raised their cups and had a seemingly splendid time.

But then again, perhaps I was right. Before the evening 47 ended, Tadao-san slipped me an envelope. "In case you wish to leave the autobike, to continue, alone, by train," he said. Inside, was a staggering sum of money.

After midnight, Sachiko-san led me to her daughters' room. 48 It was the room of teenagers, a sweet jumble of stuffed animals and pinups of popular singers. Several pencil sketches were carefully mounted on one wall. Through a window, I saw the crescent moon.

"Come Yuri-chan." Sachiko-san led me to the sketches. 49 "Come and see your past."

The drawings were light, romantic renderings, of princesses 50 all gowned and gloved.

"Your mother lived here briefly, when she was a girl," 51 Sachiko-san explained. "These are her drawings. My daughters found them in storage and thought them pretty." She paused in reflection. "Your young mother's dreams have been rescued and honored, mounted here on my little ones' wall."

Through the open window came the sound of a bamboo 52 flute. Sachiko-san looked at me with the warmth of a sister. She touched my hair gently and smiled. "The hearts of young girls," she whispered to me, "their visions, forever, the same."

1992

CHAPTER 7

Illustration

Why Don't We Complain?

William F. Buckley, Jr.

It was the very last coach and the only empty seat on the entire train, so there was no turning back. The problem was to breathe. Outside, the temperature was below freezing. Inside the railroad car the temperature must have been about 85 degrees. I took off my overcoat, and a few minutes later my jacket, and noticed that the car was flecked with the white shirts of the passengers. I soon found my hand moving to loosen my tie. From one end of the car to the other, as we rattled through Westchester County, we sweated; but we did not moan. 1

I watched the train conductor appear at the head of the car. "Tickets, all tickets, please!" In a more virile age, I thought, the passengers would seize the conductor and strap him down on a seat over the radiator to share the fate of his patrons. He shuffled down the aisle, picking up tickets, punching commutation cards. *No one addressed a word to him.* He approached my seat, and I drew a deep breath of resolution. "Conductor," I began with a considerable edge to my voice. . . . Instantly the doleful eyes of my seatmate turned tiredly from his newspaper to fix me with a resentful stare: what question could be so important as to justify my sibilant intrusion into his stupor? I was shaken by those eyes. I am incapable of making a discreet fuss, so I mumbled a question about what time we were due in Stamford (I didn't even ask whether it would be before or after dehydra- 2

tion could be expected to set in), got my reply, and went back
to my newspaper and to wiping my brow.

The conductor had nonchalantly walked down the gaunt-   3
let of eighty sweating American freemen, and not one of them
had asked him to explain why the passengers in that car had
been consigned to suffer. There is nothing to be done when the
temperature *outdoors* is 85 degrees, and indoors the air conditioner has broken down; obviously when that happens there is
nothing to do, except perhaps curse the day that one was born.
But when the temperature outdoors is below freezing, it takes
a positive act of will on somebody's part to set the temperature
indoors at 85. Somewhere a valve was turned too far, a furnace
overstocked, a thermostat maladjusted: something that could
easily be remedied by turning off the heat and allowing the
great outdoors to come indoors. All this is so obvious. What is
not obvious is what has happened to the American people.

It isn't just the commuters, whom we have come to visual-   4
ize as a supine breed who have got on to the trick of suspend-
ing their sensory faculties twice a day while they submit to the
creeping dissolution of the railroad industry. It isn't just they
who have given up trying to rectify irrational vexations. It is the
American people everywhere.

A few weeks ago at a large movie theatre I turned to my   5
wife and said, "The picture is out of focus." "Be quiet," she answered. I obeyed. But a few minutes later I raised the point
again, with mounting impatience. "It will be all right in a
minute," she said apprehensively. (She would rather lose her
eyesight than be around when I make one of my infrequent
scenes.) I waited. It was *just* out of focus—not glaringly out, but
out. My vision is 20-20, and I assume that is the vision, ad-
justed, of most people in the movie house. So, after hectoring
my wife throughout the first reel, I finally prevailed upon her
to admit that it was off, and very annoying. We then settled
down, coming to rest on the presumption that: a) someone connected with the management of the theatre must soon notice the
blur and make the correction; or b) that someone seated near
the rear of the house would make the complaint in behalf of
those of us up front; or c) that—any minute now—the entire

house would explode into catcalls and foot stamping, calling dramatic attention to the irksome distortion.

What happened was nothing. The movie ended, as it had 6 begun *just* out of focus, and as we trooped out, we stretched our faces in a variety of contortions to accustom the eye to the shock of normal focus.

I think it is safe to say that everybody suffered on that oc- 7 casion. And I think it is safe to assume that everyone was expecting someone else to take the initiative in going back to speak to the manager. And it is probably true even that if we had supposed the movie would run right through the blurred image, someone surely would have summoned up the purposive indignation to get up out of his seat and file his complaint.

But notice that no one did. And the reason no one did is be- 8 cause we are all increasingly anxious in America to be unobtrusive, we are reluctant to make our voices heard, hesitant about claiming our rights; we are afraid that our cause is unjust, or that if it is not unjust, that it is ambiguous; or if not even that, that it is too trivial to justify the horrors of a confrontation with Authority; we will sit in an oven or endure a racking headache before undertaking a head-on, I'm-here-to-tell-you complaint. That tendency to passive compliance, to a heedless endurance, is something to keep one's eyes on—in sharp focus.

I myself can occasionally summon the courage to complain, 9 but I cannot, as I have intimated, complain softly. My own instinct is so strong to let the thing ride, to forget about it—to expect that someone will take the matter up, when the grievance is collective, in my behalf—that it is only when the provocation is at a very special key, whose vibrations touch simultaneously a complexus of nerves, allergies, and passions, that I catch fire and find the reserves of courage and assertiveness to speak up. When that happens, I get quite carried away. My blood gets hot, my brow wet, I become unbearably and unconscionably sarcastic and bellicose; I am girded for a total showdown.

Why should that be? Why could not I (or anyone else) on 10 that railroad coach have said simply to the conductor, "Sir"—I take that back: that sounds sarcastic—"Conductor, would you be good enough to turn down the heat? I am extremely hot. In fact, I tend to get hot every time the temperature reaches 85 degr—" Strike that last sentence. Just end it with the simple statement that you are extremely hot, and let the conductor infer the cause.

Every New Year's Eve I resolve to do something about the 11 Milquetoast in me and vow to speak up, calmly, for my rights, and for the betterment of our society, on every appropriate occasion. Entering last New Year's Eve I was fortified in my resolve because that morning at breakfast I had had to ask the waitress three times for a glass of milk. She finally brought it— after I had finished my eggs, which is when I don't want it any more. I did not have the manliness to order her to take the milk back, but settled instead for a cowardly sulk, and ostentatiously refused to drink the milk—though I later paid for it—rather than state plainly to the hostess, as I should have, why I had not drunk it, and would not pay for it.

So by the time the New Year ushered out the Old, riding in 12 on my morning's indignation and stimulated by the gastric juices of resolution that flow so faithfully on New Year's Eve, I rendered my vow. Henceforward I would conquer my shyness, my despicable disposition to supineness. I would speak out like a man against the unnecessary annoyances of our time.

Forty-eight hours later, I was standing in line at the ski re- 13 pair store in Pico Peak, Vermont. All I needed, to get on with my skiing, was the loan, for one minute, of a small screwdriver, to tighten a loose binding. Behind the counter in the workshop were two men. One was industriously engaged in servicing the complicated requirements of a young lady at the head of the line, and obviously he would be tied up for quite a while. The other—"Jiggs," his workmate called him—was a middle-aged man, who sat in a chair puffing a pipe, exchanging small talk with his working partner. My pulse began its telltale acceleration. The minutes ticked on. I stared at the idle shopkeeper, hoping to shame him into action, but he was impervious to my telepathic reproof and continued his small talk with his friend, brazenly insensitive to the nervous demands of six good men who were raring to ski.

Suddenly my New Year's Eve resolution struck me. It was 14

now or never. I broke from my place in line and marched to the counter. I was going to control myself. I dug my nails into my palms. My effort was only partially successful.

"If you are not too busy," I said icily, "would you mind   15 handing me a screwdriver?"

Work stopped and everyone turned his eyes on me, and I   16 experienced that mortification I always feel when I am the center of centripetal shafts of curiosity, resentment, perplexity.

But the worst was yet to come. "I am sorry, sir," said Jiggs   17 deferentially, moving the pipe from his mouth. "I am not supposed to move. I have just had a heart attack." That was the signal for a great whirring noise that descended from heaven. We looked, stricken, out the window, and it appeared as though a cyclone had suddenly focused on the snowy courtyard between the shop and the ski lift. Suddenly a gigantic army helicopter materialized, and hovered down to a landing. Two men jumped out of the plane carrying a stretcher, tore into the ski shop and lifted the shopkeeper onto the stretcher. Jiggs bade his companion goodby, was whisked out the door, into the plane, up to the heavens, down—we learned—to a near-by army hospital. I looked up manfully—into a score of man-eating eyes. I put the experience down as a reversal.

As I write this, on an airplane, I have run out of paper and   18 need to reach into my briefcase under my legs for more. I cannot do this until my empty lunch tray is removed from my lap. I arrested the stewardess as she passed empty-handed down the aisle on the way to the kitchen to fetch the lunch trays for the passengers up forward who haven't been served yet. "Would you please take my tray?" "Just a *moment*, sir!" she said, and marched on sternly. Shall I tell her that since she is headed for the kitchen *anyway*, it could not delay the feeding of the other passengers by more than two seconds necessary to stash away my empty tray? Or remind her that not fifteen minutes ago she spoke unctuously into the loudspeaker the words undoubtedly devised by the airline's highly paid public relations counselor: "If there is anything I or Miss French can do for you to make your trip more enjoyable, *please* let us—" I have run out of paper.

I think the observable reluctance of the majority of Ameri- 19
cans to assert themselves in minor matters is related to our increased sense of helplessness in an age of technology and centralized political and economic power. For generations,
Americans who were too hot, or too cold, got up and did something about it. Now we call the plumber, or the electrician, or
the furnace man. The habit of looking after our own needs obviously had something to do with the assertiveness that characterized the American family familiar to readers of American
literature. With the technification of life goes our direct responsibility for our material environment, and we are conditioned to adopt a position of helplessness not only as regards
the broken air conditioner, but as regards the overheated train.
It takes an expert to fix the former, but not the latter; yet these
distinctions, as we withdraw into helplessness, tend to fade
away.

Our notorious political apathy is a related phenomenon. 20
Every year, whether the Republican or the Democratic Party is
in office, more and more power drains away from the individual to feed vast reservoirs in far-off places; and we have less and
less say about the shape of events which shape our future. From
this alienation of personal power comes the sense of resignation
with which we accept the political dispensations of a powerful
government whose hold upon us continues to increase.

An editor of a national weekly news magazine told me a few 21
years ago that as few as a dozen letters of protest against an editorial stance of his magazine was enough to convene a plenipo-
tentiary meeting of the board of editors to review policy. "So
few people complain, or make their voices heard," he explained
to me, "that we assume a dozen letters represent the inarticu-
lated views of thousands of readers." In the past ten years, he
said, the volume of mail has noticeably decreased, even though
the circulation of his magazine has risen.

When our voices are finally mute, when we have finally 22
suppressed the natural instinct to complain, whether the vexa-
tion is trivial or grave, we shall have become automatons, incapable of feeling. When Premier Khrushchev first came to this
country late in 1959 he was primed, we are informed, to expe-

rience the bitter resentment of the American people against his tyranny, against his persecutions, against the movement which is responsible for the great number of American deaths in Korea, for billions in taxes every year, and for life everlasting on the brink of disaster; but Khrushchev was pleasantly surprised, and reported back to the Russian people that he had been met with overwhelming cordiality (read: apathy), except, to be sure, for "a few fascists who followed me around with their wretched posters, and should be horsewhipped."

I may be crazy, but I say there would have been lots more   23 posters in a society where train temperatures in the dead of winter are not allowed to climb to 85 degrees without complaint.

1961

Does America Still Exist?

Richard Rodriguez

For the children of immigrant parents the knowledge comes   1 easier. America exists everywhere in the city—on billboards, frankly in the smell of French fries and popcorn. It exists in the pace: traffic lights, the assertions of neon, the mysterious bong-bong-bong through the atriums of department stores. America exists as the voice of the crowd, a menacing sound—the high nasal accent of American English.

When I was a boy in Sacramento (California, the fifties),   2 people would ask me, "Where you from?" I was born in this country, but I knew the question meant to decipher my darkness, my looks.

My mother once instructed me to say, "I am an American   3 of Mexican descent." By the time I was nine or ten, I wanted to say, but dared not reply, "I am an American."

Immigrants come to America and, against hostility or mere   4 loneliness, they recreate a homeland in the parlor, tacking up postcards or calendars of some impossible blue—lake or sea or sky. Children of immigrant parents are supposed to perch on a hyphen between two countries. Relatives assume the achievement as much as anyone. Relatives are, in any case, surprised when the child begins losing old ways. One day at the family picnic the boy wanders away from their spiced food and faceless stories to watch other boys play baseball in the distance.

There is sorrow in the American memory, guilty sorrow for 5 having left something behind—Portugal, China, Norway. The American story is the story of immigrant children and of their children—children no longer able to speak to grandparents. The memory of exile becomes inarticulate as it passes from generation to generation, along with wedding rings and pocket watches—like some mute stone in a wad of old lace. Europe. Asia. Eden.

But, it needs to be said, if this is a country where one stops 6 being Vietnamese or Italian, this is a country where one begins to be an American. America exists as a culture and a grin, a faith and a shrug. It is clasped in a handshake, called by a first name.

As much as the country is joined in a common culture, how- 7 ever, Americans are reluctant to celebrate the process of assimilation. We pledge allegiance to diversity. America was born Protestant and bred Puritan, and the notion of community we share is derived from a seventeenth-century faith. Presidents and the pages of ninth-grade civics readers yet proclaim the orthodoxy: We are gathered together—but as individuals, with separate pasts, distinct destinies. Our society is as paradoxical as a Puritan congregation: We stand together, alone.

Americans have traditionally defined themselves by what 8 they refused to include. As often, however, Americans have struggled, turned in good conscience at last to assert the great Protestant virtue of tolerance. Despite outbreaks of nativist frenzy, America has remained an immigrant country, open and true to itself.

Against pious emblems of rural America—soda fountain, 9 Elks hall, Protestant church, and now shopping mall—stands the cold-hearted city, crowded with races and ambitions, curious laughter, much that is odd. Nevertheless, it is the city that has most truly represented America. In the city, however, the

millions of singular lives have had no richer notion of whole-
ness to describe them than the idea of pluralism.

"*Where you from?*" *the American asks the immigrant child.*   10
"*Mexico,*" *the boy learns to say.*

Mexico, the country of my blood ancestors, offers formal   11
contrast to the American achievement. If the United States was
formed by Protestant individualism, Mexico was shaped by a
medieval Catholic dream of one world. The Spanish journeyed
to Mexico to plunder, and they may have gone, in God's name,
with an arrogance peculiar to those who intend to convert. But
through the conversion, the Indian converted the Spaniard. A
new race was born, the *mestizo*, wedding European to Indian.
José Vasconcelos, the Mexican philosopher, has celebrated this
New World creation, proclaiming it the "cosmic race."

Centuries later, in a San Francisco restaurant, a Mexican-   12
American lawyer of my acquaintance says, in English, over *salade
niçoise,* that he does not intend to assimilate into gringo society.
His claim is echoed by a chorus of others (Italian-Americans,
Greeks, Asians) in this era of ethnic pride. The melting pot has
been retired, clanking, into the museum of quaint disgrace,
alongside Aunt Jemima and the Katzenjammer Kids. But resistance to assimilation is characteristically American. It only makes
clear how inevitable the process of assimilation actually is.

For generations, this has been the pattern. Immigrant par-   13
ents have sent their children to school (simply, they thought) to
acquire the "skills" to survive in the city. The child returned
home with a voice his parents barely recognized or understood,
couldn't trust, and didn't like.

In Eastern cities—Philadelphia, New York, Boston, Balti-   14
more—class after class gathered immigrant children to women
(usually women) who stood in front of rooms full of children,
changing children. So also for me in the 1950s. Irish-Catholic
nuns. California. The old story. The hyphen tipped to the right,
away from Mexico and toward a confusing but true American
identity.

I speak now in the chromium American accent of my gram-   15
mar school classmates—Billy Reckers, Mike Bradley, Carol
Schmidt, Kathy O'Grady. . . . I believe I became like my classmates, became German, Polish, and (like my teachers) Irish.

And because assimilation is always reciprocal, my classmates got something of me. (I mean sad eyes; belief in the Indian Virgin; a taste for sugar skulls on the Feast of the Dead.) In the blending, we became what our parents could never have been, and we carried America one revolution further.

"Does America still exist?" Americans have been asking [16] the question for so long that to ask it again only proves our continuous link. But perhaps the question deserves to be asked with urgency—now. Since the black civil rights movement of the 1960s, our tenuous notion of a shared public life has deteriorated notably.

The struggle of black men and women did not eradicate [17] racism, but it became the great moment in the life of America's conscience. Water hoses, bulldogs, blood—the images, rendered black, white, rectangular, passed into living rooms.

It is hard to look at a photograph of a crowd taken, say, in [18] 1890 or in 1930 and not notice the absence of blacks. (It becomes an impertinence to wonder if America *still* exists.)

In the sixties, other groups of Americans learned to cham- [19] pion their rights by analogy to the black civil rights movement. But the heroic vision faded. Dr. Martin Luther King Jr. had spoken with Pauline eloquence of a nation that would unite Christian and Jew, old and young, rich and poor. Within a decade, the struggles of the 1960s were reduced to a bureaucratic competition for little more than pieces of a representational pie. The quest for a portion of power became an end in itself. The metaphor for the American city of the 1970s was a committee: one black, one woman, one person under thirty. . . .

If the small town had sinned against America by too neatly [20] defining who could be an American, the city's sin was a romantic secession. One noticed the romanticism in the antiwar movement—certain demonstrators who demonstrated a lack of tact or desire to persuade and seemed content to play secular protestants. One noticed the romanticism in the competition among members of "minority groups" to claim the status of Primary Victim. To Americans unconfident of their common identity, minority standing became a way of asserting individuality. Middle-class Americans—men and women clearly not the primary victims of social oppression—brandished their suffering with exuberance.

The dream of a single society probably died with *The Ed Sullivan Show*. The reality of America persists. Teenagers pass through big-city high schools banded in racial groups, their collars turned up to a uniform shrug. But then they graduate to jobs at the phone company or in banks, where they end up working alongside people unlike themselves. Typists and tellers walk out together at lunchtime. 21

It is easier for us as Americans to believe the obvious fact of our separateness—easier to imagine the black and white Americans prophesied by the Kerner report (broken glass, street fires)—than to recognize the reality of a city street at lunchtime. Americans are wedded by proximity to a common culture. The panhandler at one corner is related to the pamphleteer at the next who is related to the banker who is kin to the Chinese old man wearing an MIT sweatshirt. In any true national history, Thomas Jefferson begets Martin Luther King Jr. who begets the Gray Panthers. It is because we lack a vision of ourselves entire—the city street is crowded and we are each preoccupied with finding our own way home—that we lack an appropriate hymn. 22

Under my window now passes a little white girl softly rehearsing to herself a Motown obbligato. 23

1984

A Few Kind Words for Superstition

Robertson Davies

In grave discussions of "the renaissance of the irrational" in our time, superstition does not figure largely as a serious challenge to reason or science. Parapsychology, UFO's, miracle 1

cures, transcendental meditation and all the paths to instant en-
lightenment are condemned, but superstition is merely de-
plored. It is because it has an unacknowledged hold on so many
of us?

Few people will admit to being superstitious; it implies   2
naïveté or ignorance. But I live in the middle of a large university, and I see superstition in its four manifestations, alive and
flourishing among people who are indisputably rational and
learned.

You did not know that superstition takes four forms? The-   3
ologians assure us that it does. First is what they call Vain Ob-
servances, such as not walking under a ladder, and that kind of
thing. Yet I saw a deeply learned professor of anthropology,
who had spilled some salt, throwing a pinch of it over his left
shoulder; when I asked him why, he replied, with a wink, that
it was "to hit the Devil in the eye." I did not question him further about his belief in the Devil: but I noticed that he did not
smile until I asked him what he was doing.

The second form is Divination, or consulting oracles. An-   4
other learned professor I know, who would scorn to settle a
problem by tossing a coin (which is a humble appeal to Fate to
declare itself), told me quite seriously that he had resolved a
matter related to university affairs by consulting the I Ching.
And why not? There are thousands of people on this continent
who appeal to the I Ching, and their general level of education
seems to absolve them of superstition. Almost, but not quite.
The I Ching, to the embarrassment of rationalists, often gives
excellent advice.

The third form is Idolatry, and universities can show plenty   5
of that. If you have ever supervised a large examination room,
you know how many jujus, lucky coins and other bringers of
luck are placed on the desks of the candidates. Modest idolatry, but what else can you call it?

The fourth form is Improper Worship of the True God. A   6
while ago, I learned that every day, for several days, a $2 bill
(in Canada we have $2 bills, regarded by some people as un-
lucky) had been tucked under a candlestick on the altar of a college chapel. Investigation revealed that an engineering student,

worried about a girl, thought that bribery of the Deity might help. When I talked with him, he did not think he was pricing God cheap, because he could afford no more. A reasonable argument, but perhaps God was proud that week, for the scientific oracle went against him.

Superstition seems to run, a submerged river of crude religion, below the surface of human consciousness. It has done so for as long as we have any chronicle of human behavior, and although I cannot prove it, I doubt if it is more prevalent today than it has always been. Superstition, the theologians tell us, comes from the Latin *supersisto,* meaning to stand in terror of the Deity. Most people keep their terror within bounds, but they cannot root it out, nor do they seem to want to do so.   7

The more the teaching of formal religion declines, or takes a sociological form, the less God appears to great numbers of people as a God of Love, resuming his older form of a watchful, minatory power, to be placated and cajoled. Superstition makes its appearance, apparently unbidden, very early in life, when children fear that stepping on cracks in the sidewalk will bring ill fortune. It may persist even among the greatly learned and devout, as in the case of Dr. Samuel Johnson, who felt it necessary to touch posts that he passed in the street. The psychoanalysts have their explanation, but calling a superstition a compulsion neurosis does not banish it.   8

Many superstitions are so widespread and so old that they must have risen from a depth of the human mind that is indifferent to race or creed. Orthodox Jews place a charm on their door-posts; so do (or did) the Chinese. Some peoples of Middle Europe believe that when a man sneezes, his soul, for that moment, is absent from his body, and they hasten to bless him, lest the soul be seized by the Devil. How did the Melanesians come by the same idea? Superstition seems to have a link with some body of belief that far antedates the religions we know—religions which have no place for such comforting little ceremonies and charities.   9

People who like disagreeable historical comparisons recall that when Rome was in decline, superstition proliferated wildly, and that something of the same sort is happening in our   10

Western world today. They point to the popularity of astrology, and it is true that sober newspapers that would scorn to deal in love philters carry astrology columns and the fashion magazines count them among their most popular features. But when has astrology not been popular? No use saying science discredits it. When has the heart of man given a damn for science?

Superstition in general is linked to man's yearning to know   11 his fate, and to have some hand in deciding it. When my mother was a child, she innocently joined her Roman Catholic friends in killing spiders on July 11, until she learned that this was done to ensure heavy rain the day following, the anniversary of the Battle of Boyne, when the Orangemen would hold their parade. I knew an Italian, a good scientist, who watched every morning before leaving his house, so that the first person he met would not be a priest or a nun, as this would certainly bring bad luck.

I am not one to stand aloof from the rest of humanity in this   12 matter, for when I was a university student, a gypsy woman with a child in her arms used to appear every year at examination time, and ask a shilling of anyone who touched the Lucky Baby; that swarthy infant cost me four shillings altogether, and I never failed an examination. Of course, I did it merely for the joke—or so I thought then. Now, I am humbler.

1978

The Patterns of Eating

Peter Farb and George Armelagos

Among the important societal rules that represent one com-   1 ponent of cuisine are table manners. As a socially instilled form of conduct, they reveal the attitudes typical of a society. Changes in table manners through time, as they have been documented for western Europe, likewise reflect fundamental changes in human relationships. Medieval courtiers saw their table manners as distinguishing them from crude peasants; but by modern standards, the manners were not exactly refined. Feudal lords used their unwashed hands to scoop food from a common bowl and they passed around a single goblet from which all drank. A finger or two would be extended while eating, so as to be kept free of grease and thus available for the next course, or for dipping into spices and condiments—possibly accounting for today's "polite" custom of extending the finger while holding a spoon or small fork. Soups and sauces were commonly drunk by lifting the bowl to the mouth; several diners frequently ate from the same bread trencher. Even lords and nobles would toss gnawed bones back into the common dish, wolf down their food, spit onto the table (preferred conduct called for spitting under it), and blew their noses into the tablecloth.

By about the beginning of the sixteenth century, table manners began to move in the direction of today's standards. The importance attached to them is indicated by the phenomenal success of a treatise, *On Civility in Children,* by the philosopher Erasmus, which appeared in 1530; reprinted more than thirty times in the next six years, it also appeared in numerous translations. Erasmus' idea of good table manners was far from modern, but it did represent an advance. He believed, for example, that an upper class diner was distinguished by putting only three fingers of one hand into the bowl, instead of the entire hand in the manner of the lower class. Wait a few moments after being seated before you dip into it, he advises. Do not poke around in your dish, but take the first piece you touch. Do not put chewed food from the mouth back on your plate; instead, throw it under the table or behind your chair.

By the time of Erasmus, the changing table manners reveal a fundamental shift in society. People no longer ate from the same dish or drank from the same goblet, but were divided from one another by a new wall of constraint. Once the spontaneous, direct, and informal manners of the Middle Ages had been repressed, people began to feel shame. Defecation and urination were now regarded as private activities; handkerchiefs came into use for blowing the nose; nightclothes were now worn, and bedrooms were set apart as private areas. Before the sixteenth century, even nobles ate in their vast kitchens; only then did a special room designated for eating come into use away from the bloody sides of meat, the animals about to be slaughtered, and the bustling servants. These new inhibitions became the essence of "civilized" behavior, distinguishing adults from children, the upper classes from the lower, and Europeans from the "savages" then being discovered around the world. Restraint in eating habits became more marked in the centuries that followed. By about 1800, napkins were in common use, and before long they were placed on the thighs rather than wrapped around the neck; coffee and tea were no longer slurped out of the saucer; bread was genteelly broken into small pieces with the fingers rather than cut into large chunks with a knife.

Numerous paintings that depict meals—with subjects such as the Last Supper, the wedding at Cana, or Herod's feast— show what dining tables looked like before the seventeenth century. Forks were not depicted until about 1600 (when Jacopo Bassano painted one in a Last Supper), and very few spoons were shown. At least one knife is always depicted—an especially large one when it is the only one available for all the guests—but small individual knives were often at each place. Tin disks or oval pieces of wood had already replaced the bread trenchers. This change in eating utensils typified the new table manners in Europe. (In many other parts of the world, no utensils at all were used. In the Near East, for example, it was traditional to bring food to the mouth with the fingers of the right hand, the left being unacceptable because it was reserved for wiping the buttocks.) Utensils were employed in part because of a change in the attitude toward meat. During the Middle Ages, whole sides of meat, or even an entire dead animal, had been brought to the table and then carved in view of the diners. Beginning in the seventeenth century, at first in France but later elsewhere, the practice began to go out of fashion. One reason was that the family was ceasing to be a production unit that did its own slaughtering; as that function was transferred to specialists outside the home, the family became essentially a consumption unit. In addition, the size of the family was decreasing, and consequently whole animals, or even large parts of them, were uneconomical. The cuisines of Europe reflected these social and economic changes. The animal origin of meat dishes was concealed by the arts of preparation. Meat itself became distasteful to look upon, and carving was moved out of sight to the kitchen. Comparable changes had already taken place in Chinese cuisine, with meat being cut up beforehand, unobserved by the diners. England was an exception to the change in Europe, and in its former colonies—the United States, Canada, Australia, and South Africa—the custom has persisted of bringing a joint of meat to the table to be carved.

Once carving was no longer considered a necessary skill   5
among the well-bred, changes inevitably took place in the use of the knife, unquestionably the earliest utensil used for manipulating food. (In fact, the earliest English cookbooks were not so much guides to recipes as guides to carving meat.) The attitude of diners toward the knife, going back to the Middle Ages and the Renaissance, had always been ambivalent. The knife served as a utensil, but it offered a potential threat because it was also a weapon. Thus taboos were increasingly placed upon its use: It was to be held by the point with the blunt handle presented; it was not to be placed anywhere near the face; and most important, the uses to which it was put were sharply restricted. It was not to be used for cutting soft foods such as boiled eggs or fish, or round ones such as potatoes, or to be lifted from the table for courses that did not need it. In short, good table manners in Europe gradually removed the threatening aspect of the knife from social occasions. A similar change had taken place much earlier in China when the warrior was supplanted by the scholar as a cultural model. The knife was banished completely from the table in favor of chopsticks, which is why the Chinese came to regard Europeans as barbarians at their table who "eat with swords."

The fork in particular enabled Europeans to separate them-   6
selves from the eating process, even avoiding manual contact with their food. When the fork first appeared in Europe, toward

the end of the Middle Ages, it was used solely as an instrument for lifting chunks from the common bowl. Beginning in the sixteenth century, the fork was increasingly used by members of the upper classes—first in Italy, then in France, and finally in Germany and England. By then, social relations in western Europe had so changed that a utensil was needed to spare diners from the "uncivilized" and distasteful necessity of picking up food and putting it into the mouth with the fingers. The addition of the fork to the table was once said to be for reasons of hygiene, but this cannot be true. By the sixteenth century people were no longer eating from a common bowl but from their own plates, and since they also washed their hands before meals, their fingers were now every bit as hygienic as a fork would have been. Nor can the reason for the adoption of the fork be connected with the wish not to soil the long ruff that was worn on the sleeve at the time, since the fork was also adopted in various countries where ruffs were not then in fashion.

Along with the appearance of the fork, all table utensils ⁷ began to change and proliferate from the sixteenth century onward. Soup was no longer eaten directly from the dish, but each diner used an individual spoon for that purpose. When a diner wanted a second helping from the serving dish, a ladle or a fresh spoon was used. More and more special utensils were developed for each kind of food: soup spoons, oyster forks, salad forks, two-tined fondue forks, blunt butter knives, special utensils for various desserts and kinds of fruit, each one differently shaped, of a different size, with differently numbered prongs and with blunt or serrated edges. The present European pattern eventually emerged, in which each person is provided with a table setting of as many as a dozen utensils at a full-course meal. With that, the separation of the human body from the taking of food became virtually complete. Good table manners dictated that even the cobs of maize were to be held by prongs inserted in each end, and the bones of lamb chops covered by ruffled paper pantalettes. Only under special conditions—as when Western people consciously imitate an earlier stage in culture at a picnic, fish fry, cookout, or campfire—do they still tear food apart with their fingers and their teeth, in a nostalgic reenactment of eating behaviors long vanished.

Today's neighborhood barbecue recreates a world of sharing and hospitality that becomes rarer each year. We regard as a curiosity the behavior of hunters in exotic regions. But every year millions of North Americans take to the woods and lakes to kill a wide variety of animals—with a difference, of course: What hunters do for survival we do for sport (and also for proof of masculinity, for male bonding, and for various psychological rewards). Like hunters, too, we stuff ourselves almost whenever food is available. Nibbling on a roasted ear of maize gives us, in addition to nutrients, the satisfaction of participating in culturally simpler ways. A festive meal, however, is still thought of in Victorian terms, with the dominant male officiating over the roast, the dominant female apportioning vegetables, the extended family gathered around the table, with everything in its proper place—a revered picture, as indeed it was so painted by Norman Rockwell, yet one that becomes less accurate with each year that passes.

1980

The Anthropology of Manners

Edward T. Hall

> *The Goops they lick their fingers*
> *and the Goops they lick their knives;*
> *They spill their broth on the table cloth—*
> *Oh, they lead disgusting lives.*
> *The Goops they talk while eating,*
> *and loud and fast they chew;*
> *And that is why I'm glad that I*
> *am not a Goop—are you?*

In Gelett Burgess' classic on the Goops we have an example of what anthropologists call "an enculturating device"—a means of conditioning the young to life in our society. Having been taught the lesson of the goops from childhood (with or without the aid of Mr. Burgess) Americans are shocked when they go abroad and discover whole groups of people behaving like goops—eating with their fingers, making noises and talking while eating. When this happens, we may (1) remark on the barbarousness or quaintness of the "natives" (a term cordially disliked all over the world) or (2) try to discover the nature and meaning of the differences in behavior. One rather quickly discovers that what is good manners in one context may be bad in the next. It is to this point that I would like to address myself.

The subject of manners is complex; if it were not, there   2
would not be so many injured feelings and so much misunderstanding in international circles everywhere. In any society the code of manners tends to sum up the culture—to be a frame of reference for all behavior. Emily Post goes so far as to say: "There is not a single thing that we do, or say, or choose, or use, or even think, that does not follow or break one of the exactions of taste, or tact, or ethics of good manners, or etiquette—call it what you will." Unfortunately many of the most important standards of acceptable behavior in different cultures are elusive: they are intangible, undefined and unwritten.

An Arab diplomat who recently arrived in the U.S. from the   3
Middle East attended a banquet which lasted several hours. When it was over, he met a fellow countryman outside and suggested they go get something to eat, as he was starving. His friend, who had been in this country for some time, laughed and said: "But, Habib, didn't you know that if you say, 'No, thank you,' they think you really don't want any?" In an Arab country etiquette dictates that the person being served must refuse the proffered dish several times, while his host urges him repeatedly to partake. The other side of the coin is that Americans in the Middle East, until they learn better, stagger away from banquets having eaten more than they want or is good for them.

When a public-health movie of a baby being bathed in a   4
bathinette was shown in India recently, the Indian women who saw it were visibly offended. They wondered how people could be so inhuman as to bathe a child in stagnant (not running) water. Americans in Iran soon learn not to indulge themselves in their penchant for chucking infants under the chin and re-

marking on the color of their eyes, for the mother has to pay to have the "evil eye" removed. We also learn that in the Middle East you don't hand people things with your left hand, because it is unclean. In India we learn not to touch another person, and in Southeast Asia we learn that the head is sacred.

In the interest of intercultural understanding various U.S. Government agencies have hired anthropologists from time to time as technical experts. The State Department especially has pioneered in the attempt to bring science to bear on this difficult and complex problem. It began by offering at the Foreign Service Institute an intensive four-week course for Point 4 technicians. Later these facilities were expanded to include other foreign service personnel.

The anthropologist's job here is not merely to call attention to obvious taboos or to coach people about types of thoughtless behavior that have very little to do with culture. One should not need an anthropologist to point out, for instance, that it is insulting to ask a foreigner: "How much is this in real money?" Where technical advice is most needed is in the interpretation of the unconscious aspects of a culture—the things people do automatically without being aware of the full implications of what they have done. For example, an ambassador who has been kept waiting for more than half an hour by a foreign visitor needs to understand that if his visitor "just mutters an apology" this is not necessarily an insult. The time system in the foreign country may be composed of different basic units, so that the visitor is not as late as he may appear to us. You must know the time system of the country to know at what point apologies are really due.

Twenty years of experience in working with Americans in foreign lands convinces me that the real problem in preparing them to work overseas is not with taboos, which they catch on to rather quickly, but rather with whole congeries of habits and attitudes which anthropologists have only recently begun to describe systematically.

Can you remember tying your shoes this morning? Could you give the rules for when it is proper to call another person by his first name? Could you describe the gestures you make in

conversation? These examples illustrate how much of our behavior is "out of awareness," and how easy it is to get into trouble in another culture.

Nobody is continually aware of the quality of his own voice,   9
the subtleties of stress and intonation that color the meaning of
his words or the posture and distance he assumes in talking to
another person. Yet all these are taken as cues to the real nature
of an utterance, regardless of what the words say. A simple il-
lustration is the meaning in the tone of voice. In the U.S. we raise
our voices not only when we are angry but also when we want
to emphasize a point, when we are more than a certain distance
from another person, when we are concluding a meeting and
so on. But to the Chinese, for instance, overloudness of the voice
is most characteristically associated with anger and loss of self-
control. Whenever we become really interested in something,
they are apt to have the feeling we are angry, in spite of many
years' experience with us. Very likely most of their interviews
with us, however cordial, seem to end on a sour note when we
exclaim heartily: "WELL, I'M CERTAINLY GLAD YOU
DROPPED IN, MR. WONG."

The Latin Americans, who as a rule take business seriously,   10
do not understand our mixing business with informality and
recreation. We like to put our feet up on the desk. If a stranger
enters the office, we take our feet down. If it turns out that the
stranger and we have a lot in common, up go the feet again—
a cue to the other fellow that we feel at ease. If the office boy enters, the feet stay up; if the boss enters and our relationship with
him is a little strained at the moment, they go down. To a Latin
American this whole behavior is shocking. All he sees in it is insult or just plain rudeness.

Differences in attitudes toward space—what would be ter-   11
ritoriality in lower forms of life—raise a number of other interesting points. U.S. women who go to live in Latin America all
complain about the "waste" of space in the houses. On the other
hand, U.S. visitors to the Middle East complain about crowding, in the houses and on the streetcars and buses. Everywhere
we go space seems to be distorted. When we see a gardener in
the mountains of Italy planting a single row on each of six sep-

arate terraces, we wonder why he spreads out his crop so that he has to spend half his time climbing up and down. We overlook the complex chain of communication that would be broken if he didn't cultivate alongside his brothers and his cousin and if he didn't pass his neighbors and talk to them as he moves from one terrace to the next.

A colleague of mine was caught in a snowstorm while traveling with companions in the mountains of Lebanon. They stopped at the next house and asked to be put up for the night. The house had only one room. Instead of distributing the guests around the room, their host placed them next to the pallet where he slept with his wife—so close that they almost touched the couple. To have done otherwise in that country would have been unnatural and unfriendly. In the U.S. we distribute ourselves more evenly than many other people. We have strong feelings about touching and being crowded; in a streetcar, bus or elevator we draw ourselves in. Toward a person who relaxes and lets himself come into full contact with others in a crowded place we usually feel reactions that could not be printed on this page. It takes years for us to train our children not to crowd and lean on us. We tell them to stand up, that it is rude to slouch, not to sit so close or not to "breathe down our necks." After a while they get the point. By the time we Americans are in our teens we can tell what relationship exists between a man and woman by how they walk or sit together. 12

In Latin America, where touching is more common and the basic units of space seem to be smaller, the wide automobiles made in the U.S. pose problems. People don't know where to sit. North Americans are disturbed by how close the Latin Americans stand when they converse. "Why do they have to get so close when they talk to you?" "They're so pushy." "I don't know what it is, but it's something in the way they stand next to you." And so on. The Latin Americans, for their part, complain that people in the U.S. are distant and cold—*retraídos* (withdrawing and uncommunicative). 13

An analysis of the handling of space during conversations shows the following: A U.S. male brought up in the Northeast stands 18 to 20 inches away when talking face to face to a man 14 he does not know very well; talking to a woman under similar circumstances, he increases the distance about four inches. A distance of only eight to 13 inches between males is considered either very aggressive or indicative of a closeness of a type we do not ordinarily want to think about. Yet in many parts of Latin America and the Middle East distances which are almost sexual in connotation are the only ones at which people can talk comfortably. In Cuba, for instance, there is nothing suggestive in a man's talking to an educated woman at a distance of 13 inches. If you are a Latin American, talking to a North American at the distance he insists on maintaining is like trying to talk across a room.

To get a more vivid idea of this problem of the comfortable 15 distance, try starting a conversation with a person eight or 10 feet away or one separated from you by a wide obstruction in a store or other public place. Any normally encultured person can't help trying to close up the space, even to the extent of climbing over benches or walking around tables to arrive within comfortable distance. U.S. businessmen working in Latin America try to prevent people from getting uncomfortably close by barricading themselves behind desks, typewriters or the like, but their Latin American office visitors will often climb up on desks or over chairs and put up with loss of dignity in order to establish a spatial context in which interaction can take place for them.

The interesting thing is that neither party is specifically 16 aware of what is wrong when the distance is not right. They merely have vague feelings of discomfort or anxiety. As the Latin American approaches and the North American backs away, both parties take offense without knowing why. When a North American, having had the problem pointed out to him, permits the Latin American to get close enough, he will immediately notice that the latter seems much more at ease.

My own studies of space and time have engendered con- 17 siderable cooperation and interest on the part of friends and colleagues. One case recently reported to me had to do with a group of seven-year-olds in a crowded Sunday-school classroom. The children kept fighting. Without knowing quite what was involved, the teacher had them moved to a larger room. The fighting stopped. It is interesting to speculate as to what would have happened had the children been moved to a smaller room.

The embarrassment about intimacy in space applies also to 18 the matter of addressing people by name. Finding the proper distance in the use of names is even more difficult than in space, because the rules for first-naming are unbelievably complex. As a rule we tend to stay on the "mister" level too long with Latins and some others, but very often we swing into first naming too quickly, which amounts to talking down to them. Whereas in the U.S. we use Mr. with the surname, in Latin America the first and last names are used together and señor (Sr.) is a title. Thus when one says, "My name is Sr. So-and-So," it is interpreted to mean, "I am the Honorable, his Excellency So-and-So." It is no wonder that when we stand away, barricade ourselves behind our desks (usually a reflection of status) and call ourselves mister, our friends to the south wonder about our so-called "good neighbor" policy and think of us as either high-hat or unbelievably rude. Fortunately most North Americans learn some of these things after living in Latin America for a while, but the aversion to being touched and to touching sometimes persists after 15 or more years of residence and even under such conditions as intermarriage.

The difference in sense of time is another thing of which we 19 are not aware. An Iranian, for instance, is not taught that it is rude to be late in the same way that we in the U.S. are. In a general way we are conscious of this, but we fail to realize that their time system is structured differently from ours. The different cultures simply place different values on the time units.

Thus let us take as a typical case of the North European time 20 system (which has regional variations) the situation in the urban eastern U.S. A middle-class business man meeting another of equivalent rank will ordinarily be aware of being two minutes early or late. If he is three minutes late, it will be noted as significant but usually neither will say anything. If four minutes late, he will mutter something by way of apology; at five minutes he will utter a full sentence of apology. In other words, the major unit is a five-minute block. Fifteen minutes is the smallest significant period for all sorts of arrangements and it is used very commonly. A half hour of course is very significant, and if you spend three quarters of an hour or an hour, either the business you transact or the relationship must be important. Normally it is an insult to keep a public figure or a person of significantly higher status than yourself waiting even two or three minutes, though the person of higher position can keep you waiting or even break an appointment.

Now among urban Arabs in the Eastern Mediterranean, to   21 take an illustrative case of another time system, the unit that corresponds to our five-minute period is 15 minutes. Thus when an Arab arrives nearly 30 minutes after the set time, by his reckoning he isn't even "10 minutes" late yet (in our time units). Stated differently, the Arab's tardiness will not amount to one significant period (15 minutes in our system). An American normally will wait no longer than 30 minutes (two significant periods) for another person to turn up in the middle of the day. Thereby he often unwittingly insults people in the Middle East who want to be his friends.

How long is one expected to stay when making a duty call   22 at a friend's house in the U.S.? While there are regional variations, I have observed that the minimum is very close to 45 minutes, even in the face of pressing commitments elsewhere, such as a roast in the oven. We may think we can get away in 30 minutes by saying something about only stopping for "a minute," but usually we discover that we don't feel comfortable about leaving until 45 minutes have elapsed. I am referring to afternoon social calls; evening calls last much longer and operate according to a different system. In Arab countries an American paying a duty call at the house of a desert sheik causes consternation if he gets up to leave after half a day. There a duty call lasts three days—the first day to prepare the feast, the second for the feast itself and the third to taper off and say farewell. In the first half day the sheik has barely had time to slaughter the sheep for the feast. The guest's departure would leave the host frustrated.

There is a well-known story of a tribesman who came to   23 Kabul, the capital of Afghanistan, to meet his brother. Failing to find him, he asked the merchants in the market place to tell his brother where he could be found if the brother showed up. A year later the tribesman returned and looked again. It developed that he and his brother had agreed to meet in Kabul but had failed to specify what year! If the Afghan time system were structured similarly to our own, which it apparently is not, the brother would not offer a full sentence of apology until he was five years late.

Informal units of time such as "just a minute," "a while," "later," "a long time," "a spell," "a long, long time," "years" and so on provide us with the culturological equivalent of Evil-Eye Fleegle's "double-whammy" (in *Li'l Abner*). Yet these expressions are not as imprecise as they seem. Any American who has worked in an office with someone else for six months can usually tell within five minutes when that person will be back if he says, "I'll be gone for a while." It is simply a matter of learning from experience the individual's system of time indicators. A reader who is interested in communications theory can fruitfully speculate for a while on the very wonderful way in which culture provides the means whereby the receiver puts back all the redundant material that was stripped from such a message. Spelled out, the message might go somewhat as follows: "I am going downtown to see So-and-So about the Such-and-Such contract, but I don't know what the traffic conditions will be like or how long it will take me to get a place to park nor do I know what shape So-and-So will be in today, but taking all this into account I think I will be out of the office about an hour but don't like to commit myself, so if anyone calls you can say I'm not sure how long I will be; in any event I expect to be back before 4 o'clock."

Few of us realize how much we rely on built-in patterns to interpret messages of this sort. An Iranian friend of mine who came to live in the U.S. was hurt and puzzled for the first few years. The new friends he met and liked would say on parting: "Well, I'll see you later." He mournfully complained: "I kept expecting to see them, but the 'later' never came." Strangely enough we ourselves are exasperated when a Mexican can't tell us precisely what he means when he uses the expression *mañana*.

The role of the anthropologist in preparing people for ser- 26
vice overseas is to open their eyes and sensitize them to the subtle qualities of behavior—tone of voice, gestures, space and time
relationships—that so often build up feelings of frustration and
hostility in other people with a different culture. Whether we
are going to live in a particular foreign country or travel in
many, we need a frame of reference that will enable us to observe and learn the significance of differences in manners.
Progress is being made in this anthropological study, but it is
also showing us how little is known about human behavior.

1955

Distancing the Homeless

Jonathan Kozol

It is commonly believed by many journalists and politicians 1
that the homeless of America are, in large part, former patients
of large mental hospitals who were deinstitutionalized in the
1970s—the consequence, it is sometimes said, of misguided liberal opinion, which favored the treatment of such persons in
community-based centers. It is argued that this policy, and the
subsequent failure of society to build such centers or to provide
them in sufficient number, is the primary cause of homelessness
in the United States.

Those who work among the homeless do not find that ex- 2
planation satisfactory. While conceding that a certain number
of the homeless are, or have been, mentally unwell, they believe
that, in the case of most unsheltered people, the primary reason is economic rather than clinical. The cause of homelessness,
they say with disarming logic, is the lack of homes and of income with which to rent or acquire them.

They point to the loss of traditional jobs in industry (two 3
million every year since 1980) and to the fact that half of those

who are laid off end up in work that pays a poverty-level wage. They point to the parallel growth of poverty in families with children, noting that children, who represent one quarter of our population, make up forty percent of the poor; since 1968, the number of children in poverty has grown by three million, while welfare benefits to families with children have declined by 35 percent.

And they note, too, that these developments have coincided   4 with a time in which the shortage of low-income housing has intensified as the gentrification of our major cities has accelerated. Half a million units of low-income housing have been lost each year to condominium conversion as well as to arson, demolition, or abandonment. Between 1978 and 1980, median rents climbed 30 percent for people in the lowest income sector, driving many of these families into the streets. After 1980, rents rose at even faster rates. In Boston, between 1982 and 1984, over 80 percent of the housing units renting below three hundred dollars disappeared, while the number of units renting above six hundred dollars nearly tripled.

Hard numbers, in this instance, would appear to be of   5 greater help than psychiatric labels in telling us why so many people become homeless. Eight million American families now pay half or more of their income for rent or a mortgage. Six million more, unable to pay rent at all, live doubled up with others. At the same time, federal support for low-income housing dropped from $30 billion (1980) to $9 billion (1986). Under Presidents Ford and Carter, five hundred thousand subsidized private housing units were constructed. By President Reagan's second term, the number had dropped to twenty-five thousand. "We're getting out of the housing business, period," said a deputy assistant secretary of the Department of Housing and Urban Development in 1985.

One year later, the *Washington Post* reported that the num-   6 ber of homeless families in Washington, D.C., had grown by 500 percent over the previous twelve months. In New York City, the waiting list for public housing now contains two hundred thousand names. The waiting is eighteen years.

Why, in the face of these statistics, are we impelled to find   7 a psychiatric explanation for the growth of homelessness in the United States?

A misconception, once it is implanted in the popular imagination, is not easy to uproot, particularly when it serves a useful social role. The notion that the homeless are largely psychotics who belong in institutions, rather than victims of displacement at the hands of enterprising realtors, spares us from the need to offer realistic solutions to the fact of deep and widening extremes of wealth and poverty in the United States. It also enables us to tell ourselves that the despair of homeless people bears no intimate connection to the privileged existence we enjoy—when, for example, we rent or purchase one of those restored town-houses that once provided shelter for people now huddled in the street.   8

But there may be another reason to assign labels to the destitute. Terming economic victims "psychotic" or "disordered" helps to place them at a distance. It says that they aren't quite like us—and, more important, that we could not be like them. The plight of homeless families is a nightmare. It may not seem natural to try to banish human beings from our midst, but it is natural to try to banish nightmares from our minds.   9

So the rituals of clinical contamination proceed uninterrupted by the economic facts described above. Research that addresses homelessness as an *injustice* rather than as a medical *misfortune* does not win the funding of foundations. And the research which is funded, defining the narrowed borders of permissible debate, diverts our attention from the antecedent to the secondary cause of homelessness. Thus it is that perfectly ordinary women whom I know in New York City—people whose depression or anxiety is a realistic consequence of months and even years in crowded shelters or the streets—are interrogated by invasive research scholars in an effort to decode their poverty, to find clinical categories for their despair and terror, to identify the secret failing that lies hidden in their psyche.   10

Many pregnant women without homes are denied prenatal care because they constantly travel from one shelter to another. Many are anemic. Many are denied essential dietary supplements by recent federal cuts. As a consequence, some of   11

their children do not live to see their second year of life. Do these
mothers sometimes show signs of stress? Do they appear dis-
organized, depressed, disordered? Frequently. They are im-
mobilized by pain, traumatized by fear. So it is no surprise that
when researchers enter the scene to ask them how they "feel,"
the resulting reports tell us that the homeless are emotionally
unwell. The reports do not tell us we have *made* these people
ill. They do not tell us that illness is a natural response to intolerable conditions. Nor do they tell us of the strength and the re-
silience that so many of these people still retain despite the miseries they must endure. They set these men and women apart
in capsules labeled "personality disorder" or "psychotic,"
where they no longer threaten our complacence.

I visited Haiti not many years ago, when the Duvalier fam-   12
ily was still in power. If an American scholar were to have made
a psychological study of the homeless families living in the
streets of Port-au-Prince—sleeping amidst rotten garbage,
bathing in open sewers—and if he were to return to the United
States to tell us that the reasons for their destitution were "behavioral problems" or "a lack of mental health," we would be
properly suspicious. Knowledgeable Haitians would not
merely be suspicious. They would be enraged. Even to initiate
such research when economic and political explanations present
themselves so starkly would appear grotesque. It is no less so
in the United States.

One of the more influential studies of this nature was car-   13
ried out in 1985 by Ellen Bassuk, a psychiatrist at Harvard University. Drawing upon interviews with eight homeless parents,
Dr. Bassuk contends, according to the *Boston Globe,* that "90
percent [of these people] have problems other than housing
and poverty that are so acute they would be unable to live successfully on their own." She also precludes the possibility that
illness, where it does exist, may be provoked by destitution.
"Our data," she writes, "suggest that mental illness tends to pre-
cede homelessness." She concedes that living in the streets can
make a homeless person's mental illness worse; but she insists
upon the fact of prior illness.

The executive director of the Massachusetts Commission on   14

Children and Youth believes that Dr. Bassuk's estimate is far too
high. The staff of Massachusetts Human Services Secretary Phillip
Johnston believes the appropriate number is closer to 10 percent.

In defending her research, Bassuk challenges such critics by   15
claiming that they do not have data to refute her. This may be
true. Advocates for the homeless do not receive funds to defend
the sanity of the people they represent. In placing the burden
of proof upon them, Dr. Bassuk has created an extraordinary di-
alectic: How does one prove that people aren't unwell? What
homeless mother would consent to enter a procedure that might
"prove" her mental health? What overburdened shelter operator would divert scarce funds to such an exercise? It is an unnatural, offensive, and dehumanizing challenge.

Dr. Bassuk's work, however, isn't the issue I want to raise   16
here; the issue is the use or misuse of that work by critics of the
poor. For example, in a widely syndicated essay published in
1986, the newspaper columnist Charles Krauthammer argued
that the homeless are essentially a deranged segment of the
population and that we must find the "political will" to isolate
them from society. We must do this, he said, "whether they like
it or not." Arguing even against the marginal benefits of homeless shelters, Krauthammer wrote: "There is a better alternative,
however, though no one dares speak its name." Krauthammer
dares: that better alternative, he said, is "asylum."

One of Mr. Krauthammer's colleagues at the *Washington*   17
Post, the columnist George Will, perceives the homeless as a
threat to public cleanliness and argues that they ought to be consigned to places where we need not see them. "It is," he says,
"simply a matter of public hygiene" to put them out of sight.
Another journalist, Charles Murray, writing from the vantage
point of a social Darwinist, recommends the restoration of the
almshouses of the 1800s. "Granted Dickensian horror stories
about almshouses," he begins, there were nonetheless "good
almshouses"; he proposes "a good correctional 'halfway
house' " as a proper shelter for a mother and child with no
means of self-support.

In the face of such declarations, the voices of those who   18
work with and know the poor are harder to hear.

Manhattan Borough President David Dinkins made the fol- 19 lowing observation on the basis of a study commissioned in 1986: "No facts support the belief that addiction or behavioral problems occur with more frequency in the homeless family population than in a similar socioeconomic population. Homeless families are not demographically different from other public assistance families when they enter the shelter system . . . Family homelessness is typically a housing and income problem: the unavailability of affordable housing and the inadequacy of public assistance income."

In a "hypothetical world," write James Wright and Julie 20 Lam of the University of Massachusetts, "where there were no alcoholics, no drug addicts, no mentally ill, no deinstitutionalization, . . . indeed, no personal social pathologies at all, there would still be a formidable homelessness problem, simply because at this stage in American history, there is not enough low-income housing" to accommodate the poor.

New York State's respected commissioner of social ser- 21 vices, Cesar Perales, makes the point in fewer words: "Homelessness is less and less a result of personal failure, and more and more is caused by larger forces. There is no longer affordable housing in New York City for people of poor and modest means."

Even the words of medical practitioners who care for home- 22 less people have been curiously ignored. A study published by the Massachusetts Medical Society, for instance, has noted that the most frequent illnesses among a sample of the homeless population, after alcohol and drug use, are trauma (31 percent), upper respiratory disorders (28 percent), limb disorders (19 percent), mental illness (16 percent), skin diseases (15 percent), hypertension (14 percent), and neurological illnesses (12 percent). (Excluded from this tabulation are lead poisoning, malnutrition, acute diarrhea, and other illnesses especially common among homeless infants and small children.) Why, we may ask, of all these calamities, does mental illness command so much political and press attention? The answer may be that the label of mental illness places the destitute outside the sphere of ordinary life. It personalizes an anguish that is public in its genesis; it individualizes a misery that is both general in cause and general in application.

The rate of tuberculosis among the homeless is believed to   23
be ten times that of the general population. Asthma, I have learned in countless interviews, is one of the most common causes of discomfort in the shelters. Compulsive smoking, exacerbated by the crowding and the tension, is more common in the shelters than in any place that I have visited except prison. Infected and untreated sores, scabies, diarrhea, poorly set limbs, protruding elbows, awkwardly distorted wrists, bleeding gums, impacted teeth, and other untreated dental problems are so common among children in the shelters that one rapidly forgets their presence. Hunger and emaciation are everywhere. Children as well as adults can bring to mind the photographs of people found in camps for refugees of war in 1945. But these miseries bear no stigma, and mental illness does. It conveys a stigma in the Soviet Union. It conveys a stigma in the United States. In both nations the label is used, whether as a matter of deliberate policy or not, to isolate and treat as special cases those who, by deed or word or sheer presence, represent a threat to national complacence. The two situations are obviously not identical, but they are enough alike to give Americans reason for concern.

Last summer, some twenty-eight thousand homeless peo-   24
ple were afforded shelter by the city of New York. Of this number, twelve thousand were children and six thousand were parents living together in families. The average child was six years old, the average parent twenty-seven. A typical homeless family included a mother with two or three children, but in about one-fifth of these families two parents were present. Roughly ten thousand single persons, then, made up the remainder of the population of the city's shelters.

These proportions vary somewhat from one area of the na-   25
tion to another. In all areas, however, families are the fastest-growing sector of the homeless population, and in the Northeast they are by far the largest sector already. In Massachusetts, three-fourths of the homeless now are families with children;

in certain parts of Massachusetts—Attleboro and Northampton, for example—the proportion reaches ninety percent. Two-thirds of the homeless children studied recently in Boston were less than five years old.

Of an estimated two to three million homeless people na- 26
tionwide, about 500,000 are dependent children, according to Robert Hayes, counsel to the National Coalition for the Homeless. Including their parents, at least 750,000 homeless people in America are family members.

What is to be made, then, of the supposition that the home- 27
less are primarily the former residents of mental hospitals, persons who were carelessly released during the 1970s? Many of them are, to be sure. Among the older men and women in the streets and shelters, as many as one-third (some believe as many as one-half) may be chronically disturbed, and a number of these people were deinstitutionalized during the 1970s. But in a city like New York, where nearly half the homeless are small children with an average age of six, to operate on the basis of such a supposition makes no sense. Their parents, with an average age of twenty-seven, are not likely to have been hospitalized in the 1970s, either.

Nor is it easy to assume, as was once the case, that single 28
men—those who come closer to fitting the stereotype of the homeless vagrant, the drifting alcoholic of an earlier age—are the former residents of mental hospitals. The age of homeless men has dropped in recent years; many of them are only twenty-one to twenty-eight years old. Fifty percent of homeless men in New York City shelters in 1984 were there for the first time. Most had previously had homes and jobs. Many had never before needed public aid.

A frequently cited set of figures tells us that in 1955, the av- 29
erage daily census of nonfederal psychiatric institutions was 677,000, and that by 1984, the number had dropped to 151,000. Subtract the second number from the first, conventional logic tells us, and we have an explanation for the homelessness of half a million people. A closer look at the same number offers us a different lesson.

The sharpest decline in the average daily census of these in- 30 stitutions occurred prior to 1978, and the largest part of that decline, in fact, appeared at least a decade earlier. From 677,000 in 1955, the census dropped to 378,000 in 1972. The 1974 census was 307,000. In 1976 it was 230,000; in 1977 it was 211,000; and in 1978 it was 190,000. In no year since 1978 has the average daily census dropped by more than 9,000 persons, and in the six-year period from 1978 to 1984, the total decline was 39,000 persons. Compared with a decline of 300,000 from 1955 to 1972, and of nearly 200,000 more from 1972 to 1978, the number is small. But the years since 1980 are the period in which the present homeless crisis surfaced. Only since 1983 have homeless individuals overflowed the shelters.

If the large numbers of the homeless lived in hospitals be- 31 fore they reappeared in subway stations and in public shelters, we need to ask where they were and what they had been doing from 1972 to 1980. Were they living under bridges? Were they waiting out the decade in the basements of deserted buildings?

No. The bulk of those who had been psychiatric patients 32 and were released from hospitals during the 1960s and early 1970s had been living in the meantime in low-income housing, many in skid-row hotels or boarding houses. Such housing— commonly known as SRO (single-room occupancy) units—was drastically diminished by the gentrification of our cities that began in 1970. Almost 50 percent of SRO housing was replaced by luxury apartments or by office buildings between 1970 and 1980, and the remaining units have been disappearing at even faster rates. As recently as 1986, after New York City had issued a prohibition against conversion of such housing, a well-known developer hired a demolition team to destroy a building in Times Square that had previously been home to indigent people. The demolition took place in the middle of the night. In order to avoid imprisonment, the developer was allowed to make a philanthropic gift to homeless people as a token of atonement. This incident, bizarre as it appears, reminds us that the profit motive for displacement of the poor is very great in every major city. It also indicates a more realistic explanation for the growth of homelessness during the 1980s.

Even for those persons who are ill and were deinstitution- 33
alized during the decades before 1980, the precipitating cause
of homelessness in 1987 is not illness but loss of housing. SRO
housing, unattractive as it may have been, offered low-cost
sanctuaries for the homeless, providing a degree of safety and
mutual support for those who lived within them. They were a
demeaning version of the community health centers that society had promised; they were the de facto "halfway houses" of
the 1970s. For these people too, then—at most half of the homeless single persons in America—the cause of homelessness is
lack of housing.

A writer in the *New York Times* describes a homeless woman 34
standing on a traffic island in Manhattan. "She was evicted
from her small room in the hotel just across the street," and she
is determined to get revenge. Until she does, "nothing will
move her from that spot. . . . Her argumentativeness and her
angry fixation on revenge, along with the apparent absence of
hallucinations, mark her as a paranoid." Most physicians, I
imagine, would be more reserved in passing judgment with so
little evidence, but this author makes his diagnosis without hesitation. "The paranoids of the street," he says, "are among the
most difficult to help."

Perhaps so. But does it depend on who is offering the help? 35
Is anyone offering to help this woman get back her home? Is it
crazy to seek vengeance for being thrown into the street? The
absence of anger, some psychiatrists believe, might indicate
much greater illness.

The same observer sees additional symptoms of pathology 36
("negative symptoms," he calls them) in the fact that many
homeless persons demonstrate a "gross deterioration in their
personal hygiene" and grooming, leading to "indifference" and
"apathy." Having just identified one woman as unhealthy because she is so far from being "indifferent" as to seek revenge,
he now sees apathy as evidence of illness; so consistency is not
what we are looking for in this account. But how much less indifferent might the homeless be if those who decide their fate
were less indifferent themselves? How might their grooming

and hygiene be improved if they were permitted access to a public toilet?

In New York City, as in many cities, homeless people are 37 denied the right to wash in public bathrooms, to store their few belongings in a public locker, or, in certain cases, to make use of public toilets altogether. Shaving, cleaning of clothes, and other forms of hygiene are prohibited in the men's room of Grand Central Station. The terminal's three hundred lockers, used in former times by homeless people to secure their goods, were removed in 1986 as "a threat to public safety," according to a study made by the New York City Council.

At one-thirty every morning, homeless people are ejected 38 from the station. Many once attempted to take refuge on the ramp that leads to Forty-second Street because it was protected from the street by wooden doors and thus provided some degree of warmth. But the station management responded to this challenge in two ways. The ramp was mopped with a strong mixture of ammonia to produce a noxious smell, and when the people sleeping there brought cardboard boxes and newspapers to protect them from the fumes, the entrance doors were chained wide open. Temperatures dropped some nights to ten degrees. Having driven these people to the streets, city officials subsequently determined that their willingness to risk exposure to cold weather could be taken as further evidence of mental illness.

At Pennsylvania Station in New York, homeless women 39 are denied the use of toilets. Amtrak police come by and herd them off each hour on the hour. In June 1985, Amtrak officials issued this directive to police: "It is the policy of Amtrak to not allow the homeless and undesirables to remain. . . . Officers are encouraged to eject all undesirables. . . . Now is the time to train and educate them that their presence will not be tolerated as cold weather sets in." In an internal memo, according to CBS, an Amtrak official asked flatly: "Can't we get rid of this trash?"

I have spent many nights in conversation with the women 40 who are huddled in the corridors and near the doorway of the public toilets in Penn Station. Many are young. Most are cogent. Few are dressed in the familiar rags suggested by the term *bag ladies.* Unable to bathe or use the toilets in the station, almost all are in conditions of intolerable physical distress. The sight of clusters of police officers, mostly male, guarding a toilet from use by homeless women speaks volumes about the public conscience of New York.

Where do these women defecate? How do they bathe? What 41 will we do when, in her physical distress, a woman finally disrobes in public and begins to urinate right on the floor? "Gross deterioration," someone will call it, evidence of mental illness. In the course of an impromptu survey in the streets last September, Mayor Koch observed a homeless woman who had soiled her own clothes. Not only was the woman crazy, said the mayor, but those who differed with him on his diagnosis must be crazy, too. "I am the number one social worker in this town— with sanity," said he.

It may be that this woman was psychotic, but the mayor's 42 comment says a great deal more about his sense of revulsion and the moral climate of a decade in which words like these may be applauded than about her mental state.

A young man who had lost his job, then his family, then his 43 home, all in the summer of 1986, spoke with me for several hours in Grand Central Station on the weekend following Thanksgiving. "A year ago," he said, "I never thought that somebody like me would end up in a shelter. Nothing you've ever undergone prepares you. You walk into the place [a shelter on the Bowery]—the smell of sweat and urine hits you like a wall. Unwashed bodies and the look of absolute despair on many, many faces there would make you think you were in Dante's Hell. . . . What you fear is that you will be here forever. You do not know if it is ever going to end. You think to yourself: it is a dream and I will awake. Sometimes I think: it's an experiment. They are watching you to find out how much you can take. . . . I was a pretty stable man. Now I tremble when I meet somebody in the ordinary world. I'm trembling right now. . . . For me, the loss of work and loss of wife had left me rocking. Then the welfare regulations hit me. I began to feel that I would be reduced to trash. . . . Half the people that I know are suffering from chest infections and sleep deprivation. The lack of sleep leaves you debilitated, shaky. You exaggerate your fears. If a psychiatrist came along he'd say that I was crazy. But I was an ordinary man. There was nothing wrong with me. I lost my kids. I lost my home. Now would you say that I was crazy if I told you I was feeling sad?"

"If the plight of homeless adults is the shame of America," writes Fred Hechinger in the *New York Times,* "the lives of homeless children are the nation's crime." 44

In November 1984, a fact already known to advocates for the homeless was given brief attention by the press. Homeless families, the *New York Times* reported, "mostly mothers and young children, have been sleeping on chairs, counters, and floors of the city's emergency welfare offices." Reacting to such reports, the mayor declared: "The woman is sitting on a chair or on a floor. It is not because we didn't offer her a bed. We provide a shelter for every single person who knocks on our door." On the same day, however, the city reported that in the previous eleven weeks it had been unable to give shelter to 153 families, and in the subsequent year, 1985, the city later reported that about two thousand children slept in welfare offices because of lack of shelter space. 45

Some eight hundred homeless infants in New York City, reported the National Coalition for the Homeless, "routinely go without sufficient food, cribs, health care, and diapers." The lives of these children "are put at risk," while "high-risk pregnant women" are repeatedly forced to sleep in unsafe "barracks shelters" or welfare offices called Emergency Assistance Units (EAUs). "Coalition monitors, making sporadic random checks, found eight women in their *ninth* month of pregnancy sleeping in EAUs. . . . Two women denied shelter began having labor contractions at the EAU." In one instance, the Legal Aid Society was forced to go to court after a woman lost her child by miscarriage while lying on the floor of a communal bathroom in a shelter which the courts had already declared unfit to house pregnant women. 46

The coalition also reported numerous cases in which homeless mothers were obliged to choose between purchasing food or diapers for their infants. Federal guidelines issued in 1986 47 deepened the nutrition crisis faced by mothers in the welfare shelters by counting the high rent paid to the owners of the buildings as a part of family income, rendering their residents ineligible for food stamps. Families I interviewed who had received as much as $150 in food stamps monthly in June 1986 were cut back to $33 before Christmas.

"Now you're hearing all kinds of horror stories," said President Reagan, "about the people that are going to be thrown out in the snow to hunger and [to] die of cold and so forth. . . . We haven't cut a single budget." But in the four years leading up to 1985, according to the *New Republic,* Aid to Families with Dependent Children had been cut by $4.8 billion, child nutrition programs by $5.2 billion, food stamps by $6.8 billion. The federal government's authority to help low-income families with housing assistance was cut from $30 billion to $11 billion in Reagan's first term. In his fiscal 1986 budget, the president proposed to cut that by an additional 95 percent.

"If even one American child is forced to go to bed hungry at night," the president said on another occasion, "that is a national tragedy. We are too generous a people to allow this." But in the years since the president spoke these words, thousands of poor children in New York alone have gone to bed too sick to sleep and far too weak to rise the next morning to attend a public school. Thousands more have been unable to attend school at all because their homeless status compels them to move repeatedly from one temporary shelter to another. Even in the affluent suburbs outside New York City, hundreds of homeless children are obliged to ride as far as sixty miles twice a day in order to obtain an education in the public schools to which they were originally assigned before their families were displaced. Many of these children get to school too late to eat their breakfast; others are denied lunch at school because of federal cuts in feeding programs.

Many homeless children die—and others suffer brain damage—as a direct consequence of federal cutbacks in prenatal programs, maternal nutrition, and other feeding programs. The parents of one such child shared with me the story of the year in which their child was delivered, lived, and died. The child, weighing just over four pounds at birth, grew deaf and blind soon after, and for these reasons had to stay in the hospital for several months. When he was released on Christmas Eve of 1984, his mother and father had no home. He lived with his parents in the shelters, subways, streets, and welfare offices of New York City for four winter months, and was readmitted to the hospital in time to die in May 1985.

When we met and spoke the following year, the father told 51 me that his wife had contemplated and even attempted suicide after the child's death, while he had entertained the thought of blowing up the welfare offices of New York City. I would tell him that to do so would be illegal and unwise. I would never tell him it was crazy.

"No one will be turned away," says the mayor of New York 52 City, as hundreds of young mothers with their infants are turned from the doors of shelters season after season. That may sound to some like denial of reality. "Now you're hearing all these stories," says the president of the United States as he denies that anyone is cold or hungry or unhoused. On another occasion he says that the unsheltered "are homeless, you might say, by choice." That sounds every bit as self-deceiving.

The woman standing on the traffic island screaming for re- 53 venge until her room has been restored to her sounds relatively healthy by comparison. If three million homeless people did the same, and all at the same time, we might finally be forced to listen.

1988

On a Greek Holiday

Alice Bloom

The only interesting question on a trip for me is—what sus- 1 tains life elsewhere? How deep does it go? Can one see it? This hope, this anticipation, is forcibly blocked. Henry Miller, in

193—, stood in Epidaurus, alone, in a "weird solitude," and felt the "great heart of the world beat." We stand at Epidaurus with several thousand others, some of whom are being called "my chickens" by their tour guide who calls herself "your mother hen," whose counterpart, this time at Delphi, explains several times that what is being looked at is the "bellybutton of the world, okay? The Greeks thought, this is the bellybutton of the world, okay?" "These stones all look alike to me," someone grumbles. There is no help for it; we're there with guidebooks ourselves; but this fact—tourism is big business—and others, throw us back, unwilling, into contemplation of our own dull home-soul, our dull bodily comforts, our own dull dwindling purse, our own dull resentments; because the other—in this case, Greece—is either rapidly disappearing or else, self-protective, is retreating so far it has disappeared. You can get there, but you can't get at it.

For instance, a study of travel posters and brochures, which   2 in the process of setting dates and buying tickets always precedes a trip, shows us, by projection into these pictured, toothy, tourist bodies, having some gorgeous piece of ingestion: the yellow beach, the mossy blue ruin, a dinner table laden with food and red wine of the region, dancing, skiing, golfing, shopping, waving to roadside natives as our rented car sails by, as though we only go to play, as though all we do here at home is work, as though, for two or four weeks abroad, we seek regression.

Also in the posters, but as part of the landscape, there are   3 the natives—whether Spanish, Greek, Irish, etc.—costumed as attractions, performing in bouzouki or bag-pipe bands, or doing some picturesque and nonindustrial piece of work such as fishing, weaving, selling colorful cheap goods in open-air markets, herding sheep or goats. The journey promised by the posters and brochures is a trip into everyone's imaginary past: one's own, drained of the normal childhood content of fear, death, space, hurt, abandonment, perplexity, and so forth, now presented as the salesmen think we think it should have been: one in which we only ate, slept, and played in the eternal sun under the doting care of benevolent elders.

And we are shown the benevolent elders, the imaginary na-   4

tives who also, for a handsome fee, exist now, in the present of
the trip we are about to take. ("Take" is probably a more telling
verb here than we think.) They exist in a past where they are
pictured having grown cheerfully old and wise doing only
harmless, enjoyable, pre-industrial, clean, self-employed, open-
air work, in pink crinkled cheeks, merry eyes, and wonderful
quaint clothes, with baskets, nets, toyshaped boats, flower
boxes, cottages, sheep crooks, country roads, white-washed
walls, tea shop signs, and other paraphernalia of the pastoral
wish. I have never seen a travel poster showing natives of the
country enjoying their own food or beaches or ski-jumps or
hotel balconies; nor have I ever seen a travel poster showing the
natives working the nightshift in the Citroën factory, either.

The natives in the posters (are they Swiss, Mexican, Chilean,   5
Turkish models?) are happy parent figures, or character dolls,
and their faces, like the faces of the good parents we are supposed to have dreamed, show them pleased with their own lot,
busy but not too busy with a job that they obviously like, content with each other, and warmly indulgent of our need to play,
to be fed good, clean food on time, and to be tucked into a nice
bed at the end of our little day. They are the childhood people
that also existed in early grammar-school readers, and nowhere
else: adults in your neighborhood, in the identifiable costumes
of their humble tasks, transitional-object people, smiling milk-
man, friendly aproned store-owner in his small friendly store,
happy mailman happy to bring your happy mail, happy
mommy, icons who make up a six-year-old's school-enforced
dream town, who enjoy doing their nonindustrial, unmysteri-
ous tasks: mail, milk, red apple, cooky, just for you, so you can
learn to decipher: See, Jip, see.

A travel remark I have always savored came from someone   6
surprised in love for a place, just returned from a month in the
Far East (no longer tagged "the mysterious," I've noticed), and
who was explaining this trip at a party. She said, "I just loved
Japan. It was so authentic and Oriental." Few people would go
quite so naked as that, but the charm of her feelings seemed just
right. Perhaps she had expected Tokyo to be more or less a
larger version of the Japanese Shop in the Tokyo Airport. It is

somewhat surprising that she found it to be anything much more.

One of the hushed-tone moral superiority stories, the aren't-we-advanced stories told by those lucky enough to travel in Soviet Russia, has to do with that government's iron management of the trip. There are people who can't be met, buildings that can't be entered, upper story windows that can't be photographed, streets that can't be strolled, districts that can't be crossed, cities in which it is impossible to spend the night, and so on. However, our notions of who we are and what comforts we demand and what conditions we'll endure, plus any country's understandably garbled versions of who we are, what we want, and what we'll pay for, are far more rigid than the strictures of any politburo because such strictures don't say "This is you, this is what you must want," but "This is what you can't, under any circumstances, do." That, though it inhibits movement, and no doubt in some cases prevents a gathering of or understanding of some crucial or desired bit of information, has at least the large virtue of defining the tourist as potentially dangerous. What we meet most of the time, here and abroad, is a definition of ourselves as harmless, spoiled babies, of low endurance and little information, minimal curiosity, frozen in infancy, frozen in longing, terrified for our next square meal and clean bed, and whose only potential danger is that we might refuse to be separated from our money.

Suppose, for a moment, that tourism—the largest "industry" in Greece (it employs, even more than shipping, the most people)—were also the largest industry in America. Not just in Manhattan or Washington, D.C., or Disneyland or Disneyworld or at the Grand Canyon or Niagara Falls, but in every motel, hotel, restaurant, in every McDonald's and Colonel Sanders and Howard Johnson's and Mom & Pop's, in every bar and neighborhood hang-out, truck stop, gas station, pharmacy, department store, museum, church, historical site, battleground, in every taxi, bus, subway, train, plane, in every public building, in post offices and banks and public bathrooms, on every street in every city, town, village and hamlet from West Jones-

port, Maine, to Centralia, Illinois, to Parachute, Colorado, and
every stop in between and beyond, just as it is in Greece:
tourists.

Suppose that every other business establishment across the   9
country therefore found it in their best interest to become a sou-
venir shop, selling cheap, mass-produced "gifts" for the tourists
to take back home that, back home, would announce that they
had visited America. What images would we mass produce for
them? Millions of little bronzed Liberty Bells? Tepees? St. Louis
Arches? Streetcars named "Desire"? Statues of Babe Ruth? of
Liberty? of Daniel Boone? In Greece we saw miniature bottles
of ouzo encased in tiny plastic replicas of the temple of Athena
Nike. Could we do something so clever, and immediately rec-
ognizable, with miniatures of bourbon? Encase them in tiny
plastic Washington Monuments? Lincoln Memorials? Would
we feel misrepresented?

Third, suppose that a sizable portion of these tourists want-   10
ing gifts, toilets, rooms, baths, meals, dollars, film, drinks,
stamps, directions, are Greek; or else, let us suppose that we assumed, that whether actually Greek or not, wherever they come
from they speak Greek as a second language. Assume, therefore,
that our map and traffic and road signs, postings of instruction
and information, advertisements, timetables, directions—
"stop," "go," "hot," "cold," "men," "women," "open," "closed,"
"yes," "no,"—to name a few rudiments of life, plus all the
menus in all those sandwich counters, truck stops, fast-food out-
lets, lunch rooms, and so forth, had to be in Greek as well as in
English. We have never been, so far, an occupied country,
whether by forces enemy or not. Undoubtedly, if we were, as
an ongoing fact of our "in-season" summer months, we Americans, having to offer our multitudinous wares in Greek, would
come up with items as hilarious as those we collected from the
English side of Greek menus: baygon and egs. Xamberger
steake. Veat. Orange juise. Rost beef. Shrimp carry. Potoes,
Spaggeti. Morcoroni. And our favorite, Fried Smooth Hound.
(This turned out to be a harmless local fish, much to the disappointment of our children, born surrealists.)

Suppose that we had to post Bar Harbor, Plum Island, Chin-   11

coteague, Key West, Bay St. Louis, Galveston, Big Sur and Seat-
tle beaches with "No Nakedness Allowed" signs, but that the
Greeks and other tourists, freed from the cocoons of air-
conditioned tour buses, armed with sun-oil in every degree of
protection, rushed beachwards past the signs and stripped to
their altogether, anyway? Would our police sit quietly in the
shade and drink with other men and turn, literally, their khaki-
clad rumps to the beach, as did the Greek police?

And food. Suppose we had to contrive to feed them, these   12
hungry hordes? They will come here, as we go there, entrenched
in their habits and encumbered with fears of being cheated,
fears of indigestion, of recurrent allergies, of breaking their
diets, of catching American trots, of being poisoned by our
water, fattened by our grease and starch, put off by our feeding schedules, sickened by something weird or local. Suppose
we decided, out of some semiconscious, unorganized, but national canniness, that what these tourists really want is our cobbled version of their national foods. Whom will we please: the
English who want their teas at four, or the Italians who want
supper at nine at night? Or both? And what will we cook and
serve, and how will we spell it?

Or suppose they want to eat "American" food. What tastes   13
like us? What flavors contain our typicality, our history, our he-
roes, our dirt, our speeches, our poets, our battles, our national
shames? The hot dog? Corn on the cob? I have eaten, barring
picnics and occasional abstention, probably about 130 meals in
Greece. And Greek food, I feel somewhat qualified to say, contains their history, and tastes of sorrow and triumph, of olive
oil and blood, in about equal amounts. It is the most astound-
ing and the most boring food that I, an eater, have ever eaten.

Greek food is tragic. Why? Because each bite is a chomp into   14
history, our history. Why? Because this lunch—small fish,
cheese, olives, wine, bread—exactly this lunch, and tomorrow's
lunch—fish, cheese, olives, wine, bread—has been eaten since
the time of the glory that will someday be called Greece, the
glory that existed for a moment, the glory that Greece was, and
the glory that mankind—for Greece is that, not Greek, but
mankind—might yet be. Each bite is archaeological, into fine

layers of millennia: fish, oil, cheese, wine, bread—in the par-
taking we join, on the back of the tongue, Amazon forces and
single crazy saints, mythical men who married their mythical
mothers, and men, and mothers, who today and tomorrow only
dream of it.

One uses a big word like "timeless" with caution, if at all.   15
But there is nothing timely about two things in Greece; therefore it is not rhetorical to claim that, in Greece, the quality of the
heat of the sun on the skin and the quality of the food in the
mouth are perhaps as close as we can come to the taste of "time-
lessness." Along with the oldest human question—how can we
make God happy?—this sun and this food are among the most
ancient sensations recorded.

Under this summer sun every meal, beginning with break-   16
fast, is eaten in 100 degrees of heat and hotter—115, 120—by afternoon. The meal, any one of them, is composed of food that
grows best in this climate and yet is entirely unsuited to it as
daily refreshment. No one could possibly, certainly not a tourist,
need this oil-soaked food for fuel in mid-July. It tastes and feels,
though, like fuel: heavy, shiny, slow-moving food, purple,
brown, red: tomatoes, eggplants, fish, lamb, olives, black wine,
blinding white cheese, much bread. We eat this three times a
day; three times a day the tourists eat it and the Greeks eat it.
Everyone seems to look forward to the next meal, and all
around our table, where we eat again with relish, are others eating with relish, sometimes even with a look of reprieve and relief. And there is no escape from it. Who would risk whatever
"shrimp carry" might be? There is no ordering something else—
a salad of lettuce for a change, or a thin chicken sandwich. There
is nothing but this food with its taste and texture of ancient days,
of old crimes, forbidden loves, of something tinny and resigned,
something of both gluttony and renunciation.

In addition to being a tragic cuisine, a sacramental cuisine,   17
it is also practical, cheap, crude, and uninventive. The raw materials are without equal: eggplants hang with the burnish of
Dutch interiors; the fish still flap as they are headed oilwards;
the lamb chop's mother befouls the yard next to your table;
fruit so perfect, so total, that the scent of a single peach in a paper

bag perfumes the whole room overnight and brings tears of love
of God to the eyes. On a walk into the hills, meadows of thyme
and mint and basil are idly crushed under heel. What happens
to all this in the pot is a miracle of transformation, of negligence
or brutality; or possibly, stubborn evidence of some otherwise
lost political knowledge of what draws out the best, most noble,
and most beautiful in the masses.

For the food is destroyed, each meal, in the process from   18
vine or net or garden to violent table. Its facts are these: it has
always been eaten thus, with the exception of the late-coming
tomato. It is—lamb, eggplant, olive, fish, white cheese—even
now, perfectly indigenous. It is plain cooking. It is cooked for
hours, all day; oil is poured on without restraint, discretion, or
mercy. Every morsel is the same temperature and consistency
by the time it reaches the palate. In a profound way, it is stupid
food, overfeeding the flesh while tasting as though one should
renounce the flesh forever.

We did not, to be fair, eat in a single Greek home. However,   19
we were careful to eat where the Greeks ate, and the Greeks eat
out—in family groups, starched, ironed, slicked-down heads,
whited summer shoes, strictly disciplined children; or in tense,
dark groups of greedy, hasty men; which is how, as families or
as men, the Greeks travel through the day. From the second-
story, open-air, Greek-family-filled restaurant where we ate
most of our meals while on the island, we could, if we had a
table near the edge, throw our bread scraps, if we had any left
over, straight down into the blue-green sea for the melon and
dove-colored fish to mouth; and we could watch the evening
sky turn from the day's bleached-out white to a pale English
blue, then to lime-green streaked with apricot, and finally, with
the fall of night, to a grape-purple that rose, in that instant, up
from the sea.

1983

CHAPTER 8

Cause and Effect

How Do You Know It's Good?

Marya Mannes

Suppose there were no critics to tell us how to react to a pic-   1
ture, a play, or a new composition of music. Suppose we wandered innocent as the dawn into an art exhibition of unsigned
paintings. By what standards, by what values would we decide
whether they were good or bad, talented or untalented, suc-
cesses or failures? How can we ever know that what we think
is right?

For the last fifteen or twenty years the fashion in criticism   2
or appreciation of the arts has been to deny the existence of any
valid criteria and to make the words "good" or "bad" irrelevant,
immaterial, and inapplicable. There is no such thing, we are
told, as a set of standards, first acquired through experience and
knowledge and later imposed on the subject under discussion.
This has been a popular approach, for it relieves the critic of the
responsibility of judgment and the public of the necessity of
knowledge. It pleases those resentful of disciplines, it flatters the
empty-minded by calling them open-minded, it comforts the
confused. Under the banner of democracy and the kind of
equality which our forefathers did *not* mean, it says, in effect,
"Who are you to tell us what *is* good or bad?" This is the same
cry used so long and so effectively by the producers of mass
media who insist that it is the public, not they, who decides
what it wants to hear and see, and that for a critic to say that

this program is bad and *this* program is good is purely a reflection of personal taste. Nobody recently has expressed this philosophy more succinctly than Dr. Frank Stanton, the highly intelligent president of CBS television. At a hearing before the Federal Communications Commission, this phrase escaped him under questioning: "One man's mediocrity is another man's good program."

There is no better way of saying "No values are absolute." ₃ There is another important aspect to this philosophy of *laissez faire:* It is the fear, in all observers of all forms of art, of guessing wrong. This fear is well come by, for who has not heard of the contemporary outcries against artists who later were called great? Every age has its arbiters who do not grow with their times, who cannot tell evolution from revolution or the difference between frivolous faddism, amateurish experimentation, and profound and necessary change. Who wants to be caught *flagrante delicto* with an error of judgment as serious as this? It is far safer, and certainly easier, to look at a picture or a play or a poem and to say "This is hard to understand, but it may be good," or simply to welcome it as a new form. The word "new"—in our country especially—has magical connotations. What is new must be good; what is old is probably bad. And if a critic can describe the new in language that nobody can understand, he's safer still. If he has mastered the art of saying nothing with exquisite complexity, nobody can quote him later as saying anything.

But all these, I maintain, are forms of abdication from the ₄ responsibility of judgment. In creating, the artist commits himself; in appreciating, you have a commitment of your own. For after all, it is the audience which makes the arts. A climate of appreciation is essential to its flowering, and the higher the expectations of the public, the better the performance of the artist. Conversely, only a public ill-served by its critics could have accepted as art and as literature so much in these last years that has been neither. If anything goes, everything goes; and at the bottom of the junkpile lie the discarded standards too.

But what are these standards? How do you get them? How ₅ do you know they're the right ones? How can you make a clear pattern out of so many intangibles, including that greatest one, the very private I?

Well for one thing, it's fairly obvious that the more you read and see and hear, the more equipped you'll be to practice that art of association which is at the basis of all understanding and judgment. The more you live and the more you look, the more aware you are of a consistent pattern—as universal as the stars, as the tides, as breathing, as night and day—underlying everything. I would call this pattern and this rhythm an order. Not order—*an* order. Within it exists an incredible diversity of forms. Without it lies chaos—the wild cells of destruction—sickness. It is in the end up to you to distinguish between the diversity that is health and the chaos that is sickness, and you can't do this without a process of association that can link a bar of Mozart with the corner of a Vermeer painting, or a Stravinsky score with a Picasso abstraction; or that can relate an aggressive act with a Franz Kline painting and a fit of coughing with a John Cage composition. 6

There is no accident in the fact that certain expressions of art live for all time and that others die with the moment, and although you may not always define the reasons, you can ask the questions. What does an artist say that is timeless; how does he say it? How much is fashion, how much is merely reflection? Why is Sir Walter Scott so hard to read now, and Jane Austen not? Why is baroque right for one age and too effulgent for another? 7

Can a standard of craftsmanship apply to art of all ages, or does each have its own, and different, definitions? You may have been aware, inadvertently, that craftsmanship has become a dirty word these years because, again, it implies standards—something done well or done badly. The result of this convenient avoidance is a plenitude of actors who can't project their voices, singers who can't phrase their songs, poets who can't communicate emotion, and writers who have no vocabulary—not to speak of painters who can't draw. The dogma now is that craftsmanship gets in the way of expression. You can do better if you don't know *how* you do it, let alone *what* you're doing. 8

I think it is time you helped reverse this trend by trying to 9 rediscover craft: the command of the chosen instrument, whether it is a brush, a word, or a voice. When you begin to detect the difference between freedom and sloppiness, between serious experimentation and egotherapy, between skill and slickness, between strength and violence, you are on your way to separating the sheep from the goats, a form of segregation denied us for quite a while. All you need to restore it is a small bundle of standards and a Geiger counter that detects fraud, and we might begin our tour of the arts in an area where both are urgently needed: contemporary painting.

I don't know what's worse: to have to look at acres of bad   10
art to find the little good, or to read what the critics say about it all. In no other field of expression has so much double-talk flourished, so much confusion prevailed, and so much nonsense been circulated: further evidence of the close interdependence between the arts and the critical climate they inhabit. It will be my pleasure to share with you some of this double-talk so typical of our times.

Item one: preface for a catalogue of an abstract painter: 11
"Time-bound meditation experiencing a life; sincere with   12
plastic piety at the threshold of hallowed arcana; a striving for pure ideation giving shape to inner drive; formalized patterns where neural balances reach a fiction." End of quote. Know what this artist paints like now?

Item two: a review in the *Art News:*   13
". . . a weird and disparate assortment of material, but the   14
monstrosity which bloomed into his most recent cancer of aggregations is present in some form everywhere. . . ." Then, later, "A gluttony of things and processes terminated by a glorious constipation."

Item three, same magazine, review of an artist who welds   15
automobile fragments into abstract shapes:

"Each fragment . . . is made an extreme of human exasper-   16
ation, torn at and fought all the way, and has its rightness of form as if by accident. *Any technique that requires order or discipline would just be the human ego.* No, these must be egoless, uncontrolled, undesigned and different enough to give you a bang—fifty miles an hour around a telephone pole. . . ."

"Any technique that requires order or discipline would just   17
be the human ego." What does he mean—"just be"? What are
they really talking about? Is this journalism? Is it criticism? Or
is it that other convenient abdication from standards of performance and judgment practiced by so many artists and critics
that they, like certain writers who deal only in sickness and depravity, "reflect the chaos about them"? Again, whose chaos?
Whose depravity?

I had always thought that the prime function of art was to   18
create order *out* of chaos—again, not the order of neatness or
rigidity or convention or artifice, but the order of clarity by
which one will and one vision could draw the essential truth out
of apparent confusion. I still do. It is not enough to use parts of
a car to convey the brutality of the machine. This is as slavishly
representative, and just as easy, as arranging dried flowers
under glass to convey nature.

Speaking of which, i.e., the use of real materials (burlap, old   19
gloves, bottletops) in lieu of pigment, this is what one critic had
to say about an exhibition of Assemblage at the Museum of
Modern Art last year:

> Spotted throughout the show are indisputable works of art,
> accounting for a quarter or even a half of the total display. But
> the remainder are works of non-art, anti-art, and art substitutes
> that are the aesthetic counterparts of the social deficiencies that
> land people in the clink on charges of vagrancy. These aesthetic
> bankrupts . . . have no legitimate ideological roof over their heads
> and not the price of a square intellectual meal, much less a spir-
> itual sandwich, in their pockets.

I quote these words of John Canaday of *The New York Times*   20
as an example of the kind of criticism which puts responsibility to an intelligent public above popularity with an intellectual
coterie. Canaday has the courage to say what he thinks and the
capacity to say it clearly: two qualities notably absent from his
profession.

Next to art, I would say that appreciation and evaluation in   21
the field of music is the most difficult. For it is rarely possible
to judge a new composition at one hearing only. What seems

confusing or fragmented at first might well become clear and organic a third time. Or it might not. The only salvation here for the listener is, again, an instinct born of experience and association which allows him to separate intent from accident, design from experimentation, and pretense from conviction. Much of contemporary music is, like its sister art, merely a reflection of the composer's own fragmentation: an absorption in self and symbols at the expense of communication with others. The artist, in short, says to the public: If you don't understand this, it's because you're dumb. I maintain that you are not. You may have to go part way or even halfway to meet the artist, but if you must go the whole way, it's his fault, not yours. Hold fast to that. And remember it too when you read new poetry, that estranged sister of music.

> A multitude of causes, unknown to former times, are now acting with a combined force to blunt the discriminating powers of the mind, and, unfitting it for all voluntary exertion, to reduce it to a state of almost savage torpor. The most effective of these causes are the great national events which are daily taking place and the increasing accumulation of men in cities, where the uniformity of their occupations produces a craving for extraordinary incident, which the rapid communication of intelligence hourly gratifies. To this tendency of life and manners, the literature and theatrical exhibitions of the country have conformed themselves.

This startlingly applicable comment was written in the year 1800 by William Wordsworth in the preface to his "Lyrical Ballads"; and it has been cited by Edwin Muir in his recently published book "The Estate of Poetry." Muir states that poetry's effective range and influence have diminished alarmingly in the modern world. He believes in the inherent and indestructible qualities of the human mind and the great and permanent objects that act upon it, and suggests that the audience will increase when "poetry loses what obscurity is left in it by attempting greater themes, for great themes have to be stated clearly." If you keep that firmly in mind and resist, in Muir's words, "the vast dissemination of secondary objects that isolate us from the natural world," you have gone a long way toward equipping yourself for the examination of any work of art.

When you come to theatre, in this extremely hasty tour of 23 the arts, you can approach it on two different levels. You can bring to it anticipation and innocence, giving yourself up, as it were, to the life on the stage and reacting to it emotionally, if the play is good, or listlessly, if the play is boring; a part of the audience organism that expresses its favor by silence or laughter and its disfavor by coughing and rustling. Or you can bring to it certain critical faculties that may heighten, rather than diminish, your enjoyment.

You can ask yourselves whether the actors are truly in their 24 parts or merely projecting themselves; whether the scenery helps or hurts the mood; whether the playwright is honest with himself, his characters, and you. Somewhere along the line you can learn to distinguish between the true creative act and the false arbitrary gesture; between fresh observation and stale cliché; between the avant-garde play that is pretentious drivel and the avant-garde play that finds new ways to say old truths.

Purpose and craftsmanship—end and means—these are the 25 keys to your judgment in all the arts. What is this painter trying to say when he slashes a broad band of black across a white canvas and lets the edges dribble down? Is it a statement of violence? Is it a self-portrait? If it is *one* of these, has he made you believe it? Or is this a gesture of the ego or a form of therapy? If it shocks you, what does it shock you into?

And what of this tight little painting of bright flowers in a 26 vase? Is the painter saying anything new about flowers? Is it different from a million other canvases of flowers? Has it any life, any meaning, beyond its statement? Is there any pleasure in its forms or texture? The question is not whether a thing is abstract or representational, whether it is "modern" or conventional. The question, inexorably, is whether it is good. And this is a decision which only you, on the basis of instinct, experience, and association, can make for yourself. It takes independence and courage. It involves, moreover, the risk of wrong decision and the humility, after the passage of time, of recognizing it as such. As we grow and change and learn, our attitudes can change too, and what we once thought obscure or "difficult" can later emerge as coherent and illuminating. Entrenched prejudices, obdurate opinions are as sterile as no opinions at all.

Yet standards there are, timeless as the universe itself. And 27 when you have committed yourself to them, you have acquired a passport to that elusive but immutable realm of truth. Keep it with you in the forests of bewilderment. And never be afraid to speak up.

1962

Pain Is Not the Ultimate Enemy

Norman Cousins

Americans are probably the most pain-conscious people on 1 the face of the earth. For years we have had it drummed into us—in print, on radio, over television, in everyday conversation—that any hint of pain is to be banished as though it were the ultimate evil. As a result, we are becoming a nation of pill-grabbers and hypochondriacs, escalating the slightest ache into a searing ordeal.

We know very little about pain and what we don't know 2 makes it hurt all the more. Indeed, no form of illiteracy in the United States is so widespread or costly as ignorance about pain—what it is, what causes it, how to deal with it without panic. Almost everyone can rattle off the names of at least a dozen drugs that can deaden pain from every conceivable cause—all the way from headaches to hemorrhoids. There is far less knowledge about the fact that about 90 percent of pain is self-limiting, that it is not always an indication of poor health, and that, most frequently, it is the result of tension, stress, worry, idleness, boredom, frustration, suppressed rage, insufficient sleep, overeating, poorly balanced diet, smoking, excessive drinking, inadequate exercise, stale air, or any of the other abuses encountered by the human body in modern society.

The most ignored fact of all about pain is that the best way 3 to eliminate it is to eliminate the abuse. Instead, many people reach almost instinctively for the painkillers—aspirins, barbiturates, codeines, tranquilizers, sleeping pills, and dozens of other analgesics or desensitizing drugs.

Most doctors are profoundly troubled over the extent to 4 which the medical profession today is taking on the trappings of a pain-killing industry. Their offices are overloaded with people who are morbidly but mistakenly convinced that something dreadful is about to happen to them. It is all too evident that the campaign to get people to run to a doctor at the first sign of pain has boomeranged. Physicians find it difficult to give adequate attention to patients genuinely in need of expert diagnosis and treatment because their time is soaked up by people who have nothing wrong with them except a temporary indisposition or a psychogenic ache.

Patients tend to feel indignant and insulted if the physician 5 tells them he can find no organic cause of pain. They tend to interpret the term "psychogenic" to mean that they are complaining of nonexistent symptoms. They need to be educated about the fact that many forms of pain have no underlying physical cause but are the result, as mentioned earlier, of tension, stress, or hostile factors in the general environment. Sometimes a pain may be a manifestation of "conversion hysteria" . . . the name given by Jean Charcot to physical symptoms that have their origins in emotional disturbances.

Obviously, it is folly for an individual to ignore symptoms 6 that could be a warning of a potentially serious illness. Some people are so terrified of getting bad news from a doctor that they allow their malaise to worsen, sometimes past the point of no return. Total neglect is not the answer to hypochondria. The only answer has to be increased education about the way the human body works, so that more people will be able to steer an intelligent course between promiscuous pill-popping and irresponsible disregard of genuine symptoms.

Of all forms of pain, none is more important for the indi- 7 vidual to understand than the "threshold" variety. Almost everyone has a telltale ache that is triggered whenever tension or fatigue reaches a certain point. It can take the form of a migraine-type headache or a squeezing pain deep in the abdomen or cramps or a pain in the lower back or even pain in the joints. The individual who has learned how to make the correlation between such threshold pains and their cause doesn't panic when they occur; he or she does something about relieving the stress and tension. Then, if the pain persists despite the absence of apparent cause, the individual will telephone the doctor.

If ignorance about the nature of pain is widespread, ignorance about the way pain-killing drugs work is even more so. What is not generally understood is that many of the vaunted pain-killing drugs conceal the pain without correcting the underlying condition. They deaden the mechanism in the body that alerts the brain to the fact that something may be wrong. The body can pay a high price for suppression of pain without regard to its basic cause.

Professional athletes are sometimes severely disadvantaged by trainers whose job it is to keep them in action. The more famous the athlete, the greater the risk that he or she may be subjected to extreme medical measures when injury strikes. The star baseball pitcher whose arm is sore because of a torn muscle or tissue damage may need sustained rest more than anything else. But his team is battling for a place in the World Series; so the trainer or team doctor, called upon to work his magic, reaches for a strong dose of Butazolidine or other powerful pain suppressants. Presto, the pain disappears! The pitcher takes his place on the mound and does superbly. That could be the last game, however, in which he is able to throw a ball with full strength. The drugs didn't repair the torn muscle or cause the damaged tissue to heal. What they did was to mask the pain, enabling the pitcher to throw hard, further damaging the torn muscle. Little wonder that so many star athletes are cut down in their prime, more the victims of overzealous treatment of their injuries than of the injuries themselves.

The king of all painkillers, of course, is aspirin. The U.S.

Food and Drug Administration permits aspirin to be sold without prescription, but the drug, contrary to popular belief, can be dangerous and, in sustained doses, potentially lethal. Aspirin is self-administered by more people than any other drug in the world. Some people are aspirin-poppers, taking ten or more a day. What they don't know is that the smallest dose can cause internal bleeding. Even more serious perhaps is the fact that aspirin is antagonistic to collagen, which has a key role in the formation of connective tissue. Since many forms of arthritis involve disintegration of the connective tissues, the steady use of aspirin can actually intensify the underlying arthritic condition.

Aspirin is not the only pain-killing drug, of course, that is known to have dangerous side effects. Dr. Daphne A. Roe, of Cornell University, at a medical meeting in New York City in 1974, presented startling evidence of a wide range of hazards associated with sedatives and other pain suppressants. Some of these drugs seriously interfere with the ability of the body to metabolize food properly, producing malnutrition. In some instances, there is also the danger of bone-marrow depression, interfering with the ability of the body to replenish its blood supply. 11

Pain-killing drugs are among the greatest advances in the history of medicine. Properly used, they can be a boon in alleviating suffering and in treating disease. But their indiscriminate and promiscuous use is making psychological cripples and chronic ailers out of millions of people. The unremitting barrage of advertising for pain-killing drugs, especially over television, has set the stage for a mass anxiety neurosis. Almost from the moment children are old enough to sit upright in front of a television screen, they are being indoctrinated into the hypochondriac's clamorous and morbid world. Little wonder so many people fear pain more than death itself. 12

It might be a good idea if concerned physicians and educators could get together to make knowledge about pain an important part of the regular school curriculum. As for the populace at large, perhaps some of the same techniques used by public-service agencies to make people cancer-conscious can be used to counteract the growing terror of pain and illness in general. People ought to know that nothing is more remarkable 13 about the human body than its recuperative drive, given a modicum of respect. If our broadcasting stations cannot provide equal time for responses to the pain-killing advertisements, they might at least set aside a few minutes each day for common-sense remarks on the subject of pain. As for the Food and Drug Administration, it might be interesting to know why an agency that has energetically warned the American people against taking vitamins without prescriptions is doing so little to control over-the-counter sales each year of billions of pain-killing pills, some of which can do more harm than the pain they are supposed to suppress.

1979

My Wood

E. M. Forster

A few years ago I wrote a book which dealt in part with the   1
difficulties of the English in India. Feeling that they would have had no difficulties in India themselves, the Americans read the book freely. The more they read it the better it made them feel, and a cheque to the author was the result. I bought a wood with the cheque. It is not a large wood—it contains scarcely any trees, and it is intersected, blast it, by a public footpath. Still, it is the first property that I have owned, so it is right that other people should participate in my shame, and should ask themselves, in accents that will vary in horror, this very important question: What is the effect of property upon the character? Don't let's touch economics; the effect of private ownership upon the community as a whole is another question—a more important question, perhaps, but another one. Let's keep to psychology. If you own things, what's their effect on you? What's the effect on me of my wood?

In the first place, it makes me feel heavy. Property does have   2 this effect. Property produces men of weight, and it was a man of weight who failed to get into the Kingdom of Heaven. He was not wicked, that unfortunate millionaire in the parable, he was only stout; he stuck out in front, not to mention behind, and as he wedged himself this way and that in the crystalline entrance and bruised his well-fed flanks, he saw beneath him a comparatively slim camel passing through the eye of a needle and being woven into the robe of God. The Gospels all through couple stoutness and slowness. They point out what is perfectly obvious, yet seldom realized: that if you have a lot of things you cannot move about a lot, that furniture requires dusting, dusters require servants, servants require insurance stamps, and the whole tangle of them makes you think twice before you accept an invitation to dinner or go for a bathe in the Jordan. Sometimes the Gospels proceed further and say with Tolstoy that property is sinful; they approach the difficult ground of asceticism here, where I cannot follow them. But as to the immediate effects of property on people, they just show straightforward logic. It produces men of weight. Men of weight cannot, by definition, move like the lightning from the East unto the West, and the ascent of a fourteen-stone bishop into a pulpit is thus the exact antithesis of the coming of the Son of Man. My wood makes me feel heavy.

In the second place, it makes me feel it ought to be larger.   3

The other day I heard a twig snap in it. I was annoyed at   4
first, for I thought that someone was blackberrying, and depreciating the value of the undergrowth. On coming nearer, I saw it was not a man who had trodden on the twig and snapped it, but a bird, and I felt pleased. My bird. The bird was not equally pleased. Ignoring the relation between us, it took fright as soon as it saw the shape of my face, and flew straight over the boundary hedge into a field, the property of Mrs. Henessy, where it sat down with a loud squawk. It had become Mrs. Henessy's bird. Something seemed grossly amiss here, something that would not have occurred had the wood been larger. I could not afford to buy Mrs. Henessy out, I dared not murder her, and limitations of this sort beset me on every side. Ahab did not want that vineyard—he only needed it to round off his property, preparatory to plotting a new curve—and all the land

around my wood has become necessary to me in order to round
off the wood. A boundary protects. But—poor little thing—the
boundary ought in its turn to be protected. Noises on the edge
of it. Children throw stones. A little more, and then a little more,
until we reach the sea. Happy Canute! Happier Alexander! And
after all, why should even the world be the limit of possession?
A rocket containing a Union Jack, will, it is hoped, be shortly
fired at the moon. Mars. Sirius. Beyond which. . . . But these im-
mensities ended by saddening me. I could not suppose that my
wood was the destined nucleus of universal dominion—it is so
very small and contains no mineral wealth beyond the blackberries. Nor was I comforted when Mrs. Henessy's bird took
alarm for the second time and flew clean away from us all,
under the belief that it belonged to itself.

In the third place, property makes its owner feel that he 5
ought to do something to it. Yet he isn't sure what. A restless-
ness comes over him, a vague sense that he has a personality to
express—the same sense which, without any vagueness, leads
the artist to an act of creation. Sometimes I think I will cut down
such trees as remain in the wood, at other times I want to fill up
the gaps between them with new trees. Both impulses are pretentious and empty. They are not honest movements towards
money-making or beauty. They spring from a foolish desire to
express myself and from an inability to enjoy what I have got.
Creation, property, enjoyment form a sinister trinity in the
human mind. Creation and enjoyment are both very very good,
yet they are often unattainable without a material basis, and at
such moments property pushes itself in as a substitute, saying,
"Accept me instead—I'm good enough for all three." It is not
enough. It is, as Shakespeare said of lust, "The expense of spirit
in a waste of shame": it is "Before, a joy proposed; behind, a
dream." Yet we don't know how to shun it. It is forced on us by
our economic system as the alternative to starvation. It is also
forced on us by an internal defect in the soul, by the feeling that
in property may lie the germs of self-development and of exquisite or heroic deeds. Our life on earth is, and ought to be, material and carnal. But we have not yet learned to manage our
materialism and carnality properly; they are still entangled with

the desire for ownership, where (in the words of Dante) "Possession is one with loss."

And this brings us to our fourth and final point: the black- 6
berries.

Blackberries are not plentiful in this meagre grove, but they 7
are easily seen from the public footpath which traverses it, and
all too easily gathered. Foxgloves, too—people will pull up the
foxgloves, and ladies of an educational tendency even grub for
toadstools to show them on the Monday in class. Other ladies,
less educated, roll down the bracken in the arms of their gentlemen friends. There is paper, there are tins. Pray, does my
wood belong to me or doesn't it? And, if it does, should I not
own it best by allowing no one else to walk there? There is a
wood near Lyme Regis, also cursed by a public footpath, where
the owner has not hesitated on this point. He has built high
stone walls each side of the path, and has spanned it by bridges,
so that the public circulate like termites while he gorges on the
blackberries unseen. He really does own his wood, this able
chap. Dives in Hell did pretty well, but the gulf dividing him
from Lazarus could be traversed by vision, and nothing traverses it here. And perhaps I shall come to this in time. I shall
wall in and fence out until I really taste the sweets of property.
Enormously stout, endlessly avaricious, pseudo-creative, in-
tensely selfish, I shall weave upon my forehead the quadruple
crown of possession until those nasty Bolshies come and take
it off again and thrust me aside into the outer darkness.

1936

Watching the Grasshopper
Get the Goodies

Ellen Goodman

I don't usually play the great American game called Cate- 1
gories. There are already too many ways to divide us into op-

posing teams, according to age, race, sex and favorite flavors. Every time we turn around, someone is telling us that the whole country is made up of those who drive pick-up trucks and those who do not, and then analyzing what this means in terms of the Middle East.

Still, it occurs to me that if we want to figure out why people are angry right now, it's not a bad idea to see ourselves as a nation of planners and nonplanners. It's the planners these days who are feeling penalized, right down to their box score at the bank. 2

The part of us which is most visibly and vocally infuriated by inflation, for example, isn't our liberal or conservative side but, rather, our planning side. Inflation devastates our attempts to control our futures—to budget and predict and expect. It particularly makes fools out of the people who saved then to buy now. To a certain extent, it rewards instant gratification and makes a joke out of our traditional notions of preparation. 3

It is no news bulletin that the people who dove over their heads into the real-estate market a few years ago are now generally better off than those who dutifully decided to save up for a larger down payment. With that "larger down payment" they can now buy two double-thick rib lambchops and a partridge in a pear tree. 4

But inflation isn't the only thing that leaves the planners feeling betrayed. There are other issues that find them actively pitched against the nonplanners. 5

We all know families who saved for a decade to send their kids to college. A college diploma these days costs about the same amount as a Mercedes-Benz. Of course, the Mercedes lasts longer and has a higher trade-in value. But the most devoted parent can be infuriated to discover that a neighboring couple who spent its income instead of saving is now eligible for college financial aid, while they are not. To the profligate go the spoils. 6

This can happen anywhere on the economic spectrum. There is probably only one mother in the annals of the New York welfare rolls to save up a few thousand dollars in hopes of getting off aid. But she would have been better off spending it. When she was discovered this year, the welfare department took the money back. She, too, was penalized for planning. 7

In these crimped times, the Planned Parents of the Purse are 8
increasingly annoyed at other parents—whether they are
unwed or on welfare or just prolific. For the first time in my own
town, you can hear families with few children complaining out
loud at the tax bill for the public schooling of families with
many children.

One man I heard even suggesting charging tuition for the 9
third child. He admitted, "It's not a very generous attitude, I
know. But I'm not feeling very generous these days." He is suffering from planner's warts.

At the same time I've talked with friends whose parents pre- 10
pared, often with financial difficulty, for their "old age" and illness. They feel sad when this money goes down a nursing home
drain, but furious when other people who didn't save get this
same care for free.

Now we are all aware that if many people don't plan their 11
economic lives, it may be because they can't. It does no one any
good to keep the cashless out of college, to stash the old and
poor into elderly warehouses, to leave the "extra" children illiterate. We do want to help others, but we also want our own
efforts to make a difference.

There is nothing that grates a planner more than seeing a 12
nonplanner profit. It's as if the ant had to watch the grasshop-
per get the goodies.

Our two notions about what's fair end up on opposite sides. 13
It isn't fair if the poor get treated badly, and it isn't fair if those
who work and save, plan and postpone aren't given a better
shake. We want the winners to be the deserving. Only there is
no divining rod for the deserving.

The hard part is to create policies that are neither unkind 14
nor insane. It is, after all, madness not to reward the kind of behavior we want to encourage. If we want the ranks of the planners to increase in this massive behavior-modification program
called society, we have to give them the rewards, instead of the
outrage.

1981

White Guilt

Shelby Steele

I don't remember hearing the phrase "white guilt" very   1
much before the mid-1960s. Growing up black in the 1950s, I
never had the impression that whites were much disturbed by
guilt when it came to blacks. When I would stray into the wrong
restaurant in pursuit of a hamburger, it didn't occur to me that
the waitress was unduly troubled by guilt when she asked me
to leave. I can see now that possibly she was, but then all I saw
was her irritability at having to carry out so unpleasant a task.
If there was guilt, it was mine for having made an imposition
of myself. I can remember feeling a certain sympathy for such
people, as if I was victimizing them by drawing them out of an
innocent anonymity into the unasked-for role of racial policemen. Occasionally they came right out and asked me to feel
sorry for them. A caddymaster at a country club told my brother
and me that he was doing us a favor by not letting us caddy at
this white club and that we should try to understand his position, "put yourselves in my shoes." Our color had brought this
man anguish and, if a part of that anguish was guilt, it was not
as immediate to me as my own guilt. I smiled at the man to let
him know he shouldn't feel bad and then began my long walk
home. Certainly I also judge him a coward, but in that era his
cowardice was something I had to absorb.

In the 1960s, particularly the black-is-beautiful late 1960s,   2
this absorption of another's cowardice was no longer necessary. The lines of moral power, like plates in the earth, had
shifted. White guilt became so palpable you could see it on people. At the time what it looked like to my eyes was a remarkable loss of authority. And what whites lost in authority, blacks
gained. You cannot feel guilty about anyone without giving
away power to them. Suddenly, this huge vulnerability had
opened up in whites and, as a black, you had the power to step
right into it. In fact, black power all but demanded that you do
so. What shocked me in the late 1960s, after the helplessness I

had felt in the fifties, was that guilt had changed the nature of the white man's burden from the administration of inferiors to the uplift of equals—from the obligations of dominance to the urgencies of repentance.

I think what made the difference between the fifties and six- 3 ties, at least as far as white guilt was concerned, was that whites underwent an archetypal Fall. Because of the immense turmoil of the civil rights movement, and later the blackpower move- ment, whites were confronted for more than a decade with their willingness to participate in, or comply with, the oppression of blacks, their indifference to human suffering and denigration, their capacity to abide evil for their own benefit and in the de- fiance of their own sacred principles. The 1964 Civil Rights Bill that bestowed equality under the law on blacks was also, in a certain sense, an admission of white guilt. Had white society not been wrong, there would have been no need for such a bill. In this bill the nation acknowledged its fallenness, its lack of racial innocence, and confronted the incriminating self-knowledge that it had rationalized for many years a flagrant injustice. De- nial is a common way of handling guilt, but in the 1960s there was little will left for denial except in the most recalcitrant whites. With this defense lost there was really only one road back to innocence—through actions and policies that would bring redemption.

In the 1960s the need for white redemption from racial guilt 4 became the most powerful, yet unspoken, element in America's social-policy-making process, first giving rise to the Great So- ciety and then to a series of programs, policies, and laws that sought to make black equality and restitution a national mis- sion. Once America could no longer deny its guilt, it went after redemption, or at least the look of redemption, and did so with a vengeance. Yet today, some twenty years later, study after study tells us that by many measures the gap between blacks and whites is widening rather than narrowing. A University of Chicago study indicates that segregation is more entrenched in American cities today than ever imagined. A National Research Council study notes the "status of blacks relative to whites (in housing and education) has stagnated or regressed since the

early seventies." A follow-up to the famous Kerner Commission
Report warns that blacks are as much at risk today of becoming a "nation within a nation" as we were twenty years ago,
when the original report was made.

I think the white need for redemption has contributed to   5
this tragic situation by shaping our policies regarding blacks in
ways that may deliver the look of innocence to society and its
institutions but that do very little actually to uplift blacks. The
specific effect of this hidden need has been to bend social policy more toward reparation for black oppression than toward
the much harder and more mundane work of black uplift and
development. Rather than facilitate the development of blacks
to achieve parity with whites, these programs and policies—af-
firmative action is a good example—have tended to give blacks
special entitlements that in many cases are of no use because
blacks lack the development that would put us in a position to
take advantage of them. I think the reason there has been more
entitlement than development is (along with black power) the
unacknowledged white need for redemption—not true redemption, which would have concentrated policy on black development, but the appearance of redemption, which requires
only that society, in the name of development, seem to be paying back its former victims with preferences. One of the effects
of entitlements, I believe, has been to encourage in blacks a dependency both on entitlements and on the white guilt that generates them. Even when it serves ideal justice, bounty from another man's guilt weakens. While this is not the only factor in
black "stagnation" and "regression," I believe it is one very po-
tent factor.

It is easy enough to say that white guilt too often has the ef-   6
fect of bending social policies in the wrong direction. But what
exactly is this guilt, and how does it work in American life?

I think white guilt, in its broad sense, springs from a knowl-   7
edge of ill-gotten advantage. More precisely, it comes from the
juxtaposition of this knowledge with the inevitable gratitude
one feels for being white rather than black in America. Given
the moral instincts of human beings, it is all but impossible to
enjoy an ill-gotten advantage, much less to feel at least secretly

grateful for it, without consciously or unconsciously experiencing guilt. If, as Kierkegaard writes, "innocence is ignorance," then guilt must always involve knowledge. White Americans *know* that their historical advantage comes from the subjugation of an entire people. So, even for whites today for whom racism is anathema, there is no escape from the knowledge that makes for guilt. Racial guilt simply accompanies the condition of being white in America.

I do not believe that this guilt is a crushing anguish for most   8
whites, but I do believe it constitutes a continuing racial vulnerability—an openness to racial culpability—that is a thread in white life, sometimes felt, sometimes not, but ever present as a potential feeling. In the late 1960s almost any black could charge this vulnerability with enough current for a white person to feel it. I had a friend who had developed this activity into a sort of specialty. I don't think he meant to be mean, though certainly he was mean. I think he was, in that hyperbolic era, exhilarated by the discovery that his race, which had long been a liability, now gave him a certain edge—that white guilt was the true force behind black power. To feel this power he would sometimes set up what he called "race experiments." Once I watched him stop a white businessman in the men's room of a large hotel and convince him to increase his tip to the black attendant from one to twenty dollars.

My friend's tactic was very simple, even corny. Out of the   9
attendant's earshot he asked the man simply to look at the attendant, a frail, elderly, and very dark man in a starched white smock that made the skin on his neck and face look as leathery as a turtle's. He sat listlessly, pathetically, on a straight-backed chair next to a small table on which sat a stack of hand towels and a silver plate for tips. Since the attendant offered no service whatever beyond the handing out of towels, one could only conclude the hotel management offered his lowly presence as flattery to their patrons, as an opportunity for that easy noblesse oblige that could reassure even the harried and weary traveling salesman of his superior station. My friend was quick to make this point to the businessman and to say that no white man would do this job. But when the businessman put the single

back in his wallet and took out a five, my friend only sneered. Did he understand the tragedy of a life spent this way, of what it must be like to earn one's paltry living as a symbol of inferiority? And did he realize that his privilege as an affluent white businessman (ironically he had just spent the day trying to sell a printing press to the Black Muslims for their newspaper *Mohammed Speaks*) was connected to the deprivation of this man and others like him?

But then my friend made a mistake that ended the game. In the heat of argument, which until then had only been playfully challenging, he inadvertently mentioned his father. This stopped the victim cold and his eyes turned inward. "What about your father?" the businessman asked. My friend replied, "He had a hard life, that's all." "How did he have a hard life?" the businessman asked. Now my friend was on the defensive. I knew he did not get along with his father, a bitter man who worked nights in a factory and demanded that the house be dark and silent all day. My friend blamed his father's bitterness on racism, but I knew he had not meant to exploit his own pain in this silly "experiment." Things had gotten too close to home, but he didn't know how to get out of the situation without losing face. Now, caught in his own trap, he did what he least wanted to do. He gave forth the rage he truly felt to a white stranger in a public men's room. "My father never had a chance," he said with the kind of anger that could easily turn to tears. "He never had a freakin' chance. Your father had all the goddamn chances, and you know he did. You sell printing presses to black people and make thousands and your father probably lives down in Fat City, Florida, all because you're white." On and on he went in this vein, using—against all that was honorable in him—his own profound racial pain to extract a flash of guilt from a white man he didn't even know.

He got more than a flash. The businessman was touched. His eyes became mournful, and finally he simply said, "You're right. Your people got a raw deal." He took a twenty dollar bill from his wallet and walked over and dropped it in the old man's tip plate. When he was gone my friend and I could not look at the old man, nor could we look at each other.

It is obvious that this was a rather shameful encounter for   12
all concerned—my friend and I, as his silent accomplice, trading on our racial pain, tampering with a stranger for no reason,
and the stranger then buying his way out of the situation for
twenty dollars, a sum that was generous by one count and
cheap by another. It was not an encounter of people but of historical grudges and guilts. Yet, when I think about it now
twenty years later, I see that it had all the elements of a paradigm that I believe has been very much at the heart of racial
policy-making in America since the 1960s.

My friend did two things that made this businessman vul-   13
nerable to his guilt—that brought his guilt into the situation as a
force. First he put this man in touch with his own knowledge of
his ill-gotten advantage as a white. The effect of this was to dis-
allow the man any pretense of racial innocence, to let him know
that, even if he was not the sort of white who used the word *nigger* around the dinner table, he still had reason to feel racial guilt.
But, as disarming as this might have been, it was too abstract to
do much more than crack open this man's vulnerability, to expose him to the logic of white guilt. This was the five-dollar, intellectual sort of guilt. The twenty dollars required something
more visceral. In achieving this, the second thing my friend did
was something he had not intended to do, something that ultimately brought him as much shame as he was doling out: He
made a display of his own racial pain and anger. (What brought
him shame was not the pain and anger, but his trading on them
for what turned out to be a mere twenty bucks.) The effect of this
display was to reinforce the man's knowledge of ill-gotten advantage, to give credibility and solidity to it by putting a face on
it. Here was human testimony, a young black beside himself at
the thought of his father's racially constricted life. The pain of one
man evidenced the knowledge of the other. When the businessman listened to my friend's pain, his racial guilt—normally only
one source of guilt lying dormant among others—was called out
like a neglected debt he would finally have to settle. An ill-gotten
advantage is not hard to bear—it can be marked up to fate—until
it touches the genuine human pain it has brought into the world.
This is the pain that hardens guilty knowledge.

Such knowledge is a powerful influence when it becomes   14
conscious. What makes it so powerful is the element of fear
that guilt always carries, the fear of what the guilty knowledge
says about us. Guilt makes us afraid for ourselves, and thus generates as much self-preoccupation as concern for others. The nature of this preoccupation is always the redemption of innocence, the reestablishment of good feeling about oneself.

In this sense, the fear for the self that is buried in all guilt is   15
a pressure toward selfishness. It can lead us to put our own need
for innocence above our concern for the problem that made us
feel guilt in the first place. But this fear for the self does not only
inspire selfishness; it also becomes a pressure to *escape* the guilt-
inducing situation. When selfishness and escapism are at work,
we are no longer interested in the source of our guilt and, therefore, no longer concerned with an authentic redemption from
it. Then we only want the look of redemption, the gesture of
concern that will give us the appearance of innocence and escape from the situation. Obviously the businessman did not
put twenty dollars in the tip plate because he thought it would
uplift black Americans. He did it selfishly for the appearance
of concern and for the escape it afforded him.

This is not to say that guilt is never the right motive for   16
doing good works or showing concern, only that it is a very dangerous one because of its tendency to draw us into self-
preoccupation and escapism. Guilt is a civilizing emotion when
the fear for the self that it carries is contained—a containment
that allows guilt to be more selfless and that makes genuine concern possible. I think this was the kind of guilt that, along with
the other forces, made the 1964 Civil Rights Bill possible. But
since then I believe too many of our social policies related to race
have been shaped by the fearful underside of guilt.

Black power evoked white guilt and made it a force in   17
American institutions, very much in the same way as my friend
brought it to life in the businessman. Few people volunteer for
guilt. Usually others make us feel it. It was the expression of
black anger and pain that hardened the guilty knowledge of
white ill-gotten advantage. And black power—whether from
militant fringe groups, the civil rights establishment, or big city

political campaigns—knew exactly the kind of white guilt it was after. It wanted to trigger the kind of white guilt in which whites fear for their own decency and innocence; it wanted the guilt of white self-preoccupation and escapism. Always at the heart of black power, in whatever form, has been a profound anger at what was done to blacks and an equally profound feeling that there should be reparations. But a sober white guilt (in which fear for the self is still contained) seeks a strict fairness—the 1964 Civil Rights Bill that guaranteed equality under the law. It is of little value when one is after more than fairness. So black power made its mission to have whites fear for their innocence, to feel a visceral guilt from which they would have to seek a more profound redemption. In such redemption was the possibility of black reparation. Black power upped the ante on white guilt.

With black power, all of the elements of the hidden paradigm that shape America's race-related social policy were in place. Knowledge of ill-gotten advantage could now be shown and deepened by black power into the sort of guilt from which institutions could only redeem themselves by offering more than fairness—by offering forms of reparation and compensation for past injustice. I believe this bent our policies toward racial entitlements at the expense of racial development. In 1964, one of the assurances Senator Hubert Humphrey and others had to give Congress to get the landmark Civil Rights Bill passed was that the bill would not in any way require employers to use racial preferences to rectify racial imbalances. But this was before the explosion of black power in the late 1960s, before the hidden paradigm was set in motion. After black power, racial preferences became the order of the day. 18

If this paradigm brought blacks entitlements, it also brought the continuation of the most profound problem in American society, the invisibility of blacks as a people. The white guilt that this paradigm elicits is the kind of guilt that preoccupies whites with their own innocence and pressures them toward escapism—twenty dollars in the plate and out the door. With this guilt, as opposed to the contained guilt of genuine concern, 19 whites tend to see only their own need for quick redemption. Blacks then become a means to this redemption and, as such, they must be seen as generally "less than" others. Their needs are "special," "unique," "different." They are seen exclusively along the dimension of their victimization, so that they become "different" people with whom whites can negotiate entitlements but never fully see as people like themselves. Guilt that preoccupies people with their own innocence blinds them to those who make them feel guilty. This, of course, is not racism, and yet it has the same effect as racism since it makes blacks something of a separate species for whom normal standards and values do not automatically apply.

Nowhere is this more evident today than in American universities. At some of America's most elite universities administrators have granted concessions in response to black student demands (black power) that all but sanction racial separatism on campus—black "theme" dorms, black student unions, black yearbooks, homecoming dances, and so forth. I don't believe administrators sincerely believe in these separatist concessions. Most of them are liberals who see racial separatism as wrong. But black student demands pull administrators into the paradigm of self-preoccupied white guilt, whereby they seek a quick redemption by offering special entitlements that go beyond fairness. As a result, black students become all but invisible to them. Though blacks have the lowest grade point average of any racial group in American universities, administrators never sit down with them and "demand" in kind that black students bring their grades up to par. The paradigm of white guilt makes the real problems of black students secondary to the need for white redemption. It also cuts administrators off from their own values, which would most certainly discourage racial separatism and encourage higher academic performance for black students. Lastly, it makes for escapist policies. There is no difference between giving black students a separate lounge and leaving twenty dollars in the tip plate on the way out the door.

1990

Where Have All the
Parents Gone?

Barbara Dafoe Whitehead

"Invest in kids," George Bush mused during his 1988 pres-   1
idential campaign, "I like it." Apparently so do others. A growing number of corporate CEOs and educators, elected officials
and child-welfare advocates have embraced the same language.
"Invest in kids" is the bumper-sticker for an important new
cause, aptly tagged the *kids as capital* argument. It runs as follows:

America's human capital comes in two forms: the active   2
work force and the prospective work force. The bulk of tomorrow's workers are today's children, of course. So children make
up much of the stockpile of America's potential human capital.

If we look at them as tomorrow's workers, we begin to ap-   3
preciate our stake in today's children. They will determine
when we can retire, how well we can live in retirement, how
generous our health insurance will be, how strong our social
safety net, how orderly our society. What's more, today's children will determine how successfully we compete in the global
economy. They will be going head-to-head against Japanese,
Korean, and West German children.

Unfortunately, American children aren't prepared to run   4
the race, let alone win it. Many are illiterate, undernourished,
impaired, unskilled, poor. Consider the children who started
first grade in 1986: 14 percent were illegitimate; 15 percent were
physically or emotionally handicapped; 15 percent spoke another language other than English; 28 percent were poor; and
fully 40 percent could be expected to live in a single-parent
home before they reached eighteen. Given falling birth rates,
this future work force is small—all the more reason to worry
about its poor quality. So "invest in kids" is not the cry of the
soft-hearted altruist but the call of the hardheaded realist.

Kids as capital has caught on because it responds to a broad   5 set of national concerns. Whether one is worried about the rise of the underclass, the decline of the family, our standing in the global economy, the nation's level of educational performance, or intergenerational conflict, *kids as capital* seems to offer an answer.

Further, *kids as capital* offers the rationale for a new coalition   6 for child-welfare programs. The argument reaches beyond the community of traditional children's advocates and draws business into the child-saving fold. American corporations clearly have a stake in tomorrow's work force as they don't have in today's children. *Kids as capital* gives the toughminded, fifty-five-year-old CEO a reason to "care" about the eight-year-old, Hispanic school girl.

Nevertheless, the argument left unchallenged could easily   7 become yet another "feel-good" formula that doesn't work. Worse, it could end up betraying those it seeks to save—the nation's children.

First, *kids as capital* departs from a classic American vision   8 of the future. Most often, our history has been popularly viewed as progressive, with each generation breaking with and improving on the past. As an immigrant nation, we have always measured our progress through the progress of our children; they have been the bearers of the dream.

Kids as capital turns this optimistic view on its head. It con-   9 jures up a picture of a dark and disorderly future. Essentially, kids as capital is dystopic—closer to the spirit of *Blade Runner* and *Black Rain* than *Wizard of Oz* or *It's a Wonderful Life*. Children, in this view, do not bear the dream. They carry the seeds of our destruction. In short, *kids as capital* plays on our fears, rather than our hopes. It holds out the vision of a troubled future in order to secure a safer and more orderly present.

There is something troubling, too, in such an instrumental   10 view of children. To define them narrowly as tomorrow's wonders is to strip them of their full status as humans, as children: Kids can't be kids; they can only be embryonic workers. And treating *kids as capital* makes it easier to measure them solely through IQ tests, class standing, SAT scores, drop-out ratios, physical fitness tests. This leaves no place in the society for the

slow starter, the handicapped, the quirky, and the noncon-
forming.

Yet kids-as-capital has an even more serious flaw. It evades 11
the central fact of life for American children: They have parents.

As we all know, virtually every child in America grows up 12
in a family with one or more parents. Parents house children.
Parents feed children. Parents clothe children. Parents nurture
and protect children. Parents instruct children in everything
from using a fork to driving a car. To be sure, there have been
vast changes in family life, and, increasingly, parents must depend on teachers, doctors, day-care workers, and technology to
help care for and educate their children. Even so, these changes
haven't altered one fundamental fact: In American society, parents still bear the primary responsibility for the material and
spiritual welfare of children. As our teachers and counselors
and politicians keep reminding us, everything begins at home.
So, if today's children are in trouble, it's because today's parents are in trouble.

As recently as a dozen years ago, it was the central argu- 13
ment of an ambitious report by the Carnegie Council on Children. The Council put it plainly: "The best way to help children
tomorrow is to support parents today." Yet, that view has been
lost. The *kids as capital* argument suppresses the connection between parents and children. It imagines that we can improve
the standing of children without improving the standing of the
parents. In the new rhetoric, it is hard even to find the word
"parent." Increasingly, kids are portrayed as standing alone
out there somewhere, cosmically parent-free.

As a result, *kids as capital* ignores rather than addresses one 14
of the most important changes in American life: the decline in
the power and standing of the nation's parents.

Only a generation ago, parents stood at the center of soci- 15
ety. First of all, there were so many of them—fully half the nation's households in 1960 were parent households with one or
more children under eighteen. Moreover, parents looked
alike—Dad worked and Mom stayed at home. And parents
marched through the stages of childbearing and child rearing
in virtual lockstep: Most couples who married in the 1940s and

1950s finished having their 3.2 children by the time they were in their late twenties.

Their demographic dominance meant two things: First, it made for broad common ground in child rearing. Parents could do a great deal to support each other in raising the new generation. They could, and did, create a culture hospitable to children. Secondly, it made for political clout. When so many adults were parents and so many parents were part of an expanding consumer economy, private and public interests converged. The concerns of parents—housing, health, education—easily found their way into the national agenda. Locally, too, parents were dominant. In some postwar suburbs like Levittown, Pennsylvania, three-quarters of all residents were either parents or children under ten. Not surprisingly, there was little dissent when it came to building a new junior high or establishing a summer recreation program or installing a new playground. What's more, parents and kids drove the consumer economy. Every time they bought a pair of sneakers or a new bike, they were acting in the nation's best interest.

Behind this, of course, lurked a powerful pronatal ideology. Parenthood was the definitive credential of adulthood. More than being married, more than getting a job, it was having a child that baptized you as an adult in postwar America. In survey after survey, postwar parents rated children above marriage itself as the greatest reward of private life. For a generation forced to make personal sacrifices during the Depression and the war, having children and pursuing a private life represented a new kind of freedom.

By the 1970s, parents no longer enjoyed so central a place in the society. To baby boom children, postwar family life seemed suffocating and narrow. Women, in particular, wanted room to breathe. The rights movements of the sixties and seventies overturned the pronatal ideology, replacing it with an ideology of choice. Adults were free to choose among many options: single, married, or divorced; career-primary or career-secondary; parent, stepparent, or child-free.

Thus, parenthood lost its singular status. It no longer served as the definitive credential of maturity and adult achievement.

In fact, as careers and personal fulfillment beckoned, parent-hood seemed just the opposite: a serious limitation on personal growth and success. As Gloria Steinem put it, "I either gave birth to someone else or I gave birth to myself."

As the pronatal ideology vanished, so did the close con-   20
nection between private families and the public interest. Rais-ing children was no longer viewed as a valuable contribution to the society, an activity that boosted the economy, built citi-zen participation, and increased the nation's confidence in the future. Instead, it became one option among many. No longer a moral imperative, child rearing was just another "lifestyle choice."

Viewed this way, raising children looked like an economic   21
disaster. Starting out, parents had to shell out $3,000 for basic prenatal care and maternity costs; $3,000–$5,000 per child for day care; and $2,500 for the basic baby basket of goods and ser-vices. Crib-to-college costs for middle-class Americans could run as high as $135,000 per child. And, increasingly, the period of economic dependency for children stretched well beyond age eighteen. College tuitions and start-up subsidies for the new college graduate became part of the economic burden of parenthood. In an ad campaign, Manufacturers Hanover Trust gave prospective parents fair warning: "If you want a bundle of joy; you'll need a bundle of money."

Hard-pressed younger Americans responded to these new   22
realities in several ways. Some simply chose not to have chil-dren. Others decided to have one or two, but only after they had a good job and solid prospects. Gradually, the number of par-ent households in the nation declined from one-half to one-third, and America faced a birth dearth.

For those who chose the parent option, there was only one   23
way to face up to the new economic pressures of child rearing: work longer and harder outside the home. For all but the ex-tremely well-off, a second income became essential. But in struggling to pay the bills, parents seemed to be short-changing their children in another way. They weren't taking their moral responsibilities seriously enough. They weren't spending enough time with their kids. They weren't reading to the chil-

dren or playing with the kids or supervising homework. And, most important, they weren't teaching good values.

This emerging critique marked a dramatic change in the 24 way society viewed parents. In the postwar period, the stereotypical parent was self-sacrificing, responsible, caring, attentive—an impossible standard, to be sure, but one that lent enormous popular support and approval to adults engaged in the messy and difficult work of raising children. Cruel, abusive, self-absorbed parents might exist, but the popular culture failed to acknowledge them. It was not until parents began to lose their central place in the society that this flattering image faded. Then, quite rapidly, the dominant image of The Good Parent gave way to a new and equally powerful image—the image of The Bad Parent.

The shift occurred in two stages. The first-stage critique 25 emerged in the seventies and focused on an important new figure: the working mother. Working mothers were destroying their children and the family, conservative critics charged. They weren't feeding kids wholesome meals, they weren't taking the kids to church, they weren't serving as moral exemplars. Liberals sided with working mothers, but conceded that they were struggling with some new and difficult issues: Was day care as good as mother care? Was quality time good enough? Were the rewards of twelve-hour workdays great enough to make up for the loss of sleep and leisure-time? Where did the mother of a feverish child belong—at the crib or at her desk?

On the whole, the first-stage critique was a sympathetic cri- 26 tique. In its view, parents might be affected by stress and guilt, but they weren't yet afflicted by serious pathology. After all, in the seventies, the nation's most suspect drug was laetrile, not crack or ice. Divorce was still viewed as a healthy alternative to an unhappy family life. But as the eighties began, a darker image of parents appeared. In the second-stage critique, . . . parents became toxic.

Day after day, throughout the eighties, Americans con- 27 fronted an ugly new reality. Parents were hurting and murdering their children. Day after day, the newspapers brought yet another story of a child abandoned or battered. Day after day, the local news told of a child sexually abused by a father or a stepfather or a mother's boyfriend. Week by week, the national media brought us into courtrooms where photographs of battered children were held up to the camera. The sheer volume of stories suggested an epidemic of historic proportion. In even the most staid publications, the news was sensational. The *New York Times* carried bizarre stories usually found only in tabloids: a father who tortured his children for years; a mother who left her baby in a suitcase in a building she then set on fire; parents who abandoned babies dead or alive, in toilets, dumpsters, and alleyways.

Drug use among parents was one clear cause of abuse. And,   28 increasingly child abuse and drug abuse were linked in the most direct way possible. Pregnant women were battering their children in the womb, delivering drugs through their umbilical cords. Nightly images of crack-addicted babies in neonatal units destroyed any lingering public sympathy for mothers of the underclass. And as the highly publicized Joel Steinberg case made clear, middle-class parents, too, took drugs and killed babies. Even those parents who occasionally indulged were causing their children harm. The Partnership for a Drug-Free America ran ads asking: "With millions of parents doing drugs, is it any wonder their kids are too?"

More than drugs, it was divorce that lay at the heart of   29 middle-class parental failure. It wasn't the crackhouse but the courthouse that was the scene of their collapse. Parents engaged in bitter custody battles. Parents kidnapped their own children. Parents used children as weapons against each other or simply walked away from their responsibilities. In an important new study on the long-term effects of divorce, Judith Wallerstein challenged the earlier notion that divorce is healthy for kids. She studied middle-class families for fifteen years after divorce and came up with some startling findings: Almost half of the children in the study entered adulthood as worried, underachieving, self-deprecating, and sometimes angry young men and women; one in four experienced a severe and enduring drop in their standard of living; three in five felt rejected by at least one parent. Her study concluded: "Divorce is almost always more devastating for children than for their parents. . . . [W]hile divorce can rescue a parent from an intolerable situation, it can fail to rescue the children."

As a group, today's parents have been portrayed as selfish 30 and uncaring: Yuppie parents abandon the children to the au pair; working parents turn their kids over to the mall and the video arcade; single parents hang a key around their kids' necks and a list of emergency numbers on the refrigerator. Even in the healthiest families, parents fail to put their children first.

The indictment of parents is pervasive. In a survey by the 31 Carnegie Foundation, 90 percent of a national sample of public school teachers say a lack of parental support is a problem in their classrooms. Librarians gathered at a national convention to draft a new policy to deal with the problem of parents who send unattended children to the library after school. Daycare workers complain to Ann Landers that all too often parents hand over children with empty stomachs and full diapers. Everywhere, parents are flunking the most basic tests.

Declining demographically, hard-pressed economically, 32 and disarrayed politically, parents have become part of the problem. For proponents of the *kids as capital* argument, the logic is clear: Why try to help parents—an increasingly marginal and unsympathetic bunch—when you can rescue their children?

To blame parents for larger social changes is nothing new. 33 In the past, child-saving movements have depended on building a public consensus that certain parents have failed. Child reformers in the Progressive Era, for example, were able to expand the scope of public sector responsibility for the welfare of children by exploiting mainstream fears about immigrant parents and their child-rearing practices. But what is new is the sense that the majority of parents—up and down the social ladder—are failing. Even middle-class parents, once solid, dependable caretakers of the next generation, don't seem to be up to the job.

By leaving parents out of the picture, *kids as capital* conjures 34 up the image of our little workers struggling against the little workers of Germany and the little workers of Japan. But this picture is obviously false. For the little workers of Germany and Japan have parents too. The difference is that their parents are strongly valued and supported by the society for their contributions *as parents*. We won't be facing up to reality until we are ready to pit our parents against their parents, and thus our family policy against theirs.

1990

If Hitler Asked You to Electrocute a Stranger, Would You? Probably

Philip Meyer

In the beginning, Stanley Milgram was worried about the 1
Nazi problem. He doesn't worry much about the Nazis anymore. He worries about you and me, and, perhaps, himself a little bit too.

Stanley Milgram is a social psychologist, and when he 2
began his career at Yale University in 1960 he had a plan to prove, scientifically, that Germans are different. The Germans-are-different hypothesis has been used by historians, such as William L. Shirer, to explain the systematic destruction of the Jews by the Third Reich.

The appealing thing about this theory is that it makes those 3
of us who are not Germans feel better about the whole business. Obviously, you and I are not Hitler, and it seems equally obvious that we would never do Hitler's dirty work for him. But now, because of Stanley Milgram, we are compelled to wonder. Milgram developed a laboratory experiment which provided a systematic way to measure obedience. His plan was to try it out in New Haven on Americans and then go to Germany and try it out on Germans. He was strongly motivated by scientific cu-

riosity, but there was also some moral content in his decision to pursue this line of research, which was, in turn, colored by his own Jewish background. If he could show that Germans are more obedient than Americans, he could then vary the conditions of the experiment and try to find out just what it is that makes some people more obedient than others. With this understanding, the world might, conceivably, be just a little bit better.

But he never took his experiment to Germany. He never ⁴ took it any farther than Bridgeport. The first finding, also the most unexpected and disturbing finding, was that we Americans are an obedient people: not blindly obedient, and not blissfully obedient, just obedient. "I found so much obedience," says Milgram softly, a little sadly, "I hardly saw the need for taking the experiment to Germany."

There is something of the theatre director in Milgram, and ⁵ his technique, which he learned from one of the old masters in experimental psychology, Solomon Asch, is to stage a play with every line rehearsed, every prop carefully selected, and everybody an actor except one person. That one person is the subject of the experiment. The subject, of course, does not know he is in a play. He thinks he is in real life.

The experiment worked like this: If you were an innocent ⁶ subject in Milgram's melodrama, you read an ad in the newspaper or received one in the mail asking for volunteers for an educational experiment. The job would take about an hour and pay $4.50. So you make an appointment and go to an old Romanesque stone structure on High Street with the imposing name of The Yale Interaction Laboratory. It looks something like a broadcasting studio. Inside, you meet a young, crew-cut man in a laboratory coat who says he is Jack Williams, the experimenter. There is another citizen, fiftyish, Irish face, an accountant, a little overweight, and very mild and harmless-looking. This other citizen seems nervous and plays with his hat while the two of you sit in chairs side by side and are told that the $4.50 checks are yours no matter what happens. Then you listen to Jack Williams explain the experiment.

It is about learning, says Jack Williams in a quiet, knowl- ⁷ edgeable way. Science does not know much about the conditions under which people learn and this experiment is to find out about negative reinforcement. Negative reinforcement is getting punished when you do something wrong, as opposed to positive reinforcement which is getting rewarded when you do something right. The negative reinforcement in this case is electric shock.

Then Jack Williams takes two pieces of paper, puts them in 8 a hat, and shakes them up. One piece of paper is supposed to say, "Teacher" and the other, "Learner." Draw one and you will see which you will be. The mild-looking accountant draws one, holds it close to his vest like a poker player, looks at it, and says, "Learner." You look at yours. It says, "Teacher." You do not know that the drawing is rigged, and both slips say "Teacher." The experimenter beckons to the mild-mannered "learner."

"Want to step right in here and have a seat, please?" he says. 9 "You can leave your coat on the back of that chair . . . roll up your right sleeve, please. Now what I want to do is strap down your arms to avoid excessive movement on your part during the experiment. This electrode is connected to the shock generator in the next room.

"And this electrode paste," he says, squeezing some stuff 10 out of a plastic bottle and putting it on the man's arm, "is to provide a good contact and to avoid a blister or burn. Are there any questions now before we go into the next room?"

You don't have any, but the strapped-in "learner" does. 11

"I do think I should say this," says the learner. "About two 12 years ago, I was at the veterans' hospital . . . they detected a heart condition. Nothing serious, but as long as I'm having these shocks, how strong are they—how dangerous are they?"

Williams, the experimenter, shakes his head casually. "Oh, 13 no," he says. "Although they may be painful, they're not dangerous. Anything else?"

Nothing else. And so you play the game. The game is for 14 you to read a series of word pairs: for example, blue-girl, nice-day, fat-neck. When you finish the list, you read just the first word in each pair and then a multiple-choice list of four other words, including the second word of the pair. The learner, from his remote, strapped-in position, pushes one of four switches to indicate which of the four answers he thinks is the right one. If he gets it right, nothing happens and you go on to the next one. If he gets it wrong, you push a switch that buzzes and gives him an electric shock. And then you go to the next word. You start with 15 volts and increase the number of volts by 15 for each wrong answer. The control board goes from 15 volts on one end to 450 volts on the other. So that you know what you are doing, you get a test shock yourself, at 45 volts. It hurts. To further keep you aware of what you are doing to that man in there, the board has verbal descriptions of the shock levels, ranging from "Slight Shock" at the left-hand side, through "Intense Shock" in the middle, to "Danger: Severe Shock" toward the far right. Finally, at the very end, under 435- and 450-volt switches, there are three ambiguous X's. If, at any point, you hesitate, Mr. Williams calmly tells you to go on. If you still hesitate, he tells you again.

Except for some terrifying details, which will be explained in a moment, this is the experiment. The object is to find the shock level at which you disobey the experimenter and refuse to pull the switch. 15

When Stanley Milgram first wrote this script, he took it to fourteen Yale psychology majors and asked them what they thought would happen. He put it this way: Out of one hundred persons in the teacher's predicament, how would their break-off points be distributed along the 15-to-450-volt scale? They thought a few would break off very early, most would quit someplace in the middle and a few would go all the way to the end. The highest estimate of the number out of one hundred who would go all the way to the end was three. Milgram then informally polled some of his fellow scholars in the psychology department. They agreed that very few would go to the end. Milgram thought so too. 16

"I'll tell you quite frankly," he says, "before I began this experiment, before any shock generator was built, I thought that most people would break off at 'Strong Shock' or 'Very Strong Shock.' You would get only a very, very small proportion of people going out to the end of the shock generator, and they would constitute a pathological fringe." 17

In his pilot experiments, Milgram used Yale students as 18

subjects. Each of them pushed the shock switches, one by one, all the way to the end of the board.

So he rewrote the script to include some protests from the   19
learner. At first, they were mild, gentlemanly, Yalie protests, but, "it didn't seem to have as much effect as I thought it would or should," Milgram recalls. "So we had more violent protestation on the part of the person getting the shock. All of the time, of course, what we were trying to do was not to create a macabre situation, but simply to generate disobedience. And that was one of the first findings. This was not only a technical deficiency of the experiment, that we didn't get disobedience. It really was the first finding: that obedience would be much greater than we had assumed it would be and disobedience would be much more difficult than we had assumed."

As it turned out, the situation did become rather macabre.   20
The only meaningful way to generate disobedience was to have the victim protest with great anguish, noise, and vehemence. The protests were tape-recorded so that all the teachers ordinarily would hear the same sounds and nuances, and they started with a grunt at 75 volts, proceeded through a "Hey, that really hurts," at 125 volts, got desperate with, "I can't stand the pain, don't do that," at 180 volts, reached complaints of heart trouble at 195, an agonized scream at 285, a refusal to answer at 315, and only heart-rending, ominous silence after that.

Still, sixty-five percent of the subjects, twenty- to fifty-year-   21
old American males, everyday, ordinary people, like you and me, obediently kept pushing those levers in the belief that they were shocking the mild-mannered learner, whose name was Mr. Wallace, and who was chosen for the role because of his innocent appearance, all the way up to 450 volts.

Milgram was now getting enough disobedience so that he   22
had something he could measure. The next step was to vary the circumstances to see what would encourage or discourage obedience.

He put the learner in the same room with the teacher. He   23
stopped strapping the learner's hand down. He rewrote the script so that at 150 volts the learner took his hand off the shock

plate and declared that he wanted out of the experiment. He rewrote the script some more so that the experimenter then told the teacher to grasp the learner's hand and physically force it down on the plate to give Mr. Wallace his unwanted electric shock.

"I had the feeling that very few people would go on at that 24 point, if any," Milgram says. "I thought that would be the limit of obedience that you would find in the laboratory."

It wasn't.   25

Although seven years have now gone by, Milgram still re- 26 members the first person to walk into the laboratory in the newly rewritten script. He was a construction worker, a very short man. "He was so small," says Milgram, "that when he sat on the chair in front of the shock generator, his feet didn't reach the floor. When the experimenter told him to push the victim's hand down and give the shock, he turned to the experimenter, and he turned to the victim, his elbow went up, he fell down on the hand of the victim, his feet kind of tugged to one side, and he said, 'Like this, boss?' Zzumph!"

The experiment was played out to its bitter end. Milgram 27 tried it with forty different subjects. And thirty percent of them obeyed the experimenter and kept on obeying.

"The protests of the victim were strong and vehement, he 28 was screaming his guts out, he refused to participate, and you had to physically struggle with him in order to get his hand down on the shock generator," Milgram remembers. But twelve out of forty did it.

Milgram took his experiment out of New Haven. Not to 29 Germany, just twenty miles down the road to Bridgeport. Maybe, he reasoned, the people obeyed because of the prestigious setting of Yale University.

The new setting was a suite of three rooms in a run-down 30 office building in Bridgeport. The only identification was a sign with a fictitious name: "Research Associates of Bridgeport." Questions about professional connections got only vague answers about "research for industry."

Obedience was less in Bridgeport. Forty-eight percent of the 31 subjects stayed for the maximum shock, compared to sixty-five percent at Yale. But this was enough to prove that far more than Yale's prestige was behind the obedient behavior.

For more than seven years now, Stanley Milgram has been trying to figure out what makes ordinary American citizens so obedient. The most obvious answer—that people are mean, nasty, brutish and sadistic—won't do. The subjects who gave the shocks to Mr. Wallace to the end of the board did not enjoy it. They groaned, protested, fidgeted, argued, and in some cases, were seized by fits of nervous, agitated giggling. 32

"They even try to get out of it," says Milgram, "but they are somehow engaged in something from which they cannot liberate themselves. They are locked into a structure, and they do not have the skills or inner resources to disengage themselves." 33

Milgram's theory assumes that people behave in two different operating modes as different as ice and water. He does not rely on Freud or sex or toilet-training hang-ups for this theory. All he says is that ordinarily we operate in a state of autonomy, which means we pretty much have and assert control over what we do. But in certain circumstances, we operate under what Milgram calls a state of agency (after agent, n . . . one who acts for or in the place of another by authority from him; a substitute; a deputy. —*Webster's Collegiate Dictionary*). A state of agency, to Milgram, is nothing more than a frame of mind. 34

"There's nothing bad about it, there's nothing good about it," he says. "It's a natural circumstance of living with other people. . . . I think of a state of agency as a real transformation of a person; if a person has different properties when he's in that state, just as water can turn to ice under certain conditions of temperature, a person can move to the state of mind that I call agency . . . the critical thing is that you see yourself as the instrument of the execution of another person's wishes. You do not see yourself as acting on your own. And there's a real transformation, a real change of properties of the person." 35

So, for most subjects in Milgram's laboratory experiments, the act of giving Mr. Wallace his painful shock was necessary, even though unpleasant, and besides they were doing it on behalf of somebody else and it was for science. 36

Stanley Milgram has his problems, too. He believes that in ₃₇ the laboratory situation, he would not have shocked Mr. Wallace. His professional critics reply that in his real-life situation he has done the equivalent. He has placed innocent and naïve subjects under great emotional strain and pressure in selfish obedience to his quest for knowledge. When you raise this issue with Milgram, he has an answer ready. There is, he explains patiently, a critical difference between his naïve subjects and the man in the electric chair. The man in the electric chair (in the mind of the naïve subject) is helpless, strapped in. But the naïve subject is free to go at any time.

Immediately after he offers this distinction, Milgram antic- ₃₈ ipates the objection.

"It's quite true," he says, "that this is almost a philosophic ₃₉ position, because we have learned that some people are psychologically incapable of disengaging themselves. But that doesn't relieve them of the moral responsibility."

The parallel is exquisite. "The tension problem was unex- ₄₀ pected," says Milgram in his defense. But he went on anyway. The naïve subjects didn't expect the screaming protests from the strapped-in learner. But they went on.

"I had to make a judgment," says Milgram. "I had to ask ₄₁ myself, was this harming the person or not? My judgment is that it was not. Even in the extreme cases, I wouldn't say that permanent damage results."

Sound familiar? "The shocks may be painful," the experi- ₄₂ menter kept saying, "but they're not dangerous."

After the series of experiments was completed, Milgram ₄₃ sent a report of the results to his subjects and a questionnaire, asking whether they were glad or sorry to have been in the experiment. Eighty-three and seven-tenths percent said they were glad and only 1.3 percent were sorry; 15 percent were neither sorry nor glad. However, Milgram could not be sure at the time of the experiment that only 1.3 percent would be sorry.

Kurt Vonnegut Jr. put one paragraph in the preface to ₄₄ *Mother Night,* in 1966, which pretty much says it for the people with their fingers on the shock-generator switches, for you and me, and maybe even for Milgram. "If I'd been born in Germany," Vonnegut said, "I suppose I would have *been* a Nazi, bopping Jews and gypsies and Poles around, leaving boots sticking out of snowbanks, warming myself with my sweetly virtuous insides. So it goes."

Just so. One thing that happened to Milgram back in New   45
Haven during the days of the experiment was that he kept running into people he'd watched from behind the one-way glass. It gave him a funny feeling, seeing those people going about their everyday business in New Haven and knowing what they would do to Mr. Wallace if ordered to. Now that his research results are in and you've thought about it, you can get this funny feeling too. You don't need one-way glass. A glance in your own mirror may serve just as well.

1970

Nubian Diet Revealed at Last

Kathy A. Svitil

The Nubians were kings once: They built pyramids and   1
temples; carved delicate statues and jewelry; controlled trade along the Nile; and for a century or so, beginning in the eighth century B.C., even ruled Egypt, their neighbor to the north.

Mostly, though, the Nubians have been pawns, invaded by   2
the Persians and Assyrians, dominated by the Egyptians—and finally flooded.

When the Aswan High Dam was completed in 1970, the   3
reservoir it created inundated thousands of square miles of land along the banks of the Nile, from Egypt south into the Sudan.

Nearly all of what was once the Lower Nubian heartland is   4
now Lake Nasser.

Before the flood, however, teams of archaeologists from   5 around the world flocked to the region, hurriedly salvaging what they could of the Nubian past.

They recovered tons of ancient artifacts—including the en- 6 tire Temple of Dendur—and, even more remarkably, hundreds of ancient Nubians.

Most of these mummies were ordinary folk, buried in the 7 desert and accidentally preserved by the blistering heat and dry sands.

Their bodies dried out so fast that not only the bones but 8 also the skin, hair and muscle were saved from decomposition.

And preserved along with the mummies, says Christine 9 White, a physical anthropologist at the University of Western Ontario, is a record of what the ancient Nubians ate—even in the last weeks of their lives.

White gleaned that particular bit of information from the 10 mummies' hair.

Researchers already knew that the ancient Nubians' diet 11 was inadequate. Besides evidence of arthritis, tumors and parasites, the mummies show clear signs of malnutrition, iron-deficiency anemia and osteoporosis.

Yet what that diet consisted of has been something of a 12 mystery.

Despite the intensive excavation, no physical evidence— 13 plant or animal remains—was ever recovered.

White has now extracted that physical evidence from the 14 mummies themselves by looking at the isotope signatures of their tissue: the distinctive ratios of heavy nitrogen atoms to light ones and of heavy to light carbon that humans acquire from the plants and animals they eat.

White studied 167 mummies from a site along the west 15 bank of the Nile in the Wadi Halfa region of northern Sudan.

The oldest mummies dated from the period between 350 16 B.C. and A.D. 350, when Lower Nubia was ruled by the Meroitic Empire of Upper Nubia.

White first looked at the mummies' nitrogen signature to 17 find out their source of protein (which is rich in nitrogen).

Grasses and the cows that eat them have a relatively low 18

ratio of heavy nitrogen 15 to nitrogen 14; scrubs and bushes and the goats and sheep that browse on them in the Nubian Desert have a higher ratio. Most of the mummies, White found, had eaten these desert animals rather than cattle.

Some had partaken more than others: Male mummies con-   19 tained more nitrogen 15 relative to their body weight than did females. Apparently, the men of ancient Nubia got more than their fair share of the meat.

The ancient Nubians did not just ranch in the desert. They   20 also made it bloom—and with crops that aren't easy to grow in hot, arid conditions.

The ratio of carbon 13 to carbon 12 in the mummies from   21 the Meroitic period, White says, shows that fully 84 percent of the Nubians' plant intake consisted of "C3" foods such as wheat, barley and fruit—all of which require more water than is normally available in the Nubian Desert.

The Nubians, White figures, must therefore have been irri-   22 gating their crops, probably using the ox-driven waterwheel— a sort of Ferris wheel with buckets that dumped water from the Nile into irrigation channels. It was invented in Mesopotamia and brought to Lower Nubia by Meroitic settlers.

Lower Nubia, White speculates, may have been an agricul-   23 tural hinterland that produced wheat and barley for Meroe. That might explain why mummies dating from after the fall of the Meroitic Empire around A.D. 350 ate about 9 percent fewer C3 plants than their forebears.

"When the Meroitic Empire fell," White says, "the Nubians,   24 who no longer had to grow so much wheat and barley, may have reverted to a more traditional diet of C4 plants, like sorghum and millet."

Such grains are much easier to grow in the desert than C3   25 crops, even with irrigation.

Today in the Wadi Halfa, wheat and barley are grown in the   26 fall and winter, with the aid of irrigation and the annual flood- ing of the Nile, while sorghum and millet are planted in the spring and harvested beginning in early June.

Could the same crop rotation, White wondered, have been   27 occurring over a thousand years ago?

The mummies' hair said yes. 28

Until White's work, only bone had been used in isotopic 29
analyses, and bone takes between 25 and 30 years to replace its
store of isotopes—making its isotope signature "just a homog-
enized version of what was consumed over a lifetime," as White
puts it.

But isotopes show up in hair two weeks after they're con- 30
sumed. Thus isotope signatures from a hair shaft can reveal any
changes in diet that occurred while the hair was growing.

White cut hair from 14 post-Meroe mummies into 3.25-inch- 31
long segments, each segment representing about two months'
growth.

She found that the isotopic signature fluctuated dramati- 32
cally between segments, indicating that the person had alter-
nated between periods of eating mostly C3 plants and ones of
relying on C4 plants.

Furthermore, by looking at the hair closest to the scalp, 33
White could tell what the future mummies had eaten just weeks
before they died.

Nearly two-thirds of them had been eating C4 plants. That 34
suggested they died after the sorghum and millet harvest in
June, but before the wheat and barley harvest in the winter.

Why would more Nubians have died during summer? 35

Because of heat and malnutrition, White says. 36

C4 plants aren't as nutritious as C3 plants; sorghum is low 37
in vitamin B, for instance, and vitamin B deficiency increases the
incidence of pellagra, a disease that causes gastrointestinal and
neurological problems.

Moreover, by the end of summer in Nubia, even C4 crops 38
are scarce.

Today more residents of the Nubian Desert die in summer 39
than during any other time of year. One thousand years ago,
their ancestors may have faced the same hardships.

1995

CHAPTER 9

Analogy

The Myth of the Cave

Plato

And now, I said, let me show in a figure how far our nature 1
is enlightened or unenlightened:—Behold! human beings living
in an underground den, which has a mouth open toward the light
and reaching all along the den; here they have been from their
childhood, and have their legs and necks chained so that they
cannot move, and can only see before them, being prevented by
the chains from turning round their heads. Above and behind
them a fire is blazing at a distance, and between the fire and the
prisoners there is a raised way; and you will see, if you look, a
low wall built along the way, like the screen which marionette
players have in front of them, over which they show the puppets.

I see. 2

And do you see, I said, men passing along the wall carry- 3
ing all sorts of vessels, and statues and figures of animals made
of wood and stone and various materials, which appear over the
wall? Some of them are talking, others silent.

You have shown me a strange image, and they are strange 4
prisoners.

Like ourselves, I replied; and they see only their own shad- 5
ows, or the shadows of one another, which the fire throws on
the opposite wall of the cave?

True, he said; how could they see anything but the shadows 6
if they were never allowed to move their heads?

342

And of the objects which are being carried in like manner 7
they would only see the shadows?

Yes, he said. 8

And if they were able to converse with one another, would 9
they not suppose that they were naming what was actually before them?

Very true. 10

And suppose further that the prison had an echo which 11
came from the other side, would they not be sure to fancy when
one of the passers-by spoke that the voice which they heard
came from the passing shadow?

No question, he replied. 12

To them, I said, the truth would be literally nothing but the 13
shadows of the images.

That is certain. 14

And now look again, and see what will naturally follow if 15
the prisoners are released and disabused of their error. At first,
when any of them is liberated and compelled suddenly to stand
up and turn his neck round and walk and look toward the light,
he will suffer sharp pains; the glare will distress him, and he will
be unable to see the realities of which in his former state he had
seen the shadows; and then conceive some one saying to him,
that what he saw before was an illusion, but that now, when he
is approaching nearer to being and his eye is turned toward
more real existence, he has a clearer vision—what will be his
reply? And you may further imagine that his instructor is pointing to the objects as they pass and requiring him to name
them—will he not be perplexed? Will he not fancy that the
shadows which he formerly saw are truer than the objects which
are now shown to him?

Far truer. 16

And if he is compelled to look straight at the light, will he 17
not have a pain in his eyes which will make him turn away to
take refuge in the objects of vision which he can see, and which
he will conceive to be in reality clearer than the things which
are now being shown to him?

True, he said. 18

And suppose once more, that he is reluctantly dragged up 19

a steep and rugged ascent, and held fast until he is forced into the presence of the sun himself, is he not likely to be pained and irritated? When he approaches the light his eyes will be dazzled, and he will not be able to see anything at all of what are now called realities.

Not all in a moment, he said.   20

He will require to grow accustomed to the sight of the upper   21 world. And first he will see the shadows best, next the reflections of men and other objects in the water, and then the objects themselves; then he will gaze upon the light of the moon and the stars and the spangled heaven; and he will see the sky and the stars by night better than the sun or the light of the sun by day?

Certainly.   22

Last of all he will be able to see the sun, and not mere re-   23 flections of him in the water, but he will see him in his own proper place, and not in another; and he will contemplate him as he is.

Certainly.   24

He will then proceed to argue that this is he who gives the   25 season and the years, and is the guardian of all that is in the visible world, and in a certain way the cause of all things which he and his fellows have been accustomed to behold?

Clearly, he said, he would first see the sun and then reason   26 about him.

And when he remembered his old habitation, and the wis-   27 dom of the den and his fellow-prisoners, do you not suppose that he would felicitate himself on the change, and pity them?

Certainly, he would.   28

And if they were in the habit of conferring honors among   29 themselves on those who were quickest to observe the passing shadows and to remark which of them went before, and which followed after, and which were together; and who were therefore best able to draw conclusions as to the future, do you think that he would care for such honors and glories, or envy the possessors of them? Would he not say with Homer,

> Better to be the poor servant of a poor master,

and to endure anything, rather than think as they do and live after their manner?

Yes, he said, I think that he would rather suffer anything 30
than entertain these false notions and live in this miserable
manner.

Imagine once more, I said, such a one coming suddenly out 31
of the sun to be replaced in his old situation; would he not be
certain to have his eyes full of darkness?

To be sure, he said. 32

And if there were a contest, and he had to compete in mea- 33
suring the shadows with the prisoners who had never moved
out of the den, while his sight was still weak, and before his eyes
had become steady (and the time which would be needed to acquire this new habit of sight might be very considerable), would
he not be ridiculous? Men would say of him that up he went
and down he came without his eyes; and that it was better not
even to think of ascending; and if any one tried to loose another
and lead him up to the light, let them only catch the offender,
and they would put him to death.

No question, he said. 34

This entire allegory, I said, you may now append, dear 35
Glaucon, to the previous argument; the prison-house is the
world of sight, the light of the fire is the sun, and you will not
misapprehend me if you interpret the journey upwards to be
the ascent of the soul into the intellectual world according to my
poor belief, which, at your desire, I have expressed—whether
rightly or wrongly God knows. But, whether true or false, my
opinion is that in the world of knowledge the idea of good appears last of all, and is seen only with an effort; and, when seen,
is also inferred to be the universal author of all things beautiful
and right, parent of light and of the lord of light in this visible
world, and the immediate source of reason and truth in the intellectual; and that this is the power upon which he who would
act rationally either in public or private life must have his eye
fixed.

I agree, he said, as far as I am able to understand you. 36

Moreover, I said, you must not wonder that those who at- 37
tain to this beatific vision are unwilling to descend to human
affairs; for their souls are ever hastening into the upper world
where they desire to dwell; which desire of theirs is very natural, if our allegory may be trusted.

Yes, very natural.   38

And is there anything surprising in one who passes from   39
divine contemplations to the evil state of man, misbehaving
himself in a ridiculous manner; if, while his eyes are blinking
and before he has become accustomed to the surrounding darkness, he is compelled to fight in courts of law, or in other places,
about the images or the shadows of images of justice, and is endeavoring to meet the conceptions of those who have never yet
seen absolute justice?

Anything but surprising, he replied.   40

Any one who has common sense will remember that the be-   41
wilderments of the eyes are of two kinds, and arise from two
causes, either from coming out of the light or from going into
the light, which is true of the mind's eye, quite as much as of
the bodily eye; and he who remembers this when he sees any
one whose vision is perplexed and weak, will not be too ready
to laugh; he will first ask whether that soul of man has come out
of the brighter life, and is unable to see because unaccustomed
to the dark, or having turned from darkness to the day is dazzled by excess of light. And he will count the one happy in his
condition and state of being, and he will pity the other; or, if he
have a mind to laugh at the soul which comes from below into
the light, there will be more reason in this than in the laugh
which greets him who returns from above out of the light into
the den.

That, he said, is a very just distinction.   42

ca. 373 B.C.

The Myth of Sisyphus

Albert Camus

The gods had condemned Sisyphus to ceaselessly rolling a   1
rock to the top of a mountain, whence the stone would fall back

of its own weight. They had thought with some reason that there is no more dreadful punishment than futile and hopeless labor.

If one believes Homer, Sisyphus was the wisest and most 2 prudent of mortals. According to another tradition, however, he was disposed to practice the profession of highwayman. I see no contradiction in this. Opinions differ as to the reasons why he became the futile laborer of the underworld. To begin with, he is accused of a certain levity in regard to the gods. He stole their secrets. Aegina, the daughter of Aesopus, was carried off by Jupiter. The father was shocked by that disappearance and complained to Sisyphus. He, who knew of the abduction, offered to tell about it on condition that Aesopus would give water to the citadel of Corinth. To the celestial thunderbolts he preferred the benediction of water. He was punished for this in the underworld. Homer tells us also that Sisyphus had put Death in chains. Pluto could not endure the sight of his deserted, silent empire. He dispatched the god of war, who liberated Death from the hands of her conqueror.

It is said also that Sisyphus, being near to death, rashly 3 wanted to test his wife's love. He ordered her to cast his unburied body into the middle of the public square. Sisyphus woke up in the underworld. And there, annoyed by an obedience so contrary to human love, he obtained from Pluto permission to return to earth in order to chastise his wife. But when he had seen again the face of this world, enjoyed water and sun, warm stones and the sea, he no longer wanted to go back to the infernal darkness. Recalls, signs of anger, warnings were of no avail. Many years more he lived facing the curve of the gulf, the sparkling sea, and the smiles of earth. A decree of the gods was necessary. Mercury came and seized the impudent man by the collar and, snatching him from his joys, led him forcibly back to the underworld, where his rock was ready for him.

You have already grasped that Sisyphus is the absurd hero. 4 He *is*, as much through his passions as through his torture. His scorn of the gods, his hatred of death, and his passion for life won him that unspeakable penalty in which the whole being is exerted toward accomplishing nothing. This is the price that must be paid for the passions of this earth. Nothing is told us about Sisyphus in the underworld. Myths are made for the imagination to breathe life into them. As for this myth, one sees merely the whole effort of a body straining to raise the huge stone, to roll it and push it up a slope a hundred times over; one sees the face screwed up, the cheek tight against the stone, the shoulder bracing the clay-covered mass, the foot wedging it, the fresh start with arms outstretched, the wholly human security of two earth-clotted hands. At the very end of his long effort measured by skyless space and time without depth, the purpose is achieved. Then Sisyphus watches the stone rush down in a few moments toward that lower world whence he will have to push it up again toward the summit. He goes back down to the plain.

It is during that return, that pause, that Sisyphus interests 5 me. A face that toils so close to stones is already stone itself! I see that man going back down with a heavy yet measured step toward the torment of which he will never know the end. That hour like a breathing-space which returns as surely as his suffering, that is the hour of consciousness. At each of those moments when he leaves the heights and gradually sinks toward the lairs of the gods, he is superior to his fate. He is stronger than his rock.

If this myth is tragic, that is because its hero is conscious. 6 Where would his torture be, indeed, if at every step the hope of succeeding upheld him? The workman of today works every day in his life at the same tasks, and this fate is no less absurd. But it is tragic only at the rare moments when it becomes conscious. Sisyphus, proletarian of the gods, powerless and rebellious, knows the whole extent of his wretched condition: it is what he thinks of during his descent. The lucidity that was to constitute his torture at the same time crowns his victory. There is no fate that cannot be surmounted by scorn.

If the descent is thus sometimes performed in sorrow, it can 7 also take place in joy. This word is not too much. Again I fancy Sisyphus returning toward his rock, and the sorrow was in the beginning. When the images of earth cling too tightly to memory, when the call of happiness becomes too insistent, it happens that melancholy rises in man's heart: this is the rock's victory, this is the rock itself. The boundless grief is too heavy to bear. These are our nights of Gethsemane. But crushing truths perish from being acknowledged. Thus, Oedipus at the outset obeys fate without knowing it. But from the moment he knows, his tragedy begins. Yet at the same moment, blind and desperate, he realizes that the only bond linking him to the world is the cool hand of a girl. Then a tremendous remark rings out: "Despite so many ordeals, my advanced age and the nobility of my soul make me conclude that all is well." Sophocles' Oedipus, like Dostoevsky's Kirilov, thus gives the recipe for the absurd victory. Ancient wisdom confirms modern heroism.

One does not discover the absurd without being tempted   8
to write a manual of happiness. "What! by such narrow ways—?" There is but one world, however. Happiness and the absurd are two sons of the same earth. They are inseparable. It would be a mistake to say that happiness necessarily springs from the absurd discovery. It happens as well that the feeling of the absurd springs from happiness. "I conclude that all is well," says Oedipus, and that remark is sacred. It echoes in the wild and limited universe of man. It teaches that all is not, has not been, exhausted. It drives out of this world a god who had come into it with dissatisfaction and a preference for futile sufferings. It makes of fate a human matter, which must be settled among men.

All Sisyphus' silent joy is contained therein. His fate belongs   9
to him. His rock is his thing. Likewise, the absurd man, when he contemplates his torment, silences all the idols. In the universe suddenly restored to its silence, the myriad wondering little voices of the earth rise up. Unconscious, secret calls, invitations from all the faces, they are the necessary reverse and price of victory. There is no sun without shadow, and it is essential to know the night. The absurd man says yes and his effort will henceforth be unceasing. If there is a personal fate, there is no higher destiny, or at least there is but one which he concludes is inevitable and despicable. For the rest, he knows himself to be the master of his days. At that subtle moment when man

glances backward over his life, Sisyphus returning toward his rock, in that slight pivoting he contemplates that series of unrelated actions which becomes his fate, created by him, combined under his memory's eye and soon sealed by his death. Thus, convinced of the wholly human origin of all that is human, a blind man eager to see who knows that the night has no end, he is still on the go. The rock is still rolling.

I leave Sisyphus at the foot of the mountain! One always 10 finds one's burden again. But Sisyphus teaches the higher fidelity that negates the gods and raises rocks. He too concludes that all is well. This universe henceforth without a master seems to him neither sterile nor futile. Each atom of that stone, each mineral flake of that night-filled mountain, in itself forms a world. The struggle itself toward the heights is enough to fill a man's heart. One must imagine Sisyphus happy.

1955

"But a Watch in the Night": A Scientific Fable

James C. Rettie

Out beyond our solar system there is a planet called Coper- 1 nicus. It came into existence some four or five billion years before the birth of our Earth. In due course of time it became inhabited by a race of intelligent men.

About 750 million years ago the Copernicans had devel- 2 oped the motion picture machine to a point well in advance of the stage that we have reached. Most of the cameras that we now use in motion picture work are geared to take twenty-four pictures per second on a continuous strip of film. When such film is run through a projector, it throws a series of images on the screen and these change with a rapidity that gives the visual impression of normal movement. If a motion is too swift for the human eye to see it in detail, it can be captured and artificially slowed down by means of the slow-motion camera. This one is geared to take many more shots per second—ninety-six or even more than that. When the slow motion film is projected at the normal speed of twenty-four pictures per second, we can see just how the jumping horse goes over a hurdle.

What about motion that is too slow to be seen by the human 3 eye? That problem has been solved by the use of the time-lapse camera. In this one, the shutter is geared to take only one shot per second, or one per minute, or even one per hour—depending upon the kind of movement that is being photographed. When the time-lapse film is projected at the normal speed of twenty-four pictures per second, it is possible to see a bean sprout growing up out of the ground. Time-lapse films are useful in the study of many types of motion too slow to be observed by the unaided, human eye.

The Copernicans, it seems, had time-lapse cameras some 4 757 million years ago and they also had superpowered telescopes that gave them a clear view of what was happening upon this Earth. They decided to make a film record of the life history of Earth and to make it on the scale of one picture per year. The photography has been in progress during the last 757 million years.

In the near future, a Copernican interstellar expedition will 5 arrive upon our Earth and bring with it a copy of the time-lapse film. Arrangements will be made for showing the entire film in one continuous run. This will begin at midnight of New Year's Eve and continue day and night without a single stop until midnight of December 31. The rate of projection will be twenty-four pictures per second. Time on the screen will thus seem to move at the rate of twenty-four years per second; 1440 years per minute; 86,400 years per hour; approximately two million years per day; and sixty-two million years per month. The normal lifespan of individual man will occupy about three seconds. The full period of earth history that will be unfolded on the screen (some 757 million years) will extend from what the geologists call Pre-Cambrian times up to the present. This will, by no means, cover the full time-span of the earth's geological history but it will embrace the period since the advent of living organisms.

During the months of January, February, and March the picture will be desolate and dreary. The shape of the land masses and the oceans will bear little or no resemblance to those that we know. The violence of geological erosion will be much in evidence. Rains will pour down on the land and promptly go booming down to the seas. There will be no clear streams anywhere except where the rains fall upon hard rock. Everywhere on the steeper ground the stream channels will be filled with boulders hurled down by rushing waters. Raging torrents and dry stream beds will keep alternating in quick succession. High mountains will seem to melt like so much butter in the sun. The shifting of land into the seas, later to be thrust up as new mountains, will be going on at a grand scale. 6

Early in April there will be some indication of the presence of single-celled living organisms in some of the warmer and sheltered coastal waters. By the end of the month it will be noticed that some of these organisms have become multicellular. A few of them, including the Trilobites, will be encased in hard shells. 7

Toward the end of May, the first vertebrates will appear, but they will still be aquatic creatures. In June about 60 per cent of the land area that we know as North America will be under water. One broad channel will occupy the space where the Rocky Mountains now stand. Great deposits of limestone will be forming under some of the shallower seas. Oil and gas deposits will be in process of formation—also under shallow seas. On land there will still be no sign of vegetation. Erosion will be rampant, tearing loose particles and chunks of rock and grinding them into sand and silt to be sped out by the streams into bays and estuaries. 8

About the middle of July the first land plants will appear and take up the tremendous job of soil building. Slowly, very slowly, the mat of vegetation will spread, always battling for its life against the power of erosion. Almost foot by foot, the plant life will advance, lacing down with its root structures whatever 9 pulverized rock material it can find. Leaves and stems will be giving added protection against the loss of the soil foothold. The increasing vegetation will pave the way for the land animals that will live upon it.

Early in August the seas will be teeming with fish. This will [10] be what geologists call the Devonian period. Some of the races of these fish will be breathing by means of lung tissue instead of through gill tissues. Before the month is over, some of the lung fish will go ashore and take on a crude lizard-like appearance. Here are the first amphibians.

In early September the insects will put in their appearance. [11] Some will look like huge dragonflies and will have a wing spread of 24 inches. Large portions of the land masses will now be covered with heavy vegetation that will include the primitive spore-propagating trees. Layer upon layer of this plant growth will build up, later to appear as the coal deposits. About the middle of this month, there will be evidence of the first seed-bearing plants and the first reptiles. Heretofore, the land animals will have been amphibians that could reproduce their kind only by depositing a soft egg mass in quiet waters. The reptiles will be shown to be freed from the aquatic bond because they can reproduce by means of a shelled egg in which the embryo and its nurturing liquids are sealed and thus protected from destructive evaporation. Before September is over, the first dinosaurs will be seen—creatures destined to dominate the animal realm for about 140 million years and then to disappear.

In October there will be series of mountain uplifts along [12] what is now the eastern coast of the United States. A creature with feathered limbs—half bird and half reptile in appearance—will take itself into the air. Some small and rather unpretentious animals will be seen to bring forth their young in a form that is a miniature replica of the parents and to feed these young on milk secreted by mammary glands in the female parent. The emergence of this mammalian form of animal life will be recognized as one of the great events in geologic time. October will also witness the high water mark of the dinosaurs—creatures ranging in size from that of the modern goat to monsters like

Brontosaurus that weighed some 40 tons. Most of them will be placid vegetarians, but a few will be hideous-looking carnivores, like Allosaurus and Tyrannosaurus. Some of the herbivorous dinosaurs will be clad in bony armor for protection against their flesh-eating comrades.

November will bring pictures of a sea extending from the 13 Gulf of Mexico to the Arctic in space now occupied by the Rocky Mountains. A few of the reptiles will take to the air on bat-like wings. One of these, called Pteranodon, will have a wingspread of 15 feet. There will be a rapid development of the modern flowering plants, modern trees, and modern insects. The dinosaurs will disappear. Toward the end of the month there will be a tremendous land disturbance in which the Rocky Mountains will rise out of the sea to assume a dominating place in the North American landscape.

As the picture runs on into December it will show the mam- 14 mals in command of the animal life. Seed-bearing trees and grasses will have covered most of the land with a heavy mantle of vegetation. Only the areas newly thrust up from the sea will be barren. Most of the streams will be crystal clear. The turmoil of geologic erosion will be confined to localized areas. About December 25 will begin the cutting of the Grand Canyon by the Colorado River. Grinding down through layer after layer of sedimentary strata, this stream will finally expose deposits laid down in Pre-Cambrian times. Thus in the walls of that canyon will appear geological formations dating from recent times to the period when the Earth had no living organisms upon it.

The picture will run on through the latter days of December 15 and even up to its final day with still no sign of mankind. The spectators will become alarmed in the fear that man has somehow been left out. But not so; sometime about noon on December 31 (one million years ago) will appear a stooped, massive creature of man-like proportions. This will be Pithecanthropus, the Java ape man. For tools and weapons he will have nothing but crude stone and wooden clubs. His children will live a precarious existence threatened on the one side by hostile animals and on the other by tremendous climatic changes. Ice sheets—in places 4000 feet deep—will form in the northern parts of North

America and Eurasia. Four times this glacial ice will push southward to cover half the continents. With each advance the plant
and animal life will be swept under or pushed southward. With
each recession of the ice, life will struggle to reestablish itself in
the wake of the retreating glaciers. The woolly mammoth, the
musk ox, and the caribou all will fight to maintain themselves
near the ice line. Sometimes they will be caught and put into cold
storage—skin, flesh, blood, bones and all.

The picture will run on through supper time with still very   16
little evidence of man's presence on the earth. It will be about 11
o'clock when Neanderthal man appears. Another half hour will
go by before the appearance of Cro-Magnon man living in caves
and painting crude animal pictures on the walls of his dwelling.
Fifteen minutes more will bring Neolithic man, knowing how
to chip stone and thus produce sharp cutting edges for spears
and tools. In a few minutes more it will appear that man has domesticated the dog, the sheep and, possibly, other animals. He
will then begin the use of milk. He will also learn the arts of basket weaving and the making of pottery and dugout canoes.

The dawn of civilization will not come until about five or   17
six minutes before the end of the picture. The story of the Egyptians, the Babylonians, the Greeks, and the Romans will unroll
during the fourth, the third, and the second minute before the
end. At 58 minutes and 43 seconds past 11:00 P.M. (just 1 minute
and 17 seconds before the end) will come the beginning of the
Christian era. Columbus will discover the new world 20 seconds
before the end. The Declaration of Independence will be signed
just 7 seconds before the final curtain comes down.

In those few moments of geologic time will be the story of   18
all that has happened since we became a nation. And what a
story it will be! A human swarm will sweep across the face of
the continent and take it away from the . . . red men. They will
change it far more radically than it has ever been changed before in a comparable time. The great virgin forests will be seen
going down before ax and fire. The soil, covered for eons by its
protective mantle of trees and grasses, will be laid bare to the
ravages of water and wind erosion. Streams that had been flowing clear will, once again, take up a load of silt and push it

toward the seas. Humus and mineral salts, both vital elements of productive soil, will be seen to vanish at a terrifying rate. The railroads and highways and cities that will spring up may divert attention, but they cannot cover up the blight of man's recent activities. In great sections of Asia, it will be seen that man must utilize cow dung and every scrap of available straw or grass for fuel to cook his food. The forests that once provided wood for this purpose will be gone without a trace. The use of these agricultural wastes for fuel, in place of returning them to the land, will be leading to increasing soil impoverishment. Here and there will be seen a dust storm darkening the landscape over an area a thousand miles across. Man-creatures will be shown counting their wealth in terms of bits of printed paper representing other bits of a scarce but comparatively useless yellow metal that is kept buried in strong vaults. Meanwhile, the soil, the only real wealth that can keep mankind alive on the face of this earth is savagely being cut loose from its ancient moorings and washed into the seven seas.

We have just arrived upon this earth. How long will we 19 stay?

1950

Body Ritual Among the Nacirema

Horace Miner

The anthropologist has become so familiar with the diver- 1 sity of ways in which different peoples behave in similar situations that he is not apt to be surprised by even the most exotic customs. In fact, if all of the logically possible combinations of behavior have not been found somewhere in the world, he is apt to suspect that they must be present in some yet undescribed tribe. This point has, in fact, been expressed with respect to clan organization by Murdock.* In this light, the magical beliefs and practices of the Nacirema present such unusual aspects that it seems desirable to describe them as an example of the extremes to which human behavior can go.

Professor Linton first brought the ritual of the Nacirema to 2
the attention of anthropologists twenty years ago, but the culture of this people is still very poorly understood. They are a North American group living in the territory between the Canadian Cree, the Yaqui and Tarahumare of Mexico, and the Carib and Arawak of the Antilles.† Little is known of their origin, although tradition states that they came from the east. . . .

Nacirema culture is characterized by a highly developed 3
market economy which has evolved in a rich natural habitat. While much of the people's time is devoted to economic pursuits, a large part of the fruits of these labors and a considerable portion of the day are spent in ritual activity. The focus of this activity is the human body, the appearance and health of which loom as a dominant concern in the ethos of the people. While such a concern is certainly not unusual, its ceremonial aspects and associated philosophy are unique.

The fundamental belief underlying the whole system appears to be that the human body is ugly and that its natural tendency is to debility and disease. Incarcerated in such a body, man's only hope is to avert these characteristics through the use of the powerful influences of ritual and ceremony. Every household has one or more shrines devoted to this purpose. The more powerful individuals in the society have several shrines in their houses and, in fact, the opulence of a house is often referred to in terms of the number of such ritual centers it possesses. Most houses are of wattle and daub construction, but the shrine rooms of the more wealthy are walled with stone. Poorer families imitate the rich by applying pottery plaques to their shrine walls.

*American anthropologist George Peter Murdock (b. 1897), authority on primitive cultures.

†Native American tribes formerly inhabiting the Saskatchewan region of Canada, the Sonora region of Mexico, and the West Indies.

While each family has at least one such shrine, the rituals   5
associated with it are not family ceremonies but are private and
secret. The rites are normally only discussed with children, and
then only during the period when they are being initiated into
these mysteries. I was able, however, to establish sufficient rap-
port with the natives to examine these shrines and to have the
rituals described to me.

The focal point of the shrine is a box or chest which is built   6
into the wall. In this chest are kept the many charms and magical potions without which no native believes he could live.
These preparations are secured from a variety of specialized
practitioners. The most powerful of these are the medicine men,
whose assistance must be rewarded with substantial gifts. However, the medicine men do not provide the curative potions for
their clients, but decide what the ingredients should be and
then write them down in an ancient and secret language. This
writing is understood only by the medicine men and by the
herbalists who, for another gift, provide the required charm.

The charm is not disposed of after it has served its purpose,   7
but is placed in the charm-box of the household shrine. As these
magical materials are specific for certain ills, and the real or
imagined maladies of the people are many, the charm-box is
usually full to overflowing. The magical packets are so numerous that people forget what their purposes were and fear to use
them again. While the natives are very vague on this point, we
can only assume that the idea in retaining all the old magical
materials is that their presence in the charm-box, before which
the body rituals are conducted, will in some way protect the
worshipper.

Beneath the charm-box is a small font. Each day every mem-   8
ber of the family, in succession, enters the shrine room, bows
his head before the charm-box, mingles different sorts of holy
water in the font, and proceeds with a brief rite of ablution. The
holy waters are secured from the Water Temple of the community, where the priests conduct elaborate ceremonies to
make the liquid ritually pure.

In the hierarchy of magical practitioners, and below the   9
medicine men in prestige, are specialists whose designation is

best translated "holy-mouth-men." The Nacirema have an almost pathological horror of and fascination with the mouth, the
condition of which is believed to have a supernatural influence
on all social relationships. Were it not for the rituals of the
mouth, they believe that their teeth would fall out, their gums
bleed, their jaws shrink, their friends desert them, and their
lovers reject them. They also believe that a strong relationship
exists between oral and moral characteristics. For example,
there is a ritual ablution of the mouth for children which is supposed to improve their moral fiber.

The daily body ritual performed by everyone includes a 10
mouth-rite. Despite the fact that these people are so punctilious
about care of the mouth, this rite involves a practice which
strikes the uninitiated stranger as revolting. It was reported to
me that the ritual consists of inserting a small bundle of hog
hairs into the mouth, along with certain magical powders, and
then moving the bundle in a highly formalized series of gestures.

In addition to the private mouth-rite, the people seek out a 11
holy-mouth-man once or twice a year. These practitioners have
an impressive set of paraphernalia, consisting of a variety of
augers, awls, probes, and prods. The use of these objects in the
exorcism of the evils of the mouth involves almost unbelievable
ritual torture of the client. The holy-mouth-man opens the
client's mouth and, using the above mentioned tools, enlarges
any holes which decay may have created in the teeth. Magical
materials are put into these holes. If there are not naturally occurring holes in the teeth, large sections of one or more teeth are
gouged out so that the supernatural substance can be applied.
In the client's view, the purpose of these ministrations is to ar-
rest decay and to draw friends. The extremely sacred and traditional character of the rite is evident in the fact that the natives return to the holy-mouth-men year after year, despite the
fact that their teeth continue to decay.

It is to be hoped that, when a thorough study of the 12
Nacirema is made, there will be careful inquiry into the personality structure of these people. One has but to watch the
gleam in the eye of a holy-mouth-man, as he jabs an awl into

an exposed nerve, to suspect that a certain amount of sadism is involved. If this can be established, a very interesting pattern emerges, for most of the population shows definite masochistic tendencies. It was to these that Professor Linton referred in discussing a distinctive part of the daily body ritual which is performed only by men. This part of the rite involves scraping and lacerating the surface of the face with a sharp instrument. Special women's rites are performed only four times during each lunar month, but what they lack in frequency is made up in barbarity. As part of this ceremony, women bake their heads in small ovens for about an hour. The theoretically interesting point is that what seems to be a preponderantly masochistic people have developed sadistic specialists.

The medicine men have an imposing temple, or latipso, in   13
every community of any size. The more elaborate ceremonies required to treat very sick patients can only be performed at this temple. These ceremonies involve not only the thaumaturge but a permanent group of vestal maidens who move sedately about the temple chambers in distinctive costume and headdress.

The latipso ceremonies are so harsh that it is phenomenal   14
that a fair proportion of the really sick natives who enter the temple ever recover. Small children whose indoctrination is still incomplete have been known to resist attempts to take them to the temple because "that is where you go to die." Despite this fact, sick adults are not only willing but eager to undergo the protracted ritual purification, if they can afford to do so. No matter how ill the supplicant or how grave the emergency, the guardians of many temples will not admit a client if he cannot give a rich gift to the custodian. Even after one has gained admission and survived the ceremonies, the guardians will not permit the neophyte to leave until he makes still another gift.

The supplicant entering the temple is first stripped of all his   15
or her clothes. In everyday life the Nacirema avoids exposure of his body and its natural functions. Bathing and excretory acts are performed only in the secrecy of the household shrine, where they are ritualized as part of the body-rites. Psychologi-

cal shock results from the fact that body secrecy is suddenly lost upon entry into the latipso. A man, whose own wife has never seen him in an excretory act, suddenly finds himself naked and assisted by a vestal maiden while he performs his natural functions into a sacred vessel. This sort of ceremonial treatment is necessitated by the fact that the excreta are used by a diviner to ascertain the course and nature of the client's sickness. Female clients, on the other hand, find their naked bodies are subjected to the scrutiny, manipulation and prodding of the medicine men.

Few supplicants in the temple are well enough to do anything but lie on their hard beds. The daily ceremonies, like the rites of the holy-mouth-men, involve discomfort and torture. With ritual precision, the vestals awaken their miserable charges each dawn and roll them about on their beds of pain while performing ablutions, in the formal movements of which the maidens are highly trained. At other times they insert magic wands in the supplicant's mouth or force him to eat substances which are supposed to be healing. From time to time the medicine men come to their clients and jab magically treated needles into their flesh. The fact that these temple ceremonies may not cure, and may even kill the neophyte, in no way decreases the people's faith in the medicine men. 16

There remains one other kind of practitioner, known as a "listener." This witchdoctor has the power to exorcise the devils that lodge in the heads of people who have been bewitched. The Nacirema believe that parents bewitch their own children. Mothers are particularly suspected of putting a curse on children while teaching them the secret body rituals. The counter-magic of the witchdoctor is unusual in its lack of ritual. The patient simply tells the "listener" all his troubles and fears, beginning with the earliest difficulties he can remember. The memory displayed by the Nacirema in these exorcism sessions is truly remarkable. It is not uncommon for the patient to bemoan the rejection he felt upon being weaned as a babe, and a few individuals even see their troubles going back to the traumatic effects of their own birth. 17

In conclusion, mention must be made of certain practices 18 which have their base in native esthetics but which depend upon the pervasive aversion to the natural body and its functions. There are ritual fasts to make fat people thin and ceremonial feasts to make thin people fat. Still other rites are used to make women's breasts larger if they are small, and smaller if they are large. General dissatisfaction with breast shape is symbolized in the fact that the ideal form is virtually outside the range of human variation. A few women afflicted with almost inhuman hypermammary development are so idolized that they make a handsome living by simply going from village to village and permitting the natives to stare at them for a fee.

Reference has already been made to the fact that excretory 19 functions are ritualized, routinized, and relegated to secrecy. Natural reproductive functions are similarly distorted. Intercourse is taboo as a topic and scheduled as an act. Efforts are made to avoid pregnancy by the use of magical materials or by limiting intercourse to certain phases of the moon. Conception is actually very infrequent. When pregnant, women dress so as to hide their condition. Parturition takes place in secret, without friends or relatives to assist, and the majority of women do not nurse their infants.

Our review of the ritual life of the Nacirema has certainly 20 shown them to be a magic-ridden people. It is hard to understand how they have managed to exist so long under the burdens which they have imposed upon themselves. But even such exotic customs as these take on real meaning when they are viewed with the insight provided by Malinowski when he wrote:

"Looking from far and above, from our high places of safety 21 in the developed civilization, it is easy to see all the crudity and irrelevance of magic. But without its power and guidance early man could not have mastered his practical difficulties as he has done, nor could man have advanced to the higher stages of civilization."

1956

The Cosmic Prison

Loren Eiseley

"A name is a prison, God is free," once observed the Greek   1
poet Nikos Kazantzakis. He meant, I think, that valuable though
language is to man, it is by very necessity limiting, and creates
for man an invisible prison. Language implies boundaries. A
word spoken creates a dog, a rabbit, a man. It fixes their nature
before our eyes; henceforth their shapes are, in a sense, our own
creation. They are no longer part of the unnamed shifting architecture of the universe. They have been transfixed as if by
sorcery, frozen into a concept, a word. Powerful though the
spell of human language has proven itself to be, it has laid
boundaries upon the cosmos.

No matter how far-ranging some of the mental probes that   2
man has philosophically devised, by his own created nature he
is forced to hold the specious and emerging present and transform it into words. The words are startling in their immediate
effectiveness, but at the same time they are always finally im-
prisoning because man has constituted himself a prison keeper.
He does so out of no conscious intention, but because for immediate purposes he has created an unnatural world of his
own, which he calls the cultural world, and in which he feels at
home. It defines his needs and allows him to lay a small im-
mobilizing spell upon the nearer portions of his universe. Nevertheless, it transforms that universe into a cosmic prison house
which is no sooner mapped than man feels its inadequacy and
his own.

He seeks then to escape, and the theory of escape involves   3
bodily flight. Scarcely had the first moon landing been achieved
before one U.S. senator boldly announced: "We are the masters
of the universe. We can go anywhere we choose." This statement was widely and editorially acclaimed. It is a striking example of the comfort of words, also of the covert substitutions
and mental projections to which they are subject. The cosmic
prison is not made less so by a successful journey of some two

hundred and forty thousand miles in a cramped and primitive vehicle.

To escape the cosmic prison man is poorly equipped. He has 4 to drag portions of his environment with him, and his life span is that of a mayfly in terms of the distances he seeks to penetrate. There is no possible way to master such a universe by flight alone. Indeed such a dream is a dangerous illusion. This may seem a heretical statement, but its truth is self-evident if we try seriously to comprehend the nature of time and space that I sought to grasp when held up to view the fiery messenger that flared across the zenith in 1910. "Seventy-five years," my father had whispered in my ear, "seventy-five years and it will be racing homeward. Perhaps you will live to see it again. Try to remember."

And so I remembered. I had gained a faint glimpse of the 5 size of our prison house. Somewhere out there beyond a billion miles in space, an entity known as a comet had rounded on its track in the black darkness of the void. It was surging homeward toward the sun because it was an eccentric satellite of this solar system. If I lived to see it it would be but barely, and with the dimmed eyes of age. Yet it, too, in its long traverse, was but a flitting mayfly in terms of the universe the night sky revealed.

So relative is the cosmos we inhabit that, as we gaze upon 6 the outer galaxies available to the reach of our telescopes, we are placed in about the position that a single white blood cell in our bodies would occupy, if it were intelligently capable of seeking to understand the nature of its own universe, the body it inhabits. The cell would encounter rivers ramifying into miles of distance seemingly leading nowhere. It would pass through gigantic structures whose meaning it could never grasp—the brain, for example. It could never know there was an outside, a vast being on a scale it could not conceive of and of which it formed an infinitesimal part. It would know only the pouring tumult of the creation it inhabited, but of the nature of that great beast, or even indeed that it was a beast, it could have no conception whatever. It might examine the liquid in which it floated and decide, as in the case of the fall of Lucretius's atoms, that the pouring of obscure torrents had created its world.

It might discover that creatures other than itself swam in the   7
torrent. But that its universe was alive, had been born and was
destined to perish, its own ephemeral existence would never
allow it to perceive. It would never know the sun; it would explore only through dim tactile sensations and react to chemical
stimuli that were borne to it along the mysterious conduits of
the arteries and veins. Its universe would be centered upon a
great arborescent tree of spouting blood. This, at best, generations of white blood cells by enormous labor and continuity
might succeed, like astronomers, in charting.

They could never, by any conceivable stretch of the imagi-   8
nation, be aware that their so-called universe was, in actuality,
the prowling body of a cat or the more time-enduring body of a
philosopher, himself engaged upon the same quest in a more gigantic world and perhaps deceived proportionately by greater
vistas. What if, for example, the far galaxies man observes make
up, across void spaces of which even we are atomically composed, some kind of enormous creature or cosmic snowflake
whose exterior we will never see? We will know more than the
phagocyte in our bodies, but no more than that limited creature
can we climb out of our universe, or successfully enhance our
size or longevity sufficiently to thrust our heads through the confines of the universe that terminates our vision.

Some further "outside" will hover elusively in our thought,   9
but upon its nature, or even its reality, we can do no more than
speculate. The phagocyte might observe the salty turbulence of
an eternal river system, Lucretius the fall of atoms creating mo-
mentary living shapes. We suspiciously sense, in the concept of
the expanding universe derived from the primordial atom—the
monobloc—some kind of oscillating universal heart. At the instant of its contraction we will vanish. It is not given us, nor can
our science recapture, the state beyond the monobloc, nor
whether we exist in the diastole of some inconceivable being.
We know only a little more extended reality than the hypothetical creature below us. Above us may lie realms it is beyond
our power to grasp.

1970

Shouting "Fire!"

Alan M. Dershowitz

When the Reverend Jerry Falwell learned that the Supreme   1
Court had reversed his $200,000 judgment against *Hustler* mag-
azine for the emotional distress that he had suffered from an
outrageous parody, his response was typical of those who seek
to censor speech: "Just as no person may scream 'Fire!' in a
crowded theater when there is no fire, and find cover under the
First Amendment, likewise, no sleazy merchant like Larry Flynt
should be able to use the First Amendment as an excuse for ma-
liciously and dishonestly attacking public figures, as he has so
often done."

Justice Oliver Wendell Holmes's classic example of unpro-   2
tected speech—falsely shouting "Fire!" in a crowded theater—
has been invoked so often, by so many people, in such diverse
contexts, that it has become part of our national folk language.
It has even appeared—most appropriately—in the theater: in
Tom Stoppard's play *Rosencrantz and Guildenstern Are Dead* a
character shouts at the audience, "Fire!" He then quickly explains: "It's all right—I'm demonstrating the misuse of free
speech." Shouting "Fire!" in the theater may well be the only
jurisprudential analogy that has assumed the status of a folk argument. A prominent historian recently characterized it as "the
most brilliantly persuasive expression that ever came from
Holmes's pen." But in spite of its hallowed position in both the
jurisprudence of the First Amendment and the arsenal of political discourse, it is and was an inapt analogy, even in the context in which it was originally offered. It has lately become—
despite, perhaps even because of, the frequency and
promiscuousness of its invocation—little more than a caricature
of logical argumentation.

The case that gave rise to the "Fire!"-in-a-crowded-theater   3
analogy, *Schenck v. United States,* involved the prosecution of
Charles Schenck, who was the general secretary of the Socialist
party in Philadelphia, and Elizabeth Baer, who was its record-

ing secretary. In 1917 a jury found Schenck and Baer guilty of attempting to cause insubordination among soldiers who had been drafted to fight in the First World War. They and other party members had circulated leaflets urging draftees not to "submit to intimidation" by fighting in a war being conducted on behalf of "Wall Street's chosen few."

Schenck admitted, and the Court found, that the intent of the pamphlets' "impassioned language" was to "influence" draftees to resist the draft. Interestingly, however, Justice Holmes noted that nothing in the pamphlet suggested that the draftees should use unlawful or violent means to oppose conscription: "In form at least [the pamphlet] confined itself to peaceful measures, such as a petition for the repeal of the act" and an exhortation to exercise "your right to assert your opposition to the draft." Many of its most impassioned words were quoted directly from the Constitution. 4

Justice Holmes acknowledged that "in many places and in ordinary times the defendants, in saying all that was said in the circular, would have been within their constitutional rights." "But," he added, "the character of every act depends upon the circumstances in which it is done." And to illustrate that truism he went on to say: 5

> The most stringent protection of free speech would not protect a man in falsely shouting fire in a theater, and causing a panic. It does not even protect a man from an injunction against uttering words that may have all the effect of force.

Justice Holmes then upheld the convictions in the context of a wartime draft, holding that the pamphlet created "a clear and present danger" of hindering the war effort while our soldiers were fighting for their lives and our liberty. 6

The example of shouting "Fire!" obviously bore little relationship to the facts of the Schenck case. The Schenck pamphlet contained a substantive political message. It urged its draftee readers to *think* about the message and then—if they so chose—to act on it in a lawful and nonviolent way. The man who shouts "Fire!" in a crowded theater is neither sending a political message nor inviting his listener to think about what he has said and 7 decide what to do in a rational, calculated manner. On the contrary, the message is designed to force action *without* contemplation. The message "Fire!" is directed not to the mind and the conscience of the listener but, rather, to his adrenaline and his feet. It is a stimulus to immediate *action*, not thoughtful reflection. It is—as Justice Holmes recognized in his follow-up sentence—the functional equivalent of "uttering words that may have all the effect of force."

Indeed, in that respect the shout of "Fire!" is not even speech, in any meaningful sense of that term. It is a *clang* sound, the equivalent of setting off a nonverbal alarm. Had Justice Holmes been more honest about his example, he would have said that freedom of speech does not protect a kid who pulls a fire alarm in the absence of a fire. But that obviously would have been irrelevant to the case at hand. The proposition that pulling an alarm is not protected speech certainly leads to the conclusion that shouting the word "fire" is also not protected. But the core analogy is the nonverbal alarm, and the derivative example is the verbal shout. By cleverly substituting the derivative shout for the core alarm, Holmes made it possible to analogize one set of words to another—as he could not have done if he had begun with the self-evident proposition that setting off an alarm bell is not free speech.

The analogy is thus not only inapt but also insulting. Most Americans do not respond to political rhetoric with the same kind of automatic acceptance expected of schoolchildren responding to a fire drill. Not a single recipient of the Schenck pamphlet is known to have changed his mind after reading it. Indeed, one draftee, who appeared as a prosecution witness, was asked whether reading a pamphlet asserting that the draft law was unjust would make him "immediately decide that you must erase that law." Not surprisingly, he replied, "I do my own thinking." A theatergoer would probably not respond similarly if asked how he would react to a shout of "Fire!"

Another important reason why the analogy is inapt is that Holmes emphasizes the factual falsity of the shout "Fire!" The Schenck pamphlet, however, was not factually false. It contained political opinions and ideas about the causes of the war and about appropriate and lawful responses to the draft. As the Supreme Court recently reaffirmed (in *Falwell v. Hustler*), "The First Amendment recognizes no such thing as a 'false' idea." Nor does it recognize false opinions about the causes of or cures for war.

A closer analogy to the facts of the Schenck case might have been provided by a person's standing outside a theater, offering the patrons a leaflet advising them that in his opinion the theater was structurally unsafe, and urging them not to enter but to complain to the building inspectors. That analogy, however, would not have served Holmes's argument for punishing Schenck. Holmes needed an analogy that would appear relevant to Schenck's political speech but that would invite the conclusion that censorship was appropriate. 11

Unsurprisingly, a war-weary nation—in the throes of a know-nothing hysteria over immigrant anarchists and socialists—welcomed the comparison between what was regarded as a seditious political pamphlet and a malicious shout of "Fire!" Ironically, the "Fire!" analogy is nearly all that survives from the Schenck case; the ruling itself is almost certainly not good law. Pamphlets of the kind that resulted in Schenck's imprisonment have been circulated with impunity during subsequent wars. 12

Over the past several years I have assembled a collection of instance—cases, speeches, arguments—in which proponents of censorship have maintained that the expression at issue is "just like" or "equivalent to" falsely shouting "Fire!" in a crowded theater and ought to be banned, "just as" shouting "Fire!" ought to be banned. The analogy is generally invoked, often with self-satisfaction, as an absolute argument-stopper. It does, after all, claim the high authority of the great Justice Oliver Wendell Holmes. I have rarely heard it invoked in a convincing, or even particularly relevant, way. But that, too, can claim lineage from the great Holmes. 13

Not unlike Falwell, with his silly comparison between shouting "Fire!" and publishing an offensive parody, courts and commentators have frequently invoked "Fire!" as an anal- 14

ogy to expression that is not an automatic stimulus to panic. A
state supreme court held that "Holmes's aphorism . . . applies
with equal force to pornography"—in particular to the exhibition of the movie *Carmen Baby* in a drive-in theater in close
proximity to highways and homes. Another court analogized
"picketing . . . in support of a secondary boycott" to shouting
"Fire!" because in both instances "speech and conduct are
brigaded." In the famous Skokie case one of the judges argued
that allowing Nazis to march through a city where a large number of Holocaust survivors live "just might fall into the same category as one's 'right' to cry fire in a crowded theater."

Outside court the analogies become even more badly 15
stretched. A spokesperson for the New Jersey Sports and Ex-
position Authority complained that newspaper reports to the
effect that a large number of football players had contracted cancer after playing in the Meadowlands—a stadium atop a land-
fill—were the "journalistic equivalent of shouting fire in a
crowded theater." An insect researcher acknowledged that his
prediction that a certain amusement park might become roach-
infested "may be tantamount to shouting fire in a crowded theater." The philosopher Sidney Hook, in a letter to the *New York
Times* bemoaning a Supreme Court decision that required a
plaintiff in a defamation action to prove that the offending statement was actually false, argued that the First Amendment does
not give the press carte blanche to accuse innocent persons "any
more than the First Amendment protects the right of someone
falsely to shout fire in a crowded theater."

Some close analogies to shouting "Fire!" or setting off an 16
alarm are, of course, available: calling in a false bomb threat; di-
aling 911 and falsely describing an emergency; making a loud,
gun-like sound in the presence of the President; setting off a
voice-activated sprinkler system by falsely shouting "Fire!" In
one case in which the "Fire!" analogy was directly to the point,
a creative defendant tried to get around it. The case involved a
man who calmly advised an airline clerk that he was "only here
to hijack the plane." He was charged, in effect, with shouting
"Fire!" in a crowded theater, and his rejected defense—as
quoted by the court—was as follows: "If we built fire-proof the-

aters and let people know about this, then the shouting of 'Fire!' would not cause panic."

Here are some more-distant but still related examples: the 17 recent incident of the police slaying in which some members of an onlooking crowd urged a mentally ill vagrant who had taken an officer's gun to shoot the officer; the screaming of racial epithets during a tense confrontation; shouting down a speaker and preventing him from continuing his speech.

Analogies are, by their nature, matters of degree. Some are 18 closer to the core example than others. But any attempt to analogize political ideas in a pamphlet, ugly parody in a magazine, offensive movies in a theater, controversial newspaper articles, or any of the other expressions and actions catalogued above to the very different act of shouting "Fire!" in a crowded theater is either self-deceptive or self-serving.

The government does, of course, have some arguably le- 19 gitimate bases for suppressing speech which bear no relationship to shouting "Fire!" It may ban the publication of nuclear-weapon codes, of information about troop movements, and of the identity of undercover agents. It may criminalize extortion threats and conspiratorial agreements. These expressions may lead directly to serious harm, but the mechanisms of causation are very different from that at work when an alarm is sounded. One may also argue—less persuasively, in my view—against protecting certain forms of public obscenity and defamatory statements. Here, too, the mechanisms of causation are very different. None of these exceptions to the First Amendment's exhortation that the government "shall make no law . . . abridging the freedom of speech, or of the press" is anything like falsely shouting "Fire!" in a crowded theater; they all must be justified on other grounds.

A comedian once told his audience, during a stand-up rou- 20 tine, about the time he was standing around a fire with a crowd of people and got in trouble for yelling "Theater, theater!" That, I think, is about as clever and productive a use as anyone has ever made of Holmes's flawed analogy.

1989

Am I Blue?

Alice Walker

For about three years my companion and I rented a small   1
house in the country that stood on the edge of a large meadow
that appeared to run from the end of our deck straight into the
mountains. The mountains, however, were quite far away, and
between us and them there was, in fact, a town. It was one of
the many pleasant aspects of the house that you never really
were aware of this.

It was a house of many windows, low, wide, nearly floor to   2
ceiling in the living room, which faced the meadow, and it was
from one of these that I first saw our closest neighbor, a large
white horse, cropping grass, flipping its mane, and ambling
about—not over the entire meadow, which stretched well out
of sight of the house, but over the five or so fenced-in acres that
were next to the twenty-odd that we had rented. I soon learned
that the horse, whose name was Blue, belonged to a man who
lived in another town, but was boarded by our neighbors next
door. Occasionally, one of the children, usually a stocky
teenager, but sometimes a much younger girl or boy, could be
seen riding Blue. They would appear in the meadow, climb up
on his back, ride furiously for ten or fifteen minutes, then get
off, slap Blue on the flanks, and not be seen again for a month
or more.

There were many apple trees in our yard, and one by the   3
fence that Blue could almost reach. We were soon in the habit
of feeding him apples, which he relished, especially because by
the middle of summer the meadow grasses—so green and suc-
culent since January—had dried out from lack of rain, and Blue
stumbled about munching the dried stalks half-heartedly.
Sometimes he would stand very still just by the apple tree, and
when one of us came out he would whinny, snort loudly, or
stamp the ground. This meant, of course: I want an apple.

It was quite wonderful to pick a few apples, or collect those   4
that had fallen to the ground overnight, and patiently hold

them, one by one, up to his large, toothy mouth. I remained as thrilled as a child by his flexible dark lips, huge, cubelike teeth that crunched the apples, core and all, with such finality, and his high, broad-breasted *enormity;* beside which, I felt small indeed. When I was a child, I used to ride horses, and was especially friendly with one named Nan until the day I was riding and my brother deliberately spooked her and I was thrown, head first, against the trunk of a tree. When I came to, I was in bed and my mother was bending worriedly over me; we silently agreed that perhaps horseback riding was not the safest sport for me. Since then I have walked, and prefer walking to horseback riding—but I had forgotten the depth of feeling one could see in horses' eyes.

I was therefore unprepared for the expression in Blue's. 5 Blue was lonely. Blue was horribly lonely and bored. I was not shocked that this should be the case; five acres to tramp by yourself, endlessly, even in the most beautiful of meadows— and his was—cannot provide many interesting events, and once rainy season turned to dry that was about it. No, I was shocked that I had forgotten that human animals and nonhuman animals can communicate quite well; if we are brought up around animals as children we take this for granted. By the time we are adults we no longer remember. However, the animals have not changed. They are in fact *completed* creations (at least they seem to be, so much more than we) who are not likely to change; it is their nature to express themselves. What else are they going to express? And they do. And, generally speaking, they are ignored.

After giving Blue the apples, I would wander back to the 6 house, aware that he was observing me. Were more apples not forthcoming then? Was that to be his sole entertainment for the day? My partner's small son had decided he wanted to learn how to piece a quilt; we worked in silence on our respective squares as I thought . . .

Well, about slavery: about white children, who were raised 7 by black people, who knew their first all-accepting love from black women, and then, when they were twelve or so, were told they must "forget" the deep levels of communication between

themselves and "mammy" that they knew. Later they would be
able to relate quite calmly, "My old mammy was sold to another
good family." "My old mammy was———— ————." Fill in the
blank. Many more years later a white woman would say: "I
can't understand these Negroes, these blacks. What do they
want? They're so different from us."

And about the Indians, considered to be "like animals" by the   8
"settlers" (a very benign euphemism for what they actually
were), who did not understand their description as a compliment.

And about the thousands of American men who marry   9
Japanese, Korean, Filipina, and other non-English-speaking
women and of how happy they report they are, *"blissfully,"*
until their brides learn to speak English, at which point the mar-
riages tend to fall apart. What then did the men see, when they
looked into the eyes of the women they married, before they
could speak English? Apparently only their own reflections.

I thought of society's impatience with the young. "Why are   10
they playing the music so loud?" Perhaps the children have listened to much of the music of oppressed people their parents
danced to before they were born, with its passionate but soft
cries for acceptance and love, and they have wondered why
their parents failed to hear.

I do not know how long Blue had inhabited his five beau-   11
tiful, boring acres before we moved into our house; a year after
we had arrived—and had also traveled to other valleys, other
cities, other worlds—he was still there.

But then, in our second year at the house, something hap-   12
pened in Blue's life. One morning, looking out the window at
the fog that lay like a ribbon over the meadow, I saw another
horse, a brown one, at the other end of Blue's field. Blue appeared to be afraid of it, and for several days made no attempt
to go near. We went away for a week. When we returned, Blue
had decided to make friends and the two horses ambled or galloped along together, and Blue did not come nearly as often to
the fence underneath the apple tree.

When he did, bringing his new friend with him, there was   13
a different look in his eyes. A look of independence, of self-
possession, of inalienable *horse*ness. His friend eventually be-

came pregnant. For months and months there was, it seemed to me, a mutual feeling between me and the horses of justice, of peace. I fed apples to them both. The look in Blue's eyes was one of unabashed "this is *it*ness."

It did not, however, last forever. One day, after a visit to   14
the city, I went out to give Blue some apples. He stood waiting, or so I thought, though not beneath the tree. When I shook the tree and jumped back from the shower of apples, he made no move. I carried some over to him. He managed to half-crunch one. The rest he let fall to the ground. I dreaded looking into his eyes—because I had of course noticed that Brown, his partner, had gone—but I did look. If I had been born into slavery, and my partner had been sold or killed, my eyes would have looked like that. The children next door explained that Blue's partner had been "put with him" (the same expression that old people used, I had noticed, when speaking of an ancestor during slavery who had been impregnated by her owner) so that they could mate and she conceive. Since that was accomplished, she had been taken back by her owner, who lived somewhere else.

Will she be back? I asked.   15

They didn't know.   16

Blue was like a crazed person. Blue *was*, to me, a crazed per-   17
son. He galloped furiously, as if he were being ridden, around and around his five beautiful acres. He whinnied until he couldn't. He tore at the ground with his hooves. He butted himself against his single shade tree. He looked always and always toward the road down which his partner had gone. And then, occasionally, when he came up for apples, or I took apples to him, he looked at me. It was a look so piercing, so full of grief, a look so *human*, I almost laughed (I felt too sad to cry) to think there are people who do not know that animals suffer. People like me who have forgotten, and daily forget, all that animals try to tell us. "Everything you do to us will happen to you; we are your teachers, as you are ours. We are one lesson" is essentially it, I think. There are those who never once have even considered animals' rights: those who have been taught that animals actually want to be used and abused by us, as small

children "love" to be frightened, or women "love" to be mutilated and raped. . . . They are the great-grandchildren of those
who honestly thought, because someone taught them this:
"Women can't think," and "niggers can't faint." But most disturbing of all, in Blue's large brown eyes was a new look more
painful than the look of despair: the look of disgust with human
beings, with life; the look of hatred. And it was odd what the
look of hatred did. It gave him, for the first time, the look of a
beast. And what that meant was that he had put up a barrier
within to protect himself from further violence; all the apples
in the world wouldn't change that fact.

And so Blue remained, a beautiful part of our landscape, 18
very peaceful to look at from the window, white against the
grass. Once a friend came to visit and said, looking out on the
soothing view: "And it *would* have to be a *white* horse; the very
image of freedom." And I thought, yes, the animals are forced
to become for us merely "images" of what they once so beauti-
fully expressed. And we are used to drinking milk from containers showing "contented" cows, whose real lives we want to
hear nothing about, eating eggs and drumsticks from "happy"
hens, and munching hamburgers advertised by bulls of integrity who seem to command their fate.

As we talked of freedom and justice one day for all, we sat 19
down to steaks. I am eating misery, I thought, as I took the first
bite. And spit it out.

1986

Gawk Shows

Nicols Fox

I remember the dusty heat of late summer, the yellow and 1
white tent, and the barker strutting on the platform. His voice
rose above the sounds of the carnival, hinting of the wonders

within the tent, wonders painted in cheap colors on the cracked backdrop: the two-headed baby, the world's fattest man, the bearded woman. I remember the sideshows. I thought they were long behind us.

I turn on the television and see an astonishing sight: a woman. Her soul is beautiful. It penetrates the atmosphere, even across airwaves. Her body is not. It is covered with the lumps and bumps of Elephant Man disease. Sally Jessy Raphael, wearing her trademark red spectacles, cocks her blond head and asks what the woman's life is like. A window is opened into pain. There are more victims of the disease sitting in the audience. We are treated to its various manifestations. We are horrified and amazed: We gawk.

Phil Donahue interviews tiny, wizened children. They have progeria, "the aging disease." With their outsize, hairless heads and huge eyes imparting solemnity and even wisdom, they offer us themselves as a sacrifice to our curiosity. We are compelled into silence, fascinated. We are back in the tent.

While I was living in Europe in the late sixties and early seventies, friends often asked me to tell them what to expect when they visited America. "Think of America as a carnival," I would tell them. "An unending carnival." This was the only way I knew to explain my country. Not just the quality of light and landscape but the excess, the enthusiasm, the love of excitement. We want no limitations on what we can have, on what we can do. We deny ourselves nothing—no objects, no sensations. "The pursuit of happiness": What other nation has made it an absolute right?

The carnival plays on, and we have returned to the sideshows—minus the honesty that made no pretense about what lay behind the curtain, the honesty that divided the world into those who were able to resist satisfying their curiosity at the expense of others and those who were not. Gawking is painted in shades of solicitude now. We justify much in the name of compassion, but we are in fact being entertained in the same ancient tradition. Gawk shows sell.

"I offer no apology," says Donahue. "These children have been unmercifully pressured by their very distinctive appear-

ance." The purpose of the show? "To humanize people who
have suffered. It becomes a vehicle for examining our prejudices. Just because it may be true that this kind of show draws
a crowd does not condemn it," he says.

For Sally Jessy Raphael the rationale is the same: "Teaching   7
the lessons of compassion. Man's triumph over adversity."

These are noble thoughts, and not entirely hypocritical.   8
Compassion and understanding are always in short supply.
There is an outside chance that some of each might be spread
around in this exercise. We may also be witnessing exploitation.
"These children are risking their lives to be here," says Sally, introducing children who will die if exposed to light. What may
she be risking if they don't appear? As Donahue says, "If I don't
draw a crowd, I could be parking cars for a living."

Donahue is open about the dilemma: "Americans are more   9
interested in Madonna than Managua. The country suffers, in
my opinion, from the diminished interest in serious news.
Whichever way you look at it we have a culture of decay." It's
tricky playing two sides at once. "It's like walking on eggs. I
don't want to be a dead hero," he says.

We watch our cultural demise in living color.   10

Do you find yourself addicted to sex with prostitutes? Tell   11
Oprah Winfrey and her audience all about it. Did you engage
in an affair with your priest? Have your breast implants started
slipping? Geraldo Rivera wants to know. Do you wish you
could reverse your sex-change operation? Are you a celebrity
subject to diarrhea at odd moments? Does your mother keep
stealing your boyfriends? We care, we are interested. Whatever
your problem, there's a television talk show that will accommodate you.

Donahue, Oprah, Sally, Geraldo: They are the virtuosos of   12
voyeurism, lifting the skirts of our culture, peering into the closets, airing the national soiled linen. Sally thinks of her program
as a kind of updated town meeting—the modern version of
something we no longer have. Electronic gossip, in other
words—the national back fence. Wishful thinking.

As Americans we've been indulging in an orgy of self-   13
analysis and self-revelation—coupled with a natural curiosity

now totally unbridled. We've become a society hooked on the bizarre and the astonishing—living in a perpetual state of "Can you top this?" Transvestite men marry women on Sally's show, thus proving an important point, one we all needed to know: Sixty-five percent of all transvestites are not homosexual.

Nothing is sacred. There are no memories, no mysteries too 14 precious to reveal. A woman discusses her husband's sexual addiction. Geraldo asks the husband for details—and gets them. There is nothing we won't share, or watch someone else share, with a million strangers.

We have invented a new social contract on the talk shows: 15 Lay bare your body, your bed, your soul, your emotions, your worst fears, your innermost secrets, and we will give you a moment or two of fame. Every sacrifice can and should be made to the video god.

Are there topics too hot to talk about?   16

"How to blow up your local post office," says Donahue. 17 He'd draw the line there.

There is no topic Sally wouldn't consider if it "concerns the 18 human condition." She draws the line only at being boring. We have to want to watch it. So we set the agenda.

Donahue, a man obviously in conflict between his natural 19 honesty and better instincts and his ambition, admits that his audience calls the shots. Devoting a recent show to strippers—both male and female—he says, "It must be ratings week. I don't want to do these shows . . . they make me." Sure they do. But who is making us watch?

Freedom of expression is not the issue here. Nobody's sug- 20 gesting censorship or even paternalistic decisions based on what someone else thinks is good for us. The issue is honesty—honesty about why we watch. The talk shows are merely giving us what we want. The question is, Why do we want it?

In some cultures it was thought that illness or bad luck 21 could be transferred from one person to another by magic. James G. Frazer, in his classic work *The Golden Bough,* told of one example: "To get rid of warts, take a string and make as many knots in it as you have warts. Then lay the string under a stone. Whoever treads upon the stone will get the warts, and you will be rid of them." Something like that draws us to the tent. We confirm our own normalcy because our worst fears have been manifested in someone else—the visual equivalent of burying the string. Or, if we see ourselves in someone who has survived our common plight, we are reassured; we are not alone.

There is no slouching into the tent today. We walk in shame- 22 lessly, casting off inhibitions in the name of openness.

The new openness has, in fact, turned out to be an empty 23 promise. Are things any better than they were two decades ago? Has drug abuse or wife abuse or child abuse declined as we have learned more? Are we any happier thinking that a friend who takes a drink is a potential alcoholic, that every stranger is a child-snatcher?

How has this new compassion we are teaching been made 24 evident? Ask the parents who have three HIV-positive sons and found their house burned down because of it. Ask the people who cluster over the grates of subways in our largest cities. If you were a trapped whale or a little girl down a well, solici- tude would flow your way in great waves. It still helps to be cute or little or white or furry or totally nonthreatening when you're looking for compassion—or pretty, when you want a bone mar- row transplant.

The potential is there on the TV talk shows for real enter- 25 tainment—and for service. Oprah scored with a terrific show on female comics. Programs on health matters or economic ques- tions are valuable. During the first days of the war in the Per- sian Gulf, Donahue aired shows that were serious and impor- tant contributions to our understanding of the conflict. "I do have a conscience," he says.

Geraldo, however, ever subject to the temptations of the 26 flesh, spoiled what could have been a serious discussion of breast implants by having Jessica Hahn as the honored guest and by fondling examples of the implants interminably. Does he have it right? Are we a people who need to watch breast im- plants being fondled?

What happens when we set aside our last taboo? What hap- 27 pens when we've finally been titillated to a terminal numbness, incapable of shock, on the prowl for a new high? What manner of stimulation will we need next? Are we addicted? Talk show codependent?

Which topic affects us more: the discussion of the S & L cri- 28 sis Donahue did last summer or the interviews with the strippers? Which do you think got the better ratings?

In a free society we get what we want. We shouldn't be sur- 29 prised when we end up with what we deserve. But we can't transfer blame. It's not the hosts' fault—it's the viewers'.

1991

CHAPTER 10

Argument

A Modest Proposal

Jonathan Swift

It is a melancholy object to those who walk through this 1
great town or travel in the country, when they see the streets,
the roads, and cabin doors, crowded with beggars of the female
sex, followed by three, four, or six children, all in rags and im-
portuning every passenger for an alms. These mothers, instead
of being able to work for their honest livelihood, are forced to
employ all their time in strolling to beg sustenance for their
helpless infants: who as they grow up either turn thieves for
want of work, or leave their dear native country to fight for the
pretender in Spain, or sell themselves to the Barbadoes.

I think it is agreed by all parties that this prodigious num- 2
ber of children in the arms, or on the backs, or at the heels of
their mothers, and frequently of their fathers, is in the present
deplorable state of the kingdom a very great additional grievance; and, therefore, whoever could find out a fair, cheap, and
easy method of making these children sound, useful members
of the commonwealth, would deserve so well of the public as
to have his statue set up for a preserver of the nation.

But my intention is very far from being confined to provide 3
only for the children of professed beggars; it is of a much greater
extent, and shall take in the whole number of infants at a certain age who are born of parents in effect as little able to support them as those who demand our charity in the streets.

As to my own part, having turned my thoughts for many 4 years upon this important subject, and maturely weighed the several schemes of our projectors, I have always found them grossly mistaken in their computation. It is true, a child just dropped from its dam may be supported by her milk for a solar year, with little other nourishment; at most not above the value of 2s., which the mother may certainly get, or the value in scraps, by her lawful occupation of begging; and it is exactly at one year old that I propose to provide for them in such a manner as instead of being a charge upon their parents or the parish, or wanting food and raiment for the rest of their lives, they shall on the contrary contribute to the feeding, and partly to the clothing, of many thousands.

There is likewise another great advantage in my scheme, 5 that it will prevent those voluntary abortions, and that horrid practice of women murdering their bastard children, alas! too frequent among us! sacrificing the poor innocent babes I doubt more to avoid the expense than the shame, which would move tears and pity in the most savage and inhuman breast.

The number of souls in this kingdom being usually reck- 6 oned one million and a half, of these I calculate there may be about 200,000 couple whose wives are breeders; from which number I subtract 30,000 couple who are able to maintain their own children (although I apprehend there cannot be so many, under the present distress of the kingdom); but this being granted, there will remain 170,000 breeders. I again subtract 50,000 for those women who miscarry, or whose children die by accident or disease within the year. There only remain 120,000 children of poor parents annually born. The question therefore is, how this number shall be reared and provided for? which, as I have already said, under the present situation of affairs, is utterly impossible by all the methods hitherto proposed. For we can neither employ them in handicraft or agriculture; we neither build houses (I mean live in the country) nor cultivate land; they can very seldom pick up a livelihood by stealing, till they arrive at six years old, except where they are of towardly parts; although I confess they learn the rudiments much earlier; during which time they can, however, be properly looked upon

only as probationers; as I have been informed by a principal
gentleman in the county of Cavan, who protested to me that he
never knew above one or two instances under the age of six,
even in a part of the kingdom so renowned for the quickest pro-
ficiency in that art.

I am assured by our merchants, that a boy or a girl before   7
twelve years old is no saleable commodity; and even when they
come to this age they will not yield above 31. or 31.2s. 6d. at most
on the exchange; which cannot turn to account either to the
parents or kingdom, the charge of nutriment and rags having
been at least four times that value.

I shall now therefore humbly propose my own thoughts,   8
which I hope will not be liable to the least objection.

I have been assured by a very knowing American of my ac-   9
quaintance in London, that a young healthy child well nursed
is at a year old a most delicious, nourishing, and wholesome
food, whether stewed, roasted, baked, or broiled; and I make
no doubt that it will equally serve in a fricassee or a ragout.

I do therefore humbly offer it to public consideration that   10
of the 120,000 children already computed, 20,000 may be reserved for breed, whereof only one-fourth part to be males;
which is more than we allow to sheep, black cattle, or swine;
and my reason is, that these children are seldom the fruits of
marriage, a circumstance not much regarded by our savages;
therefore one male will be sufficient to serve four females.
That the remaining 100,000 may, at a year old, be offered in
sale to the persons of quality and fortune through the kingdom; always advising the mother to let them suck plentifully
in the last month, so as to render them plump and fat for a
good table. A child will make two dishes at an entertainment
for friends; and when the family dines alone, the fore or hind
quarter will make a reasonable dish, and seasoned with a little pepper or salt will be very good boiled on the fourth day,
especially in winter.

I have reckoned upon a medium that a child just born will   11
weigh 12 pounds, and in a solar year, if tolerably nursed, will
increase to 28 pounds.

I grant this food will be somewhat dear, and therefore very 12 proper for landlords, who, as they have already devoured most of the parents, seem to have the best title to the children.

Infant's flesh will be in season throughout the year, but 13 more plentiful in March, and a little before and after: for we are told by a grave author, an eminent French physician, that fish being a prolific diet, there are more children born in Roman Catholic countries about nine months after Lent than at any other season; therefore, reckoning a year after Lent, the markets will be more glutted than usual, because the number of popish infants is at least three to one in this kingdom: and therefore it will have one other collateral advantage, by lessening the number of papists among us.

I have already computed the charge of nursing a beggar's 14 child (in which list I reckon all cottagers, laborers, and four-fifths of the farmers) to be about 2s. per annum, rags included; and I believe no gentleman would repine to give 10s. for the carcass of a good fat child, which, as I have said, will make four dishes of excellent nutritive meat, when he has only some particular friend or his own family to dine with him. Thus the squire will learn to be a good landlord, and grow popular among the tenants; the mother will have 8s. net profit, and be fit for work till she produces another child.

Those who are more thrifty (as I must confess the times require) may flay the carcass; the skin of which artificially dressed 15 will make admirable gloves for ladies, and summer boots for fine gentlemen.

As to our city of Dublin, shambles may be appointed for this 16 purpose in the most convenient parts of it, and butchers we may be assured will not be wanting: although I rather recommend buying the children alive, and dressing them hot from the knife as we do roasting pigs.

A very worthy person, a true lover of his country, and 17 whose virtues I highly esteem, was lately pleased in discoursing on this matter to offer a refinement upon my scheme. He said that many gentlemen of this kingdom, having of late destroyed their deer, he conceived that the want of venison might be well supplied by the bodies of young lads and maidens, not exceeding fourteen years of age nor under twelve; so great a number of both sexes in every country being now ready to starve for want of work and service; and these to be disposed of by their parents, if alive, or otherwise by their nearest relations. But with due deference to so excellent a friend and so deserving a patriot, I cannot be altogether in his sentiments; for as to the males, my American acquaintance assured me from frequent experience that their flesh was generally tough and lean, like that of our schoolboys by continual exercise, and their taste disagreeable; and to fatten them would not answer the charge. Then as to the females, it would, I think, with humble submission be a loss to the public, because they soon would become breeders themselves; and besides, it is not improbable that some scrupulous people might be apt to censure such a practice (although indeed very unjustly), as a little bordering upon cruelty; which, I confess, has always been with me the strongest objection against any project, how well so-ever intended.

But in order to justify my friend, he confessed that this expedient was put into his head by the famous Psalmanazar, a native of the island Formosa, who came from thence to London about twenty years ago: and in conversation told my friend, that in his country when any young person happened to be put to death, the executioner sold the carcass to persons of quality as a prime dainty; and that in his time the body of a plump girl of fifteen, who was crucified for an attempt to poison the emperor, was sold to his imperial majesty's prime minister of state, and other great mandarins of the court, in joints from the gibbet, at 400 crowns. Neither indeed can I deny, that if the same use were made of several plump young girls in this town, who without one single groat to their fortunes cannot stir without a chair, and appear at the playhouse and assemblies in foreign fineries which they never will pay for, the kingdom would not be the worse. 18

Some persons of a desponding spirit are in great concern 19 about that vast number of poor people, who are aged, diseased, or maimed, and I have been desired to employ my thoughts what course may be taken to ease the nation of so grievous an encumbrance. But I am not in the least pain upon that matter, because it is very well known that they are every day dying and rotting by cold and famine, and filth and vermin, as fast as can be reasonably expected. And as to the young laborers, they are now in as hopeful a condition: they cannot get work, and consequently pine away for want of nourishment, to a degree that if at any time they are accidentally hired to common labor, they have not strength to perform it; and thus the country and themselves are happily delivered from the evils to come.

I have too long digressed, and therefore shall return to my 20 subject. I think the advantages by the proposal which I have made are obvious and many, as well as of the highest importance.

For first, as I have already observed, it would greatly lessen 21 the number of papists, with whom we are yearly overrun, being the principal breeders of the nation as well as our most dangerous enemies; and who stay at home on purpose to deliver the kingdom to the Pretender, hoping to take their advantage by the absence of so many good Protestants, who have chosen rather to leave their country than stay at home and pay tithes against their conscience to an Episcopal curate.

Secondly, The poor tenants will have something valuable 22 of their own, which by law may be made liable to distress and help to pay their landlord's rent, their corn and cattle being already seized, and money a thing unknown.

Thirdly, Whereas the maintenance of 100,000 children from 23 two years old and upward, cannot be computed at less than 10s. a-piece per annum, the nation's stock will be thereby increased £50,000 per annum, beside the profit of a new dish introduced to the tables of all gentlemen of fortune in the kingdom who have any refinement in taste. And the money will circulate among ourselves, the goods being entirely of our own growth and manufacture.

Fourthly, The constant breeders beside the gain of 8s. ster- 24 ling per annum by the sale of their children, will be rid of the charge of maintaining them after the first year.

Fifthly, This food would likewise bring great custom to tav- 25
erns, where the vintners will certainly be so prudent as to pro-
cure the best receipts for dressing it to perfection, and consequently have their houses frequented by all the fine gentlemen,
who justly value themselves upon their knowledge in good eating; and a skilful cook who understands how to oblige his
guests, will contrive to make it as expensive as they please.

Sixthly, This would be a great inducement to marriage, 26
which all wise nations have either encouraged by rewards or
enforced by laws and penalties. It would increase the care and
tenderness of mothers toward their children, when they were
sure of a settlement for life to the poor babes, provided in some
sort by the public, to their annual profit instead of expense. We
should see an honest emulation among the married women,
which of them would bring the fattest child to the market. Men
would become as fond of their wives during the time of their
pregnancy as they are now of their mares in foal, their cows in
calf, their sows when they are ready to farrow; nor offer to beat
or kick them (as is too frequent a practice) for fear of a miscarriage.

Many other advantages might be enumerated. For instance, 27
the addition of some thousand carcasses in our exportation of
barreled beef, the propagation of swine's flesh, and improvement in the art of making good bacon, so much wanted among
us by the great destruction of pigs, too frequent at our table;
which are no way comparable in taste or magnificence to a well-
grown, fat, yearling child, which roasted whole will make a considerable figure at a lord mayor's feast or any other public entertainment. But this and many others I omit, being studious of
brevity.

Supposing that 1,000 families in this city would be constant 28
customers for infants' flesh, besides others who might have it
at merry-meetings, particularly at weddings and christenings,
I compute that Dublin would take off annually about 20,000 carcasses; and the rest of the kingdom (where probably they will
be sold somewhat cheaper) the remaining 80,000.

I can think of no one objection that will possibly be raised 29 against this proposal, unless it should be urged that the number of people will be thereby much lessened in the kingdom. This I freely own, and it was indeed one principal design in offering it to the world. I desire the reader will observe, that I calculate my remedy for this one individual kingdom of Ireland and for no other than ever was, is, or I think ever can be upon earth. Therefore let no man talk to me of other expedients: of taxing our absentees at 5s. a pound: of using neither clothes nor household furniture except what is of our own growth and manufacture: of utterly rejecting the materials and instruments that promote foreign luxury: of curing the expensiveness of pride, vanity, idleness, and gaming in our women: of introducing a vein of parsimony, prudence, and temperance: of learning to love our country, in the want of which we differ even from Laplander and the inhabitants of Topinamboo: of quitting our animosities and factions, nor acting any longer like the Jews, who were murdering one another at the very moment their city was taken: of being a little cautious not to sell our country and conscience for nothing: of teaching landlords to have at least one degree of mercy toward their tenants: lastly, of putting a spirit of honesty, industry, and skill into our shopkeepers; who, if a resolution could now be taken to buy only our native goods, would immediately unite to cheat and exact upon us in the price, the measure, and the goodness, nor could ever yet be brought to make one fair proposal of just dealing, though often and earnestly invited to it.

Therefore I repeat, let no man talk to me of these and the like expedients, till he has at least some glimpse of hope that there will be ever some hearty and sincere attempt to put them in practice. 30

But as to myself, having been wearied out for many years 31 with offering vain, idle, visionary thoughts, and at length utterly despairing of success, I fortunately fell upon this proposal; which, as it is wholly new, so it has something solid and real, of no expense and little trouble, full in our own power, and whereby we can incur no danger in disobliging England. For this kind of commodity will not bear exportation, the flesh being of too tender a consistence to admit a long continuance in salt, although perhaps I could name a country which would be glad to eat up our whole nation without it.

After all, I am not so violently bent upon my own opinion 32 as to reject any offer proposed by wise men, which shall be found equally innocent, cheap, easy, and effectual. But before something of that kind shall be advanced in contradiction to my scheme, and offering a better, I desire the author or authors will be pleased maturely to consider two points. First, as things now stand, how they will be able to find food and raiment for 100,000 useless mouths and backs. And secondly, there being a round million of creatures in human figure throughout this kingdom, whose subsistence put into a common stock would leave them in debt 2,000,000*l*. sterling, adding those who are beggars by profession to the bulk of farmers, cottagers, and laborers, with the wives and children who are beggars in effect; I desire those politicians who dislike my overture, and may perhaps be so bold as to attempt an answer, that they will first ask the parents of these mortals, whether they would not at this day think it a great happiness to have been sold for food at a year old in the manner I prescribe, and thereby have avoided such a perpetual scene of misfortunes as they have since gone through by the oppression of landlords, the impossibility of paying rent without money or trade, the want of common sustenance, with neither house nor clothes to cover them from the inclemencies of the weather, and the most inevitable prospect of entailing the like or greater miseries upon their breed for ever.

I profess, in the sincerity of my heart, that I have not the least 33 personal interest in endeavoring to promote this necessary work, having no other motive than the public good of my country, by advancing our trade, providing for infants, relieving the poor, and giving some pleasure to the rich. I have no children by which I can propose to get a single penny; the youngest being nine years old, and my wife past childbearing.

1714

The Great Person-Hole Cover Debate: A Modest Proposal for Anyone Who Thinks the Word "He" Is Just Plain Easier . . .

Lindsy Van Gelder

I wasn't looking for trouble. What I was looking for, actu- 1
ally, was a little tourist information to help me plan a camping
trip to New England.

But there it was, on the first page of the 1979 edition of the 2
State of Vermont *Digest of Fish and Game Laws and Regulations:*
a special message of welcome from one Edward F. Kehoe, commissioner of the Vermont Fish and Game Department, to the
reader and would-be camper, *i.e.,* me.

This person (*i.e.,* me) is called "the sportsman." 3

"We have no 'sportswomen, sportspersons, sportsboys, or 4
sportsgirls,' " Commissioner Kehoe hastened to explain, obviously anticipating that some of us sportsfeminists might feel a
bit overlooked. "But," he added, "we are pleased to report that
we do have many great sportsmen who are women, as well as
young people of both sexes."

It's just that the Fish and Game Department is trying to 5
keep things "simple and forthright" and to respect "long-
standing tradition." And anyway, we really ought to be flat-
tered, "sportsman" being "a meaningful title being earned by
a special kind of dedicated man, woman, or young person, as
opposed to just any hunter, fisherman, or trapper."

I have heard this particular line of reasoning before. In fact, 6
I've heard it so often that I've come to think of it as The Great
Person-Hole Cover Debate, since gender-neutral manholes are
invariably brought into the argument as evidence of the lengths
to which humorless, Newspeak-spouting feminists will go to
destroy their mother tongue.

Consternation about woman-handling the language comes 7

from all sides. Sexual conservatives who see the feminist movement as a unisex plot and who long for the good olde days of
vive la différence, when men were men and women were women,
nonetheless do not rally behind the notion that the term
"mankind" excludes women.

But most of the people who choke on expressions like   8
"spokesperson" aren't right-wing misogynists, and this is what
troubles me. Like the undoubtedly well-meaning folks at the
Vermont Fish and Game Department, they tend to reassure you
right up front that they're only trying to keep things "simple"
and to follow "tradition," and that some of their best men are
women, anyway.

Usually they wind up warning you, with great sincerity,   9
that you're jeopardizing the worthy cause of women's rights by
focusing on "trivial" side issues. I would like to know how anything that gets people so defensive and resistant can possibly
be called "trivial," whatever else it might be.

The English language is alive and constantly changing.   10
Progress—both scientific and social—is reflected in our language, or should be.

Not too long ago, there was a product called "flesh-colored"   11
Band-Aids. The flesh in question was colored Caucasian. Once
the civil rights movement pointed out the racism inherent in the
name, it was dropped. I cannot imagine reading a thoughtful,
well-intentioned company policy statement explaining that
while the Band-Aids would continue to be called "flesh-
colored" for old time's sake, black and brown people would
now be considered honorary whites and were perfectly welcome to use them.

Most sensitive people manage to describe our national re-   12
ligious traditions as "Judeo-Christian," even though it takes a
few seconds longer to say than "Christian." So why is it such a
hardship to say "he or she" instead of "he"?

I have a modest proposal for anyone who maintains that   13
"he" is just plain easier: since "he" has been the style for several centuries now—and since it really includes everybody anyway, right?—it seems only fair to give "she" a turn. Instead of
having to ponder over the intricacies of, say, "Congressman"

versus "Congress person" versus "Representative," we can simplify things by calling them all "Congresswoman."

Other clarifications will follow: "a woman's home is her cas- 14 tle..." "a giant step for all womankind".... "all women are created equal".... "Fisherwoman's Wharf." ...

And don't be upset by the business letter that begins "Dear 15 Madam," fellas. It means you, too.

1980

Four-Letter Words Can Hurt You

Barbara Lawrence

Why should any words be called obscene? Don't they all de- 1 scribe natural human functions? Am I trying to tell them, my students demand, that the "strong, earthy, gut-honest"—or, if they are fans of Norman Mailer, the "rich, liberating, existential"—language they use to describe sexual activity isn't preferable to "phony-sounding, middle-class words like 'intercourse' and 'copulate?'" "Cop You Late!" they say with fancy inflections and gagging grimaces. "Now, what is *that* supposed to mean?"

Well, what is it supposed to mean? And why indeed should 2 one group of words describing human functions and human organs be acceptable in ordinary conversation and another, describing presumably the same organs and functions, be tabooed—so much so, in fact, that some of these words still cannot appear in print in many parts of the English-speaking world?

The argument that these taboos exist only because of "sex- 3 ual hangups" (middle-class, middle-age, feminist), or even that they are a result of class oppression (the contempt of the Nor-

man conquerors for the language of their Anglo-Saxon serfs),
ignores a much more likely explanation, it seems to me, and that
is the sources and functions of the words themselves.

The best known of the tabooed sexual verbs, for example,   4
comes from the German *ficken,* meaning "to strike"; combined,
according to Partridge's etymological dictionary *Origins,* with
the Latin sexual verb *futuere;* associated in turn with the Latin
fustis, "a staff or cudgel"; the Celtic *buc,* "a point, hence to
pierce"; the Irish *bot,* "the male member"; the Latin *battuere,* "to
beat"; the Gaelic *batair,* "a cudgeller"; the Early Irish *bualaim,* "I
strike"; and so forth. It is one of what etymologists sometimes
call "the sadistic group of words for the man's part in copula-
tion."

The brutality of this word, then, and its equivalents   5
("screw," "bang," etc.), is not an illusion of the middle class or
a crotchet of Women's Liberation. In their origins and imagery
these words carry undeniably painful, if not sadistic, implications, the object of which is almost always female. Consider, for
example, what a "screw" actually does to the wood it penetrates; what a painful, even mutilating, activity this kind of
analogy suggests. "Screw" is particularly interesting in this context, since the noun, according to Partridge, comes from words
meaning "groove," "nut," "ditch," "breeding sow," "scrofula"
and "swelling," while the verb, besides its explicit imagery, has
antecedent associations to "write on," "scratch," "scarify," and
so forth—a revealing fusion of a mechanical or painful action
with an obviously denigrated object.

Not all obscene words, of course, are as implicitly sadistic   6
or denigrating to women as these, but all that I know seem to
serve a similar purpose: to reduce the human organism (especially the female organism) and human functions (especially
sexual and procreative) to their least organic, most mechanical
dimension; to substitute a trivializing or deforming resemblance
for the complex human reality of what is being described.

Tabooed male descriptives, when they are not openly den-   7
igrating to women, often serve to divorce a male organ or function from any significant interaction with the female. Take the
word "testes," for example, suggesting "witnesses" (from the

Latin *testis*) to the sexual and procreative strengths of the male organ; and the obscene counterpart of this word, which suggests little more than a mechanical shape. Or compare almost any of the "rich," "liberating" sexual verbs, so fashionable today among male writers, with that much-derided Latin word "copulate" ("to bind or join together") or even that Anglo-Saxon phrase (which seems to have had no trouble surviving the Norman Conquest) "make love."

How arrogantly self-involved the tabooed words seem in 8 comparison to either of the other terms, and how contemptuous of the female partner. Understandably so, of course, if she is only a "skirt," a "broad," a "chick," a "pussycat" or a "piece." If she is, in other words, no more than her skirt, or what her skirt conceals; no more than a breeder, or the broadest part of her; no more than a piece of human being or a "piece of tail."

The most severely tabooed of all the female descriptives, in 9 cidentally, are those like a "piece of tail," which suggest (either explicitly or through antecedents) that there is no significant difference between the female channel through which we are all conceived and born and the anal outlet common to both sexes— a distinction that pornographers have always enjoyed obscuring.

This effort to deny women their biological identity, their in- 10 dividuality, their humanness, is such an important aspect of obscene language that one can only marvel at how seldom, in an era preoccupied with definitions of obscenity, this fact is brought to our attention. One problem, of course, is that many of the people in the best position to do this (critics, teachers, writers) are so reluctant today to admit that they are angered or shocked by obscenity. Bored, maybe, unimpressed, aesthetically displeased, but—no matter how brutal or denigrating the material—never angered, never shocked.

And yet how eloquently angered, how piously shocked 11 many of these same people become if denigrating language is used about any minority group other than women; if the obscenities are racial or ethnic, that is, rather than sexual. Words like "coon," "kike," "spic," "wop," after all, deform identity, deny individuality and humanness in almost exactly the same way that sexual vulgarisms and obscenities do.

No one that I know, least of all my students, would fail to   12
question the values of a society whose literature and entertainment rested heavily on racial or ethnic pejoratives. Are the values of a society whose literature and entertainment rest as heavily as ours on sexual pejoratives any less questionable?

1973

Should This Student Have Been Expelled?

Nat Hentoff

*The day that Brown denies any student freedom of speech is the day I
give up my presidency of the university.*
            —Vartan Gregorian, president of Brown University,
                                    February 20, 1991

Doug Hann, a varsity football player at Brown, was also   1
concentrating on organizational behavior and management and
business economics. On the night of October 18, 1990, Hann, a
junior, was celebrating his twenty-first birthday, and in the
process had imbibed a considerable amount of spirits.

At one point, Hann shouted into the air, "Fuck you, nig-   2
gers!" It was aimed at no one in particular but apparently at all
black students at Brown. Or in the world. A freshman leaned
out a dormitory window and asked him to stop being so loud
and offensive.

Hann, according to reporters on the *Brown Daily Herald*,   3
looked up and yelled, "What are you, a faggot?" Hann then noticed an Israeli flag in the dorm. "What are you, a Jew?" he
shouted. "Fucking Jew!"

Hann had achieved the hat trick of bigotry. (In hockey, the   4
hat trick is scoring three goals in a game.) In less than a minute,

Hann had engaged in racist, anti-Semitic, and homophobic insults.

He wasn't through. As reported by Smita Nerula in the   5
Brown Daily Herald, the freshman who had asked Hann to cool
it recruited a few people from his dorm "and followed Hann
and his friends.

"This resulted in a verbal confrontation outside of Way-   6
land Arch. At this time, [Hann] was said to have turned to one
of the freshman's friends, a black woman, and shouted, 'My parents own your people.' "

To the Jewish student, or the student he thought was Jew-   7
ish, Hann said, "Happy Hanukkah."

There are reports that at this juncture Hann tried to fight   8
some of the students who had been following him. But, the
Brown Daily Herald reports, he "was held back by one of his
friends, while [another] friend stretched his arm across the Wayland Gates to keep the students from following Hann."

John Howard Crouch—a student and Brown chapter sec-   9
retary of the American Civil Liberties Union there—tells me that
because Hann had friends restraining him, "nobody seriously
expected fighting, regardless of anyone's words."

Anyway, there was no physical combat. Just words. Awful   10
words, but nothing more than speech. (Nor were there any
threats.)

This was not the first time Hann's graceful drunken lan-   11
guage had surfaced at Brown. Two years before, in an argument
with a black student at a fraternity bar, Hann had called the student a "nigger." Thereupon he had been ordered to attend a race
relations workshop and to get counseling for possible alcohol
abuse. Obviously, he has not been rehabilitated.

Months went by after Hann's notorious birthday celebra-   12
tion as Brown's internal disciplinary procedures cranked away.
(To steal a phrase from Robert Sherrill, Brown's way of reaching decisions in these matters is to due process as military music
is to music. But that's true of any college or university I know
anything about.)

At last, the Undergraduate Disciplinary Council (five fac-   13
ulty or administration members and five students) ruled that

Doug Hann was to leave the university forevermore. Until two years ago, it was possible for a Brown student to be dismissed, which meant that he or she could reapply after a decent period of penance. But now, Brown has enshrined the sentence of expulsion. You may go on to assist Mother Teresa in caring for the dying or you may teach a course in feminism to 2 Live Crew, but no accomplishments, no matter how noble, will get you back into Brown once you have been expelled.

Doug Hann will wander the earth without a Brown degree for the rest of his days.   14

The president of Brown, Vartan Gregorian—formerly the   15
genial head of the New York Public Library—had the power to commute or even reverse the sentence. But the speech code under which Hann was thrown out had been proposed by Gregorian himself shortly after he was inaugurated in 1989, so he was hardly a detached magistrate.

On January 25, 1991, Vartan Gregorian affirmed, with vigor,   16
the expulsion decision by the Undergraduate Disciplinary Council.

Hann became a historic figure. Under all the "hate speech"   17
codes enacted around the country in recent years, he is the first student to actually be expelled for violating one of the codes.

The *New York Times* (February 12) reported that "Howard   18
Ehrlich, the research director of the National Institute Against Prejudice and Violence, said that he did not know of any other such expulsions, but that he was familiar with cases in which students who had harassed others were moved to other dormitories or ordered to undergo counseling."

But that takes place in *educational* institutions, whose presi-   19
dents recognize that there are students who need help, not exile.

At first, there didn't seem to be much protest among the stu-   20
dent body at Brown on free speech grounds—except for members of the Brown chapter of the ACLU and some free thinkers on the student paper, as well as some unaffiliated objectors to expelling students for what they say, not for what they do. The number of these dissenters is increasing, as we shall see.

At the student paper, however, the official tone has changed   21
from the libertarian approach of Vernon Silver, who was editor-

in-chief last semester. A February 13 *Brown Daily Herald* editorial was headed: *"Good Riddance."*

It began: "Doug Hann is gone, and the university is well to be rid of him." 22

But President Gregorian has been getting a certain amount of flack and so, smiting his critics hip and thigh, he wrote a letter to the *New York Times*. Well, that letter (printed on February 21) was actually a press release, distributed by the Brown University News Bureau to all sorts of people, including me, on February 12. There were a few changes—and that *Brown Daily Herald* editorial was attached to it—but Gregorian's declaration was clearly not written exclusively for the *Times*. 23

Is this a new policy at the *Times*—taking public relations handouts for the letters page? 24

Next week I shall include a relentlessly accurate analysis of President Gregorian's letter by the executive director of the Rhode Island ACLU. But first, an account of what Gregorian said in that letter to the *Times*. 25

President Gregorian indignantly denies that Brown has ever expelled "anyone for the exercise of free speech, nor will it ever do so." Cross his heart. 26

He then goes into self-celebration: "My commitment to free speech and condemnation of racism and homophobia are well known. . . . 27

"The university's code of conduct does not prohibit speech; it prohibits *actions*." 28

Now watch this pitiable curve ball: 29

"Offense III [of the Brown code]—which deals with harassment—prohibits inappropriate, abusive, threatening, or demeaning actions based on race, religion, gender, handicap, ethnicity, national origin, or sexual orientation." 30

In the original press release, Gregorian underlined the word *actions*. There, and in the letter to the *Times*—lest a dozing reader miss the point—Gregorian emphasizes that "The rules do not proscribe words, epithets, or slanders, they proscribe behavior." Behavior that "shows flagrant disrespect for the well-being of others or is unreasonably disruptive of the University community." 31

Consider the overbreadth and vagueness of these penalty- 32

bearing provisions. What are the definitions of "harassment," "inappropriate," "demeaning," "flagrant," "disrespect," "well-being," "unreasonably"?

Furthermore, with regard to Brown's termination of Doug 33 Hann with extreme prejudice, Gregorian is engaging in the crudest form of Orwellian newspeak. Hann was kicked out for *speech,* and only speech—not for *actions,* as Gregorian huffily insists. As for behavior, the prickly folks whose burning of the American flag was upheld by the Supreme Court were indeed engaged in behavior, but that behavior was based entirely on symbolic speech. So was Hann's. He didn't punch anybody or vandalize any property. He brayed.

Art Spitzer, legal director of the ACLU's National Capital 34 Area affiliate, wrote a personal letter to Gregorian:

"There is a very simple test for determining whether a per- 35 son is being punished for his actions or his speech. You just ask whether he would have received the same punishment if he had spoken different words while engaging in the same conduct.

"Thus, would your student have been expelled if he had 36 gotten drunk and stood in the same courtyard at the same hour of the night, shouting at the same decibel level, 'Black is Beautiful!' 'Gay is Good!' or 'Go Brown! Beat Yale!' or even 'Nuke Baghdad! Kill Saddam!'?

"I am confident," Spitzer said, that "he would not have 37 been expelled for such 'actions.' If that is correct, it follows that *he was expelled for the unsavory content of his speech,* and not for his actions. I have no doubt that you can understand this distinction. (Emphasis added.)

"Now, you are certainly entitled to believe that it is appro- 38 priate to expel a student for the content of his speech when that content is sufficiently offensive to the 'university community.' . . .

"If that is your position, why can't you deliver it forth- 39 rightly? Then the university community can have an open debate about which opinions it finds offensive, and ban them. Perhaps this can be done once a year, so that the university's rules can keep pace with the tenor of the times—after all, it wouldn't do to have outmoded rules banning procommunist or blasphemous speech still on the books, now that it's 1991. Then students and teachers applying for admission or employment at Brown will know what they are getting into.

"Your recent statements, denying the obvious, are just hyp- 40 ocritical. . . ."

And what did the *New York Times*—in a stunningly fatuous 41 February 21 editorial—say of Vartan Gregorian's sending Doug Hann into permanent exile? "A noble attempt both to govern and teach."

The *Times* editorials should really be signed, so that the rest 42 of the editorial board isn't blamed for such embarrassments.

1991

How Much Hate to Tolerate

New York Times editorial, (February 21, 1991)

Free speech and human relations seemed to collide last 1 month at Brown University when it expelled a student for racial and religious harassment. In fact, however, to judge by all that is publicly known, the school walked a fine line with sensitivity toward its complex mission.

One mission of a university is to send into the world grad- 2 uates who are tolerant of many races, faiths and cultures. Another mission is to teach the value of free expression and tolerance even for hateful ideas. But should such tolerance cover racist, sexist or homophobic speech that makes the learning environment intolerable for racial and religious minorities, women and other targets of abuse? Brown found a reasonable basis for saying, clearly, no.

Douglas Hann, white, a junior and a varsity football player, 3 had previously been disciplined for alcohol abuse and for racial insults against a black fellow student. Then, one evening last fall, he shouted racial insults in a university courtyard. A Jewish student who opened a dormitory window and called for quiet was answered with a religious insult. Later that evening Mr. Hann directed a racial insult at a black undergraduate.

The student-faculty discipline committee found him guilty 4

of three violations of student rules, including another count of alcohol abuse. Vartan Gregorian, the university's president, upheld the student's expulsion last month. He had a sound basis for doing so. If the facts are reported correctly, Mr. Hann crossed the line between merely hateful speech and hateful speech that directly confronted and insulted other undergraduates.

Some courts have found that public universities are bound 5 by the First Amendment's ban on state censorship and thus may not punish students for expressing politically incorrect or socially distasteful ideas. Brown, like other private schools, is less directly bound by the Constitution but committed to its precepts. It is trying to avoid censorship but draws a line between strong language and what the courts often call "fighting words."

In the adjacent Letters column today, Mr. Gregorian insists 6 that Brown does not punish unruly speech as such but will decide case-by-case whether a student has passed "the point at which speech becomes behavior" that flagrantly disregards the well-being of others or "subjects someone to abusive or demeaning actions."

That formula is a noble attempt both to govern and teach. 7 It offers a principled basis for disciplinary action against Mr. Hann for his direct, confrontational conduct.

The lines may not be so clearly drawn in other cases. There 8 may also be more of them in the present climate of evidently increasing student intolerance. But when bigots attack other students with ugly invective, universities, whether public or private, need not remain silent. Their presidents, like Mr. Gregorian, may denounce indecency and, in so doing, protect tolerance.

Brown Expulsion Not About Free Speech
New York Times letter to the editor, (February 21, 1991)

To the Editor:

"Student at Brown Is Expelled Under a Rule Barring 'Hate 1 Speech' " (news article, Feb. 12) suggests I have instituted "hate-speech" prohibitions at Brown University and that the expulsion of a student who shouted racial and homophobic epithets on campus last October is the first such in the nation based on restrictions of free speech. Brown University has never expelled anyone for free speech, nor will it ever do so.

My commitment to free speech and condemnation of racism   2 and homophobia are well known. In April 1989, several students were subjected to a cowardly attack of racial and homophobic graffiti. The words and slogans scrawled anonymously on doors in one of our dormitories were vicious attacks threatening the well-being and security of Brown students.

I condemned that anonymous poisoning of our commu-   3 nity and said I would prosecute vigorously and seek the expulsion of those who incite hatred or perpetuate such acts of vandalism. Nothing I said then or have done since should be construed as limiting anyone's freedom of speech, nor have I revised the university's code of conduct to that effect.

The university's code of conduct does not prohibit speech;   4 it prohibits actions, and these include behavior that "shows flagrant disrespect for the well-being of others or is unreasonably disruptive of the university community."

Offense III, which deals with harassment, prohibits inap-   5 propriate, abusive, threatening or demeaning actions based on race, religion, gender, handicap, ethnicity, national origin or sexual orientation.

"The Tenets of Community Behavior," which outline com-   6 munity standards for acceptable behavior at Brown, have been read for more than 10 years by entering students, who agree in writing to abide by them.

The rules do not proscribe words, epithets or slanders; they   7 proscribe behavior. The point at which speech becomes behavior and the degree to which that behavior shows flagrant disrespect for the well-being of others (Offense II), subjects someone to abusive or demeaning actions (Offense III) or is related to drug or alcohol use (Offense IV) is determined by a hearing to consider the circumstances of each case. The student is entitled to an appeal, which includes review by a senior officer and a decision by the president.

I cannot and will not comment about any specific case. I re-   8 gret the release of any student's name in connection with a disciplinary hearing and the exposure any case may receive in *The Brown Herald*.

Freedom-of-speech questions lie at the heart of any academic community. The very nature of the academic enterprise necessitates that universities remain partisans of heterodoxy, of a rich and full range of opinions, ideas and expression. Imposed orthodoxies of all sorts, including what is called "politically correct" speech, are anathema to our enterprise.   9

The university's most compelling challenge is to achieve a balance between the right of its individual members to operate and speak freely, and fostering respect for and adherence to community values and standards of conduct.   10

VARTAN GREGORIAN
President, Brown University
Providence, R.I., Feb. 21, 1991

I Have a Dream

Martin Luther King, Jr.

Five score years ago, a great American, in whose symbolic shadow we stand, signed the Emancipation Proclamation. This momentous decree came as a great beacon light of hope to millions of Negro slaves who had been seared in the flames of withering injustice. It came as a joyous daybreak to end the long night of captivity.   1

But one hundred years later, we must face the tragic fact that the Negro is still not free. One hundred years later, the life of the Negro is still sadly crippled by the manacles of segregation and the chains of discrimination. One hundred years later, the Negro lives on a lonely island of poverty in the midst of a vast ocean of material prosperity. One hundred years later, the   2

Negro is still languishing in the corners of American society and finds himself an exile in his own land. So we have come here today to dramatize an appalling condition.

In a sense we have come to our nation's capital to cash a 3 check. When the architects of our republic wrote the magnificent words of the Constitution and the Declaration of Independence, they were signing a promissory note to which every American was to fall heir. This note was a promise that all men would be guaranteed the unalienable rights of life, liberty, and the pursuit of happiness.

It is obvious today that America has defaulted on this 4 promissory note insofar as her citizens of color are concerned. Instead of honoring this sacred obligation, America has given the Negro people a bad check; a check which has come back marked "insufficient funds." But we refuse to believe that the bank of justice is bankrupt. We refuse to believe that there are insufficient funds in the great vaults of opportunity of this nation. So we have come to cash this check—a check that will give us upon demand the riches of freedom and the security of justice. We have also come to this hallowed spot to remind America of the fierce urgency of *now*. This is no time to engage in the luxury of cooling off or to take the tranquilizing drugs of gradualism. *Now* is the time to make real the promises of Democracy. *Now* is the time to rise from the dark and desolate valley of segregation to the sunlit path of racial justice. *Now* is the time to open the doors of opportunity to all of God's children. *Now* is the time to lift our nation from the quicksands of racial injustice to the solid rock of brotherhood.

It would be fatal for the nation to overlook the urgency of 5 the moment and to underestimate the determination of the Negro. This sweltering summer of the Negro's legitimate discontent will not pass until there is an invigorating autumn of freedom and equality. 1963 is not an end, but a beginning. Those who hope that the Negro needed to blow off steam and will now be content will have a rude awakening if the nation returns to business as usual. There will be neither rest nor tranquillity in America until the Negro is granted his citizenship rights. The whirlwinds of revolt will continue to shake the foundations of our nation until the bright day of justice emerges.

But there is something that I must say to my people who   6
stand on the warm threshold which leads into the palace of justice. In the process of gaining our rightful place we must not be guilty of wrongful deeds. Let us not seek to satisfy our thirst for freedom by drinking from the cup of bitterness and hatred. We must forever conduct our struggle on the high plane of dignity and discipline. We must not allow our creative protest to degenerate into physical violence. Again and again we must rise to the majestic heights of meeting physical force with soul force. The marvelous new militancy which has engulfed the Negro community must not lead us to a distrust of all white people, for many of our white brothers, as evidenced by their presence here today, have come to realize that their destiny is tied up with our destiny and their freedom is inextricably bound to our freedom. We cannot walk alone.

And as we walk, we must make the pledge that we shall   7
march ahead. We cannot turn back. There are those who are asking the devotees of civil rights, "When will you be satisfied?" We can never be satisfied as long as the Negro is the victim of the unspeakable horrors of police brutality. We can never be satisfied as long as our bodies, heavy with the fatigue of travel, cannot gain lodging in the motels of the highways and the hotels of the cities. We cannot be satisfied as long as the Negro's basic mobility is from a smaller ghetto to a larger one. We can never be satisfied as long as a Negro in Mississippi cannot vote and a Negro in New York believes he has nothing for which to vote. No, no, we are not satisfied, and we will not be satisfied until justice rolls down like waters and righteousness like a mighty stream.

I am not unmindful that some of you have come here out   8
of great trials and tribulations. Some of you have come fresh from narrow jail cells. Some of you have come from areas where your quest for freedom left you battered by the storms of persecution and staggered by the winds of police brutality. You

have been the veterans of creative suffering. Continue to work with the faith that unearned suffering is redemptive.

Go back to Mississippi, go back to Alabama, go back to 9 South Carolina, go back to Georgia, go back to Louisiana, go back to the slums and ghettos of our northern cities, knowing that somehow this situation can and will be changed. Let us not wallow in the valley of despair.

I say to you today, my friends, that in spite of the difficul- 10 ties and frustrations of the moment I still have a dream. It is a dream deeply rooted in the American dream.

I have a dream that one day this nation will rise up and live 11 out the true meaning of its creed: "We hold these truths to be self-evident; that all men are created equal."

I have a dream that one day on the red hills of Georgia the 12 sons of former slaves and the sons of former slaveowners will be able to sit down together at the table of brotherhood.

I have a dream that one day even the state of Mississippi, a 13 desert state sweltering with the heat of injustice and oppression, will be transformed into an oasis of freedom and justice.

I have a dream that my four little children will one day live 14 in a nation where they will not be judged by the color of their skin but by the content of their character.

I have a dream today.   15

I have a dream that one day the state of Alabama, whose 16 governor's lips are presently dripping with the words of inter-position and nullification, will be transformed into a situation where little black boys and black girls will be able to join hands with little white boys and white girls and walk together as sis-ters and brothers.

I have a dream today.   17

I have a dream that one day every valley shall be exalted, 18 every hill and mountain shall be made low, the rough places will be made plain, and the crooked places will be made straight, and the glory of the Lord shall be revealed, and all flesh shall see it together.

This is our hope. This is the faith with which I return to the 19 South. With this faith we will be able to hew out of the moun-

tain of despair a stone of hope. With this faith we will be able
to transform the jangling discords of our nation into a beautiful symphony of brotherhood. With this faith we will be able to
work together, to pray together, to struggle together, to go to
jail together, to stand up for freedom together, knowing that we
will be free one day.

This will be the day when all of God's children will be able 20
to sing with new meaning.

> My country, 'tis of thee,
> Sweet land of liberty,
>   Of thee I sing:
> Land where my fathers died,
> Land of the pilgrims' pride,
> From every mountain-side
>   Let freedom ring.

And if America is to be a great nation this must become true. 21
So let freedom ring from the prodigious hilltops of New Hamp-
shire. Let freedom ring from the mighty mountains of New
York. Let freedom ring from the heightening Alleghenies of
Pennsylvania!

Let freedom ring from the snowcapped Rockies of Col- 22
orado!

Let freedom ring from the curvaceous peaks of California! 23

But not only that; let freedom ring from Stone Mountain of 24
Georgia!

Let freedom ring from Lookout Mountain of Tennessee! 25

Let freedom ring from every hill and molehill of Mississippi. 26
From every mountainside, let freedom ring.

When we let freedom ring, when we let it ring from every 27
village and every hamlet, from every state and every city, we
will be able to speed up that day when all of God's children,
black men and white men, Jews and Gentiles, Protestants and
Catholics, will be able to join hands and sing in the words of the
old Negro spiritual, "Free at last! free at last! thank God
almighty, we are free at last!"

1963

Sex, Drugs, Disasters, and the Extinction of Dinosaurs

Stephen Jay Gould

Science, in its most fundamental definition, is a fruitful 1
mode of inquiry, not a list of enticing conclusions. The conclusions are the consequence, not the essence.

My greatest unhappiness with most popular presentations 2
of science concerns their failure to separate fascinating claims
from the methods that scientists use to establish the facts of nature. Journalists, and the public, thrive on controversial and
stunning statements. But science is, basically, a way of knowing—in P. B. Medawar's apt words, "the art of the soluble." If
the growing corps of popular science writers would focus on
how scientists develop and defend those fascinating claims, they
would make their greatest possible contribution to public understanding.

Consider three ideas, proposed in perfect seriousness to ex- 3
plain that greatest of all titillating puzzles—the extinction of dinosaurs. Since these three notions invoke the primally fascinating themes of our culture—sex, drugs, and violence—they
surely reside in the category of fascinating claims. I want to
show why two of them rank as silly speculation, while the other
represents science at its grandest and most useful.

Science works with testable proposals. If, after much com- 4
pilation and scrutiny of data, new information continues to affirm a hypothesis, we may accept it provisionally and gain confidence as further evidence mounts. We can never be completely
sure that a hypothesis is right, though we may be able to show
with confidence that it is wrong. The best scientific hypotheses
are also generous and expansive: they suggest extensions and
implications that enlighten related, and even far distant, subjects. Simply consider how the idea of evolution has influenced
virtually every intellectual field.

Useless speculation, on the other hand, is restrictive. It gen- 5
erates no testable hypothesis, and offers no way to obtain po-

tentially refuting evidence. Please note that I am not speaking
of truth or falsity. The speculation may well be true; still, if it
provides, in principle, no material for affirmation or rejection,
we can make nothing of it. It must simply stand forever as an
intriguing idea. Useless speculation turns in on itself and leads
nowhere; good science, containing both seeds for its potential
refutation and implications for more and different testable
knowledge, reaches out. But, enough preaching. Let's move on
to dinosaurs, and the three proposals for their extinction.

1. *Sex:* Testes function only in a narrow range of temperature (those of mammals hang externally in a scrotal sac because internal body temperatures are too high for their
proper function). A worldwide rise in temperature at the
close of the Cretaceous period caused the testes of dinosaurs
to stop functioning and led to their extinction by steriliza-
tion of males.

2. *Drugs:* Angiosperms (flowering plants) first evolved toward the end of the dinosaurs' reign. Many of these plants
contain psychoactive agents, avoided by mammals today as
a result of their bitter taste. Dinosaurs had neither means to
taste the bitterness nor livers effective enough to detoxify
the substances. They died of massive overdoses.

3. *Disasters:* A large comet or asteroid struck the earth
some 65 million years ago, lofting a cloud of dust into the
sky and blocking sunlight, thereby suppressing photosynthesis and so drastically lowering world temperatures that
dinosaurs and hosts of other creatures became extinct.

Before analyzing these three tantalizing statements, we   6
must establish a basic ground rule often violated in proposals
for the dinosaurs' demise. *There is no separate problem of the extinction of dinosaurs.* Too often we divorce specific events from
their wider contexts and systems of cause and effect. The fundamental fact of dinosaur extinction is its synchrony with the
demise of so many other groups across a wide range of habi-
tats, from terrestrial to marine.

The history of life has been punctuated by brief episodes of   7 mass extinction. A recent analysis by University of Chicago paleontologists Jack Sepkoski and Dave Raup, based on the best and most exhaustive tabulation of data ever assembled, shows clearly that five episodes of mass dying stand well above the "background" extinctions of normal times (when we consider all mass extinctions, large and small, they seem to fall in a regular 26-million-year cycle). The Cretaceous debacle, occurring 65 million years ago and separating the Mesozoic and Cenozoic eras of our geological time scale, ranks prominently among the five. Nearly all the marine plankton (single-celled floating creatures) died with geological suddenness; among marine invertebrates, nearly 15 percent of all families perished, including many previously dominant groups, especially the ammonites (relatives of squids in coiled shells). On land, the dinosaurs disappeared after more than 100 million years of unchallenged domination.

In this context, speculations limited to dinosaurs alone ignore the larger phenomenon. We need a coordinated explanation for a system of events that includes the extinction of dinosaurs as one component. Thus it makes little sense, though it may fuel our desire to view mammals as inevitable inheritors of the earth, to guess that dinosaurs died because small mammals ate their eggs (a perennial favorite among untestable speculations). It seems most unlikely that some disaster peculiar to dinosaurs befell these massive beasts—and that the debacle happened to strike just when one of history's five great dyings had enveloped the earth for completely different reasons.

The testicular theory, an old favorite from the 1940s, had its root in an interesting and thoroughly respectable study of temperature tolerances in the American alligator, published in the staid *Bulletin of the American Museum of Natural History* in 1946 by three experts on living and fossil reptiles—E. H. Colbert, my own first teacher in paleontology; R. B. Cowles; and C. M. Bogert.

The first sentence of their summary reveals a purpose beyond alligators: "This report describes an attempt to infer the reactions of extinct reptiles, especially the dinosaurs, to high temperatures as based upon reactions observed in the modern

alligator." They studied, by rectal thermometry, the body temperatures of alligators under changing conditions of heating
and cooling. (Well, let's face it, you wouldn't want to try sticking a thermometer under a 'gator's tongue.) The predictions
under test go way back to an old theory first stated by Galileo
in the 1630s—the unequal scaling of surfaces and volumes. As
an animal, or any object, grows (provided its shape doesn't
change), surface areas must increase more slowly than volumes—since surfaces get larger as length squared, while volumes increase much more rapidly, as length cubed. Therefore,
small animals have high ratios of surface to volume, while large
animals cover themselves with relatively little surface.

Among cold-blooded animals lacking any physiological   11
mechanism for keeping their temperatures constant, small creatures have a hell of a time keeping warm—because they lose so
much heat through their relatively large surfaces. On the other
hand, large animals, with their relatively small surfaces, may
lose heat so slowly that, once warm, they may maintain effectively constant temperatures against ordinary fluctuations of climate. (In fact, the resolution of the "hot-blooded dinosaur" controversy that burned so brightly a few years back may simply
be that, while large dinosaurs possessed no physiological mechanism for constant temperature, and were not therefore warm-
blooded in the technical sense, their large size and relatively
small surface area kept them warm.)

Colbert, Cowles, and Bogert compared the warming rates   12
of small and large alligators. As predicted, the small fellows
heated up (and cooled down) more quickly. When exposed to
a warm sun, a tiny 50-gram (1.76-ounce) alligator heated up one
degree Celsius every minute and a half, while a large alligator,
260 times bigger at 13,000 grams (28.7 pounds), took seven and
a half minutes to gain a degree. Extrapolating up to an adult 10-
ton dinosaur, they concluded that a one-degree rise in body
temperature would take eighty-six hours. If large animals absorb heat so slowly (through their relatively small surfaces),
they will also be unable to shed any excess heat gained when
temperatures rise above a favorable level.

The authors then guessed that large dinosaurs lived at or   13 near their optimum temperatures; Cowles suggested that a rise in global temperatures just before the Cretaceous extinction caused the dinosaurs to heat up beyond their optimal tolerance—and, being so large, they couldn't shed the unwanted heat. (In a most unusual statement within a scientific paper, Colbert and Bogert then explicitly disavowed this speculative extension of their empirical work on alligators.) Cowles conceded that this excess heat probably wasn't enough to kill or even to enervate the great beasts, but since testes often function only within a narrow range of temperature, he proposed that this global rise might have sterilized all the males, causing extinction by natural contraception.

The overdose theory has recently been supported by UCLA   14
psychiatrist Ronald K. Siegel. Siegel has gathered, he claims, more than 2,000 records of animals who, when given access, administer various drugs to themselves—from a mere swig of alcohol to massive doses of the big H. Elephants will swill the equivalent of twenty beers at a time, but do not like alcohol in concentrations greater than 7 percent. In a silly bit of anthropocentric speculation, Siegel states that "elephants drink, perhaps, to forget . . . the anxiety produced by shrinking rangeland and the competition for food."

Since fertile imaginations can apply almost any hot idea to   15
the extinction of dinosaurs, Siegel found a way. Flowering plants did not evolve until late in the dinosaurs' reign. These plants also produced an array of aromatic, amino-acid-based alkaloids—the major group of psychoactive agents. Most mammals are "smart" enough to avoid these potential poisons. The alkaloids simply don't taste good (they are bitter); in any case, we mammals have livers happily supplied with the capacity to detoxify them. But, Siegel speculates, perhaps dinosaurs could neither taste the bitterness nor detoxify the substances once ingested. He recently told members of the American Psychological Association: "I'm not suggesting that all dinosaurs OD'd on plant drugs, but it certainly was a factor." He also argued that death by overdose may help explain why so many dinosaur fossils are found in contorted positions. (Do not go gentle into that good night.)

Extraterrestrial catastrophes have long pedigrees in the 16
popular literature of extinction, but the subject exploded again
in 1979, after a long lull, when the father-son, physicist-geologist
team of Luis and Walter Alvarez proposed that an asteroid,
some 10 km in diameter, struck the earth 65 million years ago
(comets, rather than asteroids, have since gained favor. Good
science is self-corrective).

The force of such a collision would be immense, greater by 17
far than the megatonnage of all the world's nuclear weapons.
In trying to reconstruct a scenario that would explain the simultaneous dying of dinosaurs on land and so many creatures
in the sea, the Alvarezes proposed that a gigantic dust cloud,
generated by particles blown aloft in the impact, would so
darken the earth that photosynthesis would cease and temperatures drop precipitously. (Rage, rage against the dying of the
light.) The single-celled photosynthetic oceanic plankton, with
life cycles measured in weeks, would perish outright, but land
plants might survive through the dormancy of their seeds (land
plants were not much affected by the Cretaceous extinction,
and any adequate theory must account for the curious pattern
of differential survival). Dinosaurs would die by starvation and
freezing; small, warm-blooded mammals, with more modest requirements for food and better regulation of body temperature,
would squeak through. "Let the bastards freeze in the dark," as
bumper stickers of our chauvinistic neighbors in sunbelt states
proclaimed several years ago during the Northeast's winter oil
crisis.

All three theories, testicular malfunction, psychoactive 18
overdosing, and asteroidal zapping, grab our attention mightily. As pure phenomenology, they rank about equally high on
any hit parade of primal fascination. Yet one represents expansive science, the others restrictive and untestable speculation.
The proper criterion lies in evidence and methodology; we must
probe behind the superficial fascination of particular claims.

How could we possibly decide whether the hypothesis of 19
testicular frying is right or wrong? We would have to know
things that the fossil record cannot provide. What temperatures
were optimal for dinosaurs? Could they avoid the absorption

of excess heat by staying in the shade, or in caves? At what temperatures did their testicles cease to function? Were late Cretaceous climates ever warm enough to drive the internal temperatures of dinosaurs close to this ceiling? Testicles simply don't fossilize, and how could we infer their temperature tolerances even if they did? In short, Cowles's hypothesis is only an intriguing speculation leading nowhere. The most damning statement against it appeared right in the conclusion of Colbert, Cowles, and Bogert's paper, when they admitted: "It is difficult to advance any definite arguments against the hypothesis." My statement may seem paradoxical—isn't a hypothesis really good if you can't devise any arguments against it? Quite the contrary. It is simply untestable and unusable.

Siegel's overdosing has even less going for it. At least $_{20}$ Cowles extrapolated his conclusion from some good data on alligators. And he didn't completely violate the primary guideline of siting dinosaur extinction in the context of a general mass dying—for rise in temperature could be the root cause of a general catastrophe, zapping dinosaurs by testicular malfunction and different groups for other reasons. But Siegel's speculation cannot touch the extinction of ammonites or oceanic plankton (diatoms make their own food with good sweet sunlight; they don't OD on the chemicals of terrestrial plants). It is simply a gratuitous, attention-grabbing guess. It cannot be tested, for how can we know what dinosaurs tasted and what their livers could do? Livers don't fossilize any better than testicles.

The hypothesis doesn't even make any sense in its own $_{21}$ context. Angiosperms were in full flower ten million years before dinosaurs went the way of all flesh. Why did it take so long? As for the pains of a chemical death recorded in contortions of fossils, I regret to say (or rather I'm pleased to note for the dinosaurs' sake) that Siegel's knowledge of geology must be a bit deficient: muscles contract after death and geological strata rise and fall with motions of the earth's crust after burial—more than enough reason to distort a fossil's pristine appearance.

The impact story, on the other hand, has a sound basis in $_{22}$

evidence. It can be tested, extended, refined, and, if wrong, disproved. The Alvarezes did not just construct an arresting guess for public consumption. They proposed their hypothesis after laborious geochemical studies with Frank Asaro and Helen Michael had revealed a massive increase of iridium in rocks deposited right at the time of extinction. Iridium, a rare metal of the platinum group, is virtually absent from indigenous rocks of the earth's crust; most of our iridium arrives on extraterrestrial objects that strike the earth.

The Alvarez hypothesis bore immediate fruit. Based originally on evidence from two European localities, it led geochemists throughout the world to examine other sediments of the same age. They found abnormally high amounts of iridium everywhere—from continental rocks of the western United States to deep sea cores from the South Atlantic.   23

Cowles proposed his testicular hypothesis in the mid-1940s. Where has it gone since then? Absolutely nowhere, because scientists can do nothing with it. The hypothesis must stand as a curious appendage to a solid study of alligators. Siegel's overdose scenario will also win a few press notices and fade into oblivion. The Alvarezes' asteroid falls into a different category altogether, and much of the popular commentary has missed this essential distinction by focusing on the impact and its attendant results, and forgetting what really matters to a scientist—the iridium. If you talk just about asteroids, dust, and darkness, you tell stories no better and no more entertaining than fried testicles or terminal trips. It is the iridium—the source of testable evidence—that counts and forges the crucial distinction between speculation and science.   24

The proof, to twist a phrase, lies in the doing. Cowles's hypothesis has generated nothing in thirty-five years. Since its proposal in 1979, the Alvarez hypothesis has spawned hundreds of studies, a major conference, and attendant publications. Geologists are fired up. They are looking for iridium at all other extinction boundaries. Every week exposes a new wrinkle in the scientific press. Further evidence that the Cretaceous iridium represents extraterrestrial impact and not in-   25 digenous volcanism continues to accumulate. As I revise this essay in November 1984 (this paragraph will be out of date when the book is published), new data include chemical "signatures" of other isotopes indicating unearthly provenance, glass spherules of a size and sort produced by impact and not by volcanic eruptions, and high-pressure varieties of silica formed (so far as we know) only under the tremendous shock of impact.

My point is simply this: Whatever the eventual outcome (I 26 suspect it will be positive), the Alvarez hypothesis is exciting, fruitful science because it generates tests, provides us with things to do, and expands outward. We are having fun, battling back and forth, moving toward a resolution, and extending the hypothesis beyond its original scope.

As just one example of the unexpected, distant cross- 27 fertilization that good science engenders, the Alvarez hypothesis made a major contribution to a theme that has riveted public attention in the past few months—so-called nuclear winter. In a speech delivered in April 1982, Luis Alvarez calculated the energy that a ten-kilometer asteroid would release on impact. He compared such an explosion with a full nuclear exchange and implied that all-out atomic war might unleash similar consequences.

This theme of impact leading to massive dust clouds and 28 falling temperatures formed an important input to the decision of Carl Sagan and a group of colleagues to model the climatic consequences of nuclear holocaust. Full nuclear exchange would probably generate the same kind of dust cloud and darkening that may have wiped out the dinosaurs. Temperatures would drop precipitously and agriculture might become impossible. Avoidance of nuclear war is fundamentally an ethical and political imperative, but we must know the factual consequences to make firm judgments. I am heartened by a final link across disciplines and deep concerns—another criterion, by the way, of science at its best. A recognition of the very phenomenon that made our evolution possible by exterminating the previously dominant dinosaurs and clearing a way for the evolution of large mammals, including us, might actually help to save us from joining those magnificent beasts in contorted poses among the strata of the earth.

1984

A Step Back to the Workhouse?

Barbara Ehrenreich

The commentators are calling it a "remarkable consensus." 1 Workfare, as programs to force welfare recipients to work are known, was once abhorred by liberals as a step back toward the 17th-century workhouse or—worse—slavery. But today no political candidate dares step outdoors without some plan for curing "welfare dependency" by putting its hapless victims to work—if necessary, at the nearest Burger King. It is as if the men who run things, or who aspire to run things (and we are, unfortunately, talking mostly about men when we talk about candidates), had gone off and caucused for a while and decided on the one constituency that could be safely sacrificed in the name of political expediency and "new ideas," and that constituency is poor women.

Most of the arguments for workfare are simply the same 2 indestructible stereotypes that have been around, in one form or another, since the first public relief program in England 400 years ago: that the poor are poor because they are lazy and dissolute, and that they are lazy and dissolute because they are suffering from "welfare dependency." Add a touch of modern race and gender stereotypes and you have the image that haunts the workfare advocates: a slovenly, over-weight, black woman who produces a baby a year in order to augment her welfare checks.

But there is a new twist to this season's spurt of welfare- 3 bashing: workfare is being presented as a kind of *feminist* alternative to welfare. As Senator Daniel Patrick Moynihan (D.-N.Y.) has put it, "A program that was designed to pay mothers to stay at home with their children [i.e., welfare, or Aid to Families with Dependent Children] cannot succeed when we now observe most mothers going out to work." Never mind the startling illogic of this argument, which is on a par with saying that no woman should stay home with her children because other women do not, or that a laid-off male worker should not receive unemployment compensation because most men have been observed holding jobs. We are being asked to believe that pushing destitute mothers into the work force (in some versions of workfare, for no other compensation than the welfare payments they would have received anyway) is consistent with women's strivings toward self-determination.

Now I will acknowledge that most women on welfare—like   4
most unemployed women in general—would rather have jobs. And I will further acknowledge that many of the proponents of workfare, possibly including Senator Moynihan and the Democratic Presidential candidates, have mounted the bandwagon with the best of intentions. Welfare surely needs reform. But workfare is not the solution, because "dependency"—with all its implications of laziness and depravity—is not the problem. The problem is poverty, which most women enter in a uniquely devastating way—with their children in tow.

Let me introduce a real person, if only because real people,   5
as opposed to imaginative stereotypes, never seem to make an appearance in the current rhetoric on welfare. "Lynn," as I will call her, is a friend and onetime neighbor who has been on welfare for two years. She is also about as unlike the stereotypical "welfare mother" as one can get—which is to say that she is a fairly typical welfare recipient. She has only one child, which puts her among the 74 percent of welfare recipients who have only one or two children. She is white (not that that should matter), as are almost half of welfare recipients. Like most welfare recipients, she is not herself the daughter of a welfare recipient, and hence not part of anything that could be called an "intergenerational cycle of dependency." And like every woman on welfare I have ever talked to, she resents the bu-

reaucratic hassles that are the psychic price of welfare. But, for now, there are no alternatives.

When I first met Lynn, she seemed withdrawn and disoriented. She had just taken the biggest step of her 25 years; she had left an abusive husband and she was scared: scared about whether she could survive on her own and scared of her estranged husband. He owned a small restaurant; she was a high school dropout who had been a waitress when she met him. During their three years of marriage he had beaten her repeatedly. Only after he threw her down a flight of stairs had she realized that her life was in danger and moved out. I don't think I fully grasped the terror she had lived in until one summer day when he chased Lynn to the door of my house with a drawn gun.

Gradually Lynn began to put her life together. She got a divorce and went on welfare; she found a pediatrician who would accept Medicaid and a supermarket that would take food stamps. She fixed up her apartment with secondhand furniture and flea market curtains. She was, by my admittedly low standards, a compulsive housekeeper and an overprotective mother; and when she wasn't waxing her floors or ironing her two-year-old's playsuits, she was studying the help-wanted ads. She spent a lot of her time struggling with details that most of us barely notice—the price of cigarettes, mittens, or of a bus ticket to the welfare office—yet, somehow, she regained her sense of humor. In fact, most of the time we spent together was probably spent laughing—over the foibles of the neighbors, the conceits of men, and the snares of welfare and the rest of "the system."

Yet for all its inadequacies, Lynn was grateful for welfare. Maybe if she had been more intellectually inclined she would have found out that she was suffering from "welfare dependency," a condition that is supposed to sap the will and demolish the work ethic. But "dependency" is not an issue when it is a choice between an abusive husband and an impersonal government. Welfare had given Lynn a brief shelter in a hostile world, and as far as she was concerned, it was her ticket to *independence*.

Suppose there had been no welfare at the time when Lynn 9
finally summoned the courage to leave her husband. Suppose
she had gone for help and been told she would have to "work
off" her benefits in some menial government job (restocking the
toilet paper in rest rooms is one such "job" assigned to New
York women in a current workfare program). Or suppose, as in
some versions of workfare, she had been told she would have
to take the first available private sector job, which (for a non-
high school graduate like Lynn) would have paid near the minimum wage, or $3.35 an hour. How would she have been able
to afford child care? What would she have done for health insurance (as a welfare recipient she had Medicaid, but most low-
paying jobs offer little or no coverage)? Would she have ever
made the decision to leave her husband in the first place?

As Ruth Sidel points out in *Women and Children Last* 10
(Viking), most women who are or have been on welfare have
stories like Lynn's. They go onto welfare in response to a crisis—divorce, illness, loss of a job, the birth of an additional
child to feed—and they remain on welfare for two years or less.
They are not victims of any "welfare culture," but of a society
that increasingly expects women to both raise and support children—and often on wages that would barely support a woman
alone. In fact, even some of the most vociferous advocates of replacing welfare with workfare admit that, in their own estima-
tion, only about 15 percent of welfare recipients fit the stereotype associated with "welfare dependency": demoralization,
long-term welfare use, lack of drive, and so on.

But workfare will not help anyone, not even the presumed 11
15 percent of "bad apples" for whose sake the majority will be
penalized. First, it will not help because it does not solve the
problem that drives most women into poverty in the first place:
how to hold a job *and* care for children. Child care in a licensed,
professionally run center can easily cost as much as $100 a week
per child—more than most states now pay in welfare benefits
and (for two children) more than most welfare recipients could
expect to earn in the work force. Any serious effort to get welfare recipients into the work force would require child-care provisions at a price that would probably end up higher than the

current budget for AFDC. But none of the workfare advocates
are proposing that sort of massive public commitment to child
care.

Then there is the problem of jobs. So far, studies show that   12
existing state workfare programs have had virtually no success
in improving their participants' incomes or employment rates.
Small wonder: nearly half the new jobs generated in recent years
pay poverty-level wages; and most welfare recipients will enter
jobs that pay near the minimum wage, which is $6,900 a year—
26 percent less than the poverty level for a family of three. A menial, low-wage job may be character-building (from a middle-
class vantage point), but it will not lift anyone out of poverty.

Some of my feminist activist friends argue that it is too late   13
to stop the workfare juggernaut. The best we can do, they say,
is to try to defeat the more pernicious proposals: those that are
over-coercive, that do not offer funds for child care, or that
would relegate work clients to a "subemployee" status unprotected by federal labor and civil rights legislation. Our goal, the
pragmatists argue, should be to harness the current enthusiasm
for workfare to push for services welfare recipients genuinely
need, such as child care and job training and counseling.

I wish the pragmatists well, but for me, it would be a be-   14
trayal of women like Lynn to encourage the workfare bandwagon in any way. Most women, like Lynn, do not take up welfare as a career, but as an emergency measure in a time of
personal trauma and dire need. At such times, the last thing
they need is to be hustled into a low-wage job, and left to piece
together child care, health insurance, transportation, and all the
other ingredients of survival. In fact, the main effect of workfare may be to discourage needy women from seeking any help
at all—a disastrous result in a nation already suffering from a
child poverty rate of nearly 25 percent. Public policy should be
aimed at giving impoverished mothers (and, I would add, fathers) the help they so urgently need—not only in the form of
job opportunities, but sufficient income support to live on until
a job worth taking comes along.

Besides, there is an ancient feminist principle at stake. The   15
premise of all the workfare proposals—the more humane as

well as the nasty—is that single mothers on welfare are *not working*. But, to quote the old feminist bumper sticker, EVERY MOTHER IS A WORKING MOTHER. And those who labor to raise their children in poverty—to feed and clothe them on meager budgets and to nurture them in an uncaring world—are working the hardest. The feminist position has never been that all women must pack off their children and enter the work force, but that all women's work—in the home or on the job—should be valued and respected.

Barbara Ehrenreich's essay stimulated a lively response from Ms. *readers. The following letters were published in the February 1988 issue.*

I was absolutely thrilled when I read Barbara Ehrenreich's 16 article on workfare ("A Step Back to the Workhouse?" November 1987). As a single mother who received welfare for several years (with no child support) I'm against everything that workfare stands for. I belong to an organization called Women, Work, and Welfare, a group of current and former welfare recipients trying to empower ourselves and become a part of the decisions that affect our lives as poor women. It seems as if everybody but the welfare recipient herself has a hand in the decisions that are made.

CHERI HONKALA
Minneapolis, Minn.

I arrived in Chicago in 1952 with a husband and two chil- 17 dren from a camp in Europe. I had another child in 1953, lost a newborn in 1954, had a miscarriage, a hysterectomy, and a divorce in 1955. I never received child support. My ex-husband was remarried within two months.

I *never* received welfare. I worked in another culture, while 18 in very bad health. I found a two-room flat, had no furniture and slept for years on the floor. I even went back to school at night and had to contend with companies like Gulf Oil Corp., which did not believe in promoting women. But I just slugged on.

By the end of the sixties, I had two daughters in college, and 19
I had bought a house. My total earnings for 1970 from three jobs
came to a whopping $8,000.

A full-time minimum wage job *can* support one adult and 20
one child. One just has to learn how to do it.

URSULA SCHRAMM
Hurley, Wis.

I found myself agreeing with the problems that Barbara 21
Ehrenreich outlines in the present workfare program.

Yet deep inside a protesting rumbling exploded when I 22
read that impoverished mothers should receive sufficient income support to live on "until a job worth taking comes along."
Bullshit! Sure, we all should have the right to only work a job
we love, but how many of us can afford to wait for it? That we
are often forced to work at jobs that are not fulfilling says a lot
about our society in which more needs to be changed than just
the welfare system!

My mother was forced to go to work when I was nine years 23
old. Our family was in dire financial straits and at the age of 50
she took a job in a factory. Was that job "worth taking"? Did it
utilize her unique talents? *No!* Did it bring her personal fulfillment? *No!* Did it prevent the bank from foreclosing on our
home? *Yes!* Did it give my mother the power to overcome our
financial crisis and maintain her autonomy? *Yes!* You tell me if
it was "worth taking." That depends on what your self-respect
is worth to you.

GAIL FREI
Newtown Square, Pa.

Barbara Ehrenreich omitted a major element in her discus- 24
sion of the victimization of welfare families: the inability or un-
willingness of the legal system to award *and enforce* realistic
child support. Until it stops being easier to abandon your chil-

dren than to default on that car loan, women and those who depend on them will be welfare/workfare victims.

SUSAN MARTIN RYNARD
Durham, N.C.

I went on welfare when my daughter was three, when I left 25 my husband. I had a high school education, but had always wanted to go to college. I was 25.

So, with the help of the government, I got my B.S. in nurs- 26 ing. I worked for several years as an R.N. and then returned to school for my master's degree. For graduate school, I lived on savings, loans, and grants. The loans ($19,000 for undergrad and graduate in all) will be paid off in less than a year, in time for my daughter to begin college!

KATHRYN REID
Silverado, Calif.

Although I share Barbara Ehrenreich's concerns about 27 workfare and the plight of her friend Lynn, the conclusions she draws strike me as misguided. We live in a society where the myths of the work ethic and self-help are deeply embedded in the popular culture; where resort to the dole is frowned upon unless the need is temporary or arises from disability; where the middle-class majority feels inequitably taxed, as compared to the wealthy, to support a system that directly benefits few of its members.

Feminists and other liberals should acknowledge the 28 swelling demand for welfare reform. Our support should be conditional upon the incorporation in any welfare reform plan of provision for *quality* childcare facilities; upon the minimization of coercion; and upon further efforts to compel ex-spouses to pay their fair share of support. Nothing in this approach rules out our going ahead simultaneously with other, parallel efforts to question the mystique of work or to expose the links between welfare and poverty, on the one hand, and capitalism and the subordination of women, on the other.

DAVID G. BECKER
Hanover, N.H.

California is serious about workfare, but we call it GAIN 29 (Greater Avenues for Independence). It offers welfare recipients vocational counseling, up to two years of vocational training, and workshops in how to get and hold a job.

GAIN also pays for child care and transportation. No job 30 need be accepted by the recipient unless she/he will *net* at least as much as their AFDC grant, *including* child care, transportation, and medical insurance. And even then, they will receive funds to cover these costs for three months after they begin working to help them make the transition to the work force.

JANE KIRCHMAN
Guerneville, Calif.

Lifeboat Ethics: The Case Against Helping the Poor

Garrett Hardin

Environmentalists use the metaphor of the earth as a 1 "spaceship" in trying to persuade countries, industries and people to stop wasting and polluting our natural resources. Since we all share life on this planet, they argue, no single person or institution has the right to destroy, waste, or use more than a fair share of its resources.

But does everyone on earth have an equal right to an equal 2 share of its resources? The spaceship metaphor can be dangerous when used by misguided idealists to justify suicidal policies for sharing our resources through uncontrolled immigration and foreign aid. In their enthusiastic but unrealistic generosity, they confuse the ethics of a spaceship with those of a lifeboat.

A true spaceship would have to be under the control of a captain, since no ship could possibly survive if its course were determined by committee. Spaceship Earth certainly has no captain; the United Nations is merely a toothless tiger, with little power to enforce any policy upon its bickering members. 3

If we divide the world crudely into rich nations and poor nations, two thirds of them are desperately poor, and only one third comparatively rich, with the United States the wealthiest of all. Metaphorically each rich nation can be seen as a lifeboat full of comparatively rich people. In the ocean outside each lifeboat swim the poor of the world, who would like to get in, or at least to share some of the wealth. What should the lifeboat passengers do? 4

First, we must recognize the limited capacity of any lifeboat. For example, a nation's land has a limited capacity to support a population and as the current energy crisis has shown us, in some ways we have already exceeded the carrying capacity of our land. So here we sit, say 50 people in our lifeboat. To be generous, let us assume it has room for 10 more, making a total capacity of 60. Suppose the 50 of us in the lifeboat see 100 others swimming in the water outside, begging for admission to our boat or for handouts. We have several options: we may be tempted to try to live by the Christian ideal of being "our brother's keeper," or by the Marxist ideal of "to each according to his needs." Since the needs of all in the water are the same, and since they can all be seen as our "brothers," we could take them all into our boat, making a total of 150 in a boat designed for 60. The boat swamps; everyone drowns. Complete justice, complete catastrophe. 5

Since the boat has an unused excess capacity of 10 more passengers, we could admit just 10 more to it. But which 10 do we let in? How do we choose? Do we pick the best 10, the neediest 10, "first come, first served"? And what do we say to the 90 we 6 exclude? If we do let an extra 10 into our lifeboat, we will have lost our "safety factor," an engineering principle of critical importance. For example, if we don't leave room for excess capacity as a safety factor in our country's agriculture, a new plant disease or a bad change in the weather could have disastrous consequences.

Suppose we decide to preserve our small safety factor and   7
admit no more to the lifeboat. Our survival is then possible, although we shall have to be constantly on guard against boarding parties.

While this last solution clearly offers the only means of our   8
survival, it is morally abhorrent to many people. Some say they feel guilty about their good luck. My reply is simple: "Get out and yield your place to others." This may solve the problem of the guilt-ridden person's conscience, but it does not change the ethics of the lifeboat. The needy person to whom the guilt-ridden person yields his place will not himself feel guilty about his good luck. If he did, he would not climb aboard. The net result of conscience-stricken people giving up their unjustly held seats is the elimination of that sort of conscience from the lifeboat.

This is the basic metaphor within which we must work out   9
our solutions. Let us now enrich the image, step by step, with substantive additions from the real world, a world that must solve real and pressing problems of overpopulation and hunger.

The harsh ethics of the lifeboat become even harsher when   10
we consider the reproductive differences between the rich nations and the poor nations. The people inside the lifeboats are doubling in numbers every 87 years; those swimming around outside are doubling, on the average, every 35 years, more than twice as fast as the rich. And since the world's resources are dwindling, the difference in prosperity between the rich and the poor can only increase.

As of 1973, the U.S. had a population of 210 million people,   11
who were increasing by 0.8 percent per year. Outside our lifeboat, let us imagine another 210 million people (say the combined populations of Colombia, Ecuador, Venezuela, Morocco, Pakistan,

Thailand, and the Philippines), increasing at a rate of 3.3 percent per year. Put differently, the doubling time for this aggregate population was 21 years, compared to 87 years for the U.S.

Now suppose the U.S. agreed to pool its resources with 12 those seven countries, with everyone receiving an equal share. Initially the ratio of Americans to non-Americans in this model would be one-to-one. But consider what the ratio would be after 87 years, by which time the Americans would have doubled to a population of 420 million. By then, doubling every 21 years, the other group would have swollen to 3.54 billion. Each American would have to share the available resources with more than eight people.

But, one could argue, this discussion assumes that current 13 population trends will continue, and they may not. Quite so. Most likely the rate of population increase will decline much faster in the U.S. than it will in the other countries, and there does not seem to be much we can do about it. In sharing with "each according to his needs," we must recognize that needs are determined by population size, which is determined by the rate of reproduction, which at present is regarded as a sovereign right of every nation, poor or not. This being so, the philanthropic load created by the sharing ethic of the spaceship can only increase.

The fundamental error of spaceship ethics, and the sharing 14 it requires, is that it leads to what I call "the tragedy of the commons." Under a system of private property, people who own property recognize their responsibility to care for it, for if they don't they will eventually suffer. A farmer, for instance, will allow no more cattle in a pasture than its carrying capacity justifies. If he overloads it, erosion sets in, weeds take over, and he loses the use of the pasture.

If a pasture becomes a commons open to all, the right of each 15 to use it may not be matched by a corresponding responsibility to protect it. Asking everyone to use it with discretion will hardly do, for the considerate herdsman who refrains from overloading the commons suffers more than a selfish one who says his needs are greater. If everyone would restrain himself, all would be well; but it takes only one less than everyone to ruin a system of voluntary restraint. In a crowded world of less than perfect human beings, mutual ruin is inevitable if there are no controls. This is the tragedy of the commons.

One of the major tasks of education today should be the cre- 16 ation of such an acute awareness of the dangers of the commons that people will recognize its many varieties. For example, the air and water have become polluted because they are treated as commons. Further growth in the population or per-capita conversion of natural resources into pollutants will only make the problem worse. The same holds true for the fish of the oceans. Fishing fleets have nearly disappeared in many parts of the world; technological improvements in the art of fishing are hastening the day of complete ruin. Only the replacement of the system of the commons with a responsible system of control will save the land, air, water and oceanic fisheries.

In recent years there has been a push to create a new com- 17 mons called a World Food Bank, an international depository of food reserves to which nations would contribute according to their abilities and from which they would draw according to their needs. This humanitarian proposal received support from many liberal international groups, and from such prominent citizens as Margaret Mead, the U.N. Secretary General, and Senator Edward Kennedy.

A world food bank appeals powerfully to our humanitar- 18 ian impulses. But before we rush ahead with such a plan, let us ask if such a program would actually do more good than harm, not only momentarily but also in the long run. Those who propose a food bank usually refer to a current "emergency" or "crisis" in terms of world food supply. But what is an emergency? Although they may be infrequent and sudden, everyone knows that emergencies will occur from time to time. A well-run family, company, organization or country prepares for the likelihood of accidents and emergencies. It expects them, it budgets for them, it saves for them.

What happens if some organizations or countries budget for 19 accidents and others do not? If each country is solely responsible for its own well-being, poorly managed ones will suffer. But they can learn from experience. They may mend their ways, and learn to budget for infrequent but certain emergencies. For example, the weather varies from year to year, and periodic crop failures are certain. A wise and competent government saves out of the production of the good years in anticipation of bad years to come. Joseph taught this policy to Pharaoh in Egypt more than 2,000 years ago. Yet the great majority of the governments in the world today do not follow such a policy. They lack either the wisdom or the competence, or both. Should those nations that do manage to put something aside be forced to come to the rescue each time an emergency occurs among the poor nations?

"But it isn't their fault!" some kind-hearted liberals argue. 20
"How can we blame the poor people who are caught in an emergency? Why must they suffer for the sins of their governments?" The concept of blame is simply not relevant here. The real question is, what are the operational consequences of establishing a world food bank? If it is open to every country every time a need develops, slovenly rulers will not be motivated to take Joseph's advice. Someone will always come to their aid. Some countries will deposit food in the world food bank, and others will withdraw it. There will be almost no overlap. As a result of such solutions to food shortage emergencies, the poor countries will not learn to mend their ways, and will suffer progressively greater emergencies as their populations grow.

On the average, poor countries undergo a 2.5 percent in- 21
crease in population each year; rich countries, about 0.6 percent. Only rich countries have anything in the way of food reserves set aside, and even they do not have as much as they should. Poor countries have none. If poor countries received no food from the outside, the rate of their population growth would be periodically checked by crop failures and famines. But if they can always draw on a world food bank in time of need, their population can continue to grow unchecked, and so will their "need" for aid. In the short run, a world food bank may diminish that need, but in the long run it actually increases the need without limit.

Without some system of worldwide food sharing, the pro- 22
portion of people in the rich and poor nations might eventually

stabilize. The overpopulated poor countries would decrease in numbers while the rich countries that had room for more people would increase. But with a well-meaning system of sharing, such as a world food bank, the growth differential between the rich and the poor countries will not only persist, it will increase. Because of the higher rate of population growth in the poor countries of the world, 88 percent of today's children are born poor, and only 12 percent rich. Year by year the ratio becomes worse as the fast-reproducing poor outnumber the slow-reproducing rich.

A world food bank is thus a commons in disguise. People 23 will have more motivation to draw from it than to add to any common store. The less provident and less able will multiply at the expense of the abler and more provident, bringing eventual ruin upon all who share in the commons. Besides, any system of "sharing" that amounts to foreign aid from the rich nations to the poor nations will carry the taint of charity, which will contribute little to the world peace so devoutly desired by those who support the idea of a world food bank.

As past U.S. foreign-aid programs have amply and de- 24 pressingly demonstrated, international charity frequently inspires mistrust and antagonism rather than gratitude on the part of the recipient nation.

The modern approach to foreign aid stresses the export of 25 technology and advice, rather than money and food. As an ancient Chinese proverb goes: "Give a man a fish and he will eat for a day; teach him how to fish and he will eat for the rest of his days." Acting on this advice, the Rockefeller and Ford Foundations have financed a number of programs for improving agriculture in the hungry nations. Known as the "Green Revolution," these programs have led to the development of "miracle rice" and "miracle wheat," new strains that offer bigger harvests and greater resistance to crop damage.

Whether or not the Green Revolution can increase food pro- 26 duction as much as its champions claim is a debatable but possibly irrelevant point. Those who support this well-intended humanitarian effort should first consider some of the fundamentals of human ecology. Ironically, one man who did was the late Alan Gregg, a vice president of the Rockefeller Foundation.

Two decades ago he expressed strong doubts about the wisdom of such attempts to increase food production. He likened the growth and spread of humanity over the surface of the earth to the spread of cancer in the human body, remarking that "cancerous growths demand food, but, as far as I know, they have never been cured by getting it."

Every human born constitutes a draft on all aspects of the environment: food, air, water, forests, beaches, wildlife, scenery and solitude. Food can, perhaps, be significantly increased to meet a growing demand. But what about clean beaches, unspoiled forests, and solitude? If we satisfy a growing population's need for food, we necessarily decrease its per capita supply of the other resources needed by people.   27

India, for example, now has a population of 600 million, which increases by 15 million each year. This population already puts a huge load on a relatively impoverished environment. The country's forests are now only a small fraction of what they were three centuries ago, and floods and erosion continually destroy the insufficient farmland that remains. Every one of the 15 million new lives added to India's population puts an additional burden on the environment, and increases the economic and social costs of crowding. However humanitarian our intent, every Indian life saved through medical or nutritional assistance from abroad diminishes the quality of life for those who remain, and for subsequent generations. If rich countries make it possible, through foreign aid, for 600 million Indians to swell to 1.2 billion in a mere 28 years, as their current growth rate threatens, will future generations of Indians thank us for hastening the destruction of their environment? Will our good intentions be sufficient excuse for the consequences of our actions?   28

Without a true world government to control reproduction and the use of available resources, the sharing ethic of the spaceship is impossible. For the foreseeable future, our survival demands that we govern our actions by the ethics of a lifeboat, harsh though they may be. Posterity will be satisfied with nothing less.   29

1974

Permissions
Acknowledgments

Dabney, Virginia Bell, "The Day the Fire Came," from *Once There Was a Farm . . . : A Country Childhood Remembered* (Random House, 1990). The essay was first published in Harper's Magazine, April 1990.

Davies, Robertson, "A Few Kind Words for Superstition" by Robertson Davies. Reprinted by permission of Pendragon Ink.

Dershowitz, Alan M., "Shouting 'Fire!' " by Alan M. Dershowitz. Copyright © 1989 by Alan M. Dershowitz. First published in *The Atlantic Monthly*. Reprinted by permission.

Didion, Joan, "The Metropolitan Cathedral in San Salvador" from *Salvador* by Joan Didion. Copyright © 1983 by Joan Didion. Reprinted by permission of the author.

Dillard, Annie, "The Stunt Pilot." Copyright © 1989 by Annie Dillard. First published in *Esquire*, 1989. Reprinted by permission of the author and Blanche C. Gregory, Inc.

Dowling, Claudia Glenn, "Fire in the Sky" by Claudia Glenn Dowling and Jimmy Briggs in *Life*, December 1994. Life Magazine © Time Inc. Reprinted by permission.

Ehrenreich, Barbara, "A Step Back to The Workhouse?" by Barbara Ehrenreich. Reprinted by permission of the author.

Ehrlich, Gretel, "The Rules of the Game: Rodeo" from *The Solace of Open Spaces*. Copyright © 1985 by Gretel Ehrlich. Used by permission of Viking Penguin, a division of Penguin Books, Inc.

Eiseley, Loren, "The Cosmic Prison." Reprinted with the permission of Scribner, a Division of Simon & Schuster from *The Invisible Pyramid* by Loren Eiseley. Copyright © 1970 by Loren Eiseley.

Farb, Peter and George Armelagos, "The Patterns of Eating" from *Consuming Passions* by Peter Farb and George Armelagos. Copyright © 1980 by The Estate of Peter Farb. Reprinted by permission of Houghton Mifflin Company. All rights reserved.

Forster, E.M., "My Wood" from *Abinger Harvest*, copyright 1936 and renewed 1964 by E.M. Forster, reprinted by permission of Harcourt Brace & Company and King's College, Cambridge, and The Society of Authors as the literary representatives of the E.M. Forster Estate.

Fox, Nicols, "Gawk Shows" by Nicols Fox. Reprinted by permission of the author.

Gibbons, Euell, "How to Cook a Carp" from *Stalking the Wild Asparagus*. Copyright © 1962 used by permission of Alan C. Hood & Company, Inc. Brattleboro, Vermont, and the author's estate.

Golding, William, "Thinking as a Hobby" by William Golding from *Holiday*, August 1961. Reprinted by permission of Curtis Brown Ltd. Copyright © 1961 by William Golding, renewed.

Index of Authors
and Titles